Blue Chicago

Blue Chicago

The Search for Authenticity
in Urban Blues Clubs

DAVID GRAZIAN

The University of Chicago Press   Chicago and London

David Grazian is assistant professor of sociology at the University of Pennsylvania, where he teaches courses on popular culture and urban nightlife.

The University of Chicago Press, Chicago 60637
The University of Chicago Press, Ltd., London

12 11 10 09 08 07 06 05 04 03   1 2 3 4 5
ISBN: 0-226-30568-6 (cloth)

Library of Congress Cataloging-in-Publication Data

Grazian, David.
Blue Chicago : the search for authenticity in urban blues
    clubs / David Grazian.
        p.   cm.
Includes bibliographical references (p.   ) and index.
ISBN 0-226-30568-6 (alk. paper)
    1. Blues (Music)—Illinois—Chicago—Social aspects.
    2. Nightclubs—Illinois—Chicago. I. Title.
ML3521 .G72 2003
306.4'84—dc21   2002015511

For my parents

    Kathy Blank Grazian and Solomon Grazian

CONTENTS

All photographs by Joseph Carey.

In the context of book publishing, all acknowledgments are exercises in performing authenticity. In such moments, the author is expected to pull away from the first- or third-person narrative voice and speak freely, as a writer who has stepped outside of the confines of the text in order to extend heartfelt love and respect to friends, colleagues, and significant others. Of course, this performance of authenticity becomes somewhat shattered when the author reverts to a predictable formula for giving thanks, starting with the generosity of any relevant donors, foundations, and other financial supporters, moving on to the informants who provided the researcher with the necessary entry into their current field of study, then on to the publisher and its wise editors, followed by long lists of mentors, colleagues, and friends, and closing with a final word for one's spouse, children, parents, and other intimates. Sometimes, such acknowledgments end with a cute quip about the importance of teamwork, or a disclaimer that although such a wonderful group of people helped bring the book to life in immeasurable ways, ultimately the author will bear the responsibility for any mistakes that may remain between its pages.

Still, despite my generally contrary nature, I appreciate a good ritual as much as anyone else, and so in the present case I am only too happy to express my gratitude to a long list of contributing minds and endearing souls, beginning with the countless bartenders, performers, and bar regulars who allowed me into their lives for the duration of my research in Chicago. The staff of B.L.U.E.S. proved to be especially generous during the earlier stages of my dissertation research. Although I have hidden their identities behinds pseudonyms, I give particular thanks to the amateur and professional musicians who perform in the city's blues clubs for their willingness to be expressive in their reactions to my inquiries, generous in their time spent in early morning conversation, and kind when passing along their muted criticisms of my horn playing.

Likewise, I must thank my elementary, middle, and high school music teachers, a group of encouraging and caring professionals who truly endure in the performance of one of the more challenging and irreplaceable roles in American primary and secondary education: Karen Baron, Emile DeCosmo, Dan DiStefano, Mark Hast, John Mayola, and Harry T. Welte. Although they could not have known it at the time, the completion of my graduate work in sociology would not have been possible without their quick-witted yet patient instruction on instrumental practice, music theory, and general life lessons. They deserve a wave of thunderous applause.

In similar fashion, I thank my editors at the University of Chicago Press for their thoughtfulness and patience during this endeavor. Doug Mitchell, a drummer and spirited jazz fan himself, offered his encouragement and support from the beginning of the publication process; Robert Devens and Tim McGovern provided much needed editorial assistance; and Erin DeWitt helped to sharpen the manuscript in its final stages. Howard Becker and Richard Peterson offered sagacious wisdom in their thoughtful reviews of an earlier draft of the book. Finally, I thank the editorial board of the Press for taking a chance on a first-time author in need of a big break.

It is hardly uncommon for alumni of the graduate departments at the University of Chicago to describe their experience in Hobbesian terms; indeed, many find their academic lives there to be all too solitary, poor, nasty, and brutish, if not necessarily all that short. In the introduction to this book, I will reveal my own apprehensions with the university that eventually drove me to escape its clutches by heading to the city's blues bars; however, I am forever grateful for the education I gained while in its grip, fostered in no small part by the faculty of its Department of Sociology. My dissertation committee provided me with a firm grounding in the rigors of systematic social inquiry. I thank Wendy Griswold for her years of guidance and instruction since this project's inception, and for not throwing me and my half-baked ideas out of her office during my salad days; Andrew Abbott for introducing me to the wonders of the Chicago school of urban sociology and lending his enthusiastic support since my first years of graduate study; and Rob Sampson for his insightful comments throughout the research and writing stages of this project. I also learned a great deal from my interactions with a number of Chicago faculty members both in the classroom and on the quadrangles, including Bert Cohler, Roger Gould, Martin Riesebrodt, Leslie Salzinger, George Steinmetz, William Julius Wilson, and Dingxin Zhou. Finally, I must give special thanks to Gerald Suttles, a scholar whose knowledge and curiosity about the city knows no limits. More than anyone else, he tried to teach me how to experience the world through the eyes and mind of an ethnographer, and I can only hope that I have proven to be a worthy candidate for such a challenge.

My experience at Chicago was also enriched by my membership in an entering graduate class that any student would be proud to call their own, and I will always be indebted to my closest classmates, colleagues, and confidants from that group: Chad Broughton, John Dilts, Adrienne Falcon, Lori Hill, Marc Jolin, Jim Kales, Anne Nie, Robert Petrin, Catherine Reigle-Crumb, and Michael Rosenfeld. In addition, I thank Ari Adut, Mark Ashley, Kim Babon, Rod Coover, Maria Kefalas, Dawne Moon, Jeffrey Morenoff, and Marc Sanford, all fellow graduate students who helped enliven my intellectual as well as emotional life at Chicago. Finally, as a Chicago sociologist who found an additional home at Northwestern University, its suburban neighbor along the shores of Lake Michigan, I thank Chris Coleman, Brian Donovan, Philip Howard, and JuLeigh Petty for their wisdom and friendship.

Upon graduating from Chicago and completing a brief teaching stint there, I left the Midwest for a tenure-track position in the sociology department at the University of Pennsylvania, where I prepared the book for publication, and I thank Doug Massey and the rest of the Penn community for their support and encouragement during these final stages of the writing process. Elijah Anderson, Chuck Bosk, Jerome Hodos, and Jason Schnittker all read the entire manuscript, while Robin Leidner and Tukufu Zuberi read drafts of specific chapters and provided thoughtful criticisms and useful suggestions for revising the final manuscript draft. By the same token, the hard work of the administrative staff in the sociology department deserves my appreciation and respect. Finally, I thank Randall Collins for providing a constant stream of intellectual probing and friendly distraction from his office across the hall during my final months of rewriting and revision.

I also wish to single out a handful of friends and colleagues for going above and beyond the call of duty. Garth Bond read and polished the entire manuscript, and lent his time and energies to endless hours of obsessive conversation about the blues and popular music. Eric Klinenberg read through substantial sections of the book and offered insightful suggestions around the writing process. Sean Davis ruthlessly combed over the entire manuscript for errors and offered a sensible and balanced perspective as an impartial reader. In addition, I wish to thank a number of old and new friends outside the academic world whose thoughtful remarks, suggestions, moral support, and all-around good humor helped make this book a smarter and more down-to-earth version than the one floating in my head these many years: Meredith Broussard, Michael Cimicata, Rob Felton, David Gerridge, Jason Gottlieb, Suchi Gururaj, Julie Janus, Marci May, Matt Nolker, Guy Raviv, Aimee Strasko, Anne Sussman, Jon Wotman, and Leslie Zacharias.

Finally, I must thank Joseph Carey for his integrity as an artist, sincerity and intelligence as a colleague, and generosity and warmth as a close friend. A truly creative partner in crime, Joseph framed, shot, and developed all of the photographs for the book, and in doing so lends his own ethnographic eye to the story that follows. In our photographic excursions around Chicago, I have always been struck by his compassion for the people depicted in these pages, and throughout this process he has tirelessly questioned whether my cultural critique might perhaps, in his words, unfairly "deny the people their pleasure." Surely, the telling images of the musicians, fans, and street life of the city collected in this volume speak not only to his skill as a craftsman, but to his sympathetic and humanist vision as an artist as well.

My parents, Kathy and Solomon Grazian, have provided their unconditional love and encouragement throughout my life, and it is to them that I owe the bulk of my accomplishments, at least the good ones. I have dedicated this book to them.

These are all the wise and gracious people who helped transform this project from a weekend distraction into the book whose pages await your consideration. Any errors that remain are entirely their fault.

How Blue Can You Get

A Night in a Chicago Blues Club

It is showtime at B.L.U.E.S., and Tommy McCracken—a hefty, biracial singer and showman in his mid-sixties and one of the hardest-working performers at the club—takes a deep breath and wipes his dripping brow under his colored jet-black hair. He motions his band to lower their volume as they play behind him with a steady drumbeat while the guitar follows a slow riff, and as they quiet down, he begins preaching to his attentive audience as a minister might address his congregation.

"It's still Sunday, right? All right, I've got some things that I'll need to wait till *after* Sunday to say . . . But you know, the branch never falls too far from the tree . . . and I believe . . . I believe that if I had some water, if was standing by the water, well then, do you know what I'd do?"

He waits for the crowd to respond, and when they don't, he shouts back:

"I said . . . Do you know what I'd *do*?!"

When the crowd finally reacts, he begins to chant softly—with feeling—

"Well, I'd pull up my pants, I'd roll up my pants real high, yes, I would . . . And I'd wade in the water . . . Yes, I'd wade, I'd wade . . . I'd wade in the water, oh Lord." And he puts his hands up, palms out, and he raises his voice, shouting: "But you say, 'Hold on now . . . Wait a minute . . . How can you do that, and sing the blues? How can you wade in the water . . . and still sing the blues?' " And he smiles: "Well, I'm a-gonna tell ya . . ."

Suddenly his band mates turn to each other with looks of puzzled trepidation, as if they are not quite sure what will come out of his mouth

next, only to watch him abruptly interrupt his sermon and signal them to jump into his next number, an Earl Hooker cover—fast-paced, up-tempo—

"Have you ever . . . Have you ever seen a one-eyed woman cry?
Have you ever, have you ever seen a one-eyed woman cry?
She looks good, tears come out of one eye!"

The audience roars to McCracken's shouts and hollers as he starts to move: shaking his hips, executing a decades-old moonwalk across the stage, and following it up with yet another 1980s breakdance maneuver. Between lines he lets out a wail in his best James Brown imitation that just shakes up the room, and the eyes of his energized audience follow his awkwardly large body as he spins around, kicks down the microphone stand, and in a well-rehearsed turn of his foot, expertly lifts it back up as he comes crashing down on the stage floor into a split. Suddenly he jumps up, flexes the pectorals on his chest through his sweat-drenched shirt, and turns around, shaking his behind at the crowd to their hysterical cries. As the song comes to a close, he tucks the microphone into the front of his pants—just above his groin—and pulls his fists back and forth in time to the closing riffs, and finally takes a low bow as he thanks the audience while his band sharply slows down their tempo. Once again, he wipes the perspiration from his brow.

But the evening is not over just yet: McCracken has one more song to perform. His band is still with him, rumbling quietly behind him as he slowly starts to sway. He looks up at his audience, raises his palm, and, once again, patiently resumes his role as a preaching showman: "Now, here's what you gotta do . . . When you get home, you gotta walk in the door, and take your mate, spouse, boyfriend, girlfriend, wife, husband, significant other, and sit them down . . . and tell 'em, 'Honey, turn down the TV, 'cause we gotta talk.' Tell 'em how the kids are all grown up and in college, and you just want to sit down because you have to talk to them about something that's been on your mind all these years . . ." And so he begins:

"I've been downhearted, baby, ever since the day that we met,
I've been downhearted, baby, ever since the day that we met,
And I want to know tonight . . . 'How blue—can you get?' "

Strolling among the smiling members of his audience, he continues—

"I bought you a ten-course dinner, and you said, 'Thanks for the snack,'
I let you live in my penthouse, but you called it a shack,
I bought you a brand-new Porsche, and you said, 'I like Cadillacs . . .' "

And as the music grows louder, he starts jumping up and down in an emotional crescendo to the buildup of the B.B. King cover and belts out the rest of the lyric—again, with feeling—"*I gave you seven pretty babies, and now you wanna give them all back!*" and he gasps and cries, shouting, "*I've been so brokenhearted baby, ever since the day, ever since the day that we met . . .*

"*And I want to know tonight, 'How blue—how blue—can you get?!'*"

And the music grows louder and harder, and then suddenly comes to a grinding halt. With a flourish of his hand, his band stops playing, and in the silence of the club, he looks up to the audience and, as if to demonstrate just how blue *he* can get, resumes preaching: "Oh, *Lord* . . . All the women in the house, say 'Yeah!' " They respond to his plea, but he begs them for more, only louder: "Say '*Yeah!!!*' " After they do, he continues: "Well, all right . . . Now I want all you women to go back and remember what you learned back in grammar school, back when things didn't seem so negative . . . And I believe that you had math class, and science class, and English class, and I believe you learned what we call verbs and adverbs, adjectives, nouns, and pronouns . . . and there was a He, and there was a She . . ." and he continues to preach to the women—and the men—in his audience, imploring them to treat themselves better without giving up hope on life—"Remember, if it's too high to get over, and too low to get under, and too wide to get around, then there's just one way in and that's to get through it . . ."—and the band starts to crescendo as he buzzes, shrieks, and climbs up to a high-pitched wail—

"And I want you!" And in case the audience missed his cue, he throws his hand down fast as a signal to the band to drop a sharp yet cacophonous punch: *Bang!*

"And I need you . . ."

Bang!

"And I love you . . ."

Bang! Bang! Bang! Bang! Bang! Beads of sweat rolling down his leathered face, he raises his hands up in the air as the band plays their final drumroll of the night, and he thanks the crowd, pleading with them, "Keep drinking what you're drinking; keep thinking what you're thinking!" and he bows down his head, arms flailing, fingers pointing in all directions, and a nod to the band, who, with a slam of his hand, break into silence for the final word of the evening:

"How blue—can you get?!"

And the band plays down the closing bars; the crowd is on their feet, cheering, applauding, toasting; an exhausted Tommy McCracken staggers aside and drops for a bow and, at least for tonight, showtime is finally over.

Black and Tan Fantasy
Searching for the Chicago Blues

The thrill is gone, baby
It's gone away from me
Although I'll still live on
But so lonely I'll be.   —B.B. King, "The Thrill Is Gone"

Come on, baby, don't you want to go?
Back to that same old place, Sweet Home Chicago?
                    —Robert Johnson, "Sweet Home Chicago"

The Setting.   Welcome to B.L.U.E.S., where every night of the week, taxicabs and chartered buses bring thrill-seekers to its unassuming yet strangely alluring North Halsted Street entrance. Passing under the red-and-blue warmth of its neon sign, they step into the club to be greeted with a smile by Jack, a towering and tattooed bouncer endowed with bulging biceps revealed by the sleeveless arms of his black leather vest. On weekends patrons cram inside the club's long and narrow interior underneath the glow of yellow lamps and haze of cigarette smoke.[1]

In a neighborhood as affluent as Chicago's Lincoln Park, the run-down decor of B.L.U.E.S. seems unusually modest.[2] As one enters from the front, a small cigar humidor and peanut machine lean against the bar, which runs along the right side of the club, while a raised platform littered with shelves of splintering wood and worn black bar stools stretches along the left wall. Assorted club memorabilia, old photographs of renowned blues performers, and compact discs line the club's walls of cheap paneling and plaster. More stools and cocktail tables sit at the far end of the bar, just in front of a small stage, while dim bulbs and a neon sign advertising Old Style beer illuminate the tiny back room. A rarely used dartboard hangs off the wall and faces the club's interminably filthy men's and women's rest rooms, just inches away from the bandstand.

When B.L.U.E.S. first opened in the late 1970s, it served a blue-collar and interracial mix of regulars, and the scattershot decor of the club recalls those informal days. Above the bar hangs a television perpetually tuned to one of the city's cable sports channels. Gold tinsel and red-and-green Christmas lights hang perennially from the rafters along with an old pair of XXL blue-and-green checkered flannel boxer shorts. Seasonal decorations and colorful plastic fruit—grapes, pineapples, oranges, bananas, watermelons—swing from the glass racks behind the bartenders. Above the stage hang a selection of T-shirts for sale and a photograph of blues pianist Sunnyland Slim, a local favorite before his death a few years ago. He shares space on the stage with the club's sombrero-adorned pet mannequin, Bernice, and the blow-up doll Jack received for a recent birthday.

But in spite of its modest beginnings years ago, today B.L.U.E.S. feels like a somewhat different kind of place, in part because many of the city's local neighborhoods and their leisure establishments have undergone a palpable transformation in the past two decades with regard to the kinds of communities they serve. Whereas its early entrepreneurs made their fortunes in meatpacking, steel production, and other industries that made up Chicago's great manufacturing economy, the city once immortalized by Carl Sandburg as the "Hog Butcher for the World" has lost many of its factory jobs, and in recent years investment in Chicago has turned toward more post-industrial enterprises and cultural attractions.[3] Consequently, the city center has witnessed a surge in the local expansion of travel and leisure industries as evidenced by the growth of new hotels, convention halls, restaurants, shopping plazas, fine arts theaters, summer festivals, and the spectacular renovation of its waterfront and park areas. This economic restructuring of the city's downtown provides an upscale entertainment infrastructure for an increasingly mobile and moneyed class of consumers made up of international business travelers, white-collar employees of major corporations, convention attendees, foreign students, and vacationing families who dine, shop, and spend in the city.[4]

The presence of this growing audience for local entertainment can be observed in the demographics of the audiences who patronize the city's most prominent blues clubs. On any given weekend, B.L.U.E.S. attracts a large following among an affluent and well-heeled audience consisting mostly of out-of-towners. A large number of these customers are foreign students, international business travelers, and other professionals who hail from regions of the world as diverse as Puerto Rico, Germany, Spain, Great Britain, Poland, Australia, Algeria, and Japan. On Friday and Saturday nights, they arrive dressed in pinstriped suits and clean-cut casual wear and pack themselves into every available nook of the club. Always ready for action, they chat in the aisle, crowd up against the front windows, perch themselves in the doorway to the back room, and even linger by the rest rooms.

Like many of the city's blues bars, B.L.U.E.S. offers the strange atmospherics of a dingy, down-home tavern colonized by an airport gift shop. Three times an evening during the close of each set, the headlining band parades off the stage as Jack grabs a microphone to deliver his usual plea:

> Hey-hey, please put your hands together for the band!! Right now, the band's gonna take a brief pause for a worthy cause, but don't go anywhere, because the band will be right back for two more sets! And ladies and gentlemen, don't forget to tip your waitresses and your bartenders . . . Please be good to them, I *know* they've been good to you! And before you leave this evening— and we hope you're *not*—please don't go without picking up a B.L.U.E.S. souvenir! We have T-shirts, baseball caps, and jackets, men's boxer shorts and ladies panties, our brand-new hooded sweatshirts, and a wide selection of CDs and cassette tapes by famous local Chicago blues artists! In the meantime, please sit tight and don't go anywhere, because the band will be *right back*!!!

As suggested by Jack's announcement, the club sells trinkets ranging from the expected tourist-trap fare to the hopelessly tacky, including a women's lingerie set bearing the slogan "Don't stop now; I've got the blues!" Meanwhile, signs encourage patrons to submit their business cards for a chance to win a raffled leather jacket sporting the club's logo. This shopping-mall merchandising is even more apparent at the club's strongest local competitors, a collection of theme park–style clubs named after (and often owned and operated by) local blues heroes. At Buddy Guy's Legends, Koko Taylor's Celebrity, and Eddy "The Chief" Clearwater's Reservation Blues, patrons admire black-and-white photographs of these stars while munching on standardized southern food-court options ranging from pulled pork dripping with messy barbeque sauce to red beans and rice.

These bars compete with a variety of blues-oriented entertainment franchises located in the downtown area, where painstaking attempts are made to blur the boundary between high-society consumption and the countrified mystique of the old South. Located in the Marina City Towers complex at the Chicago River's edge, the city's House of Blues hosts blues and rock bands who play for high-paying audiences craving a more gentrified taste of the Louisiana bayou—pan-seared voodoo shrimp with rosemary corn bread and Dixie beer reduction, a filet mignon topped with a crawfish bordelaise, and sautéed curried crab cakes with cucumbers, lime zest, and a mango coulis—and who enjoy dining in the club's sky boxes, luxurious VIP section, and reserved meditation chamber. Meanwhile, at even modest honky-tonk clubs like B.L.U.E.S., roving waitresses serve customers from a cocktail menu that offers lemon-garnished *Weiss* beers, ten-dollar glasses of cabernet, champagne by the bottle, special coffee drinks, a selection of single-malt scotches and small-batch bourbons, no less than twenty-eight kinds of vodka, ten kinds of tequila, and a selection of overpriced Macanudo cigars.

As for the music itself, B.L.U.E.S. and its local counterparts rotate the same blues bands for their nightly bookings, and so while the music performed at these clubs often seems fresh to weekend visitors, it grows somewhat predictable for repeat customers. The repertoires of these local Chicago bands typically include well-known blues standards as well as rhythm-and-blues and pop hits; at B.L.U.E.S. local favorites such as Robert Johnson's "Sweet Home Chicago," Muddy Waters's "I'm Your Hoochie Coochie Man" and "Got My Mojo Working," B.B. King's "The Thrill Is Gone" and "Every Day I Have the Blues," Albert King's "Crosscut Saw," and the religiously covered "Call It Stormy Monday" draw enthusiastic applause from audience members who bounce on their bar stools while they lip-synch and play air-guitar to the music, in and out of time.

Among these songs, the most popular are those that encourage audience involvement through singing along, dancing, or trading off lyrics with the band, such as Wilson Pickett's "Mustang Sally" and Sam & Dave's "Soul Man." When performed at B.L.U.E.S., these songs energize nightclubbers who rush the dance floor and growl their well-known lyrics aloud to their dates—"Ride, Sally, ride!" "I'm a *soul* man!" Since many of these songs have been popularized by pop stars with broad crossover appeal, including, not coincidentally, the fictitious Blues Brothers, they tend to be much more familiar to a mass audience than lesser-known hits by more traditional blues recording artists like Junior Wells or Howlin' Wolf. For this reason, a rather wide range of pop songs, particularly those by black artists, finds its way into the set lists of local blues performers at the club, including Otis Redding's "(Sittin' on) The Dock of the Bay," Chuck Berry's "Johnny B. Goode," Bob Marley's "No Woman, No Cry," and just about anything by James Brown.

Perhaps not surprisingly, musicians tire of performing these same standards night after night. As Philip, a local guitarist, explains during a set break at the club:

> You mean the songs? No, we usually play the same songs . . . You know, we add a new one every three or four months, and we don't have a set order or anything. But yeah, we mostly play the same songs, and, man, I get so tired of playing them, you know, like "Got My Mojo Working," "Sweet Home Chicago," and let's see, um, "Crosscut Saw" . . . But, you know, we have to play them, because they're the songs that people know and they want to hear. I'm so sick of playing those songs.

Musicians are not only expected to include these songs in their repertoires; in fact, their inability to honor a requested favorite will often be met with hostility. One evening I stumble into Mike and Jolynn, a couple enjoying a night of drinking and schmoozing at B.L.U.E.S. As they sit in the back corner of the bar, Mike begins serenading his date along with the band as they perform "Call It Stormy Monday." He sings seductively to its opening lyrics while drawing deeply on his cigarette. He slowly exhales while turning to Jolynn as the next line comes around and tells her, coolly, " . . . But Tuesday's just as bad." In his hopes to sing along to another song, Mike starts shouting out his request to the band: "Play 'When My Heart Beats Like a Hammer'!" When the bandleader apologetically claims not to know the B.B. King song, he protests: "Oh, come on, what kind of bluesman *are* you?!" Later in the evening he continues: "I can't believe they don't know B.B. King here!" Turning to me, he shouts, "Who is, like, *the* bluesman?!!" presumably still in shock that his request has been denied.

Still, these musicians usually draw on a variety of faculties to punctuate their crowd-pleasing performances with the most well-rehearsed gimmickry. Their bag of tricks typically includes a tired set of politically incorrect jokes about oral sex, gay men, and overweight women, all sprinkled among greatest-hits medleys featuring random snippets of selected song lyrics, solos, riffs, rhythms, chords, and refrains.[5] Farrell, a local bass guitarist, recalls the onstage prowess of Son Seals, his former bandleader:

> I played with Son Seals for about a year and a half, just up until somebody shot him in the face . . . Now, he always did the same set, and always used the same jokes, the same lines, but he was so good at it. Somehow, he learned how to push all the right buttons on the crowd, and they just loved every minute of it—in fact, I can only remember one time that he *didn't* get a reaction from the audience. But for him, it was all about finding those buttons and knowing just how and when to push them.

In attempting to push these buttons, some bandleaders attempt to enliven their audiences by coaxing them to repeat their shouts, dance in place, or join in when the chorus comes around. One singer invokes the call-and-response style indicative of black church culture to energize his audience as they repeat after him, "C-H-I— C-A-G-O!" while another performer draws on comparable strategies of showmanship to divide up his audience into separate groups and command them to dance in the aisles, wave their arms above their heads, and sing along with him to James Brown's "Get Up (I Feel Like Being a) Sex Machine."[6] And when performers introduce "Sweet Home Chicago," the city's easiest crowd-pleaser, it is never hard to predict that they will soon have their audiences enthusiastically smiling and singing in unison on the familiar refrain: "Come on, baby, don't you want to go? Back to that same old place— Sweet Home Chicago?"

The Authenticity of the Blues.   As demonstrated by endless television commercials for new computer technologies, financial services, and Coca-Cola, everyday representations of globalization suggest that the international spread of consumer products around the world effectively works to erase age-old cultural differences among formerly traditional nations and their peoples. But in recent years sociologists, anthropologists, and other social scientists have examined how the increased global travel of media, commodities, and capital actually generates its own backlash as local communities grow ever more protective of their regional customs, collective identities, and territorial attachments.[7] Similarly, and perhaps ironically, the increased global commodification of popular culture creates an even stronger desire among many consumers for that which seems *un*commercial and therefore less affected by the strong hand of the marketplace, such as independent cinema and punk rock.

For these reasons, the increased commercialization and international popularity of the Chicago blues seem particularly fascinating. For many global consumers, the blues represents a form of cultural expression with very strong attachments to local settings and regional locations. Unlike the postmodern blur of New Age adult pop and the multiethnic world beat of the international underground rave scene, the blues evokes a deep sense of place among its fans, whether the sun-baked stickiness of the Mississippi Delta, the Creole spice of New Orleans nightlife, or the honky-tonk burliness of the South Side of Chicago. At the same time, for many listeners the blues seems to evoke a dank, stripped-down sensibility void of the silicone plasticity and blinding Day-Glo flash commonly associated with the popular cultural icons of Hollywood and MTV. To millions of fans both in America and abroad, the blues symbolizes authenticity in a cultural universe populated by virtual realities, artificial intelligences, and a dizzying sense of placelessness.

But while the popularity of the blues may represent a kind of resistance against the hypercommercialized branding of everyday life, the commodification of the blues in Chicago has set off its own backlash in recent years as disappointed critics, musicians, and audience members reject what they regard to be a loss of authenticity. Some musicians wax nostalgic for the authenticity suggested by earlier moments in this storied musical heritage. According to Jack, who headlines his own band in addition to serving as a bouncer at B.L.U.E.S., the club's affluent audiences of today seem less subculturally savvy than their earlier counterparts did in the 1970s:

> Well, back then the audience was a lot older. I mean, there were hardly any kids at all; most of the crowd was in their mid-thirties and older, and there were some seniors here too, and a lot of old hippie types. They were people who were really acquainted with the music . . . On any given night, you could imagine overhearing a thorough discussion in the back about the styles of Blind Lemon Jefferson, or Sunnyland Slim, because these people knew all about the traditions of the music. Today the audiences don't know anything about blues . . . If you mentioned Sunnyland Slim, they might think it was a drink or something.

Meanwhile, the local press echoes similar disappointment with the overall quality of the music performed in venues like B.L.U.E.S. Specifically, the repetitious performance of popular favorites like "Sweet Home Chicago" draws constant ire from local critics and other cultural authorities. In a biting *Chicago Tribune* review of the city's blues clubs, the award-winning music journalist Bill Dahl argues that renditions of canonized standards like "Sweet Home Chicago" have become shopworn staples of the new blues experience:

> Perhaps only in suburban hotel lounges can one encounter as many overworked covers as there are in the North Side blues clubs. Song list stagnation permeates live Chicago blues. Bands regularly headline top clubs while offering little to no fresh material. Set lists remain dominated by certified classics of decades past ("Sweet Home Chicago," "Every Day I Have the Blues," "Mustang Sally")—songs that long ago slipped into onstage cliché through their sheer predictability. . . . A danger looms that Chicago blues may gradually become a museum piece, embalmed in time.
>
> . . . Why is originality so scarce? For starters, the audience for the music has shifted drastically. Once the genre appealed primarily to the African-American population that spawned it, and was played principally for that audience at neighborhood taverns as an integral part of socializing (and still is, on a considerably smaller scale). Now it's regarded as hearty party music by young white fans who support it enthusiastically with their wallets but aren't always cognizant of the idiom's tradition.[8]

In fact, the hard sell of the contemporary blues club is rarely lost on many of the tourists that it attempts to target. As Wally, a vacationing patron from Australia, inquires one evening, "Is this place a real touristy club?" When he is told otherwise, he remains unconvinced: "Really? Even though they have all those T-shirts up on the wall?" When cultural products valued for their authenticity—traditional music and art, exotic foods, handmade artifacts—become transformed into commodities and souvenirs, their consumers often respond by searching even more persistently for the authenticity once symbolized by such objects.

Many music writers and journalists have written books in recent years that critique the intensified commercialization of American blues music over the past two decades, and they frequently employ this critique as a springboard to their discovery of the *real* authenticity that lurks beneath the postmodern facade of the urban entertainment marketplace. In *The Blues Route*, writer Hugh Merrill grows disenchanted with the mid-1980s atmosphere of Blues Harbor, an upscale nightclub set in Atlanta's posh Buckhead district, and at times his account reads like a eulogy; he writes: "*My God*, I thought, *is this what the blues has come to? Where's the electricity? Where's the emotion?*" In fact, Merrill finds himself so horrified by these surroundings that he takes off in his Honda for the Mississippi Delta in the hopes of rediscovering the roots of the blues and the authenticity buried deep in its rich soil and historic past.[9]

I wrote this book for a different reason. As a sociologist by trade, I am not interested as much in what is or is not authentic, as I am curious about this *search for authenticity*, the trip that Merrill and people like him take every day in the hopes of living out their fantasies of experiencing the dream world of authenticity through the medium of tourism and cultural consumption. Specifically, in this book I try to examine how the commodification and global popularity of Chicago's blues music produce a heightened desire for authenticity among fans and musicians alike. By closely observing and engaging in countless barroom conversations with the local characters who make up the social world of the urban blues club, including professional and amateur musicians, foreign and domestic tourists, bar regulars and die-hard blues fans, and bartenders and club owners, I explore how each of these groups defines and thus experiences authenticity in different ways within a context of commercialization, whether as a fantasy to fulfill, a way of life to protect, or a burden to overcome.

In doing so, my goal is to provide an understanding of the synergistic relationship between culture and commerce by revealing how the desire to experience authenticity in a postmodern world increases the popularity of the blues and other traditional forms of music, and how this popularity encourages musicians and other cultural producers to cater to this consumption in local clubs—an attempt that, ironically, drives consumers to search even *more* vigilantly for signs of authenticity untainted by the blemishes of commercialism.[10] But first, let me begin by explaining exactly how I became interested in the world of the Chicago blues, because in many ways the research for this book began with my own search for authenticity in the city's blues bars.

Searching for the Chicago Blues. The first time I attended B.L.U.E.S. was to watch Son Seals perform in early 1995 after I had begun my first year of graduate school in the Department of Sociology at the University of Chicago. A classmate had introduced me to the city's blues clubs a few weeks earlier, and ever since then I had enjoyed them immensely as a respite from the grind of reading books about urban politics and global cultural theory in the drab libraries of the university. In a way, the blues club represented a place where I could take a break from the world of sociology, free from the rigorous demands of the academic world.

But almost in spite of my attempts to carve out a space of leisure and escape for myself at places like B.L.U.E.S., I soon realized that the sociological issues covered in those books—the growing commodification of popular culture in America, the contemporary relevance of urban subcultures, the fate of race relations in the post–civil rights era, the shifting emphasis in cities from factory production to entertainment consumption—all manifested themselves in the richly textured world of the blues bar. In many ways, these bars seemed so much more vital and meaningful than the dry, jargon-laden texts familiar to any graduate student. These books attempted to analytically represent the world in crisply defined terms, while the blues club revealed the wonderful messiness of everyday life. Unlike the typeface of the printed word, the life of the bar was real: it was authentic.

But the club also felt authentic in a different way. Unlike the stuffy academic world of the university, B.L.U.E.S. seemed to exude a sense of revelry and liveliness absent from the pretentious classroom discussions and snobbish cocktail parties where graduate students and professors hobnobbed and competed for intellectual points and knowing winks and nods. Perhaps because I felt as alienated from this elitist world as any overwhelmed twenty-two-year-old probably should, the university felt like a staged arena of make-believe and artifice, where brainiacs performed for one another in dull soliloquies laced with esoteric verbiage. In contrast, the blues club promised the excitement of real action: the music was loud and fast, the audience was always drunk, and the band was usually even drunker. At the club the bartenders and bouncers didn't care how many books you had read, only whether you were having fun and paying for another round. As I took in the tactile and sensual aura of the smoke-filled bar, B.L.U.E.S. felt like the authentic blues club of my dreams.

What is authenticity? Broadly speaking, the notion of authenticity suggests two separate but related attributes. First, it can refer to the ability of a place or event to conform to an idealized representation of reality: that is, to a set of expectations regarding how such a thing ought to look, sound, and feel. At the same time, authenticity can refer to the credibility or sincerity of a performance and its ability to come off as natural and effortless. When we take vacations to faraway and exotic locales, we often seek out experiences that suggest both kinds of authenticity, whether while listening to live music or consuming some other form of entertainment. During such adventures we desire to inhabit what we imagine to be the typical, everyday worlds of our guests, and we want to experience that world without the sense that it has been manufactured for our own benefit.

The dramaturgical work of Erving Goffman provides an appropriate framework for understanding how individuals experience this kind of cultural consumption. In *The Presentation of Self in Everyday Life*, Goffman argues that all interpersonal encounters represent elaborate theatrical performances, each of us playing a series of roles as we move through life; after all, "All the world's a stage, and all the men and women merely players," as Lord Jacques reminds us in Shakespeare's *As You Like It*.[11] According to Goffman, when we players take refuge from these performances in our most private spaces, or "backstage" regions, we reveal what we imagine to be our more authentic selves to our intimates and confidants. As a result, these kinds of backstage zones are often regarded as privileged areas, and thus alluring to outsiders, which explains the mystical aura commonly attached to celebrities' dressing rooms and the VIP lounges of exclusive nightclubs. Meanwhile, for tourists vacationing in urban environments, the search for authenticity often represents a desire to gain access to the backstage regions of the city commonly hidden from mainstream public view (and therefore other tourists), whether a neighborhood located off the beaten path or a clandestine establishment known and patronized exclusively by locals.

Unfortunately, as I soon learned, the search for authenticity is always a failing prospect. First, as Goffman reminds us, *all* of social life is performed, including that which takes place in our backstage regions, as any account of a snooty VIP lounge can surely demonstrate.[12] Authenticity, therefore, is always manufactured: like life itself, it is a grand performance, and while some performances may be more convincing than others, its status as a contrivance hardly changes as a result. Second, the search for authenticity incorrectly presumes that people typically observe highly predictable, customary patterns of behavior—a conceit that tricks us into thinking that cultural worlds other than our own are homogenous and unchanging, rather than complex and contradictory. As a result, we encounter the world with a set of stereotypical ideas about how these worlds should look and feel, and we are surprised when the reality fails to conform to our expectations. Like other kinds of stereotypes, images of authenticity are idealized representations of reality, and are therefore little more than collectively produced fictions.

In this sense, authenticity itself is never an objective quality inherent in things, but simply a shared set of beliefs about the nature of things we value in the world. These beliefs are subsequently reinforced by the conscious efforts of cultural producers and consumers alike. Examples abound in recent work in cultural sociology and social history. In *Creating Country Music*, Richard A. Peterson explains how the American country music recording industry helped "fabricate" the glorified image of the cowboy in American popular culture. Dean MacCannell's *The Tourist* describes the "staged" quality of tourist attractions ranging from San Francisco's Fisherman's Wharf to the back regions of restaurant kitchens, orchestra rehearsal spaces, and Cape Kennedy. In their edited volume *The Invention of Tradition*, Eric Hobsbawm and Terence Ranger explore the manufactured nature of the various rituals and customs of the British Empire, including the Highland culture of Scotland and the royal pageantry of the monarchy.[13]

The manufactured and invented quality of authenticity in Chicago blues clubs revealed itself to me a few weeks after my initial foray into the scene. At first, my expectations regarding the natural atmosphere of B.L.U.E.S. were challenged by the commodified artifice of the club, beginning with the T-shirts and compact discs that lined the walls of the club. On subsequent visits I discovered that the bluesy melodies I loved to hear at the club were not improvised by musicians swept away by the tragedy of everyday life, but were part of a calculated list of commonly performed standards, including "Sweet Home Chicago" and, perhaps even more fitting, B.B. King's "The Thrill Is Gone."

When I explained this aspect of B.L.U.E.S. to longtime Chicago residents, they would agree with my assessment of the club but insist that if I simply looked hard enough, I could find *actual* authentic blues clubs elsewhere in the city, and some locals directed me to clubs located in isolated spots throughout the city's South Side, West Side, and so forth. But although I enjoyed attending many of those venues, I soon discovered that no matter how hard I looked, I would never find the authenticity that I sought, because my very definition of authenticity was, like *all* definitions of authenticity, based on a mix of prevailing myths and prejudices invented in the absence of actual experience. While the search for authenticity may be rooted in our desire to experience a place in all its complexities, in truth, people tend to seek out a very small set of popularized images thought to represent authenticity in spite of their frequently arbitrary and even superstitious nature.

In the context of the local blues club, these symbols of authenticity take the form of a familiar set of overblown caricatures. Authentic blues clubs are ramshackle joints with broken front doors and rattling sound systems; they are dimly lit, unbearably smoky, and smell as funky as their music sounds. They serve cheap beer and hard whiskey all night long and are located in slightly dangerous black urban neighborhoods, or else off the deserted highway, deep in the sticks. They only hire authentic-looking blues musicians, who are generally uneducated American black men afflicted by blindness, or else they walk on a wooden leg or with a secondhand crutch; as they are defiantly poor, they drive beat-up Fords and old Chevy trucks, and usually cannot read or write their own name. Their audiences are usually black as well, with the occasional white customer surfacing only if they are also sufficiently old, poor, drunk, or blind. Most of all, the surest sign of a blues club's genuine authenticity is if the working-class regulars who patronize it do not *know* it is authentic, because their lack of concern regarding such matters demonstrates that their enthusiasm for the club is truly sincere and not contrived.

Likewise, the authenticity of the blues club is always constructed in relative terms: that is, in contradistinction to someplace else. The subjective quality of the concept of authenticity gives it a certain elasticity, and therefore almost anything can be regarded as more or less authentic in relation to its competitors. The comparative nature of the concept suggests that the authenticity of objects and experiences can increase or diminish in different contexts; for example, a large downtown blues club might seem more authentic than one in a suburban shopping mall, but less authentic than a tiny neighborhood tavern, and perhaps even less authentic when the bulk of its patrons are all accountants in town for a CPA convention. Blues bars and blues music are never evaluated in absolute terms but measured comparatively along a *sliding scale of authenticity*: thus, according to the most simplistic of stereotypes, black blues musicians from Chicago's South Side are considered more authentic than upper-class whites from the North Shore suburbs, and both rate higher than the handful of Japanese American players who perform in the city. By the same token, one can achieve an intense level of authentic blues feeling in a shotgun shack, on a lonesome dirt road, or while awaiting a sentence in the electric chair, whereas singing the blues in an expensive Parisian restaurant over an exorbitant corking fee might not hit the mark nearly as high.

One of the consequences of the global diffusion of the Chicago blues is that these symbols of authenticity are recognizable throughout the world and reinforced by similarly bombastic and exaggerated representations of the blues in popular films, television shows, advertisements, and music videos. However, a cursory view of the city's contemporary blues clubs reveals a wide range of inconsistencies. First, musicians of all racial, ethnic, and class backgrounds perform in blues clubs throughout the city; in fact, for reasons that I will explain in a later chapter, *white* musicians are actually far more likely to perform in clubs located in black neighborhoods than in other areas of the city. While blues fans may imagine otherwise, local musicians generally prefer to play in high-paying downtown and suburban clubs instead of in run-down bars brimming with the markers of authenticity and urban grit. Also, the conceit that working-class blacks produce and consume the blues outside of the context of local battles over authenticity is not only elitist, but reveals the extent to which this population has been historically and unfairly viewed as anti-intellectual and hopelessly naive.

The relationship here between race and the blues deserves special attention because blackness may very well be *the* dominant signifier of authenticity in the blues. In the world of the blues, authenticity claims are frequently made about black musicians and audiences, in part because during the 1920s early record companies like Columbia designated virtually all of their secular recordings by African Americans as "blues," in order to more efficiently market their black artists in a racially segregated society—even though many of those recordings were not stylistically different from their white "hillbilly" counterparts. By demarcating all the music recorded by these artists, regardless of musical persuasion, as distinctively *black* music pressed onto vinyl as "race records," this institutional process played a significant role in eventually racializing nearly *all* popular music as either authentically black or white, regardless of singing style, lyrical content, melody, or harmony.[14]

Perhaps for this reason, it is difficult to define the specific contours of the blues genre at all, much less construct an accurate definition of authenticity in the blues. Certainly, our academic definitions of the blues style rely on idealized stereotypes that create more confusion than clarity, as demonstrated by the *Concise Oxford Dictionary of Music*'s entry:

Blues. Slow jazz song of lamentation, generally for an unhappy love affair. Usually in groups of 12 bars, instead of 8 or 16, each stanza being three lines covering 4 bars of music. Tonality predominantly major, but with the flattened 3rd and 7th of the key (the "blue notes"). Harmony tended toward the plagal or the subdominant. The earlier (almost entirely Negro) history of the Blues is traced by oral tradition as far back as the 1860s, but the form was popularized about 1911–14 by the Negro composer W.C. Handy (*St. Louis Blues, Basin Street Blues*). Composers such as Gershwin, Ravel, Copland, and Tippett have used the term to indicate a Blues-type mood rather than a strict adherence to the form. Among notable blues singers were Bessie Smith and Billie Holiday.[15]

A more extensive and technical definition appears in the *Harvard Concise Dictionary of Music:*

Blues.   Most often, a type of jazz based on a repeated harmonic progression consisting of twelve measures of 4/4 time in which measures 1–4 are on the tonic, measures 5–8 on the subdominant, measures 9–10 on the dominant, and measures 11–12 on the tonic. Although its origins among American Negroes are vocal, the blues can be either vocal or strictly instrumental. Often, though not always, the tempo is moderate or slow, in keeping with the sad or resigned character of many of the sung texts. The texts frequently consist of two statements, the first of which accompanies measures 1–4 and is repeated for measures 5–8. The melodies accompanying the harmonic progression make frequent use of the lowered third and seventh degrees (called blue notes), and like other pitches employed, these may be inflected in ways that do not conform to equal temperament. Similarly, the basic harmonic structure may be elaborated upon by means of secondary dominants and the like. Thus, the lowered seventh in the melody often occurs as an element of a seventh chord on the tonic in measure 4, which chord functions as the dominant seventh of the subdominant of measure 5. Published blues occur as early as 1912 with W.C. Handy's *Memphis Blues*. But a substantial part of the tradition is improvisatory. Ma Rainey, Bessie Smith, and Huddie "Leadbelly" Ledbetter were among the important early exponents of this tradition.

From this particular type of musical structure, the term has been extended to apply to the general style of performance with which it is associated and to the dejected state of mind frequently expressed in its texts. Early uses of the term are also not restricted to the type described above.[16]

In spite of this last caveat against making generalizations about the early blues form, these definitions are fairly specific. Not surprisingly, a lot of music that is commonly (and, I think, appropriately) called blues cannot so easily squeeze into this pigeonhole of a category, including the long list of relatively well-known eight-bar blues songs, like Brownie McGhee's "Key to the Highway 70," and sixteen-bar blues like Muddy Waters's "I'm Your Hoochie Coochie Man." (In fact, W.C. Handy's "St. Louis Blues" reverts between twelve- *and* sixteen-bar verses.) Meanwhile, a "Blues-type mood" may conjure up images of the world-weary and down-and-out, but in fact the history of the blues suggests a litany of happy-go-lucky rhythms and rhymes from the piano boogie-woogie dance music of the 1930s to the guitar hot-dogging of contemporary blues jammers.

It also hardly helps that styles as disparate as the mournful, thread-bare folksongs of Leadbelly and Son House, the cabaret singing of Bessie Smith, the orchestral jazz of Duke Ellington, the rollicking guitar of Muddy Waters, and the soul stirrings of Bobby "Blue" Bland are often lumped together as part of the same blues genre. This mess is furthered by the fact that aspects of the blues as we know it (as well as other comparable early southern musical styles) can been found in almost every American popular music form of the twentieth century, including country, bluegrass, rhythm and blues, rock 'n' roll, reggae, hip-hop, and even electronic dance music, as demonstrated by the critical success of the New York–based techno artist Moby's 1999 release *Play* and its sampling of traditional folk-blues songs like Vera Hall's "Trouble So Hard" and Bill Landford and the Landfordaires' "Run on for a Long Time." But ironically, instead of challenging the many overarching claims made in the name of authenticity, the liquidity of the blues only seems to help reinforce the commonly held assumption that any song performed by a black singer should rightfully be considered a blues song and, consequently, that the blues can only be delivered in an authentic manner by a black artist—a position that few Chicago blues musicians, white *or* black, would defend.

The Search for Authenticity.   However, while authenticity may be little more than an idealized representation of reality, it hardly means that it ceases to exist as a social fact. Although it remains a figment of our collective imagination, we still continue to employ the concept of authenticity as an organizing principle for evaluating our experiences in everyday life, and that makes it significantly meaningful and, in many ways, *real.* In this manner, authenticity shares a similar place in our hearts as love or beauty: it is an old wives' tale we tell ourselves over and over again until we believe it to be true, and as a result it gains a certain kind of power over us. As the influential Chicago sociologists W. I. Thomas and Dorothy Swaine Thomas remind us, "If men define their situations as real, they are real in their consequences."[17]

If authenticity is simply nonexistent in the material world but *does* exist as a social fact of life, then what exactly does it mean, as my book subtitle suggests, for a sociologist to "search for authenticity"? As I suggested above, as a sociologist I am not interested in attempting to complete the impossible task of evaluating what is and what is not authentic in the blues. Instead, I want to understand how different kinds of people within the world of the Chicago blues employ the concept of authenticity in their daily rounds of everyday life. How do club owners and performers attempt to manufacture authenticity for their audiences? How do consumers evaluate their experiences consuming blues in terms of authenticity? How do different kinds of musicians forge dissimilar types of artistic identities on the basis of their own multiple definitions of what constitutes an authentic blues performance or record? How do bar regulars explain their affiliation with their favorite blues clubs by employing the language of authenticity? How do each of these groups of people search for authenticity in the urban metropolis, and, more importantly, how do they know (or *think* they know) when they have found it?

In other words, as my research began, I was interested in conducting a truly sociological study of authenticity—a study that would analyze authenticity not as an objective and undeniable reality, like gravity, or the eternal hopelessness of the Chicago Cubs, but as an arbitrarily measured kind of value, like money. The search for authenticity in Chicago's blues clubs is not so much a quest for some actual material thing, but for what participants in these clubs merely imagine to be the symbols of authenticity, all manufactured, bartered, sold, and consumed within a *symbolic economy of authenticity*—that is, a specific network of commodified signs, social relations, and meanings, a world of human experience and subjectivity. I wanted to understand how this economy worked by mapping out exactly how different audiences, club regulars, musicians, bartenders, and bar owners define authenticity and then attempt to seek it out in the context of the blues club.[18]

Once I decided to embark upon this sociological study of authenticity, I began taking my visits to B.L.U.E.S. much more seriously, and while my first weeks of observation were admittedly casual and preliminary,

I eventually began working on what amounted to a year-long ethnographic study based primarily on participant observation and interviewing, both of which I conducted at local blues clubs throughout the city. I began this more formal stage of my research in January 1998 by collecting field observations at B.L.U.E.S. and its satellite club, appropriately (if unimaginatively) called B.L.U.E.S. Etcetera. About two or three times a week, I would arrive at one of these clubs shortly after their house bands began their first set, order a beer, and strike up open-ended barroom conversations with audience members, during which I would ask them about their general tastes in music, expectations of the club, and their reflections on Chicago. At the same time, I would try to document the surrounding social worlds existing within these clubs, with special attention given to the onstage performances of the entertainers employed by them.

When the clubs closed at two o'clock in the morning, I would usually head home and type up my field observations from the evening, documenting these barroom encounters to the best of my recollection. Likewise, whenever possible I attempted to jot down notes at the clubs, and frequently an intriguing conversation would send me to the men's rest room so I could scribble down a particularly juicy quote onto a cocktail napkin. In the interests of producing the most accurate account possible, I found myself constantly challenging these recollections for their veracity, particular when their accuracy seemed compromised by my beer consumption and other assorted distractions.[19]

At a certain point, I realized that my emphasis on B.L.U.E.S. and B.L.U.E.S. Etcetera, while providing me with an increasingly familiar space in which to conduct my research, could potentially hinder my ability to accurately depict the variation among blues clubs located in other regions of the city. To supplement my ethnographic study of these two venues, I conducted additional observations in thirty-six blues-oriented bars, nightclubs, restaurants, and cafés located in an ethnically diverse range of neighborhoods and entertainment zones throughout the city, including those in Grand Boulevard, Greater Grand Crossing, Irving Park, Lakeview, Lincoln Park, Lincoln Square, Logan Square, the Loop, Near North Side, Near South Side, Rogers Park, Uptown, and West Town.[20] This expansion of the study brought me to places as diverse as the Checkerboard Lounge, a well-worn tavern located in Bronzeville, one of the city's historic black districts; Smoke Daddy, a neighborhood juke joint that sits along Division Street in the gentrifying bohemia of

West Town; and a series of downtown tourists attractions such as Blue Chicago, Buddy Guy's Legends, and the House of Blues. By extending my research to these clubs, I attempted to compare and contrast how audiences and participants experienced their different environments, and where they located these clubs within their own mental maps of the city's entertainment landscape.

As the months of research at these clubs continued, I came to understand the extent to which representations of blackness figured into local definitions of authenticity in the blues. Among black Americans, the popularity of the blues has actually declined since the mid-1950s while that of soul, rhythm and blues, jazz, reggae, and hip-hop has increased over the past forty years; meanwhile, its popularity among whites has continued to increase since the 1960s, in part as a result of that decade's folk revival, the rise of blues-oriented rock music by bands like the Rolling Stones, and the heightened visibility of black culture in the wake of the post–civil rights era. Perhaps for this reason, Chicago's contemporary blues clubs serve a predominately white clientele.[21]

However, it became clear that these overwhelmingly white audiences still expected to be entertained by *black* singers and musicians, and most club owners catered to this desire by exclusively booking black bands, rather than interracial or all-white groups. Meanwhile, in the interests of meeting audience demands for the stereotypical symbols of authenticity in the blues, the performances of these black musicians came to resemble latter-day minstrel shows, a mélange of cartoonlike stock caricatures sprinkled with racially charged jokes and sexual put-ons of varying degrees of taste. This identification of blackness qua authentic culture also drove white out-of-towners and college students to black neighborhood bars like the Checkerboard Lounge, where they could consume the authenticity represented by the ghetto, just as slumming socialites flocked to Chicago's black and tan jazz cabarets during the 1920s to release themselves from the bourgeois constraints of Victorian prudishness and sobriety.[22]

Admittedly, the racism suggested by this behavior is not as clearly pronounced today as it might have been during the Jazz Age. One of the consequences of the civil rights movement is that the recent successes of multiculturalism and identity politics have increased the attractiveness of consuming black culture among whites, and, in fact, local blues clubs represent some of the most racially integrated leisure spots in the city. However, insofar as these music fans often draw on very traditional, stereotypical images of black men and women in their search for authenticity in the blues, even the most well-intentioned audiences frequently confuse the commodification of racial difference with interracial solidarity and liberalism in a post–civil rights era.

Of course, this begs the question of exactly *why* authenticity is so important to these cultural consumers. In this book I argue that in some ways these audiences collectively revere the dominant symbols of authenticity in the blues as a means of producing the currency with which they might compete against one another for the social status associated with what I like to call a *nocturnal self*—that is, a special kind of presentation of self associated with consuming urban nightlife. While sociologists are used to thinking about status in terms of the set of hierarchical categories that structure our political, economic, and occupational lives, a very real, status-conscious universe exists within downtown spaces of urban entertainment and leisure as well. A cursory view around any velvet-roped nightclub in Chicago, New York, Philadelphia, Los Angeles, or any other American city reveals a raw competitiveness to rival the great duels of medieval days and chivalrous knights. On any given weekend, a series of contests fills the evening hours: bouncers size up and challenge the social status of queued-up patrons desiring admittance; customers match wits with one another for the attention of a bartender; half-drunk men and women stumble over each other in their attempts at "scoring" (an interesting term) with their fellow revelers; ostentatious couples strive to outdo each other by publicly dramatizing the most gratuitous displays of affection; hot-tempered men challenge one another to fistfights over barely muttered insults; and so forth.

Similarly, by competing within a symbolic economy of authenticity, people can vie for all sorts of intangible rewards made more attractive by their meaning than their economic value.[23] Once the signs of authenticity have been agreed upon, the competition for what the late French sociologist Pierre Bourdieu would refer to as cultural capital—or perhaps in this case *nocturnal capital*—may commence, as thrill-seekers compete among their peers for the bragging rights that accompany the experience of authenticity. In doing so, they may present themselves to the world in the same symbolic language used to depict the nightlife of the city: that is, as cosmopolitan, subculturally savvy, and tragically hip. Of course, this competition operates according to a zero-sum game in which too many seekers of authenticity can easily spoil the fun for everyone else. This happens when a blues club recognized for its authentic qualities becomes *too* popular among travelers in search of the proverbial road-not-taken and suddenly leaves those out-of-towners tripping over each other's knapsacks, all wondering where all the damn tourists came from.

But while gaining nocturnal capital can augment how one presents oneself to *others*, it is also the case that nightclubbers search for authenticity when they look inward with the universal desire to enhance how they see *themselves*. By forging a nocturnal self in the city's bars, nightclubs, restaurants, and cafés, late-night revelers achieve a very personal kind of satisfaction that cannot simply be reduced to social status gain; rather, the self-esteem generated by their successful negotiation of the city's entertainment options seems to represent the fulfillment of a dream. In my travels through Chicago's bars, I consistently met bouncing, smiling customers who, when prompted by little more than an inviting gesture, would gush about how proud they were to have discovered for themselves the never-ending authenticity suggested by the atmosphere of a smoke-filled, dimly lit blues club. In these moments, I realized that the search for authenticity may not only stem from the fantasy of consuming that which is considered authentic, but from the desire to actually *become* authentic, to attain a sense of authenticity for oneself. While this authentic feeling may only exist as a mirage, this hardly makes it less palpable for these blues fans—again, when people define their situations as real, they are real in their consequences.

The Interpretation of Authenticity. As the months wore on, I realized that not all of the audience members I encountered in the city's blues clubs actually experienced them in the same way, and in fact they often disagreed when it came to identifying the most dominant markers of authenticity in the blues. While we tend to universalize our impressions of authenticity by assuming that it possesses natural and objective properties, in reality different kinds of audiences approach the issue of authenticity with varying degrees of intensity and focus, and sometimes rely on contradictory sets of criteria when evaluating a particular place or performance. The search for authenticity is an exercise in symbolic production in which participants frequently disagree on what specific kinds of symbols connote or suggest authenticity, and even those who agree on the symbols themselves may share different views on how they might manifest themselves in the world. In other words, different kinds of blues audiences represent what the literary critic Stanley Fish refers to as "interpretive communities," insofar as each of these groups experiences the world of the club in a somewhat different way.[24]

These differences emerged into focus when I began meeting local audience members at B.L.U.E.S. The role that these audiences play emerged early on during my fieldwork around the time I discovered that the club employed a "Good Neighbor" policy whereby customers who either worked or resided nearby received free admission every Tuesday evening. I began attending regularly, and after a few short weeks, Jack, the bouncer, started to recognize me and eventually granted me free admittance to the club on other nights as well. I then got to know some of the bartenders fairly well, and they came to know me, if only by my usual order, a $3.25 bottle of Budweiser; over time our conversations shifted from pleasant small talk to more interesting matters concerning the cultural world of the club.[25]

During these weeknight sessions at B.L.U.E.S., I was always intrigued by how different the club seemed as compared to other weekends, and I began to recognize a familiar cast of regulars made up of professional and amateur musicians, local blues fans, and the bartenders and bouncers employed by other local bars in the area. At first I was very surprised, as I had not expected that a club as tourist-oriented as B.L.U.E.S. would be able to attract a community of regulars; after all, I hardly expected to see similar local gangs at the bar areas of the Hard Rock Cafe or Planet Hollywood. I eventually got to know several of them, and soon my focus shifted from a study of out-of-towners to an exploration of how regulars conceptualized authenticity in the context of the club.

While approaching these regulars became a less daunting task as my fieldwork progressed, I still had problems meeting and developing rapport with the professional and amateur musicians who perform at these clubs. In some sense, I can attribute this difficulty to these musicians' expectations of outsiders, especially those who ask a lot of questions. Unlike bar regulars and bartenders, musicians are used to attracting newspaper reporters, entertainment columnists, and adoring music fans, and they initially gave me the cold shoulder or else a friendly but distanced greeting.

As a means of gaining their trust, I started playing the alto saxophone—quite badly, I might add—at a weekly jam session every Wednesday night at B.L.U.E.S. Etcetera. At first I was nervous about my performing abilities, as I had not really practiced much since high school, but after digging out my beginner's horn from the dusty corner of my kitchen closet and playing out of tune for a few embarrassing weeks, I found that my lack of experience actually eased my interactions with more seasoned musicians excited to mentor a new, if clumsy, protégé. In a few months' time, I expanded my study by performing at jam sessions held in different bars throughout the city. In addition, I was offered the opportunity to sit in with a number of blues bands to provide accompaniment and an occasional improvised solo during their performances at local clubs.

During this time I concentrated my efforts on interviewing black and white blues musicians in order to understand how they experience their role within the day-to-day world of the club. Because of the complicated and unpredictable schedules of these performers, I would typically conduct these interviews at the clubs in the early evening before they opened and after they closed for the night. The interviews were loosely structured and varied in degree of formality, ranging from sporadic bar conversations to organized tape-recorded interviews lasting up to several hours. I asked them to describe how they began their careers as blues artists, their experiences as performers in local clubs, and their attitudes concerning their peers, club owners, and contemporary audiences. Additionally, I asked questions pertaining to recent shifts in the production, marketing, and consumption of blues in Chicago and elicited their evaluation of these shifts in terms of the quality of the music currently performed in local clubs, the hiring practices of club owners and booking agents, and any significant changes that they felt advanced or limited their artistic integrity or commercial appeal as entertainers. They were also asked to describe how they understood their identity as musicians, their status in the local blues community, and their relations with other members of that community.

After conducting this part of the research, I discovered that like more mainstream audiences, these regulars and musicians were also very interested in authenticity but tended to define it according to a slightly different set of criteria. Regulars experience B.L.U.E.S. as a place of refuge where authenticity is measured in terms of the club's ability to represent an idealized vision of community and moral order. Like authenticity, the concept of community represents a romanticized reality that can only be identified and judged subjectively and does not exist independently of our popular assumptions regarding what "real" communities are like. In their search for authenticity, bar regulars seek out images of neighborhood tavern life when they patronize local clubs. By forging nocturnal selves that emphasize membership in such a community, these regulars can experience the blues club *as* regulars by enjoying the emotional benefits associated with the role, including a sense of individual worth. At the same time, those seduced by the authenticity often attached to the blues club attempt to join this urban community by constructing a nocturnal identity that evokes a highly extroverted aura of subcultural cool.

Meanwhile, among more professional musicians, concerns over authenticity always play a role in determining how they view their own status as musicians, but unlike their audiences, they tend to search for authenticity within the musical performance itself, as opposed to the racial ascription of the performer or the clubs where their performances occur. In doing so, some evaluate their authenticity in terms of their adherence to traditional styles of blues playing, while others define it in terms of artistic innovation and individualism. At the same time, many view popular concerns over authenticity as a hindrance that in some cases prevents them from convincing their audiences of their authenticity and in other instances constrains their ability to perform at all. In fact, for some of these performers, the sliding scale of authenticity was not the yardstick by which they measured their worth as musicians, but served as a stumbling block to their success and happiness, and thus represented a false stereotype—an expectation to be overcome, rather than achieved.

The Making of Urban Authenticity. In the first third of the twentieth century, professors and graduate students affiliated with the Department of Sociology at the University of Chicago produced a series of ethnographic monographs detailing the social and subcultural variety of the city's urban worlds—the outdoor kosher markets of the Jewish ghetto, the smoke-filled Persian coffeehouses along Wells Street, and, most relevant to the present discussion, the jazz and blues cabarets of the racially segregated region of the city that Chicago sociologists St. Clair Drake and Horace Cayton dubbed Black Metropolis.[26] As members of the influential Chicago school of urban sociology, Robert Park, Ernest Burgess, and others argued that neighborhoods, streets, and other areas of the city had a "natural history" that could be observed and documented as they evolved over time, with each stage of past development contributing to the sum total of its present form. As Park argues in *The City*, urban spaces, subcultures, and other forms of social organization are always "the outcome of a historic process in which many individuals participated without foreseeing what the ultimate product of their labors was to be."[27] To these sociologists, cities could be thought of as living, breathing ecosystems brimming with energy, rather than dead walls of concrete and asphalt.

For example, in the three most important studies of urban culture during this period—Paul Cressey's *The Taxi-Dance Hall*, Walter Reckless's *Vice in Chicago*, and Harvey Zorbaugh's *The Gold Coast and the Slum*—these researchers examined the temporal context in which subcultures quickly develop over time as a process of accumulation and change, rather than as fixed and stagnant worlds. In *The Gold Coast and the Slum*, Zorbaugh explores the pathways of immigrant enclaves and transitional neighborhoods on Chicago's Near North Side as a means of uncovering the social archaeology of these urban spaces and their entertainment zones. For example, in a chapter on Towertown, the downtown area's pseudo-bohemian artist colony packed with cheap galleries and grungy tearooms, he describes the neighborhood as a work in progress, from its early days when intellectual giants like Sherwood Anderson and Carl Sandburg strolled its sidewalks, to its late 1920s present, a time of commercialized eccentricity and staged authenticity where high-society types took organized guided tours of local dives and run-down studio spaces.[28]

The commercialization of the Chicago blues is similarly a work in progress, and I attempted to uncover its past by asking musicians and longtime bar regulars to recall their early days of misspent youth fraternizing in the city's blues bars and taverns. As they would often wax nostalgic about hanging out in clubs during the 1960s and 1970s by recollecting those moments in oral narratives refracted through rose-tinted lenses, I was able to follow their search for authenticity over time by critically examining how their memories of this not-too-distant past, both real and imagined, continue to shape their current perspective on the commercialization of the current blues scene. I supplemented this fieldwork with more traditional historical research by relying on documents found in the permanent collections of the Chicago Historical Society and the Harold Washington Public Library, including the Chicago Blues Archive, housed at the latter institution. These documents included old music festival programs, photographs, newspaper clippings, and a collection of sixty guidebooks to the city published between 1945 and 1995.

With the help of this archival and ethnographic material, I was able to reconstruct a cultural history of the rise of the Chicago blues bar as a tourist attraction, with special emphasis on how this history has been shaped by the needs of commerce, the search for authenticity, and its promotion in the local mainstream and alternative press. I discovered that the blues became popular among local white audiences in the hippie enclave of Old Town during the rise of the 1960s counterculture and the New Left. Ironically, despite the popularity of the blues in Chicago's Black Belt since the 1920s, civic boosters only began incorporating the city's cultural heritage as the so-called "Home of the Blues" or "Blues Capital of the World" into its overall image in the late 1960s after *white* audiences began patronizing blues bars in this North Side neighborhood, after which it became economically and politically viable for local elites to appropriate for their own ends. Meanwhile, more alternative voices like the *Chicago Reader* suggested that blues fans trek to the city's black neighborhoods to find the authenticity represented by the aforementioned stereotypical images of blackness. Of course, today the city wholeheartedly embraces its blues legacy and its popularity around the globe; after all, cities often rely on their ability to connote a successful image of authenticity, staged or otherwise, in order to increase their status in the global tourism economy and benefit from the increased revenue and cultural capital that this prestige provides.

Books like *The Gold Coast and the Slum* are still admired today because they attempt to understand how the city operates as a process of cumulative change within the local context of time and space. However, one of the problems inherent in their ecological model of urbanism is their lack of attention to how powerful political forces existing *outside* the context of the immediate neighborhood environment impact local cultures in crucial ways. If Zorbaugh, Park, and others had placed more emphasis on the role that centralized city governance, institutionalized racism, and the collusion of local entrepreneurial and political elites all play in molding the cultural and commercial landscapes of cities, their work might have better illuminated the larger sociological forces that truly lend shape to the urban environment.

In fact, the authenticity represented by Chicago's blues heritage does not reflect the city's "natural" legacy, but a manufactured image of Chicago, promoted in local brochures, guidebooks, newspapers, and tacky souvenir kiosks that dot hotel lobbies throughout the central business district. In order to document how the city draws on popular representations of authenticity to market itself to the world as the "Home of the Blues," I left the noisy din of B.L.U.E.S. and the Checkerboard Lounge to begin examining how the city represents the blues in more officially sanctioned settings like the Chicago Cultural Center; the city's Neighborhood Tours program, which takes visitors on bus trips through South Side ghetto communities and other local areas; and the Chicago Blues Festival held annually along the downtown lakefront in Grant Park. Through a variety of ethnographic endeavors ranging from conducting interviews with public officials to performing blues standards with marginalized street musicians on the outskirts of the festival, I explored how Chicago's local government and civic boosters appropriate its local blues heritage as a means of marketing the city to out-of-towners as an idealized world of authenticity. In doing so, I found that the city had commodified its musical and ethnic populism as officially sponsored cultural attractions in order to increase local tourism revenues, all while masking their efforts behind the rhetoric of multiculturalism and progressive politics.[29]

Black and Tan Fantasy.   The organization of the book's chapters is as follows. In chapter 1 I discuss the relationship between race and authenticity in the Chicago blues and examine how club owners, musicians, and audiences attempt to manufacture authenticity in local clubs by drawing on dominant stereotypes of black men and women. Chapter 2 focuses on how audiences create nocturnal identities for themselves as they seek out idealized images of authenticity in the city's blues bars. In chapter 3 I shift my attention from these audiences to the social world of bar regulars and their search for authenticity, while chapter 4 discusses how musicians define authenticity in the blues, particularly in a context of commercialization. Chapter 5 provides a brief history of the rise of the blues club as a tourist attraction, and in chapter 6 I move outside the context of the club to critically examine how local city boosters appropriate Chicago's blues legacy and the authenticity it represents as a means of increasing its prestige in the global tourism economy, concluding with an account of the annual Chicago Blues Festival as a site where many of the themes of the book come to a head: the commodification of the urban landscape, the global reach of American popular culture, the relationship between city politics and cultural commerce, and, of course, the search for authenticity in the Chicago blues. In chapter 7 I conclude with a short discussion about how the theoretical implications suggested by these chapters might be applied to a general understanding of how authenticity operates as an organizing principle for structuring other aspects of human experience: the rise of urban tourism in the post-industrial metropolis, the consumption of alternative forms of popular culture, and, finally, the search for authenticity within the contemporary practice of sociology.

In 1927 Duke Ellington and His Orchestra recorded "Black and Tan Fantasy," a short composition that combines the blues melodies of the

Deep South and the muted trumpets and stride piano of Harlem's jazz sound with, of all things, Chopin's Funeral March from his piano sonata in B Flat Minor. The name of the piece recalls the multiracial social world of the black and tan cabarets of the 1920s Jazz Age in which black musicians entertained racially integrated audiences in Chicago and New York, notably in the black commercial districts of Bronzeville and Harlem, respectively. In these clubs blacks and whites experienced the pleasures of Prohibition whiskey, wild dancing, and occasionally each other, insofar as these venues represented some of the few available public spaces of leisure in urban America where the races could mingle with a relative degree of freedom. It is this blurring of racial and cultural boundaries that Ellington's orchestra draws on in "Black and Tan Fantasy," with its harmonious and seamless mix of European classical music, ragtime jazz, and the Mississippi blues.[30]

Of course, like many blues songs, "Black and Tan Fantasy" carries with it a kind of melancholy humor, a bittersweet reminder of how the black and tan cabarets of Chicago's Black Belt hardly evoked the same harmoniousness suggested by the performance of this elegant yet mournful prayer for a racially united society. These clubs attracted predominately white patrons who valued the experience of "slumming" in a seemingly exotic and sexualized world represented by the era's dominant stereotypes of black men and women. For this reason, the kinds of social encounters in which whites engaged with blacks tended to be highly patronizing and offensive, and were often rooted in the misperception that black entertainers (and, to a certain extent, black customers) naturally enjoyed dancing and smiling for paying consumers as a means of sharing their god-given birthright of hot sensuality and cool soul in exchange for their humanity.[31] And so, perhaps Ellington's "Black and Tan Fantasy" not only suggests the dream of an integrated world to come, but also provides a critical commentary on the fantasy held by whites regarding the forbidden pleasures associated with black music and entertainment at that moment in American history.

The interracial mix of entertainers and customers featured in Chicago's contemporary blues clubs evokes a similar kind of sensibility. In some ways, clubs like B.L.U.E.S. and the Checkerboard Lounge represent little more than latter-day versions of the classic black-and-tans of yesteryear, with their emphasis on black minstrelsy, the commercialization of public culture, and the never-ending search for authenticity among white customers. On the other hand, a number of differences distinguish today's blues clubs from their earlier counterparts. First, as

I suggest in an earlier section of the introduction, the racially charged consumerism demonstrated by contemporary audiences is not as sharply drawn today as it might have been during the Roaring Twenties. In the current post–civil rights era, the visibility of black Americans has increased the attractiveness of consuming black culture among liberally minded, well-intentioned whites, and friendly encounters between blacks and whites at local clubs are not uncommon. Of course, this is not to say that prejudicial motivations are absent from the commodification of blackness and the proliferation of racial stereotypes in this context; however, I would point out that these contemporary settings must be viewed through the political and social realities of the present if we are to understand their internal complexities and contradictions.

Second, even a cursory view of contemporary blues clubs suggests a far more socially complicated world than might be suggested by the classic black and tan cabaret. The professional and amateur musicians who perform in today's clubs are black and white, German and Japanese. Their international audiences—composed of expatriates, immigrants, foreign students, and business travelers from the Caribbean Islands, Latin America, Continental Europe and the British Isles, North Africa, and the Far East—further complicate the traditional racial and ethnic divides suggestive of past cultural struggles and animosities. If the earliest blues music represented a global cultural hybrid of West African polyrhythms and dialects, European dance music and the rural twangs of the American South, then the contemporary climate of internationalized music production and consumption, intense differences in race, ethnicity, nationality, class, and age among local band members and audiences members, and the influence of soul, rhythm and blues, gospel, reggae, rap, zydeco, rock 'n' roll, and heavy metal on modern-day styles of performance makes for an even greater global mélange of sound, music, and interpretation in a bar like B.L.U.E.S.[32]

Finally, while the most celebrated blues and jazz clubs of the Jazz Age were pitched as tourist attractions—the Cotton Club, Ed Small's Paradise, the Dreamland Café—contemporary black-and-tans raise the commercial bar at these venues to new heights of organization and cooperation with local business and city government. While the Black Belt was always popular among Chicago's high-society crowd, today the Department of Cultural Affairs markets the city's blues clubs to tourists in their promotional brochures, and downtown hotels offer discount passes to local venues for their out-of-town guests. The Chicago Blues Festival, organized by the Mayor's Office of Special Events, attracts high-end corporate sponsorship and civic support along with an annual attendance of over 660,000 visitors for the four-day event. In fact, the city's appropriation of its blues legacy has grown so enthusiastic in recent years that the Department of Environment used it not too long ago to promote its landfill conservation and waste management strategies, drawing on its fame as the "Home of the Blues" to advertise its blue-bag recycling campaign on the sides of public city buses.

When Robert Johnson penned his well-known ode to the city, "Sweet Home Chicago," it is unclear whether this is quite what he had in mind. Duke Ellington's "Black and Tan Fantasy" may be equally elusive, although it is said that at one time it was fashionable among black Americans to sing along to the first bars of Chopin's Funeral March: "Where will we all / Be / A hundred years / From now?"[33] I can hardly offer an answer to that question, but we can certainly turn to the contemporary city of Chicago to see whether the "Home of the Blues," even today, still feels like that same old place.

Blues in Black and White
The Politics of Race and Authenticity

When the downtown nightclubs had closed, most of these Harlem places crawled with white people. These whites were just mad for Negro "atmosphere," especially some of the places which had what you might call Negro *soul*. Sometimes Negroes would talk about how a lot of whites seemed unable to have enough of being close around us, and among us—in groups. Both white men and women, it seemed, would get almost mesmerized by Negroes.

—Alex Haley, *The Autobiography of Malcolm X*

The Racial Politics of the Chicago Blues.   Musicians, critics, and fans of American blues music have always championed an ideology that regards the dialectical relationship between musician and audience as its paramount concern. They depict the blues as populist music that appeals to audiences on the basis of its ability to express a universal set of emotions, whether despair, longing, fear, or jealousy. At the same time, myths surrounding the social role of blues musicians have always emphasized their desires to please their listeners in exchange for whiskey and gin, spare change, enthusiastic applause, and sexual favors. Local blues musicians tend to internalize such myths by comporting themselves as craftsmen performing in the service of their audiences. Unlike artists in fields considered more avant-garde, such as atonal jazz or performance art, blues musicians frequently conceptualize artistic success in terms of public popularity and financial profitability.[1]

Perhaps as a result, blues musicians have traditionally structured their performances in order to meet the assumed expectations of their audiences. In Chicago the blues helped to define a certain kind of urban life for local blacks seeking refuge and entertainment in the segregated neighborhoods where they worked and resided from the time of the Great Migration until the 1960s.[2] Since South and West Side blues taverns served a steady clientele of local patrons, they were able to function as urban havens where community residents, musicians, and even the occasional white visitor could congregate and socialize. The consistency of neighborhood audiences allowed these clubs and their employees to cater to highly specific kinds of consumer tastes and demands.[3]

The populist and participatory quality of the blues at this time revealed itself in the stylistic shifts fashioned by musicians as they struggled to follow the changing demands of their audiences. During the 1920s urban vaudeville and cabaret singers emphasized the comedic and sexual elements of Tin Pan Alley numbers in order to curry favor with urban blacks and slumming whites.[4] In later years boogie-woogie pianists developed a faster syncopated blues to suit dancing crowds at rent parties and small local taverns. During the 1940s jump blues singers performed ballads at venues like the Flame Club on Chicago's South Side, and in the early 1950s musicians shifted toward perfecting a more rural sound heavily influenced by the country-blues of the Mississippi Delta.[5] While stylistic and thematic continuities (including the reliance on twelve- and sixteen-bar chord progressions, flattened third and seventh notes, backbeat rhythms, and lyrical allusions to labor, poverty, escape, love, and death) have remained in the blues idiom in spite of these changes, musicians have continually reinvented the blues tradition in order to suit the shifting tastes of their audiences.[6]

But during the 1960s the popularity of blues music in Chicago among black audiences dropped considerably. Delta-raised blues musicians such as Muddy Waters and Howlin' Wolf gradually fell out of favor among urban black audiences, who derided their countrified and somewhat old-fashioned styles of performance as "gutbucket," "low-class" music because it served as a reminder of the toil and racism of the southern plantations they had left behind. As the popularity of modern soul, rhythm and blues, doo-wop, and Motown pop music grew exponentially among black consumers during this time, radio airplay, jukebox popularity, and record and ticket sales dropped sharply for more traditional blues artists.[7]

Meanwhile, *white* audiences began listening to blues musicians with greater frequency in Chicago's black neighborhood taverns and uptown clubs, and visitors slowly began to trickle down to the city to watch them perform. The irony of this commercial shift is striking: while blues musicians like Waters had trouble packing black neighborhood *bars* in cities like Detroit and Minneapolis during the 1960s, these same artists found increased popularity among large white audiences of jazz, folk, and rock music in stadiums and concert halls across America and Europe.[8] The increased popularity of blues among whites in Chicago occurred as a result of several coinciding events. The emergent folk revival during the early 1960s revalorized rural country-blues music across the nation because its unrestrained, rustic melodies were considered a more "authentic" alternative to the highly commodified rock and pop offerings by the major record labels and commercial radio.[9] At the same time, prominent blues legends like Waters gained exposure as black popular culture grew more visible among white Americans during the rise of the civil rights movement.

But perhaps the most significant reason for the rising popularity of blues music among white audiences in Chicago is that an increasing number of white musicians performing blues locally as well as internationally made the blues seem more accessible to mainstream white audiences. These musicians included celebrated pop stars like Bob Dylan and the Rolling Stones, who incorporated a diverse selection of blues motifs and styles into their folk and rock compositions and performances. But in Chicago these musicians also included scores of white hipsters and self-proclaimed bohemians who hobnobbed with local black performers in South Side blues taverns; racially mixed areas of the city such as the famed Maxwell Street Market, where Jewish merchants sold their wares alongside black street performers and hollerers; and up-and-coming blues bars located in gentrifying North Side neighborhoods in the city.[10] Today these white performers make up a sizable proportion of Chicago's blues musicians: they include young musicians who have recently begun to establish themselves in the local music scene and more experienced players who have sustained longer, if marginal, careers in the city's blues clubs.

As a result of the newfound popularity of blues music in Chicago among white audiences, blues bars began rapidly proliferating in the North Side neighborhoods where they resided. By the mid-1980s blues musicians could find relatively steady employment performing in these establishments as they began to attract large audiences consisting of suburban professionals and international business and leisure travelers. However, by this time the local blues clubs that had formerly hosted small crowds of local residents—clubs like B.L.U.E.S.—had become transformed into full-blown tourist attractions, and many of their new patrons possessed a less differentiated set of tastes and expectations regarding the music performed in them.

Today a notable consequence of this shift is that contemporary audiences are far more likely to evaluate the performances of local blues musicians on the basis of largely symbolic distinctions—particularly race—instead of their individually based stylistic qualities or deficiencies. Specifically, for many consumers, blackness connotes an extreme sense of authenticity, or what we might call the cultural construction of "soul" as a dominant racial stereotype. It is for this reason that in Chicago, the owners of tourist-oriented blues clubs almost exclusively hire black musicians, and many rarely hire white musicians at all. Elliot, a white singer and guitarist who performs in several downtown clubs, explains:

> It's because white audiences and owners are ignorant. The owners know that tourists will ask at the door, "Well, is the band playing tonight a *black* band, or is it a *white* band?" Because the tourists only want to hear black bands, because they want to see an authentic Chicago blues band, and they think a black band is more *real*, more *authentic*. When they come to Chicago, it's like they want to go to the "Disneyland of the Blues." You know, it's like this: people want German cars, French chefs, and, well, they want their bluesmen black. It's a designer label.

In fact, while audiences appreciate the performative aspects of the musician's stage act, they nevertheless demand to hear performances based, in part, on preconceived expectations regarding the authenticity of the stereotypical black blues player.[11] As Wally, the aforementioned Australian from the introduction, asks regarding a local show in the city: "So, it'll be the real deal, then, with a big black band playing up there and all?" Likewise, white audience members frequently direct insulting remarks at nonblack artists during their performances. One night as Marc, a young white singer and harmonica player, approaches the stage for a guest appearance, an audience member shouts from the back of the bar in drunken disgust: "Don't *sound* like no blues singer! . . . Don't *look* like no blues singer!"

Meanwhile, Franz, a middle-age blues fan from Germany, disparages one white bandleader's performance for what he regards as a lack of racial authenticity; he protests: "He just sings like a million other white

guys. His voice, his singing—it is not authentic." He counters this attitude with his enthusiastic approval of a rival black bandleader: "I like
him; he is very good. He is very emotional when he sings. Very authentic,
you know?" He clarifies his position by describing the reception of blues
music abroad:

> In Germany the blues is so popular that a show like this would have to be in
> a bigger club, because there would be maybe eight hundred people there,
> and they would all be cheering the whole time. But in Germany the blues
> musicians would have to be black, because if they were white, no one would
> come to see them. They would have to be black.

This way of thinking is characteristic of the general cultural framework
employed by many of the white music enthusiasts who actively participate in Chicago's blues culture: in fact, some amateur white musicians
even deny their *own* authenticity on the basis of racial difference. During a jam session at B.L.U.E.S. Etcetera, a now-defunct satellite club of
B.L.U.E.S. formerly located on Belmont Avenue in the North Side neighborhood of Lakeview, Nick, a keyboardist and new arrival to the city
from South Carolina, expresses his frustration with his playing by sigh-
ing, "Never in my life have I felt so *white*." I remind him that there
are plenty of white musicians present at the club in addition to himself,
but he qualifies his remark by explaining that his performance itself is
"white" because it lacks emotional drive and, therefore, authenticity:
"Part of the problem for me, I guess, is that I'm pretty happy, you know,
no complaints, and so I don't really have the blues, so it's hard to play
it. Maybe if I go home and break up with my girlfriend, then at least
I'll have a *reason* to have the blues." In criticizing his own performance
by drawing on a commonly held racial stereotype, Nick gives voice to an
assumption shared by many of the audience members who attend the
city's blues clubs.

   This assumption of racial difference extends to other ethnic groups
as well. During a performance at which Philip, who is originally from
Japan, plays with a group of black musicians, Mike and Jolynn offer their
impressions. "You know that *Sesame Street* song, 'One of these things is
not like the other, one of these things just doesn't belong'?" sings Mike.
"'Cause when you see some Japanese guy, you don't think, 'Oh, blues.' . . .
That's more part of the South, really." Nodding in agreement, Jolynn
adds, "I'm actually most surprised that they let him in the band at all!"
This kind of confusion over race and authenticity extends to bar staff as

well; on the presumed relationship between Philip's Japanese roots and his musical abilities, Jack (who is white) remarks, "He's a strong guitar player, but he doesn't know the language of the blues . . . but that's not surprising, given his background. As someone who studies cultures and societies and stuff like that, you probably understand just what I'm talking about, right, Dave?"[12]

"The Great Music Robbery" and the Problem with Authenticity.

These concerns expressed in Chicago blues bars echo the nagging fears and anxieties expressed during the 1960s by both black and white cultural critics who worried that the rising popularity of white blues musicians at that time signaled a loss in the meaning and integrity of the blues idiom. As Joel Rudinow argues in an aptly titled essay that asks the question "Can white people sing the blues?" this concern typically manifests itself in two separate but related critiques.[13] First, a "proprietary" argument equates "white blues" with actual theft, or what the poet and musicologist Amiri Baraka (formerly Leroi Jones) refers to in one essay as "The Great Music Robbery":

> The more subtle functioning of black national oppression carries with it many not so delicious ironies. For instance, now that the music and the culture are no longer termed inferior or primitive as articles of faith, the notion in the last few years has been simply to *claim* it! The racist line more and more now holds white players, etc., responsible for the high points of the music. The corporations through their media and bourgeois scribblers not only continually push and emphasize the greatness of white musicians, orchestras, arrangements, approach to the music, etc., but more and more each year lay claim to the music's very creation! And of course, as responsible for most of its excellence.
>
> . . . We are now told magnanimously that R&B *influenced* Rock & Roll. Whew! My friends, Rock & Roll *is* Rhythm & Blues! We realize Fats Domino, Chuck Berry, etc., could never get as rich and famous as Elvis Presley and company who are written about as if they has actually *originated* something rather than copied. . . . So the Great Music Robbery is, boldly, an attempt by the bourgeoisie to claim and coopt, in a growingly more obvious way, black music as the creation of whites.[14]

While this approach characterizes the blues in terms of cultural and ethnic ownership, an "experiential access" argument suggests that even empathetic whites cannot truly comprehend or authentically express the subtle meanings inherent in blues music, because such an understanding can only be learned through experiencing life as a black person. Again, Baraka provides the canonical model; as he asserts in *Blues People*:

> Blues as an autonomous music had been in a sense inviolable. There was no clear way into it, i.e. its production, not its appreciation, except as concomitant with what seems to me to be the peculiar social, cultural, economic, and emotional experience of a black man in America. The idea of a white blues singer seems an even more violent contradiction of terms than the idea of a middle-class blues singer. The materials of blues were not available to the white American, even though some strange circumstance might prompt him to look for them. It was as if these materials were secret and obscure, and blues a kind of ethno-historic rite as basic as blood.[15]

While black critics like Baraka attacked white blues musicians for their lack of authenticity, the 1960s folk revival generated similar protests from white intellectuals desperate to preserve what they thought to be the last remnants of a dying African American cultural legacy. As jazz critic Ralph J. Gleason argues, "The blues is a black man's music, and whites diminish it at best or steal it at worst. In any case they have no moral right to use it."[16] In his 1960 classic study *Blues Fell This Morning*, folklorist Paul Oliver writes: "Yet the apparent fact remains that only the American black, whether purple-black or so light-skinned as to be indistinguishable from his sun-tanned white neighbor, can sing the blues."[17] Finally, as Paul Garon fervently asserts in *Blues and the Poetic Spirit*:

> The most baffling aspect of the entire phenomenon of "white blues" is the legitimacy and relevance with which its perpetuators would like to see it endowed. This single fact is evidence of the cretinously low level of mental activity which is forced upon us under the guise of the creative process . . . for in "white blues" creativity rarely makes an appearance. But can anyone pretend that "white blues" are any more creative and any less imitative than, say, reproductions of Eskimo sculptures turned out by white suburbanites? And what of these reproductions? Are they not death? Is it not clear that they are totally devoid of imagination and creativity? The same must be said for "white blues." Removed from the unique historical configurations that produced the blues, that is, the socio-economic and cultural conditions through which blues came into being, the melodic similarities produced by the white imitators appear weak, trivial, spineless and with-

out substance. . . . The question then, is not, "Can whites play (or sing) the blues?" but simply, "Why do they bother, and who cares?"[18]

Cultural authorities develop certain definitions of authenticity in particular times and places for specific political and ideological purposes. For instance, arguments about authenticity often emerge during historical moments when the meaningfulness of traditional ways of life seems challenged by the force of modernity and its by-products, including the globalization of popular culture.[19] Likewise, social groups value the transcendent quality represented by the cross-cultural exchange of rituals and symbolic practices, and therefore frequently devalue attempts by their members to "imitate" the authenticity suggested by such practices. For these reasons, blues music has been conventionally constructed in terms of racial authenticity for most of the past century by whites as well as blacks.

The central problem here is that discussions of race in terms of identity politics frequently obscure its origins as a manufactured social category. Grounded in unsubstantiated arguments about the so-called genetic inferiority of Africans and their descendants, race represents a political distinction bestowed on persons thought to possess similar traits selected from a relatively arbitrarily chosen menu of physical characteristics, such as the melanin content of the skin or hair of one's parents.[20] Because of their inherently inventive and inconsistent quality, definitions of race are always prone to change over time: thus, a number of American ethnic groups, including immigrant populations from Italy and Ireland, and Jews from eastern Europe, only "became white" after years of cultural assimilation, political and economic struggle, and competition among even less privileged minority groups.[21] In fact, as Jeffrey Melnick argues in *A Right to Sing the Blues: African Americans, Jews, and American Popular Song*, during the 1920s Jewish male entertainers employed the performance of black music styles—including ragtime, swing, and, of course, the blues—in order to reconstruct their own racial identity as whites. By writing and performing distinctly American songs and dances while, at the same time, emphasizing traits that distinguished them from their newfound African American colleagues and competitors, Jewish composers and showmen were able to gain status as nonblacks while decreasing the distance between themselves and more assimilated ethnic groups.[22]

However, many progressive black and white scholars who are critical of racial discrimination in its many forms—including Baraka and

Melnick—frequently maintain that those persons designated by our society as black *still* possess a greater ability and a more justifiable right to play the blues, and it is not hard to see why. After all, black sharecroppers developed the blues idiom in an environment where they faced the brutalizing force of racial oppression and exploitation under the laws of Jim Crow. Insofar as this music emerged as an expressive form of black protest and celebration early in the twentieth century and continued to entertain black audiences in segregated urban neighborhoods during the postwar era, perhaps it should not seem particularly unusual that blues audiences would use race as a marker of authenticity in this context.

But while this historical legacy should be remembered and honored, along with the many other contributions to American popular culture made by African Americans, it cannot possibly follow that a musician's race *causes* their artistic efforts to become more authentic and expressively rich. As Tukufu Zuberi argues in *Thicker than Blood: How Racial Statistics Lie*, race's socially ascribed nature makes it impossible for social scientists to attribute specific causal effects to racial status; rather, it is a *symptom* of a large and complex set of historical processes through which individuals are unfairly categorized as "superior" or "inferior," and moreover, like all decontextualized sociological variables, doesn't really *do* anything independently from the constellation of social factors that impact the condition of human beings in the world.[23] In fact, most sociologists would agree that in spite of its general use as a master status marker, race alone makes for a fairly poor predictor of *any* type of inherent talent or ability, including those related to music and the arts.[24]

Still, might one argue that persons who have been identified as black in American society are more capable than whites of expressing their sense of social stigma through the blues form? I would certainly submit that such an experience could give someone a particularly unique perspective on the world; however, it would be difficult to imagine how that might specifically make them a more expressive *guitar* player or better at voicing their frustrations through an AAB, twelve-bar blues lyric than, say, a finely phrased haiku. Furthermore, as critical race scholars remind us, American blacks hardly experience the trials of racial discrimination in a monolithic manner, and individuals themselves experience racism in varying ways as they move across multiple institutional and social contexts in the course of their everyday lives.[25]

More instructively, as countless black writers and musicians argue, authenticity claims rooted in notions of racial difference all too often reinforce traditional racial stereotypes of rhythmic and uncivilized blacks who radically differ from their white counterparts.[26] As Baraka himself argues in a point about "reverse patronization" in his essay "Jazz and the White Critic": "The disparaging 'all you folks got rhythm' is no less a stereotype, simply because it is proposed as a positive trait."[27] As the black jazz legend Dizzy Gillespie remarked a few years ago during an interview to the question of whether "only black people can play jazz": "No, it's not true. And if you accept that premise, well then what you're saying is that maybe black people can *only* play jazz. And black people, like anyone else, can be anything they want to be."[28]

This final point is extremely significant insofar as whites have historically drawn on stereotypes of black musicians and entertainers as a means of justifying ideologies of racial difference in American society. Perhaps more to the point, as the black feminist scholar bell hooks argues in her essay "Eating the Other," racial difference has long served as a suggestive signifier of seductive and exotic primitivism in the symbolic iconography of American popular culture. She asserts, "The commodification of Otherness has been so successful because it is offered as a new delight, more intense, more satisfying than normal ways of doing and feeling. Within commodity culture, ethnicity becomes spice, seasoning that can liven up the dull dish that is mainstream white culture."[29] Accordingly, contemporary mainstream culture frequently draws on stereotypes of blacks to produce an "alternative playground" of transgressive pleasure, one where affluent white consumers might cannibalize images of black culture, music, and sexuality in order to somehow achieve emancipation from their privileged yet alienated selves.[30]

The long history of the commercialization of the blues represents a similar set of problematic issues. The earliest fascination with blues music among folklorists and other academics drew on essentialist images of American blacks as somehow more primitive and earthy than their highly modernized white counterparts.[31] The field recordings collected by rural anthropologists after World War I revealed to them an utterly transcendent and anti-modernist world in which African religious beliefs, agricultural toil, and sexual desire manifested themselves in lyrics and rhythm.[32] In later years white beatniks and bohemians would turn to the urban blues and jazz records of black musicians like Muddy Waters and Howlin' Wolf for evidence of a soulful spirituality and chilling realism that might counter the seemingly mundane texture of their middle-class lives.[33] In a way, the "authenticity" that whites have traditionally sought in the cultural expression of American blacks repre-

sents an attempt—albeit at times quite earnest and well intentioned—
to manufacture racial difference under the guise of flattery and praise.
In contemporary blues clubs in Chicago, these attempts at fabricating
authenticity reach a critical level of intensity and effort.

**Chicago Blues Clubs and the Manufacturing of Authen-
ticity.**   In an attempt to capitalize on the popularity of blues music
among audiences in search of the authenticity suggested by blackness,
the city's most commercialized blues clubs draw on popular stereotypical
images of race with a most exaggerated enthusiasm. Like the theme-
park restaurants and crowd-pleasing entertainment meccas of Chicago's
downtown area, including its Planet Hollywood, Hard Rock Cafe, Rain-
forest Cafe, and short-lived Disney Quest franchises, the city's corporate-
run blues clubs rely on themed images, logos, and standardized cuisine to attract the widest possible range of customers.[34] At Navy Pier,
the city's recently museumized waterfront, Joe's Be-Bop Cafe and Jazz
Emporium hosts vacationers who sink into blues piano and jazz combo
sets over "soul food" options like Duke Ellington Baby Back Ribs with
Joe's Sideman Be Bop BBQ Sauce, Blow Hard Garlic Bread, and Banana
Lama Ding Dong Smoothies. Before it recently switched its name to
Isaac Hayes and mildly modified its menu, audiences at Famous Dave's
BBQ & Blues watched local blues bands pounce along a tremendously
wide stage as they gorged on Fire-Kissed Mojo Chicken, Sweet Georgia
Mama's Chopped Pork, and Onion Guitar Strings with Swingin' Spin
Dip—all served on a garbage can lid.

Meanwhile, the physical interiors of these clubs pay homage to similarly commodified images of blackness. As affluent visitors from Germany and Italy listen to local characters like Eddy "The Chief" Clearwater sing the blues in the sleek atmosphere of Blue Chicago, posters and
framed photographs of dancing crowds of black revelers cover the club's
walls along with paintings featuring caricatures of shouting blueswomen
and carnivalesque scenes from southern juke joints. On the outside exterior of the club, a large mural depicts a black blues guitarist who plays
with a cigarette dangling from his mouth and a bottle at his side. In
its efforts to market culture and place, the club sells T-shirts displaying
images such as these for eighteen dollars each, along with a special
soundtrack collection of themed compact discs produced by the club;
these items can also be purchased from the Blue Chicago Store, the
club's official souvenir shop.[35]

As for the music itself, contemporary blues musicians shape their performances in response to the expectations of consumers searching for the racial authenticity suggested by stereotypical images of Chicago blues clubs and their celebrity stars. In fact, the shticks of local blues artists often demonstrate a certain cookie-cutter homogeneity by increasingly drawing on familiar, racially charged scripts. Throughout the evening performers consistently remind their audiences of the authenticity of their "blues" experience: "If you can't get the blues, you're in the wrong place tonight!" "Are you ready to hear some real blues, or what?" "This is a blues club, not a mortuary!"

At the same time, local black artists present racially suggestive stock characters reminiscent of minstrel performances of yesteryear in exchange for abundant cheers and applause from their predominantly white audiences. Since the late eighteenth century, such figures have been used in American popular culture to reinforce ideologies regarding the sexuality and morality of blacks and whites. From the beginnings of American blackface minstrelsy in the 1790s, white actors painted with burnt cork depicted their slaves as comic buffoons, "black dandies," and "nigger wenches" in broad strokes and cruel colors in popular "coon" songs.[36] While the introduction of talented black performers in minstrelsy during Reconstruction certainly helped to temper the tastelessness commonly exhibited by these performances, the white producers and financiers who controlled the entertainment market promised the survival of fragments of blackface culture.[37] Consequently, the advertising copy and cartoons used to promote blues records in the 1920s relied on traditional images of blackness ranging from the "plantation darky" to the black "mammy" to the stylish, sporty, and hopelessly materialistic city dweller.[38]

Over the past hundred years, the stock characters presented on American commercial recordings have evolved as changes in reproduction technologies, business practices, targeted audiences, and prevailing racial stereotypes have perpetually reshaped the form and content of popular music.[39] However, contemporary blues musicians continue to employ variations on traditional black stereotypes by playing stock characters who resemble their 1920s vaudevillian counterparts.

For instance, young black musicians commonly maintain stage personae commensurate with the imagined lifestyle of the hypersexed traveling showman who cannot help but succumb to the pleasures of drink, women, and song. This figure recalls an entire lexicon of popular cultural images associated with black male sexuality employed by traditional and contemporary entertainment media, from old-time blues sides to 1970s "blaxploitation" cinema and 1990s gangsta-rap recordings.[40] As an example, at clubs like B.L.U.E.S. Vino Louden intersperses his medleys of suggestive blues numbers like "I'm Your Hoochie Coochie Man" with tall tales of sexual conquest.

"So it's Valentine's Day, and so I buy my woman some cheap candy and a dying, droopy rose, and I go to the front door of her house and I knock . . . but nobody answers! And so then I go to the back door and I knock, and I wonder if somebody is in there! Finally, my woman comes to the door and lets me in, and I ask her for some loving, and she says, 'Uh-uh.' " He imitates the sound of the rejection on his guitar and continues his kiss-and-tell confession.

"And so then I take two knee pads—I mean, uh, pillows—from the couch, and I put them on the floor, and do you know what I did?" He looks up at his audience and shouts out his question once again: "I said . . . Do you know what I *did*?" As the crowd responds to his plea, he continues his "testimonial": "I did a little something like this . . ." and he gets down on his knees and proceeds to furiously lick the strings of his guitar with his fluttering tongue, inciting howls of hysterical laughter from his audience.

Louden's sexualized performance is a common one among black musicians who play in local clubs. Vance Kelley shares tall tales about "his woman's" voluptuous hips and breasts, asks his audience, "Tell me now, all the men: Is your woman fine?" and leaves innuendo behind in his rendition of the Clarence Carter hit "Strokin' ": "I stroke it to the north / I stroke it to the south / I stroke it everywhere / I even stroke it with my mouth!" Lindsay Alexander, a local blues singer and guitarist, asks members of his audience to stick out their tongues so he can remark on their size as he instructs the men how to orally please their female partners.

Likewise, Tiger, a black male guitarist and singer in his mid-thirties, draws on his relative youthfulness and sly wit to stylize his minstrel-like performance as a self-proclaimed "candy-licking man." In his gigs at BL.U.E.S., he wears a loose-fitting athletic warm-up suit along with a brown cowboy hat, suggesting the style of a rapper from the neck down and a rodeo star from the neck up.

Tiger's performances begin relatively tame. He plays the crowd with gimmicks and chatter. He announces, "Now, if B.B. King was here, he would sound exactly like this . . ." and then launches into a convincing reproduction of a King-styled guitar solo. He repeats the line by borrowing from Stevie Ray Vaughn, Albert King, and Buddy Guy, continuing to tease the audience as he hollers: "Do y'all know about the blues out there? All right, it's test time . . . Who is this?" and he goes into a solo, and after hearing answers from the tourist-packed crowd, he says, "Wait a minute, wait a minute . . . I'm tired of people saying ZZ Top!" The answer is John Lee Hooker; next, he begins playing a T-Bone Walker riff. Throughout this charade the audience responds with surprising jubilance. But his coy shtick soon turns from playful to provocative as he plays a solo by his "friend" Jordan, a man with whom he tells the crowd he has been very intimate and has even *kissed.*

"All right, now, do you want to know who Jordan is? Jordan is me! . . . All right? Hey, so everything is cool now . . . 'cause I'm not like *that* . . . I just wanna make *that* clear . . . whew . . . *I'm all man*!" The joke receives thunderous applause from his audience as they grow even wilder. As if to offer further evidence of his "manliness," Tiger dives into his self-penned "Candy-Licking Man," with its sexual suggestiveness: "Open up your candy bars, baby / Show me all you got / Once I start licking, baby / You won't want my tongue to stop!" He then starts baiting the enthusiastic, dancing crowd, selecting women from the audience to inquire, "Is your man a candy-licking man? What kind of candy-licker is he?"

Black blues singers like Tiger who play the minstrel role of the self-assured lover tend to pepper their performances with anti-gay remarks with surprising frequency. By doing so, they attempt to build solidarity with their mainstream audiences as well as bolster their onstage personification of hypermasculinity and virility.[41] In a cultural milieu defined by racial and ethnic difference, shared sexist ideologies and homophobic prejudices operate as an available, if tasteless, basis of consensus and group cohesion for black musicians and white audience members.[42] During a slow weeknight performance, Alexander asks his audience: "How many men in the house tonight like women?" Upon receiving a lukewarm reception, he repeats the question: "I *said* . . . How many men in the house tonight like women?" When the meager crowd finally responds, he wipes his brow, "*Whew!* I was getting worried for a minute! I thought I was in the *wrong* club!" and his previously timid audience suddenly erupts in laughter. Musicians also utilize the tactic offstage: Dizzy, an elderly black singer, asserts in a conversation at B.L.U.E.S. between sets one evening (before his recent passing), "I like the ladies . . . I don't like no guys!" As he drops his hand, he embellishes: "They be swishing all the time, know what I'm saying?" Likewise, before one of his shows at B.L.U.E.S. Etcetera, he remarks:

"Hey, look at that girl over there—you see that girl over there? She looks like a party girl, like she likes to party . . . Oh yeah, that girl right there, she's from St. Louis . . . Yeah, you know I remember a few years back, this place had all dudes . . . everywhere you look, all dudes. It might as well have been a gay bar!"

Like his fellow musicians, Dizzy often takes his hypermasculine performance from the stage to the floor of the club between sets.[43] At his seventieth birthday party at B.L.U.E.S. Etcetera, he brags to a group of us in the back poolroom: "I'm seventy years old, man! Seventy! . . . But I don't need no Viagra . . . I can still do it by myself! I thank JC for that, man!" Of course, private conversations reveal that blues performers consciously manipulate their sexualized personae all the time. While Tiger never addresses the heterosexism of his show in our conversations, he *does* privately admit that he *doesn't* actually "lick candy" himself. In an interview outside the entrance to B.L.U.E.S. Etcetera, he confesses: "Ha-ha . . . 'Candy-Licker' is fun, you know . . . it's something that guys do, right? Now, it's not something that *I* do, but it's something that a lot of guys do, and so I wrote it, because I wanted to write something that was fun, that's all."

While black male musicians perform hypermasculine roles onstage, their female counterparts tend to play a series of racially charged, sexualized roles that simultaneously recall the subversive camp and feminist sensibilities of classic blues performers such as Bessie Smith, Gertrude "Ma" Rainey, and Memphis Minnie.[44] During the 1920s Jazz Age, many of the early blueswomen performed in richly elaborate costumes of gold, pearls, and rhinestones, which made them all the more exotic to their racially mixed cabaret audiences. As the "Empress of the Blues," Smith herself was known to wear an Indian headdress lavishly adorned with feathers. But at the same time, these women recorded and performed songs that expressed a brand of radical feminism unparalleled in the white entertainment world during this period. Many of these progressive songs rejected patriarchy in all its forms, including marriage and the enforced domesticity endured by most wives during this time. Their provocative and dreamlike lyrics assaulted their listeners with a steady barrage of complaints about the selfishness and cruelty of men, and their choruses often revealed a fantasy of relief from male violence and, in some cases, revenge. In the 1924 song "Hateful Blues," Bessie Smith sings of murdering her abusive and runaway husband in an act of bloody vengeance:

> Yes, I'm hateful 'cause he treats me so unkind
> If I find that man while hurt is on my mind
> If I see him I'm gon' beat him, gon' kick and bite him, too
> Gonna take my weddin' butcher, gonna cut him two and two
> The ambulance is waitin', the undertaker, too
> A suit in doctor's office, all kinds of money for you
> Ain't gonna sell him, gon' keep him for myself
> Gonna cut on him until a piece this big is left
> 'Cause my love has been abused,
> Now I got the hateful blues.[45]

These songs criticized society's denial of political and economic autonomy to women, and many specifically challenged prevailing assumptions about feminine submissiveness, giving rise to the blues song as an affirmation of sexual dominance, personal power, and a black feminist consciousness. In her 1926 recording of "Young Woman's Blues," Smith sings:

> I'm as good as any woman in your town
> I ain't no high yella, I'm a deep killer brown
> I ain't gonna marry, ain't gon' settle down
> I'm gon' drink good moonshine and run these browns down
> See that long lonesome road, Lord, you know it's gotta end
> And I'm a good woman and I can get plenty men.[46]

Meanwhile, back in contemporary Chicago, the performances of "Big Time" Sarah Streeter echo the strange mix of black minstrelsy and feminist politics represented by Bessie Smith's stage shows and recordings. A large, full-bosomed blueswoman from Coldwater, Mississippi, she often dedicates her usual standards—"Sweet Home Chicago," "The Thrill Is Gone," and her self-penned "Fannie Mae"—to the men in her audience who "love their big, sweaty, juicy ladies." Ever the performer, Big Time Sarah introduces the classic Howlin' Wolf song "The Red Rooster" in downtrodden helplessness and grief: "This one's going out to all y'all who ain't never had enough of nothin' . . . I'm an old woman and I ain't *ever* had enough of nothin'." But when a male audience member heckles her performance, Sarah quickly switches to a more aggressive role:

"Why don't I tie you up and sit on your face?! . . . I know you like it that way!"

On other evenings she can be bolder still. During Jack's birthday celebration at B.L.U.E.S., Sarah announces that she will be performing something *really* special for the crowd. After offering the aforementioned blow-up doll to Jack, she begins singing her rendition of Muddy Waters's "I'm Your Hoochie Coochie Man" and slowly unbuttons her blouse onstage—only to suddenly grab Jack's head and press his face into her tremendous cleavage. As she releases her grip and continues to sing, she invites a tourist from Japan up to the stage. She seats him below her waist as she thrusts her body into his head, and then she presses *his* face into her breasts, at which time she jokes, "I think I felt tongue . . ."

By now the audience is just in stitches, absolutely hysterical with laughter. Meanwhile, the gentleman's friend, another tourist from Japan, snaps a photograph of his buddy as she pulls yet a *third* gentleman up from the audience. Older than his two predecessors, he lets Sarah place his hands on her hips as she bumps and grinds against him, gyrating while shouting her alleged measurements, "Forty-two . . . forty-eight . . ." and suddenly she turns around to shake her behind and announces, "Sixty-eight!" as she sings, "I'm your hoochie coochie *woman* . . ." to thunderous laughter and applause from her adoring fans.

But as much as she entertains her audiences by appropriating a racially and sexually charged stock character for her onstage persona, she simultaneously asserts an enviable self-reliance. One night, after downing a series of drinks in rapid succession, Sarah offers me her stool as she turns to leave the club, only to return moments later to announce to a group of us at the bar, "I was gonna leave, but I'll stay for one thing—*money*. They gonna pay me forty-five dollars to do a couple of songs," and approaches the stage as a guest vocalist to sing "The Thrill Is Gone" and "Fannie Mae." During the latter song she begins collecting tips from her fans as she sings: "Well, they call me Fannie Mae / I've got the biggest tits in town / Well, they call me Fannie Mae / I've got the biggest tits in town / And if you don't believe me / Stop and lay your money down."

Meanwhile, a drunk male patron passes his right hand over her shoulder and his left hand on her thigh. Just as he begins groping Sarah, she turns to her microphone to assert her authority over the performance: "Now wait a minute, baby! I can get with you copping a feel, grabbing at my thigh and ass, but if you goin' down there, you better be giving me a bigger bill! . . . You be grabbing my middle leg down there!" She continues to embarrass the offending patron: "You know, if you keep this up, I will beat you! . . . Yeah, and you'd probably like that, too!"

The complexities and contradictions of Big Time Sarah's performance make for a confusing musical brew. While her improvised song lyrics recall alluring and self-deprecating images of primitive blacks in impoverished ghetto and rural settings, they simultaneously draw on the feminist sympathies of the women in her audience who respond to her strong, transgressive persona with enthusiastic laughter and approval: "I may not be Koko Taylor, but I can still sing the blues; I may not be Etta James, I may not be Patti LaBelle, I may not be Son Seals—but *I* can play a funky guitar, too . . . Can somebody give a poor girl—a low-down, dirty, back-of-the-alley, blues-singing, Mississippi-cooking woman a hand?" She frequently dedicates her songs to the women in her predominately white audience who needlessly put up with their "cheatin', lying, ugly, lazy, good-for-nothin', glass-eyed motherfucking men," and they respond in kind with shouts of solidarity and screams of delight. Meanwhile, the men in her audience offer mixed reactions ranging from gleeful to derogatory to simply confused. During one show a white gentleman snidely remarks to his friends, "Who does she think she is, Sista Souljah?" while another, bewildered by her suggestive performance, can only stammer, "So, I guess we've graduated to the R-rated music now, huh."

If black male and female performers employ highly sexualized roles during their stage acts, then elderly black musicians additionally appropriate the familiar blues theme of world-weary desperation to play down-and-out characters afflicted with bad luck. Like Sarah's "poor girl," elderly blues performers draw on iconic images of downtrodden blacks that recall the narrators of blues classics from "Nobody Knows You When You're Down and Out" to "Born Under a Bad Sign."

At seventy, an old-timer like Dizzy performs this role to great effect. In his usual dapper suit, necktie, shades, and sharp feathered hat, he sighs on the stage of B.L.U.E.S.: "I wouldn't have no luck at all if it weren't for bad luck . . . My old lady threw me out, my dog died . . ." "All right, it's confession time . . . It's about the ladies—you know what I'm talking about, the ladies? I always find myself hung up on the ladies, y'all know what I'm talking about." "I've been abused and misused, misused and abused . . . I feel so bad, I could shout . . ." At the same time, elderly men sometimes counter this down-and-out sullenness with more enthusiastic affectations. During the same performance, Dizzy struts down the aisle singing a carefree rendition of Howlin' Wolf's "Shake for

Me"—"Come on and shake it, baby . . . Shake like a willow tree!" and as he dances his way back to the stage, he opens his arms wide to shout: "I have more fun than poor people is supposed to have . . . I could even have fun in a graveyard!"

In other instances, elderly black performers take on a grandfatherly persona by offering pearls of wisdom to their audiences. A domineering, if cantankerous, figure in his big black Stetson hat, cowboy boots, and string tie, Tail Dragger chomps down hard on his cigar as he warns his enthusiastic audience: "People come up to you and try to give you some crack, and they tell you it's free. But that shit ain't free!" "Everybody's got to use their head! Even the president's got to use his head!" "I'm bald, but I don't need no hair! No woman ever wanted me 'cause I had hair!"

Selling the Urban Ghetto as a Tourist Attraction.

As the number of tourist-oriented clubs like B.L.U.E.S. proliferated in Chicago's North Side neighborhoods during the 1970s and 1980s, the city's South and West Sides witnessed a steep decline in their ability to maintain operational and successful blues bars. As a result, the North Side and downtown areas of the city have become the new centers of blues activity in Chicago, attracting many prominent musicians and their beloved audiences away from the Black Belt. However, as a strange twist of fate, this commercial shift has increased the value that audiences place on the urban "authenticity" suggested by the few blues clubs that still remain in the city's black ghetto neighborhoods. As a result, Chicago's most racially segregated and impoverished city blocks have been transformed into commodified tourist attractions.

This trend is best exemplified by the success of the Checkerboard Lounge, a South Side juke joint that regularly attracts, in addition to a fairly stable black clientele, a sizable pool of white consumers made up of suburbanites, business travelers, and members of the nearby University of Chicago community in Hyde Park. Founded in 1972 by blues legend Buddy Guy, the club survives amidst the backdrop of urban decay that for years has lined the sidewalks of Forty-third Street just off Martin Luther King Drive: a currency exchange; an abandoned Won's Fried Rice and Emporium Hair Salon; vacant lots; cheap eateries like Baby Joe's Chicken Box; dilapidated storefront churches such as the Psalm Orthodox Ministries, Christ Outreach Ministries, and the New Bethel Baptist Church; and all else that decades of depopulation, concentrated poverty, and institutional divestment have left behind.[47]

Located in the overwhelmingly black neighborhood of Grand Boulevard and promoted in citywide newspapers and travel guides, audiences trek to the Checkerboard in the hopes of finding an authentic cultural experience to rival its pricier downtown competitors.[48] In their search for the rugged authenticity suggested by images of poverty and blackness, these patrons derive satisfaction from the grittiness of the club's cheaply fashioned interior as defined by its ripped orange booths, tables lined with fading contact paper, walls covered with posters of black models in seductive poses, and bathroom floors tiled with flattened cardboard boxes from old beer cases. In comparing the Checkerboard to a local jazz club known for its elegant interior, Rajiv, a conventioneer, explains: "The Green Mill was very polished; I like this place a lot more—*especially* the decor."[49]

Like travelers searching for authenticity in other cultural contexts, many visiting patrons find the Checkerboard attractive because it offers the promise of an uncommodified, authentic space untainted by camera-clad audiences such as themselves.[50] But while the decor and atmosphere echo their black and tan fantasies of clubs like the Checkerboard, these audiences often find themselves disappointed by the realities of its cultural environment, insofar as many of the songs performed in South Side bars—James Brown's "The Big Payback," the Temptations' "My Girl"—tend to sound more like 1960s soul than traditional blues standards, and the crowds who patronize such bars tend to be cosmopolitan and diverse, rather than local and homogeneous.

This became very clear to me on a wintry Saturday night when I escorted a white professional couple from the Chicago suburb of Evanston to the Checkerboard. As our waitress writes down our drink order on a napkin, the gentleman turns to me to ask, "So, would you call this club more authentic? Is the music more authentic?" Meanwhile, his partner peers across the bar with an unsatisfied expression on her face, disappointed by the number of whites at the club: they include an enthusiastic pack of middle-aged men from New York and a gaggle of drunk college-age kids bounding across the length of the dance floor. In fact, the flow of traffic at the Checkerboard consistently replicates itself every weekend night as the early evening audience of black neighborhood patrons eventually finds itself displaced by a growing post-frat crowd as the hours wear on.

On another occasion a white graduate student from the University of Chicago campus and his friends snicker to one another about the club's strong tourist presence: "Did you see the tour bus out front?" Although

in some ways "tourists" in their own right, members of the university community frequently feel as though their status as temporary South Side residents privileges their own presence at the club over out-of-towners.[51]

As a result of its newfound popularity among affluent audiences, the Checkerboard does its best to pander to its mostly white customers by providing racially and sexually charged entertainment within its deteriorating walls. Local black acts playfully tease their female audience members with innuendo rife with hypermasculine bravado, explicit allusions to oral sex, and X-rated versions of otherwise innocuous songs such as "Hold on, I'm Comin' " and "She'll Be Comin' Round the Mountain When She Comes." Meanwhile, before his passing in 1998, James Ramsey, a popular local character dubbed the "Black Lone Ranger," strolled around the club selling home-recorded tapes featuring his renditions of blues standards such as "I'm a Man" and invited customers to pay to have their Polaroid photograph taken with him in his contemporary minstrel regalia, replete with white ten-gallon-hat and black mask.

The commercialization of the Checkerboard Lounge presents an interesting dilemma. On the one hand, like many of the city's blues bars, the club's racial mix of regulars and visitors makes the Checkerboard one of the few places in the city where blacks and whites regularly interact in a leisure-based setting. In highly segregated cities like Chicago, divisions along class, racial, and ethnic boundaries are often expressed through the consumption of leisure, and therefore it is not uncommon for the members of specific groups to patronize bars, nightclubs, and other entertainment venues apart from one another.[52] For instance, the Lincoln Park bars surrounding B.L.U.E.S. nearly all serve predominately white crowds of college students and local residents, while many lounges and taverns concentrated in racially segregated areas of Chicago's South Side and West Side specifically cater to black working- and middle-class customers. According to a number of Chicago-based ethnographic accounts, including Elijah Anderson's *A Place on the Corner* and Reuben A. Buford May's *Talking at Trena's*, black patrons rely on these kinds of local neighborhood establishments as safe havens where they can openly talk about race and other sensitive matters.[53]

However, at the Checkerboard, neighborhood patrons generally welcome customers of all races and ethnicities, along with the cosmopolitan diversity they add to the club's urbane atmosphere. In doing so, an evening there can reveal not only its lively social and aesthetic world, but also how casual encounters between black and white strangers at the club have the potential to contribute to their mutual understandings of each other's worldviews during even brief moments of social interaction.

I discovered this for myself during one of my first trips to the club. At 10 P.M. on a cold and rainy Saturday evening, I arrive at the Checkerboard Lounge with two friends. After we park in the secured lot across the street from the club and split the four-dollar parking fee, we head into the half-empty bar, pay the seven-dollar cover charge, and settle in for the evening next to an exceedingly drunk but friendly white couple at a table near the back of the club. We note the run-down decor of the club: the frayed tinsel and old neon signs hanging from the walls; the torn vinyl chairs scattered among the cracked tables; the stink of ash and smoke. The bathroom is equally messy: the floor is soaked with beer and piss, a vending machine above the toilet offers condoms and novelty sex toys, and the door doesn't appear to have a lock.

Shortly after our drunk neighbors leave the bar, a middle-aged black couple—James and Jennifer—approach our table, and we invite them to share our space. Well dressed, James sports a gorgeous hat and a shirt with a gold-buttoned collar, while Jennifer wears a pretty blouse, textured pants, and boots. Upon joining us, they clean up the cigarettes and trash left behind. After I apologize for the previous customers, Jennifer asks me, point-blank, "These people—were they white or black?" When I answer her, she laughs and remarks how she supposes there are "all different kinds of people out there."

James and Jennifer explain that although they attend shows at the Checkerboard about once or twice a month, they also enjoy downtown clubs like Buddy Guy's Legends because the latter feature multiracial crowds (as opposed to the city's North Side Lincoln Park bars) as well as good music. They live in Pill Hill, a residential neighborhood located in Calumet Heights, a black middle-class enclave on the city's South Side: James works for a paper company, while Jennifer is a bus driver for the Chicago Transit Authority. They have two daughters, ages twenty-two and seventeen, and three grandchildren from their eldest daughter. Gregarious, they buy us a round of beer as we begin an evening of conversation. As they drink cognac over ice with Budweiser for a chaser, they rave about their happy marriage and the pleasures and dramas of pregnancy and child rearing.

The couple seems to enjoy our company, and our chatter grows intimate as the night progresses. Jennifer describes the importance of church in her life and explains that she sings in the choir at the local Sweet Holy Spirit church and tells us how much she looks forward to Sunday services at 11:30 A.M. the next morning. She asks me where I first learned about the blues. During a set break, a pop-gospel song pipes in the lyric "Can I get a witness?" and as I repeat the line aloud, she instructs us, "Now, you do know where that comes from, right? That comes from the church!" We all smile at one another.

As the night wears on, James and Jennifer grow entranced by the evening's performance and begin singing along with the band and bouncing in their chairs, pressing their bodies close to each other lovingly as they dance. I ask them, "So, y'all are big blues fans, huh?" Jennifer turns to me and replies, "Well, you know, we like *all* kinds of music . . . soul, R&B, funk, jazz, gospel, blues. Yeah, you name it—we listen to *all* kinds of music."

At the Checkerboard, interactions between black and white strangers often lead to enthusiastic conversations on topics ranging from religion to work and family life, and for this reason, it is a shame that there are so few racially integrated places of leisure in the city where patrons can drink and socialize together while learning about each other's worldviews and life experiences.[54] However, not all interracial encounters at the club provide their participants with as much comfort and ease. For many customers, blues clubs represent a liberating space where they can free themselves from the inhibitions that ordinarily constrain their behavior in their everyday lives. Since the current success of the Checkerboard among affluent whites relies, in part, on the popularity of restless fantasies about black working-class culture (which are reinforced by the performances of local blues performers), white patrons frequently lose a certain degree of decorum in the process of letting their hair down at the club. The overriding problem here is not that whites patronize the Checkerboard, but that the Checkerboard is practically the *only* black club they frequent, and so they tend to rely on it as a tourist attraction as opposed to a place to socialize with black and white customers in ways that might eventually move *beyond* the search for the authenticity suggested by racial difference.

In their attempts to press the racial boundaries that structure everyday life in the urban milieu, young whites often seek out black club employees and elderly patrons as safe targets for interaction.[55] In their conversations with regulars, they attempt to push those barriers further and further in what for them represents a high-stakes (or perhaps low-stakes, as the case may be) game of social intercourse, a risky norm-breaching experiment set to music and dance steps.[56] While such patrons sometimes seem well intentioned in their furtive attempts to engage their black neighbors, these interactions too often devolve into awkward and offending interracial encounters, especially since, not surprisingly, young and old black regulars usually fail to appreciate the insensitivity that slumming audiences commonly reveal when interacting with the club's local patronage, service staff, and hired musicians.

Of course, consumers instigate these kinds of encounters in North Side blues bars as well: the incident that always comes quickest to my mind took place at Kingston Mines, when a middle-aged white clubber stood at the entranceway of the club, pointed to the face of the black bouncer on duty, and turned to his friends to joke, "Oh, come on—tell me he doesn't look *just* like Mr. T!" Still, the Checkerboard Lounge offers plenty of opportunities to observe similar kinds of behavior. One Saturday night I accompany two friends, Eric and Kate, to the club. After paying five dollars to park in the new underground garage, we head inside at about 11:30 P.M. This weekend marks the club's twenty-seventh anniversary, and so we pay an inflated cover charge of fifteen dollars for a special show headlined by blues and soul legend Bobby Rush.[57] The smoke-drenched room is packed, but we manage to find seats after the room empties out a bit at the close of the first set. The audience is racially mixed, but its members segregate themselves from one another at the edges of the room: black patrons line up at the bar and along the back of the club; white customers take the booths along the left side of the stage, and clusters of both blacks and whites scatter themselves among the long tables in the center of the smoky room. This segregation is further emphasized by differences in dress, insofar as white patrons tend to dress far more casually and carelessly than their dressier black counterparts at the club.

As we sip our bourbon, the energy of the room grows as the young announcer chants louder and louder: "Bobby *Rush*!" "Bobby *Rush*!" Rush finally makes it to the stage to perform a wildly bombastic show filled with Muddy Waters standards, including "I Just Want to Make Love to You" and "I'm Your Hoochie Coochie Man," but sung in a funk style and backed by a scantily clad chorus line of four young women. Rush incorporates these dancers into his show by licking his lips and crowing like a rooster—"Cock-a-doodle-*doooo*!"—while remarking on their bodies as they gyrate their hips to the music in time. The youngest of the dancers is nineteen, and at some point during the show, Rush turns to L. C. Thurman, the club's proprietor, and offers to have her "sit on his face" while she bumps and grinds. Later in the evening he remarks on the sex appeal of *all* women and invites an elderly black woman up to the stage to imitate the dancing of his younger chorus girls—all to thunderous applause.

Although distracted by the spectacle of the performance, my guests cannot help but notice the antics of many of the younger white patrons, whose transgressions respond to the sexual innuendo of Rush's performance. As we spot a white couple furiously necking to a blues number for all to see, Kate turns to me to describe their exhibition as its own kind of "wilding."

But the unbridled passion of these midnight lovers only provides a less ostentatious example of the rudeness displayed by their more brazen neighbors. In sloppy drunkenness, a gang of young white men raise their shouts louder and louder as one of their more enterprising members starts dancing and spinning too close to the stage for the tastes of one of the club's black security guards. Decked out in a cowboy hat, toy holster, and cap gun, the guard pulls him away from the stage and physically places him back in his chair. As the night wears on, he continues to rush the stage, only to be thwarted again and again by the guard and later by another club bouncer. Soon another guy joins his drunk friend and they begin taunting the bouncer by rushing the dance floor, quickly sitting down at the drop of his stare and getting up immediately when he turns his back.

This uneasy interaction only continues as the boys attempt to chat up the more mild-mannered, older black patrons who surround them. As one slaps the back of a hulking black gentleman, his friend invites a heavyset woman to dance. Soon, having had enough fun for one evening, the gentleman rises from his chair to cut in.

Not surprisingly, the frequent occurrence of these situations can make black regulars fairly cautious of their white neighbors across the aisle. Again, most regulars at the Checkerboard welcome the racial diversity represented by the club's multiethnic audience; however, as exemplified by Jennifer's abrupt remark, "These people—were they white or black?" such patrons understandably react to the rudeness of white customers with disapproval.

A Black and Tan Fantasy.   More than anything, these encounters suggest how fractured latter-day black and tan fantasies really are. During the Jazz Age, black and tan cabarets attracted multiracial audiences in search of bootleg liquor and the classic urban blues. But then, just as now, that experience of communion existed alongside a tense confrontation over the meanings suggested by the blues and jazz club. For blacks, the local club represented one of the few public spaces where they might be welcome and could mingle with friends, lovers, and neighbors in relative peace. But for slumming whites, these black-and-tans promised the call of the wild, a chance to experience the so-called primitiveness of black culture and its blessed gifts: the smile of the happy-go-lucky minstrel dancer, the strange whispers of beautiful women, the "jungle music" of the jazz orchestra, the intoxication promised by illegal booze and illicit drugs, and terrifying thrills of darkness and shadow. And yet, if the multiracial interaction promised in these nightspots symbolized to whites the fulfillment of an urban fantasy to contrast the sobriety of middle-class living, to black performers and patrons it often served as a curse, a constant reminder of the rigidity of the American color line, especially when such clubs became so popular among the slumming trade that black patrons found themselves crowded out of their own neighborhood establishments on the weekends, victimized by white-on-black violence, and, in some cases, banned altogether.[58]

Of course, it is undoubtedly the case that in many ways the current popularity of blues music suggests an affirmative sea change in the reception of black music and culture among whites in Chicago, one of the most historically segregated cities in America.[59] However, it is also clear that the value placed on blues by such audiences continues to derive in part from the unfortunate yet persistent power of racially charged and essentialist images of black men and women. Indeed, as white thrill-seekers bounce blindly through the sticky aisles of B.L.U.E.S. to Tiger's "Candy-Licking Man" under the dim glow of yellowed lamps, the authenticity they fetishize is in the vision of black sexuality conjured up by his song, the urban danger represented by the smoky haze of the club, the poverty symbolized by a dank blues joint and its faint smell of whiskey and urine, the rhythmic funk of Tiger's guitar playing, and, of course, the darkness of his skin. In fact, it is precisely during such moments that they will look up to the spectacle of the stage and smile, because for many of these thrill-seekers, *this* is just about as blue as you can get.

The Fashion of Their Dreams
Inventing Authenticity in the Nocturnal City

As one watches these types merge and mingle in the restaurants and studios of Towertown, one is struck by the fact that in Towertown nearly everyone plays a role, wears a masque. "Self-expression" is the avowed goal of "village" life. And where talent is lacking, self-expression runs to the playing of roles and the wearing of masques, sometimes of the most bizarre sort. . . . Behind these masques which the "villagers" present to one another and to the world one usually discovers the egocentric, the poseur, the neurotic, or the "originality" of an unimaginative nature. Occasionally, however, one finds behind these masques young persons who are struggling to live out their lives, to remake the world a bit more after the fashion of their dreams—young persons who have come from north and west and south, from farm and village and suburb, to this mobile, isolated, anonymous area of a great city where they imagine they may live their dreams.

—Harvey Zorbaugh, *The Gold Coast and the Slum*

The Fashion of Their Dreams. At B.L.U.E.S. the collective ritual performed during showtime implicates nearly all audience members as not merely spectators, but as active participants whose roles and responses shape the event as much as the musicians. As exemplified by the last chapter, their contributions are often jump-started from the stage, as when a bandleader coaxes his audience to repeat his shouts, dance in place, or join in when the chorus comes around. But at other times, the offstage antics of the club's predominantly white audience demonstrate a great deal more initiative on its part, as when dancers from the floor take to the aisles during familiar upbeat R&B numbers in their attempts to generate attention from the crowd.[1]

On one such evening at B.L.U.E.S., three attractive female patrons in skimpy and snug outfits attack the dance area in drunken abandon, and only moments later several of the club's male customers angle their way toward the stage to sneak a peek at the floor show, which, for the moment, has supplanted the evening's paid headliner. Anne, a waitress and bartender, quips, "Don't you need a different kind of license for that?" On other occasions, drunk audience members desiring the spotlight aggressively push their way up to the bandstand, seize the singer's microphone, and clamor violently to the music or an approximation thereof.

Likewise, at B.L.U.E.S. Etcetera couples of all ages neck to the music, lone women sway seductively close to the stage, and occasionally a drunk yet enterprising young customer sidles up to a woman, gets rejected, and settles for dancing with the pole stuck in the center of the floor. Dizzy describes the improvised and festive drama indicative of the scenes at both clubs:

> Well, people, they be dancing over at B.L.U.E.S. . . . Like last time we played there, on the fifteenth, there was this dude, and he was so drunk, he'd keep dancing and falling down on the floor, get back up and just fall back down again! Finally, I say to him, "Man, why don't you just stay down there? It'll be less work for you!"

Musicians, patrons, and even staff defend the outrageousness and license of the club on the seemingly least entertaining of nights. While listening to (according to almost any conceivable objective measure) a painfully unpleasant performance by a local blues artist, Aimee, a regular bartender, turns to me and remarks:

> Yeah, he is really bad. But, you know, the girl at the end of the bar was just smoking pot in the bathroom, and some couple is, like, having sex in the other bathroom in the back, so everybody's having a good time, and that's what it's all about—so you can't complain too much.

In a burlesque world where drugs, sex, alcohol, cigarettes, and loud music dominate, audiences at B.L.U.E.S. revel in a kind of liberating abandon not normally permitted during their daily rounds of occupational and family life.[2] But in spite of the club's wildly festive environment, patrons nevertheless engage in highly self-conscious behavior in their attempts at merrymaking and distraction. While the blues offers a kind of transcendent escapism for many audience members, they are constantly aware of the world from which they are trying to escape. At B.L.U.E.S. they often accompany their desires for pleasant distraction with an earnest search for a sense of purpose within the club's carnivalesque atmosphere. In their attempts to experience the world of the blues bar in an intimate and meaningful manner, audience members frequently rely on its theatrical backdrop to forge a particular kind of self, an identity that I call a *nocturnal self.*

I have coined the term *nocturnal self* to describe the personalities that pleasure-seekers craft as they negotiate their way through the nightlife of the city. In urbane restaurants, cocktail bars, and dance clubs, late-night revelers frequently engage in a kind of temporary role-playing by fashioning themselves as sexy divas and drink-swilling hipsters, dazzling sophisticates and bewitching bombshells, or other personae to contrast the regularity of their everyday lives, if only for a few hours at a time.[3] In fact, one might argue that the revived popularity of formerly antiquated fads and fashions in recent years—the revival of 1940s swing music and dancing, the comeback of the cigar and the martini, the return of platform shoes and bell-bottom jeans among dance-clubbers—speaks to this desire among cultural consumers to create fantasy worlds of make-believe through experimenting with urban styles and subcultural sensibilities at night.[4] Of course, this recycling of past styles for incorporation into present modes of cultural expression is hardly limited to our current postmodern age of nostalgia, but exemplifies how cultures in earlier epochs also idealized the past as a means of revitalizing the present.[5]

When observing the urban frontier, journalists and cultural critics generally fixate on the radical chic demonstrated by the adventures in role-playing employed by candy-ravers, drag queens, and other representative dignitaries of the underground city.[6] However, for most adults the adoption of a nocturnal self rarely suggests such a break from the normative world of everyday life. In particular, a great majority of the audiences that patronize local clubs tend to view the city's blues and jazz scene as little more than a temporary diversion from the rigors of their workaday schedules.[7] Unlike the patrons of more subterranean scenes like warehouse rave parties and punk clubs, Chicago blues audiences generally forge nocturnal identities that more or less cohere with the roles they commonly inhabit outside the club.

For instance, take George, a gregarious businessman from Long

Beach, California, whom I met at B.L.U.E.S. one Tuesday evening. I arrive at the club alone at a quarter past ten, and I immediately head to the bar for my usual bottle of Budweiser. After chatting briefly with Marci, one of the club's regular bartenders, I turn toward the stage to watch the band play its final songs of the evening's first set. In search of conversation, I stroll the smoky club to find George and his two colleagues, all in town for a relay manufacturers convention in the Illinois suburb of Oak Brook Hills. After spotting George clumsily dancing in a drunken haze in the aisle wearing his beige suit from the convention, I approach him.

"Hey, you sure look like you're having a good time!"

"Oh, yeah," he replies, "well, you can't get any of this in Long Beach, so I gotta enjoy it while it lasts. Out in California, we have mostly karaoke places—and this isn't quite karaoke, know what I'm saying? We've been stuck up at this resort in the suburbs, and we were getting really bored and just had to get out, so we headed on down here to hear some blues!"[8]

I ask him, "So, what do you like about this place?"

"Oh, this place is great, you know, they got great blues here, and it's just a small joint—that's the most important part, you know? I've seen Led Zeppelin like five times, and lots of huge rock concerts, so I don't need that anymore . . . No, this is really great." I ask George how long he plans to stay in town.

"Well, some of these guys are staying for the weekend, you know, but not me . . . I'll be heading home when the conference ends on Thursday. I've got to get back to my wife and kids."

And so it began to make sense to me that a patron like George does not actually use his moments at B.L.U.E.S. as an opportunity to forge a brand-new identity, but he does attempt to negotiate his way among a set of real and imagined roles. In the social world of B.L.U.E.S., audiences enjoy the commercialized leisure provided by live entertainment and flowing cocktails. Within that world George negotiates his way among a number of identities (reveler, traveler, suburbanite, family man), and at the club he finds himself somewhere between the concertgoer who has "seen Led Zeppelin like five times" and the faithful husband who must eventually "get back to my wife and kids." In other words, the blues club offers him a place where, in the words of the great University of Chicago sociologist Harvey Zorbaugh, he and others might temporarily "remake the world a bit more after the fashion of their dreams," even as they allow the realities of occupational and family stability to hold them in check.[9]

Simultaneously, George lives out a certain fantasy of urban leisure (and perhaps unmarried life as well) through his after-hours consumption of the blues club. According to George, one of his colleagues at the bar is on the rather uptight side, and so he and his other buddy have been trying to loosen him up with shots and song—all on the company's tab, apparently. They begin shouting in unison along with the bandleader's screeches and howls in attempted imitation; meanwhile, Megan, the regular Tuesday night waitress and the object of their failed flirtatious overtures, shoots them a look, shakes her head, and mutters to me under her breath: "These guys are starting to get *really* annoying." Then, encouraged by the invitations proffered to a pair of out-of-towners to approach the stage—one to play harmonica, another to sing Big Mama Thornton's pre-Elvis "Hound Dog"—George pulls me aside to ask me what I think of the Doors and confesses *his* fantasy of appearing before the audience to perform their rendition of the Howlin' Wolf blues classic "Back Door Man": "Do you think they would let *me* sing it up there?"

In fact, he never makes it to the stage and, to Megan's delight, eventually stumbles out the door of the club with his colleagues. Still, by drinking with work buddies, singing with strangers, hitting on waitresses, and dancing to live blues music, white-collar professionals like George experience B.L.U.E.S. according to "the fashion of their dreams," as a rustic urban playground set half a world away from the reality of their everyday lives.[10]

The Chicago Blues Club as a Tourist Attraction. If some patrons envision their experiences at B.L.U.E.S. through a looking-glass fantasy of the nocturnal metropolis, others rely on the blues club as a means of specifically consuming the city of Chicago itself, along with its heavily promoted legacy as the so-called "Home of the Blues."[11] Chicago guidebooks and city newspapers commonly accentuate the city's blues heritage in their attempts to sell publications, provide exciting, if predictable, narratives, and support local commercial enterprises and economic growth.[12] Consider the introductory passage from a contemporary guidebook that pays homage to Chicago's historic past while connecting it to the present production of the blues:

In the early part of this century, as the steel mills of Gary and Hammond and East Chicago began smoking in earnest, Chicago began to attract its now-majority black population, many from the Mississippi Delta. It's a community that has contributed greatly to the city's special flavor . . . and the creation of the urban electric blues by Muddy Waters, Little Walter . . . music that provided rock 'n roll with its heartbeat. . . . And the blues is still alive and well in Chicago.[13]

At B.L.U.E.S. the most enchanted of audience members seek out the experiences promised in local tourism literature and other guides to the city. As they cross over borders demarcating the American nation and its cities, foreign travelers draw on dominant images of Chicago in order to transform themselves into cultural conquistadors consumed by the thrill of discovering the much-hyped authenticity of the local blues club for themselves.

For instance, take Skya, an aspiring college student from Krakow, Poland. I met Skya when she and her friend Paul stole away the vacant bar stools from my corner of B.L.U.E.S. on a cold Saturday night. After trudging through a January windchill that only a Chicago winter could produce, I slowly negotiate my way through the standing-room-only crowd to a miraculously empty bar stool in a warm corner of the bar near the stage. As I lean against the club's roughly plastered wall dotted with framed photographs and exposed nail heads, I casually sip my beer as the band entertains the rowdy and rollicking audience with a selection of blues and soul standards: two hits by the recently deceased Junior Wells, "Little by Little" and "Messin' with the Kid," Albert King's "Feel Like Breaking Up Somebody's Home," and Sam Cooke's "A Change Is Gonna Come."

And then I meet Skya. After an older couple departs from their stools for closer seats, she and Paul join me in the corner of the club, and while Paul simply smiles at the band while quietly remaining fixed in his seat, the music drives Skya into a complete frenzy that leaves her bouncing on her bar stool, kicking her legs, swaying her arms, and whistling a piercing shrill between songs. As the lead singer announces, "Thank God I'm a country boy!" before launching into a slow rendition of "Tobacco Road," she remains transfixed by the show, nearly unable to separate the suggestiveness of the *performance* from the individual background traits of the *performer* as she turns to me to ask, "His voice is so great . . . So tell me—how can a person drink and smoke his whole life and still have a voice like that?"

Skya explains that she and Paul are both from Poland, but for the past few months they have been living in the suburbs with their respective distant families while studying at local universities. After a few minutes of chatter, she turns to me to gush:

"And you . . . are you from Chicago?" I nod, and she continues:

> The one thing I love the most about Chicago . . . it's the blues. I love it! . . . Tonight, this is my first time hearing blues in Chicago . . . I've always wanted to go, because the best place for blues is in Chicago, the blues orig- inated in Chicago, and so I've always wanted to go, and tonight I finally got to come . . . It's probably the most important thing I've done since I've been here. It's amazing . . . Oh, it is the *best*, I *love* it! . . . In Krakow in the south of Poland, we have a blues club, and I've been to it, but it is *nothing* compared to *this* . . . No, this is the *best*.

As she departs to freshen up, I ask Paul if tonight also marks his first trip to a blues club in the city. In his Busch Gardens T-shirt, he smiles and explains, "Yes . . . it is even the first time I've heard blues live; I missed the Blues Festival this year. I mean, I've only heard Chicago blues here on the radio—but it's *not* the same thing." Skya returns and continues to jump and shout at the stage, attracting attention from some of the other customers as the band plays on.

International visitors like Skya and Paul enjoy B.L.U.E.S. because it satiates their hunger for what they take to be a uniquely "Chicago" expe- rience, and in doing so, they employ the images of authenticity suggested by the blues performance, the urbane setting of the club, and even the dubious thrill of meeting a bona fide "local" to imagine themselves as cutting-edge pleasure-seekers who have succeeded in finding the "real" Chicago—and, in some ways, the real America as well.

In addition to attracting foreign travelers, local blues clubs appeal to natives searching for tourist destinations that might best impress their out-of-town guests. Mike and Jolynn, the couple from B.L.U.E.S. intro- duced in the two previous chapters, confess their reasons for attending the club in the first place. A Chicago local, Jolynn explains: "Well, *Chi- cago*—I mean, the blues is just so ingrained in Chicago, right? Me and my friends come here every once in a while; I have a friend who lives just down the street, and so I wanted to take Mike out for a *real* Chi- cago experience, so I brought him here." Escorting visitors to venues like B.L.U.E.S. offers residents status *as* locals: by bringing their guests to places characteristic of Chicago's distinctively urban image, hosts show off their *nocturnal capital*—that is, their savvy familiarity and intimate knowledge of the city's nightlife. In this manner, they re-create them-selves in the same image that they use to represent the city; in other words, like the blues club itself, they attempt to come off as decidedly urbane, offbeat, and hip.[14]

Of course, like many other "real" Chicago experiences—shuttling up to the observation deck of the Sears Tower, admiring the Post-Impres-sionist wing of the Art Institute, taking in an improvisational comedy show at Second City, dining at Gibsons Steak House or Gino's Pizza—few locals actually patronize the city's blues clubs during the daily rounds of their everyday lives; rather, they reserve such occasions for entertaining out-of-town guests. Like these other local pleasures, blues clubs repre-sent prioritized items on the proverbial checklist of Chicago experiences that guests and hosts alike employ when mapping the essential places of the city to be consumed.[15]

At B.L.U.E.S. I introduce myself to Dave, a black business traveler from Toronto. His local hosts are the representatives of a suburban-based health care equipment supplier, and over the past several days they have been entertaining Dave and his son by introducing them to popular spots indicative of the Chicago tourist experience. On this par-ticular evening, they treated their guests to dinner at a local steakhouse, a Chicago Bulls basketball game at the United Center, and, finally, a hop around several North Side blues clubs, including Kingston Mines and B.L.U.E.S.; apparently, the company always takes its out-of-town clients to hear blues when they visit the city. Meanwhile, Dave wears his ela-tion on his sleeve. After buying Big Time Sarah's CD and soliciting her autograph at B.L.U.E.S. as a souvenir, he enthusiastically chats about the highlights of his trip, which include spotting Bulls guard Ron Harper at a local restaurant and club-hopping to hear a handful of downtown jazz sets. As the evening wears on, Dave explains the special significance he attributes to attending blues and jazz clubs in Chicago:

> Oh yeah, I always try to come hear music when I'm in Chicago . . . Now, of course, we have great blues clubs in Toronto—most people don't know that—and there is a place in Toronto that looks just like this, and they get bands like tonight's. This band tonight was really tight, you know? This place was much better than Kingston Mines tonight. I get to see blues all the time . . . There's great music in Toronto. But you know, *this is Chicago*, which has the history, and the culture, and so it's a special thing to come here to hear blues. Like last night, I smoked a Cuban cigar and took a walk with my son, and I took him into . . . that jazz club on Rush Street, and we sat

down and he loved it, he recognized all the songs from my music collection that he heard growing up . . .

Whereas George and his friends seek out the blues club as a way of experiencing the urbanity of the city, Dave enjoys B.L.U.E.S. specifically because of the authenticity suggested by Chicago's blues and jazz heritage. While he hails from an equally cosmopolitan city and demonstrates his affection for its local entertainment, the music of Chicago impresses him more for its *symbolic* significance. As a music fan, Dave questions whether Chicago's clubs necessarily offer *better* blues and jazz performances than those in Toronto, but he affirms that his affections for such clubs derive from the historical legacy they represent to him. By drawing on celebrated images of Chicago's authenticity, Dave consumes the blues club as a means of experiencing that legacy firsthand—and in some ways, such an experience overshadows the significance he places on the actual music performed there.[16]

Dave's remarks parallel those made by many of the business travelers that I met at the club. Insofar as post-industrial economic mobility encourages increased domestic and international business travel to global cities like Chicago, local and multinational firms require a reliable network of restaurants, nightclubs, sporting events, and other cultural attractions to seduce visiting clients and partners, and blues clubs function as a popular component of that entertainment infrastructure. In fact, international business conventions often sponsor trips to blues clubs for their participants to enjoy between meetings and presentations, as revealed one evening as forty men and women from all over the world, including Finland, Denmark, and Brazil, file into B.L.U.E.S. wearing their name tags from a global environmental management conference. After staying for a spell to soak up the local color, they promptly exit just after 11 P.M. as their tour bus pulls up to the club entrance for their pickup.[17]

Conversations with foreign executives like Dave reveal the popularity of Chicago's blues legacy among international business travelers. One wintry Sunday evening at B.L.U.E.S. Etcetera, I introduce myself to a group of Japanese businesspeople, including a gregarious businessman who turns out to be a high-ranking executive of the Japanese Chamber of Commerce and Industry of Chicago, an organization representing over five hundred Japanese companies that conduct business in the city. After celebrating their annual New Year's dinner, he escorts the event's guest entertainer, Sanshi Katsura, a well-known and popular comedian in Japan, via limousine to the club for late-night kicks. Identifying me as a Chicago resident, the executive asks me in earnest about the city's blues scene: "Who is your favorite Chicago blues singer? How often do you come here? Once a week? Twice a week?" He maintains great respect for the city's blues heritage and assumes that local residents attend its clubs with regular frequency, a misleading assumption that I undoubtedly reinforced by replying that I try to attend the local blues clubs about three times a week, as demanded by my fieldwork.

But for many intercontinental visitors, an evening at a blues club represents much more than an authentic experience in Chicago, but symbolizes a quintessential *American* encounter as well. When Europeans like Skya compare Chicago blues clubs to bars in Krakow, they recognize real and imagined distinctions not only between cities, but national cultures as well. Many foreign visitors become self-styled ethnographers themselves as they attempt to ground their *own* sociological theories of urban culture in the observations they make at the club. In such instances, the roles commonly employed by sociologists and their subjects can reverse themselves as visitors come to rely on the local ethnographer as an informant and guide. In fact, many of my conversations with inquisitive audience members often shifted focus when *they* began interrogating *me* about the authenticity of particular blues clubs and performers in the city.

By experiencing the more localized world of the blues club, such pleasure-seekers draw on familiar depictions of Chicago and America to develop context-specific interpretations of its culture. After chatting up one of the bartenders and her husband for a spell one late Sunday evening at B.L.U.E.S., I introduce myself to Dickon and Chris, two rowdy English gentlemen in their thirties. Pleasant yet passionate drinkers, after talking with me for a few minutes, they order me a cocktail and inform me that on this particular evening I will be drinking as they do, shot for shot. Moments later a screwdriver is placed before me, and they continue to arrive as the night wears on.

After we have been chatting for a while, Dickon remarks: "You know, I love Americans, because in this country you can walk into a bar and have a conversation with a complete stranger. In England everyone is so reserved—they won't talk to you unless they've seen you there for six months. Not because they are ignorant, you see, but because the country is so dense, with people living on top of one another, that everyone puts up these barriers . . ."

A few drinks later Dickon pulls me aside again: "You know, Dave, Manchester is a very industrial city, right? Very working class, everyone's life is the same—go to work, go to the bars, go to work, go to the bars—and I hear that Chicago is just the same kind of place, you know? Chicago is also very industrial, very working class. It's the same kind of place."

Meanwhile, Chris seems extremely impressed with the music and in a drunken fit begins shouting at the top of his lungs, "Top banana! Top banana! You know, I've never heard the blues before in my life! And where do you go if you want to hear the blues? Where do you go? *Chicago*! So I guess I got it right on the first try—it's fucking great! I love it! Top banana!" Upon shaking hands with the band, he announces: "I never liked the blues at all . . . until tonight!" The staff of B.L.U.E.S. begins closing up at two in the morning, and I leave the boys for their journey across the street to the after-hours' glow of Kingston Mines.

In their drunken joy, Dickon and Chris internalize the nocturnal role of the ethnographer as they explore the cultural norms inscribed within the space of the club. By observing how participants behave and interact at B.L.U.E.S. while drawing upon dominant images of the working-class industrial city and the American neighborhood tavern, Dickon develops inferences about the greater local, regional, and national cultural contexts in which Chicago blues clubs operate. Meanwhile, Chris imagines his experience as authentically representative of everyday life in Chicago. In doing so, he re-creates himself anew as a late-night reveler, converted blues fan, and witness to the so-called promise of the city—at least until he and Dickon presumably get kicked out of Kingston Mines during its closing time at four in the morning.

Perhaps not surprisingly, this tourist's-eye view contrasts with more subculturally savvy orientations as defined by everyday participants in local blues clubs. While audiences emphasize Chicago's urbanity and homegrown flavor as integral to their experience at B.L.U.E.S., musicians find the symbolic distinctions represented by local clubs to be somewhat superficial. In contrast, their concerns with club spaces tend to revolve around material rather than cultural interests—wages, availability of dressing rooms, and so forth. For this reason, Chicago natives who perform locally tend not to privilege the city as a premier locale for their own bookings. In fact, while audiences venture to Chicago from all over the world in their never-ending pursuit of authenticity, musicians themselves often prefer to play *outside* the city. As touring performers, they report that audiences and club owners outside Chicago accord them with greater material—and at times, emotional—compensation than they could ever hope to receive at local blues bars. According to Tiger, local blues musicians receive kinder treatment outside the city as a result of their status *as* Chicago blues performers. In light of Dave's earlier comparison of Chicago blues clubs to venues in Toronto, Tiger's remarks seem especially poignant:

> Man, I travel all over . . . I play in Memphis, New York, Ohio . . . I love play ing on the road, because I'm tired of playing in Chicago . . . I also get treated much better on the road. I've played in town at B.L.U.E.S. and B.L.U.E.S. Et-cetera, but I don't know, I like to keep moving . . . I don't know what it is, but people don't appreciate me here, not like they do *outside* Chicago. Besides, out there they appreciate you more because you're *from* Chicago . . . Like over in Toronto, man, they treated me like a king! You know? Like I was a king!

Cultural Commerce and the Sliding Scale of Authenticity.   As I suggested in the introduction, blues fans rely on varying definitions of authenticity to structure their experiences of consumption. Downtown clubs like Blue Chicago satisfy the desires of many thrill-seekers, including those on the prowl for authenticity—or not, as is often the case. During a conversation with his friends at a downtown blues festival, an audience member comments on his evening at the House of Blues: "Yeah, we saw the Blues Brothers at the House of Blues when it opened, like John Goodman and Jim Belushi and those guys, and they were goofy, you know . . . It wasn't serious, but it was fun."[18]

However, many other nightclubbers who *do* find these kinds of establishments lacking in local flavor, and thus unworthy of their patronage, often turn to places outside the central commercial district for a heightened sense of authenticity. For these consumers, clubs located in transitional urban neighborhoods with romantic and storied reputations seem less commercialized than those in the downtown area. Audiences and tastemakers organize the city's blues clubs and their entertainment zones along what I call a *sliding scale of authenticity* from the most seemingly mainstream and commercialized places to the most authentic, exotic, and hip. In this manner, clubbers begin by patronizing bars located at the most accessible end of the spectrum and work their way up the scale (or down, as the case may be) until they reach what they determine to be a satisfactory level of authenticity. This sliding scale of authenticity represents how consumers, cultural authorities, and even some musicians rank venues and their locales in relation to one another according to their own manufactured definitions of nocturnal status and subcultural cool.

In their quest to consume the seemingly exotic allure of the underground city, rather than more traditional renderings of metropolitan sophistication, many contemporary consumers fashion themselves as urban pioneers involved in a constant project of discovery and conquest as they trailblaze through entertainment zones and former ethnic enclaves as if they were unsettled frontiers, ripe for exploration.[19] For these audiences, clubs located in neighborhoods outside the city center offer a more authentic urban experience than themed restaurants such as the House of Blues. In particular, this turn to contemporary slumming involves a search for the prototypical urban community as a symbolic space of authenticity. To this end, clubbers will measure a bar's authenticity according to its ability to project a sense of intimacy, imagined or otherwise. *Global* travelers evaluate clubs favorably by envisioning tourist attractions as unassuming and uncommercialized nightspots where *locals* regularly fraternize, instead of tourists like themselves. By internalizing myths that celebrate local neighborhoods as lively bastions of social solidarity, these "anti-tourists" take pleasure in locating and experiencing what they imagine to be islands of community in a sea of urban anomie and commodification.[20] In their search for authenticity in the city, consumers seek out places that satisfy these kinds of utopian fantasies about neighborhood life.

While South Side taverns like the Checkerboard Lounge fulfill the desires of these audiences, blues clubs located outside the downtown area in affluent *white* neighborhoods like Lincoln Park and Lakeview (home to B.L.U.E.S. and B.L.U.E.S. Etcetera, respectively) sometimes work just as well. According to Jack:

> Well, to be honest, B.L.U.E.S. is right now one of the only ones that's still around. But we'll always be successful, because this place is what the old, smoky blues clubs used to be like . . . I mean, B.L.U.E.S. has always been an authentic-style blues club, and people are always going to want that.

While Jack's remarks surely suggest a generous portrait of the club, Lincoln Park venues such as B.L.U.E.S. often *do* satisfy audience demands for local "authenticity." Suchi, a tourist from Iowa, explains her appreciation of B.L.U.E.S.: "It's smaller here, and it's cozy, you know, people seem to know each other, it's less *touristy* . . ." Lisa, a seasoned visitor from California, favors peripheral clubs like B.L.U.E.S. to larger downtown clubs and characterizes them as informal havens representative of the iconic urban community, in contradistinction to the sprawl of Los Angeles nightlife:

> I go to clubs to hear music all the time in L.A., and especially in Hollywood . . . but there's really nothing like this out there . . . I mean, out in L.A. all the clubs are so huge . . . There's just nothing like this, you know? This place is just smaller, and has a real neighborhood feel to it . . . and after going to Blue Chicago, this place seems much cooler, much more homey.

Lisa seeks out an "authentic" neighborhood bar to contrast her experience of Los Angeles, and because of its centralized downtown location and slick decor, a club like Blue Chicago fails to register as high as B.L.U.E.S. on her own personal sliding scale of authenticity. Likewise, when I run into Maria, a student from Barcelona on a ten-day tour of Chicago, she explains her touring group's decision to attend B.L.U.E.S.

"Well, today we saw *Les Miserables* . . . It was really wonderful . . . and we wanted to go someplace typical for Chicago, so we wanted to hear blues and jazz, and somebody told us this would be a good place. First we went to the House of Blues—you know the House of Blues?" I nod. "But we left, because it was too big, and you know, for *tourists*, so we came here, and it's much better, it's smaller, and more personal . . . Do people from Chicago come here a lot?"

I take a look around the room, and although a number of regulars have found their usual seats, the bar is pretty much packed wall-to-wall with out-of-towners. But Maria seems so enthralled by the fantasy of venturing into uncharted urban territory, and I just don't have the heart to burst her bubble.

"Oh, yeah," I tell her.

"Oh, good! The House of Blues was just so big, and we wanted a place that was small and more, um, typical, ah, more, um . . ."

"More real?"

"Ah, yes! *Real*! That's it!"

Although they appeal directly to the city's tourism industry, neighborhood clubs like B.L.U.E.S. continue to attract out-of-towners desiring to re-create themselves in the same cool, authentic image suggested by the prototypical smoke-filled, dimly lit blues club. In contrast, musicians often reject the "coziness" of neighborhood bars for downtown and suburban venues, and, in fact, some performers even *prefer* playing in such clubs. During a jam session at B.L.U.E.S. Etcetera, Jeffrey, a saxophonist,

admits his fondness for the Beale Street Blues Cafe, a blues club located in the Chicago suburb of Palatine:

> I don't really like playing straight blues, I like to play stuff that's more funky, like more rhythm and blues, you know, like James Brown? And at this jam session, they mostly play straight blues, you know, and the musicians here, they are usually not so good. But I go to another jam session, and it's much better . . . On Sunday nights I play at this club in Palatine—the Beale Street Blues Cafe. I know it's far away—it takes me forty-five minutes to get there by car, actually, but it's really a great place: they have a great sound system, and it's big, too, about three times the size of this place . . . and the musicians all play to a much higher standard than here. And the clientele is much more upscale there than here, you know; they have a restaurant and the food is really good, too, and there is no cover during the week. It's a really great place . . . You'll have to come out there sometime to jam.

Unlike tourists attracted to "homey" neighborhood clubs suggestive of stereotypical images of authenticity, Jeffrey prefers attending a remote suburban club "three times the size" of B.L.U.E.S. Etcetera because it serves his needs and wants as a musician. Of course, his status as an urban resident as well as a Chicago blues saxophonist makes it possible for him to enjoy Palatine's Beale Street Blues Cafe without harboring the anxious feeling that he *himself* might sink toward the wrong end of the authenticity scale. Meanwhile, Hiroshi, a blues fan from Japan, revels in the intimacy suggested by B.L.U.E.S as he carefully remarks: "I like this club very much . . . Some places, they are too big. But here, it is small, and the music and the people and the beer are all together." He clasps his hands to express this intimacy and adds, "And when the musicians come off the stage, they are right here and you can talk to them."

But while B.L.U.E.S. is, in fact, a smaller-sized club than many of its competitors, the variety of opinion among patrons suggests that they rely on their imaginations as much as their more "objective" observations when evaluating the local intimacy of the club's atmosphere. On the very same night described above, Franz, the German blues fan introduced in the last chapter, offers a less flattering evaluation of the club: "I don't like these audiences; they are all tourists. They are here for the convention—they are not die-hard blues fans. They don't listen to the blues, and they don't understand it—they do not really know how to appreciate it. And it takes away from the whole atmosphere of the place, and for me, it makes it a less enjoyable experience."

While neighborhood bars like B.L.U.E.S. appeal to many locals as well as out-of-towners, clubbers like Franz find even *these* places to be too commercialized and inauthentic for their tastes, and longtime regulars frequently echo the same concerns. During a Tuesday night show at B.L.U.E.S., Sean, a former regular, suggests how the experience of attending the club has changed for him over the past decade:

> I've been coming here for, well, twelve years now, yeah, since 1987 . . . Back then the crowd was really into it, and now the audience seems like, I don't know, it's more for "the masses." Like now, the blues is more "chic," and coming out to hear blues is more the "thing to do." For them, it's just about going out for "blues," instead of going to hear one particular artist, while back then the audience really knew about the music, and the names of people they wanted to see, and it was more authentic.

Urban Chic and the Gentrification of West Town. As a reaction to the current mainstream popularity of clubs like B.L.U.E.S., former regulars turn to clubs located in off-the-beaten-path entertainment zones a step removed from the city's affluent lakefront communities like Lincoln Park. For example, Smoke Daddy, a blues bar located in the constantly changing commercial terrain of Division Street in the recently gentrified West Town area, attracts cultural consumers seeking the urban authenticity often associated with community life, bohemian creativity, and the risk of the street. According to their own accounts of gentrification and cultural consumption in the neighborhood, young locals attempt to refashion the former immigrant enclave as a countercultural haven bristling with an unusual combination of edgy grittiness and postmodern irony.[21] Consequently, nightclubbers venture out to Smoke Daddy in search of the symbols of authenticity suggested by its surrounding neighborhood milieu and celebrated in countless hotspots, dive bars, and sexy lounges located nearby. In fact, it may be instructive to describe the general cultural life of West Town and its Division Street as a prelude to understanding exactly why Smoke Daddy succeeds among even the surliest of musicians and their cutting crews.

A collection of diverse neighborhoods that include Wicker Park, Ukrainian Village, and parts of Bucktown, the community area of West Town sits directly to the west of the Near North Side. The urban face of West Town is one of recurrent ethnic succession and neighborhood instability. In the 1960s the neighborhood provided a haven for first- and second-generation immigrants of Polish, Italian, German, and Russian Jewish descent, but the residential population underwent a radical sea change between that time and the 1990s, as the neighborhood lost nearly 40 percent of its population size and its European ethnic majority was eventually replaced by first- and second-generation Latino immigrant families.[22]

Today the cultural ecology of West Town still suggests hints of its multiethnic vibrancy. Walking down Division Street, one of the former immigrant enclave's major commercial arteries, reveals the remnants of West Town's old eastern European community life: Polish sausage shops and bakeries, Hungarian eateries, the local Czar Bar, and a prosperous Russian/Turkish bathhouse. Meanwhile, at least until recently, several local businesses catered to the specific needs of the neighborhood's Latino residents: Las Villas Bakery serves homemade *pan de Majorca* and *aqua fresca*, while the former Lorimar Produce carried fresh corn tortillas, chorizo, and household products with labels printed in Spanish. Currency exchanges, storefront churches, and liquor stores common to low-income urban neighborhoods remain on the strip.[23]

Unfortunately, many of these businesses are on their last legs, as West Town not only experienced a wave of ethnic succession in recent years but economic displacement as well, when large numbers of middle-class residents first began migrating there during the mid-1980s and subsequently increased the market land values of the area's residential properties.[24] Marked by the attempts of gentrifiers and real estate speculators to renovate existing local structures, the value of an owner-occupied housing unit in the area more than doubled during that decade, increasing from $36,482 to $74,730.[25] (In the context of Chicago's urban malaise during the 1980s, this jump is both significant and surprising, insofar as the doubling of property values in West Town represents the fifth highest rate of increase in the entire city during that time. In fact, only nine out of the city's seventy-seven community areas experienced land value increases of over 50 percent in the 1980s.)

As the residential blocks surrounding the strip continue to experience high levels of development, former neighborhood establishments like Las Villas Bakery have all but disappeared as entrepreneurs attempt to transform Division Street's ethnic streetscape into an entertainment zone that can service a more affluent set of desperately seeking consumers and cocktail loungers. Accentuated by its illuminated fish tank, bright red couches, curvy cocktail tables, and orange and red swirl-covered walls, the recently uprooted Liquid Kitty recalled the playful swank of 1960s playboy lounges, where dolled-up weekenders would sip chocolate martinis and cognacs over an eclectic mix of rock, funk, and newly revived swing. Meanwhile, just down the street at Fruits de Mer, the moneyed classes enjoy French haute cuisine with a Cuban-Pacific flair. On fine white linens, diners indulge their highbrow appetites through menu offerings which include boursin cheese pot stickers served in a sake sauce, cornmeal-rolled venison loin served with a champagne demi-glace, yucca-encrusted sea bass topped with a roasted pepper aioli, and so forth.[26] As Heidi, a server working her way through graduate school, remarks while folding linen napkins in preparation for the dinner rush: "Since I've moved here, I have definitely noticed how this area is really turning into a real scene," adding that, at the restaurant, "the customers have been very upscale: couples, families—all very rich."[27]

In contrast to Fruits de Mer, other establishments located along the Division Street strip during the late 1990s catered toward a younger cultural patronage of graduate students, would-be artists and intellectuals, and wild-eyed night owls. Phyllis' Musical Inn served the local punk music scene; readers and daydreamers pored over used books in the window of Myopic; diners carried their own bottles of wine in paper bags to Twilight, where they enjoyed trendy eclectic fare: grilled corn and cactus quesadillas with chipotle salsa, black bean hummus with watermelon, mint and feta salad, and the like. Meanwhile, just a half block south of Division on Damen Avenue, a mix of bohemian locals and suburban strays continue to drink cocktails at the Rainbo Club. As they lounge across secondhand couches, they admire the rotating work of local artists featured around the perimeter of the bar's dimmed interior.

Leo's Lunchroom attempts a similar aesthetic to match its off-kilter counterparts down the strip. At the restaurant tattooed chefs and waitresses in platform shoes and horn-rimmed glasses serve diners at the eatery's short Formica-lined counter. As the black and red bar stools blend into the checkered floor, a random mess of postcards, magazine clippings, rock 'n' roll bumper stickers, cassette tapes, a sign advertising "CIGARS 5¢," a Batman clock, and a kitschy poster featuring various cuts of pork cover the wood-paneled walls. White frosted lamps decorated with stars dangle from the ceiling. Behind the counter the servers' workspace is actually an old broken bureau under which the house stereo plays loud indie rock, funk, disco, techno, and alternative country music. By the door, flyers advertise classes for yoga, independent theater troupes, and Radical Balance, a locally based company specializing in holistic medicines. The advertisement for the latter suggests the pseudo-bohemianism of West Town's newly gentrified urban milieu: "Experience how your energy field responds to your thoughts and emotions, and Detect and correct Psychological Reversal and rebalance your energy; Tap your Body/Mind wisdom to super-charge affirmations, and Learn how to rapidly release distress and program in your goals."

Likewise, during its brief life on the strip, the Mystery Spot specialized in buying, selling, and trading all things thrifty, antiquated, and kitschy: pulp fiction titles such as *Shack Woman* and *Groovy Chick*, old Donny Osmond and Rodney Dangerfield vinyl records, 1950s-style saddle shoes, Las Vegas tapestries, and various 1980s toys, including a Michael Jackson doll, old electronic sports games, and a used 2XL toy robot. The co-owners, Henry and Anat, lived in the apartment in the back of the store. They opened the retro-savvy Mystery Spot in October 1997 with the intention of serving the younger set of new residents to the gentrifying neighborhood. Adorned in a blue leather blazer, plastic bracelet, and toy watch, Henry describes the role his store plays in the cultural ecology of Division Street:

> This neighborhood is great . . . Our biggest fear is that as the area gets more popular, more Eurotrash culture will move in, instead of blending in with what is already here . . . Down here, we wanted to provide a place more for younger people, and that's why we have free coffee and couches in the back here, so people can grab a book and just hang out, drink coffee, and get a good sense of community, you know? Because for us, that's the most important thing—community. And soon, we want to clean up the basement and use it to show sixteen-millimeter movies and have bands play, and it will have to be all underground, because it's illegal, but it's also, you know, a way to get people together to hang out and stuff . . . I know that when you own a business, it should be about money, but we would do this even if we lost money, because it's not really about money at all. Both Anat and I hold other jobs, and we wouldn't be able to keep the store open if we didn't work other jobs . . . But we just love this stuff, and we love to hunt around for it, and play with it, and turn it around and just get more stuff, because it's just so cool . . . Everything is an extension of yourself, especially if you can build an environment that expresses who you are.

This sense of play among young residents and business owners is emphasized at Jinx, a nearby coffeehouse. Open since September 1997, the spot is cutely decorated with marigold stucco walls, bight red moldings, and a neon red cat in the window. An old used couch, a jukebox playing alternative rock classics by Elvis Costello and the Pixies, a pinball machine, and a 1980s Burger Time video game occupy the back area of the coffeehouse. A blue cigarette menu is placed on every table along with booklets offering food options whose names include the "Ralph Machiato," "Fucking Good Brownies," "Toasted Cheese" and "Fancy Toasted Cheese," "Uncle Mo's Good Stuff," "A Kinder, Gentler Mussolini," "Castroville Special," a vegan-friendly soy cheese dish, and Pop-Tarts.

Julie, one of Jinx's two co-owners, contrasts Jinx to more upscale establishments located off the nearby North-Damen-Milwaukee intersection, the epicenter of West Town's most developed phase of gentrification—a distinction perhaps best exemplified in 2001 by the local presence of the MTV *Real World Chicago* house-*cum*–television studio:

> This area is totally different from the crowd at North and Damen. I'd say that the people who hang out in this area are much more educated, much more open-minded than the suburbanites who hang out at the Soul Kitchen, and places like that . . . Now, I don't know what Liquid Kitty is like, but here, there are no jocks, not a lot of fraternity action, none of the heavy-drinking guys yelling at every woman on the street. Of course, these people who come to Wicker Park during the day are completely different from the ones who come at night, and the people who come in during the week are totally different from the weekend crowd. But here, it's great . . . I think this neighborhood has an image of being dangerous, and I think that helps to keep those kinds of people away . . . The people who come in here are in their low twenties to early thirties, polite, middle-class . . . They are mostly white, but we also get a lot of local kids who come in here for ice cream and pinball, so it's mixed.[28]

Exemplified by hot spots like Jinx, Leo's Lunchroom, Liquid Kitty, and the Mystery Spot, the cultural landscape of Division Street represents a web of contradictions: neighborhood instability and ethnic displacement provide a liberating framework for young bohemians to experiment with identity; new restaurants rely on high-concept themes to generate business amidst a declining number of immigrant-run eateries and bakeries; meanwhile, other businesses attempt to represent their authenticity by relying on the rhetoric of community and the underground city. As an entertainment zone, Division Street provides a space for consumers and producers alike to construct counternormative identities and generate status on the basis of their contradictory appeals to authenticity and fantasy, postmodern play and cosmopolitan chic. Within this particular cultural context, blues clubs thrive by drawing on these same symbols of subcultural status and nocturnal capital.

Smoke Daddy and the Lifeblood of the City.   Just down the street from Jinx, a loud, red neon sign announces "WOW" to all customers as they approach Division Street's own blues club, Smoke Daddy. In step with its surrounding gentrified milieu, the nostalgic decor of the neon-lit Smoke Daddy blends in with the contrived retro-streetwise affectations of nearby nightspots. The club mimics a highway juke joint redesigned in classic Chicago style with exposed piping, frosted blocks of glass, multicolored Christmas bulb lights, and 1950s-style booths and dining sets. On the left, a long and narrow bar accentuates the railroad-car design of the club's rose-tinted interior. In the back of Smoke Daddy, a cinema poster advertising *The Man with the Golden Arm*, the film based on the novel of the same title by the storied Wicker Park author Nelson Algren, hangs along the wall by the club's small yet functional kitchen.

Like other blues clubs in the city, the interior of Smoke Daddy museumizes canonical representations of African American popular culture with great enthusiasm. Most of the club's wall hangings depict works by black movie stars and jazz, blues, and rhythm-and-blues artists: the Jayhawks' "Stranded in the Jungle," Lena Horne's "Stormy Weather," the Coasters' "Charlie Brown." Waitresses serve up oversize portions of Mississippi delights to the tables of smiling customers who feast on baby back ribs doused with hickory-smoked barbecue sauce, buttered corn-on-the-cob, red beans and rice, corn bread, and sweet potato pie. At the same time, the playful movie-set aura of Smoke Daddy echoes the atmosphere of nearby bars and trendy nightclubs. As male patrons chomp down on their cigars, their female companions sip cosmopolitans from swinging martini glasses.

But while Smoke Daddy shares many similarities with other Chicago blues clubs, striking differences make it a unique place. The club attracts an audience made up of young residents from West Town and nearby off-the-beaten-path neighborhoods, rather than middle-aged conventioneers and other business travelers. As a music venue without a cover charge, the club spends little money paying its bands and therefore attracts less commercially oriented acts whose song lists generally eschew tourist-friendly pop and soul standards in favor of classic, yet less-well-known, blues numbers from the 1940s and 1950s. During their sets these performers cram into the front of the club for lack of an actual stage; on occasion, such musicians find themselves inadvertently performing in the front doorway to the club, preventing all customers from entering or exiting without disrupting the performance.

The informal, off-kilter environment of the club contrasts with the more controlled organization of its downtown and North Side counterparts. Before shows wandering panhandlers roam the club attempting to "sell" free local newspapers. Because of the club's lack of a bouncer, teenagers frequently use heavily applied makeup and risqué clothing in desperate attempts to pass for drinking-age adults. As a spot dominated by the younger bohemian set, groups of college-age fans bearing toe and nose rings, torn jeans, sun dresses, and ankle tattoos occasionally dance barefoot near the front of the club during gigs.

Since many of the young, up-and-coming white musicians who frequent Smoke Daddy for their weeknight fun actually live in West Town's Wicker Park and Ukrainian Village, their relationship to the club parallels their close attachment toward these neighborhoods. Daniel, a guitarist and bandleader, lives in a relatively inexpensive loft apartment on nearby Milwaukee Avenue, and during the day he rides his secondhand bicycle around the neighborhood to his favorite local spots, including Las Villas Bakery. The freshly gentrified "newness" of West Town gives these young musicians a sense of cultural ownership and autonomy over the terrain of their everyday lives, from the sidewalks to local diners, clubs, and bars. At the same time, West Town's rapidly changing immigrant enclaves provide young musicians with the authenticity all too often represented by working-class community life, while the residential and economic instability of the area offers them the romanticized sense of the "raw" urbanism and danger suggested by neighborhood disruption.

Of course, this is not to suggest that these musicians necessarily have a more privileged reading of the city than anyone else; after all, in spite of their high degree of nocturnal capital relative to their out-of-town counterparts, their evaluations of authenticity still rely on the symbolic power of images of place and the stereotypes they breed. While these musicians may be savvy cultural consumers, in the end they simply exchange one set of idealized, place-based myths for another. A twelve-year resident of the area, Chad, a blues and rockabilly guitarist and singer, frequents local clubs like Smoke Daddy as a customer as well as a performer. Near closing time he describes his relationship with the changing neighborhood.

Over bottles of Rolling Rock and jukebox blues, he fondly recalls his earliest memories of West Town's Wicker Park as a "wild neighborhood" where one "could do anything":

> Well, after I graduated from high school, my parents gave me the choice of going to college to study business or moving out, and I really wanted to go to art school, so I moved in with this guy I knew in a punk band for a while in the suburbs. But then when I was nineteen I won a contest, and the prize was a scholarship for a semester at the Art Institute, so that's when I moved into the city and into Wicker Park with this crazy couple from this punk band. I'll never forget the first day I moved in. We're driving up Wood, and right on the corner there's this crazy naked guy, just standing there, man, with this look on his face . . . That was probably the first sign that this was a wild neighborhood.
>
> Back then, there wasn't anything here, and you could do *anything* . . . This place was like a ghost town. I remember walking home from work and seeing people getting shot on the street, and there were gangs . . . Like one day on my way home, when I lived on North and Western, as I'm heading back from Humboldt Park, I see this pack of about thirty Latin Kings just walking down the middle of the street like it's a parade, and they're yelling and shit . . . And there was a lot of drugs around here, a lot of heroin, and prostitutes would be trying to pick up guys right here on Division . . . This place was like the wild country, man! You know what they used to call this spot around the corner, on Wood, just a few blocks up? The "Dog Patch." Yeah, man, because abandoned wild dogs used to roam around this place in a pack, and in the winter you'd have to run through these blocks here, because those dogs were hungry, man![29]

While Chad's glorification of the urban danger of the area clearly suggests the high value he places on the symbolic authenticity of West Town's helter-skelter instability and proletarian grittiness, he also reveals his satisfaction with the opportunities that neighborhood gentrification provides:

> Then, money started coming into the neighborhood, and yuppies began moving into the neighborhood . . . I guess the biggest sign of the shift was when they opened that bank and ATM on the Damen intersection a few years back . . . I think it's cool, you know, because now there's more stuff going on, more places to play and hang out, and besides, you can make a lot more money out here now than you ever could before . . .

He concludes our conversation by maintaining that Smoke Daddy represents "the lifeblood of the city," a space for bohemian creativity and subcultural authenticity:

> The music scene here is still great, I mean, this is still a place where you can play your *own* thing . . . Man, the truth is that it's places like this that make up the lifeblood of the city, you know? Music—you can't survive without it. It's like air. They'll never be able to get rid of it all, because it's just too important.

Just as Chad idolizes Smoke Daddy as "a place where you can play your *own* thing," other performers prefer the marginalized club to more established venues because its more locally indigenous audiences appreciate the lively twang of their set lists and styles of performance. Tex, a guitarist and singer, has made a local career out of playing a slow and subtle brand of Mississippi Delta music during regular gigs at Smoke Daddy, in contrast to the party-oriented blues music commonly performed downtown. During one of his gigs at the club, I mention this to Tex: "So, you guys really stick to that early Delta sound in your show here. You don't hear that a lot in Chicago nowadays, do you?" He concurs, responding: "No, you really don't, not in many places in town. Most guys don't play this way anymore—it's more loud, violent. I prefer something a little quieter, easier to listen to, mellower, more laid-back." I reply, "Why do you think that is? Why is that other style of music is so popular?" Tex just shakes his head: "Beats me. I guess that it's just expressing the way people are feeling, you know? More violent, more angry." Bandleaders like Tex enjoy Smoke Daddy because it offers a comfortable sanctuary where they can perform the slow (if still *lyrically* violent) Delta blues and other stylistic alternatives to the more popular music frequently heard in clubs like B.L.U.E.S.[30]

Meanwhile, other musicians who perform and take refuge at Smoke Daddy mourn the loss of the shared communal atmosphere they once felt in the subcultural earthiness of local blues bars in the 1970s. In our initial conversation at Smoke Daddy, Sebastian, a local guitarist who plays in Tex's band, remarks:

> Yeah, you could go into Elsewhere [a former Lincoln Park blues club] and hear a living legend perform seven nights a week . . . Hey, you've heard of *Living Blues* magazine? Well, back then *Living Blues* would have ads for the guys playing at Elsewhere and every one of 'em would be famous, and

they would pack the house with people from the neighborhood, or real blues fans from Chicago and some from out of town, but it was always real blues fans who loved the music, and there was no House of Blues or any of that big tourist crap . . . You know, I was reading in *Chicago Magazine*, there was an article and the headline was "So, You're Tired of Doing the Same Old Blues Club Thing." Well, back then there was no "blues club thing," there weren't all these tourist clubs—it just wasn't something people were doing . . . get it? There *was* no "blues club thing." Not like now. You gotta let people know that me and [a fellow band mate] think this whole tourist thing is bullshit.

Musicians like Sebastian wear their involvement at Smoke Daddy as a badge of honor. These performers have little interest in impressing out-of-town crowds with the familiar set list of standards, and so they enjoy the club because it offers them the breathing room to play the blues any way they like. I ask Sebastian how most local musicians feel about performing at more established, higher-paying clubs in the city:

Well, to be honest, most of those guys make their living playing blues and so they go for the money. And at a place like that, a band can make like a hundred bucks a night for each guy, instead of playing at one of the West Side places—or *here*, where there is no cover—and take home thirty-five dollars apiece. Now, if a band can make like seven hundred dollars playing at the House of Blues, are they gonna care about the crowd, or the money? They're gonna care about the money.

And so, in some ways Sebastian's appreciation of Smoke Daddy stems from the same desires for authenticity harbored by his audiences, and just like the ankle tattoo–bearing college-age fans who occasionally dance barefoot near the front of the club during gigs, he uses the club as a place where *he* just might find dream fulfillment and self-rejuvenation by developing a countercultural sense of self, nocturnal or otherwise.

Like Therapy

The Blues Club as a Haven

Third places the world over share common and essential features. As one's investigations cross the boundaries of time and culture, the kinship of the Arabian coffeehouse, the German *bierstube*, the Italian *taberna*, the old country store of the American frontier, and the ghetto bar reveals itself. . . . The wonder is that so little attention has been paid to the benefits attaching to the third place. It is curious that its features and inner workings have remained virtually undescribed in this present age when they are so sorely needed and when any number of lesser substitutes are described in tiresome detail. Volumes are written on sensitivity and encounter groups, on meditation and exotic rituals for attaining states of relaxation and transcendence, on jogging and massaging. But the third place, the people's own remedy for stress, loneliness, and alienation, seems easy to ignore.   —Ray Oldenburg, *The Great Good Place*

A Cast of Regulars.   Thus far, we have explored the world of the blues club, and B.L.U.E.S. in particular, through the lens of the audience member, and in doing so, we have observed how out-of-towners seek out the symbols of authenticity suggested by fabricated images of blackness, ghetto life, and the city of Chicago itself. But while these consumers squeeze into the club's small interior on most Friday and Saturday evenings for their weekend kicks, during the rest of the week they are joined by a colorful cast of local regulars in search of a slightly different kind of authenticity. Now that we have peeled away some of its layers of manufactured authenticity, let us return to B.L.U.E.S. once again, but this time we will observe the club from the point of view of this

cast of regulars, a collection of die-hard blues fans, professional musicians, amateur players, bartenders, and other locals who inhabit the club
throughout the week not only to be entertained by the blues, but also,
as the following entry from my field notebook reveals, to check in with
friends, schmooze with acquaintances, and gossip about everybody else.

"So, Robin, how do I look tonight?"

Robin, the Tuesday night bartender, looks confused and wants to know
what Doug means, and why he is asking *her*. As for me, I've been at the bar
since about 11 P.M., and from what I can gather, Doug, who is the harmonica
player for the evening's headliner, has been spending the night confidently
chatting up his date. But now that she has left the bar for the rest room, he
is shifting from his ordinarily confident demeanor to more of an anxious
backstage role, enlisting Robin for grooming tips.

As Doug explains his desire to impress his date, I peek around the bar in
search of other members of the Tuesday night cast of regulars. Rob Hecko,
the club owner, sips coffee at his perch on the raised platform by the front
door, where he can survey his employees and customers while watching television; he chats with Mike, one of the club's bouncers enjoying an evening
off. Mark, a local booking agent and former club owner, approaches the bar
to order his usual glass of red wine. Chicago blues artist Dave Myers strikes
up a conversation with a friend of the band at the back of the club as he sells
and autographs his CD for any takers. Jay jokes at the bar with Aimee, the
other Tuesday night bartender, and Patrick, the evening's bouncer. Louis, a
local saxophonist and the organizer of the weekly jam session at B.L.U.E.S.
Etcetera, makes his rounds at the club, greeting all familiar faces. Meanwhile, Karen, a local blues photojournalist, snaps her flash down by the stage
at Tail Dragger (the blues singer introduced in chapter 1).

As the night wears on, the banter among the regulars continues, and as
I characteristically peel away the red-and-white label from my beer bottle,
I try to fashion myself as a potential member of this cast of characters. I
chat with Dizzy, asking him if he will be in attendance for the Wednesday
night jam session, and he suggests that he might consider going if Jack, his
current band mate, offers him a ride from his South Side apartment to the
North Side club. Karen soon returns to the bar and casually smooches with
her date as I exchange remarks with Suzanne, the Tuesday night waitress,
about her social life in West Town's Wicker Park neighborhood. Later Aimee
buys me my third beer as she relishes telling her tale of last Monday night's
fun at Suzanne's Academy Awards party, after which several of members of
the staff headed out to Smoke Daddy for beer and music until early in the

morning. She appears equally jovial as she details her plans to go with Hecko to catch her favorite blues artist, Lee Russell, at a show in the suburbs.

As the night progresses, Dizzy performs a few numbers on the fly, after which Tail Dragger resumes his spotlight at the front of the stage, growling in his best Howlin' Wolf imitation. He rhapsodizes mournfully about his latest stint in prison in his highly affected baritone blues voice as Jay remarks aloud to himself, "Oh, why was I in jail? Oh, I remember . . ." and he turns to Karen and adds, "because I shot somebody and killed them!" (In 1993 Tail Dragger murdered fellow Chicago blues performer Boston Blackie over a financial dispute and served four years in the Illinois State Correctional System for the crime.) Karen gestures that he shouldn't announce this news so loud, but he retorts that Tail Dragger didn't hear him and neither did anyone else . . . and the night continues on until closing.

Unlike many of the audience members who jump and shout alongside them at B.L.U.E.S., the members of this cast of regulars do not spend a lot of time thinking about the authenticity of black or white musicians, or whether their favorite B.B. King song will be performed during the second set, or how their experience at the club resonates with popular depictions of Chicago's urban nightlife. Instead, they experience the club through an alternative interpretive lens, and so they literally see a different kind of world when they enter the bar, a world populated by local acquaintances and familiar strangers. According to Marci, a bartender and manager at B.L.U.E.S.:

> Oh, yeah, well, Saturday night is amateur night, you know, all tourists, people from the suburbs. During the week it's different. I mean, there are still some tourists, but not as many. Tuesday nights are more for locals, and lots of people here are friends with the band, and it's just great—lots of my friends come, and it's just cooler.

In this chapter I want to explore how these bar regulars use the social backdrop of the club to manufacture a kind of authenticity that differs somewhat from the one discussed in the previous two chapters. Regulars reconstruct the world of the club as a haven, a place where authenticity is measured in terms of the club's ability to adequately represent a vision of urban community and moral order. As countless sociologists have pointed out, the notion of community represents a romantic and idealized form of social organization that can only be defined and evaluated subjectively, in part because, like authenticity, it does not exist independently of the set of collectively agreed-upon symbols of community, like the preponderance of friendship ties or public celebrations. Community, therefore, is not really an objective or definable set of social relations, but simply represents an ideal type of the society in which we imagine we would like to live. While a number of recent popular books, such as Alan Ehrenhalt's *The Lost City: The Forgotten Virtues of Community in America*, romanticize the stereotypical notion of community by eulogizing its alleged loss in contemporary cities, the past forty or so years have yielded a wealth of intriguing urban studies on how city dwellers manufacture community in their everyday lives. This interdisciplinary approach to urban culture places particular emphasis on the production of symbolic markers of neighborhood solidarity and social cohesion, such as the presence of public characters and their "eyes upon the street," a metaphor astutely evoked by Jane Jacobs in *The Death and Life of Great American Cities*.[1]

In the case of the Chicago blues, bar regulars seek out the vital signs of neighborhood tavern life when they patronize local clubs, such as the familiarity of strangers, the camaraderie displayed between bartender and customer, and the promoted tolerance of social differences. Like more mainstream audiences, regulars value these symbols of community because in their moments of consumption they can attempt to fulfill their own dreams of attaining a sense of authenticity, albeit an authenticity rooted in the idealism of community solidarity, rather than racial difference or urban grit. By crafting nocturnal selves that emphasize membership in such a community, bar regulars can experience the blues club *as* regulars by enjoying the emotional perks suggested by the role, including a sense of social recognition and personal worth.

Meanwhile, those seduced by the glamour associated with the blues club attempt to join this urban community by constructing a nocturnal identity that evokes a highly extroverted aura of bohemian cool. Musicians and patrons alike rely on stylized gestures, slang, and other strategies of performance in order to present themselves to one another with bold confidence and subcultural swagger. Regulars forge these identities during their social encounters at concerts and jam sessions held at local blues venues, and rely on the theatrical backdrop provided by the smoky aura of these dimly lit clubs as a suitable public setting where they can attempt to embody these roles in a convincing manner.[2]

As Marci suggests above, these encounters typically occur during weekday evenings at B.L.U.E.S., when regular patrons, die-hard blues fans, professional musicians, and staff members actively pursue one another for companionship and comfort. They stake out spaces segregated from the rest of the audience—along the bar, in front of the stage, near the bouncer's perch by the door, by the back room near the rest rooms, on the stoop just outside the front entrance—and enjoy the club as a place where they can imagine themselves as part of a collective world greater than the sum of its parts, a community of regulars.

Like authenticity itself, this community of regulars may be an elaborately produced fantasy, but in the moments of its fabrication, it becomes meaningful and palpable to these participants as part of their reality. Seasonal rituals provide such occasions; for example, B.L.U.E.S. hosts a number of special promotional events every year that bring together this usual gang of suspects, including birthday celebrations, Mardi Gras, and a summer barbecue held every August. A survival from the neighborhood's more countercultural era, the barbecue is an all-afternoon affair that continues into the evening: it is one of the few times during the year when these nocturnal characters actually socialize during the light of day. While bands play live blues inside, the usually frenetic staff enjoy a few lazy moments of lounging around outside with close friends while munching on grilled hot dogs, hamburgers, corn-on-the-cob, chili, and home-cooked picnic fare in the backyard. On a lazy summer afternoon, I discover this scene as I wander through the dank club to the sun-drenched backyard lit up with conversation and laughter. Anne, a bartender, exemplifies the spirit of the event: wearing a lei, she clutches Bernice, the club's mannequin (done up in summer wear), while downing a bottle of Rolling Rock in the hot sun and blowing bubbles carelessly on the back stairs on the club. All around her, bartenders and regulars gather in groups of friendly chatter.

After schmoozing with Anne for a few minutes, I scan the backyard for another familiar face, and I recognize Ken, a longtime regular as well as an amateur harmonica player. He explains his affection for B.L.U.E.S. amidst all the fun: "I've been coming here for, I don't know, I'd say for about the past eight, no, maybe ten years now. I guess this is my Cheers, you know? It's a bar where I can go, and I never have to sit alone. I always know that somebody will be here that I know."

The sheer familiarity of the local patrons and bartenders makes Ken feel like a member of an established community of neighbors. By comparing B.L.U.E.S. to Cheers, the Boston pub featured in the syndicated television comedy of the same name, he characterizes the club as a place where actual friendships emerge and sustain themselves over time: a bar where, as the show's theme songs reminds us, "everybody knows your name." The club serves as a meeting place where regulars maintain relationships through face-to-face encounters, and therefore expect each other to make themselves available by routinely stopping by the club during their evening rounds for a beer, a chat, or simply a quick handshake and a smile. In fact, regulars often require each other to offer excuses for their extended absences from the club.

This expectation becomes apparent when I return from an unannounced hiatus to B.L.U.E.S. Etcetera and Gigi, a regular, demands an explanation: "Hey, where have you been?!" On other occasions, musicians and regulars attempt to explain away my absences from B.L.U.E.S. One night Aimee knowingly presents me with my usual Budweiser at the bar upon my arrival and, after asking me to explain my whereabouts, lists the reasons that might explain my absence: "Hey, nice to see you! Where have you been? I was sure you were going to stop by last week . . . Is this crunch time for you guys at school? Or were you on break? Yeah, I'd figured it had to be something like that . . ."

Aimee's interest in my whereabouts also reveals a desire on her part to understand the academic world where I reside and demonstrates how regulars often attempt to bridge the cultural differences among themselves that would ordinarily divide such a diverse group of individuals. Over the course of my fieldwork, I discovered that Aimee's efforts to understand my life outside the club were common, especially among the staff. On another occasion, after I was absent from B.L.U.E.S. for an extended period of time, Jack remarked how "we haven't seen you in like two months," and when I explained that I had been busy working, he asked, "You mean for money, or is this work for school?" When I explained that I had actually been doing graduate work, he seemed less impressed, but after mulling over my response for a few seconds, he finally justified my absence in his own mind: "Oh, but the work for school will eventually *lead* to making money, right?" My conversations with Jack often revolved around these attempts to inhabit a common worldview, and so while I would question him about his experiences as a bouncer and musician, he would continue the encounter by asking me about my own work. On one such evening in particular, as I helped him pull down bar stools from the club's cocktail tables before business hours, he asked:

"So, Dave, before we start—what exactly *is* sociology? Is it the study of the human animal, or society, or what?"

"Well, yeah, I guess you could say that sociology is the study of the human animal, society, and the relationship between the two."

"Well, then I guess you've found the right place. If there's one thing we've got here at this club, it's plenty of human animals."

In the House Tonight in Love.   Among the club's cast of regulars, this menagerie of human animals not only includes customers and bar staff, but professional musicians who rely on its social world for recreation and friendly conversation as well as work. In fact, this desire for leisurely human contact often distracts musicians from their professional responsibilities. For instance, when clubs televise pivotal sporting events, players and singers often exert more energy collectively cheering on their home team than performing their sets, as I discovered in 1998 during the week that the Chicago Bulls advanced to the NBA finals for the third year in a row. I arrive at B.L.U.E.S. Etcetera early one night to catch the first half of Game 1 against the Utah Jazz on the club's large projection television screen, along with a handful of other bar regulars. Beer in hand, I relax on one of the couches near the front of the club to enjoy the game.

Suddenly, Jack, who also works at B.L.U.E.S. Etcetera, takes over at 9:30 P.M. before the end of the match-up. "Sorry, guys, I gotta put up the screen. I've got too many paying customers tonight, and so we have to start the music." Prepared to watch the entire game at the club with his buddies, one regular growls, "Man, fuck them . . . Let's just go home!" Meanwhile, as the house band begins to play, a group of us crowd around the smaller television in the back room to watch the final quarter of the game, and every couple of minutes the band's drummer sticks his head out from his perch onstage to ask, "Hey, what's the score?" and then telegraphs the update to the bass player. As I pass the stage, Louis, the band's leader and vocalist, looks up from his microphone and then, right in the middle of one of his songs, *he* asks me for the score.[3]

Like Louis, many regulars juggle occupational and social concerns simultaneously at the club, and sometimes it is hard to tell the difference between the two. For instance, Big Time Sarah, a featured entertainer at B.L.U.E.S., stops by the club nearly every evening of the week to socialize, perform, or both. Ever the businesswoman, she habitually sells her compact discs, concert tickets, and assorted souvenirs to unsuspecting patrons at the club with relentless ferocity—on one occasion, she even tried to sell me an electric razor.

Sarah's social yet enterprising nature was revealed to me one evening when I arrived the club at about 11:30 P.M. to watch an independent film crew stake out the entrance to B.L.U.E.S. to shoot a scene for a movie. The scene only required a shot of Tail Dragger getting out of a taxi, muttering a line, and walking into the club, but it was taking a long time to get the shot just right. Meanwhile, cabs kept pulling up to the club to drop off out-of-towners arriving from downtown, and so Sarah was recruited to scare off any cabbies who might disrupt the filming. When she suggested that she should be paid for her troubles, I found it difficult to ascertain whether or not she was joking. Moments later I headed inside to watch Rob Hecko, the club's owner, demand an iced coffee from the bar, and there was Sarah at his side, playfully ridiculing him for not ordering an alcoholic beverage.

Later that same evening Sarah shifted roles as she took a break from socializing around the bar area (and the never-ending movie shoot in front of the club) and headed toward the stage for an impromptu performance. As she transformed herself from a bar regular into a professional entertainer, she shouted to the audience: "How many y'all in the house tonight in love?" The crowd responded with cheers, while from behind the bar Debbie, one of the bartenders, yelled, "Love stinks!" Sarah's response was characteristic of her usual pugnacity, and, frankly, not entirely different from what one might expect to hear her utter *offstage*: "Well, even if you're not, you're gonna listen to me *anyway*!" She began her medley and announced, "Now everybody's got a blues idol, and a soul idol, and my soul idol is Aretha Franklin, and this was a song we had on in the car while I was getting a piece for the first time, and people be driving by," and then she broke into lyrics devoid of any subtlety: "We going up, down, like a seesaw . . ."

In a way, Big Time Sarah shifts so effortlessly from the bar to the stage because her performance itself is highly social, while her offstage demeanor is quite performative. The blues club is a place where regulars can achieve professional and emotional rewards simultaneously, and, in fact, this clustering of fulfilled needs is only heightened among those "in the house tonight in love," particularly when musicians, bartenders, and regulars become romantically involved with one another. In fact, this happens rather often: for a time, Aimee, a bartender, dated the bassist of one of the club's regularly featured bands, while Steve, a club bouncer and part-time musician, met his wife at B.L.U.E.S. Etcetera during a jam session where she regularly played blues guitar onstage while he worked the door. The club provides a place where these relationships can be instigated, developed, and enjoyed.

I arrive at B.L.U.E.S. on a wintry Sunday evening and spot Marci sitting at one of the bar stools enjoying a coffee drink. I approach and take the stool next to her, and we exchange greetings as she explains that tonight is her night off, and I recall that her husband, Matt, is the usual drummer for the evening's featured band. She laughs as I mention how nice it is to see her on the other side of the bar, and as we turn to the music, I notice that even though she is off the clock, she is still wearing one of her usual gray B.L.U.E.S. sweatshirts.

As the set comes to a close, I casually slide a stool away from Marci to allow her husband to join her at the bar, while I entertain myself by watching sports on the overhead cable television in silence alongside one of his band mates. At the end of the set break, Marci's husband heads back to the stage and she turns to me to ask me about my weekend: I explain how two friends announced their wedding engagement at a party the night before, and she responds by describing her relationship with Matt, noting how although he is a professional musician, he is kind enough to avoid playing his drums in the house. I ask her how they met, and she explains:

> Well, he's from here, but I met Matt in Iowa, actually, when he was playing a festival . . . I moved up here to Chicago right before we got married . . . and we used to spend a lot of time here, you know, and one day they needed someone to fill in, and I've been working here ever since . . . And it's great, I mean, all my friends hang out here, and we hang out here all the time. I even hang out here when I'm not working—it's especially nice during the week. Like this weekend, it was just so packed! And mostly with tourists, people who come and go, people that I'll never see again. And you know, they're all right, and that's all well and good . . . But during the week it's cool, you can just hang out, and see people you know, and everybody's cool, it's so much fun.

In *The Great Good Place*, Ray Oldenburg argues that pubs, taverns, cafés, and other establishments function as worlds of sociability and leisure where friends and strangers alike can enjoy the pleasures of informal public life. Oldenburg calls these environments "third places" because they provide an alternative to the two dominant settings of our everyday lives: the rigorously structured world of work and productivity, and our more privatized spaces of domesticity and family life. Clearly, blues clubs and other public drinking establishments provide a respite from job and family responsibilities for many of their regulars; however, by identifying such venues as distinctly "third" places, Oldenburg ignores the fact that commercial spaces of *leisure* are simultaneously places of *work* for their entertainers, service staffs, and other employees. Moreover, for couples like Marci and Matt, the social world of B.L.U.E.S. functions as a pseudo-domestic environment as well, because they spend so much of their time together within the confines of the club as a married couple. Just as Marci takes the opportunity of an evening off to watch her husband perform with his band, Matt will sometimes stay past closing time to help his wife clean up and close down the bar for the evening. In this manner, the blues club functions as place of leisure, work, *and* family life for these participants.[4]

But while Marci seems to easily balance her multiple worlds of work, family, and leisure to her own satisfaction, for other women a relationship with a musician can require a greater degree of self-sacrifice. For a number of reasons, professional blues musicians commonly experience greater difficulties balancing their occupational and romantic lives than those in more normative professions. Musicians typically work in bars, nightclubs, and other environments generally considered at odds with respectable middle-class family life and domestic bliss, particularly since musicians have a reputation for indulging in hard liquor and the attention of potential sexual partners, and both tend to be readily available to musicians in the clubs where they perform. Likewise, career musicians are often expected to work long, late hours and travel far distances for jobs, away from their families and loved ones.[5] As a result, a musician's work schedule and lifestyle can place heavy burdens on his romantic relationship without providing many financial or emotional benefits to the woman who loves him. This burden weighs heavy on the musician as well, as Calvin, a guitarist and vocalist, suggests when he describes his involvement with his partner, Gigi, "Yeah, it's hard, because I want to be with her, but I don't want to stifle my creative and artistic expression, you know what I'm saying?" In fact, it is often the case that the career and its alluring lifestyle win out over the relationship.[6]

To alleviate these strains, wives and girlfriends often pick up the slack by accompanying their husbands or partners to their gigs in an effort to share more face time with them. In doing so, the women involved in such relationships selflessly give up a fraction of their own personal lives to spend long hours in dark and smoky male-dominated settings. In the early morning hours, Gigi often finds herself at jam sessions tired and yawning, lamenting her need to get up in the morning for her day job at a restaurant. In fact, a romantic involvement with a blues musician can almost become an extra full-time job.

But at the same time, these women inevitably forge friendships with their mates' colleagues and other club regulars. For example, by joining Calvin regularly at weekly jam sessions at B.L.U.E.S. Etcetera and frequent gigs at B.L.U.E.S., Gigi became a regular at these clubs in her own right and nurtured intimate relationships with other musicians invested in the local blues subculture. She demonstrates her acceptance among club insiders when she and Big Time Sarah conduct their late-night ritual of sharing greasy potato chips doused with hot sauce at the bar. And so, while the romantic partners of blues musicians may suffer through late nights of loud music, they sometimes gain access to an additional social world at the club, a familiar cast of regulars.

A Brotherhood of Strangers.   The intimacy shared by club couples—from Marci and Matt, to Sarah and Gigi—contrasts with the loneliness that a good number of other regulars occasionally experience when biding their time alone at the bar while awaiting the arrival of familiar faces. During these moments regulars engage in an intricate and restless ballet in their attempts to feign comfort: shaking hands with the bouncer, ordering a beer, strolling down the length of the club in search of company, waving to the band, settling back at the bar, engaging the bartender in brief small talk, nodding to the familiar regular across the bar, walking across the club to fill up on peanuts, watching and nodding with great concentration at the evening's performance, pretending to watch the closed-captioned television terminally set to one of many cable sports channels, getting up to change seats for a different view, and so forth. Occasionally, regulars will spend an entire evening performing this elaborate dance before finally giving up and heading home. Meanwhile, others use the commonality offered by the late-night sports broadcasts overhead to jump-start conversations about boxing and hockey with nearby customers.[7]

In fact, many of the regulars at B.L.U.E.S. share a collective feeling of community rooted in a generalized familiarity with their fellow patrons rather than any deeply held sense of intimacy, and warmhearted relations based on loose mutual acquaintances and face-to-face interactions characterize many of the friendships at other local clubs as well. Indeed, while years of socializing at the same club provide regulars with amiable experiences, it is often an amiability felt among strangers. As Farrell, a guitarist and bass player, remarked to me on the night we finally introduced ourselves at B.L.U.E.S. after weeks of spotting each other at the same clubs throughout the city, "Yeah, right, nice to meet you . . . Yeah, you can see somebody at the same bar for, like, five years and never actually know their name."

In fact, the community of regulars that emerges at B.L.U.E.S. looks very much like a microcosm of urban neighborhood life itself, a cross section of the city in which neighbors recognize each other's faces, but not always their names. I like to call this seemingly paradoxical urban world a *brotherhood of strangers*, a largely male-dominated community in which weak but friendly ties provide the solidarity necessary for regulars to imagine themselves as members of a collective group. As Andy, a blues guitarist, jokes after mulling over the predominance of standard set lists among bands, "Well, actually, the answer is that there is only really one band in Chicago—Ha-ha-ha-ha!" To this, Farrell continues the joke: "Right, and it's got seventy or eighty people in it. We all have numbers—'Oh, Sammy's out with a broken hip, so let's send in this guitarist . . .' " Although relationships among local blues musicians and other regulars are often more casual than close, they persist through friendly handshakes and short-lived conversations spawned by their mutual recognition of one another as members of the same team. Consequently, while many regular patrons may spend their evenings alone at the bar, their experience is almost always enhanced by the familiarity of their surroundings. The recognition of habitual locals; the names and faces of the bouncers, waitresses, and bartenders; the chords of the standards performed by the headlining band; and the usual beer and wine list all offer the regularity desired by the club's most dedicated fixtures.[8]

While Farrell often emphasizes the ironic familiarity of strangers and the anonymity of regulars at B.L.U.E.S., his undying gratitude for the club's persistence underscores the strength of those relationships. A Chicago native in his mid-forties, he has sought refuge in the haven of B.L.U.E.S. since its opening, and he attributes his attachment to the club to the solidarity of its patrons and its treatment of regulars, which include perks such as free admission, complimentary and discounted drinks, and knowing glances and gestures. Over cold bottles of beer on a warm Monday evening, Farrell explains:

> See, the thing about this place, and the difference between this place and those other clubs, is that even if it weren't a blues club, it would still be a great bar. Just look around—this is a great bar. I remember one winter, it was one of the coldest winters in Chicago history, on the coldest night of the year, and I lived just a few blocks from here, and all the bars in the

neighborhood were closed, every single one of them. Except this one. Even Kingston Mines was closed—but B.L.U.E.S. was open, and this place was *packed.*

And of all the clubs in the city, no place treats musicians better than this place right here. No place has treated me like B.L.U.E.S. See, with the drink policy here, the musicians, the regulars, the blues fans, everybody gets free drinks. Everybody. And when you get a free drink, when the bartender buys you a drink? That comes ordered from the top down: that's the policy of the owner, and it always has been. No other bar cares more about its musicians and its regulars than this place.

Mickey's Blues.   One regular in particular who represents the close relationship between customers, musicians, and staff at B.L.U.E.S., at least as described above by Farrell, is a quirky nocturnal character named Mickey. Mickey has been frequenting the city's blues clubs for the past twenty-five years in his characteristically disheveled garb: a wrinkled brown shirt with a pocket full of pens, a stained black cap loaded with buttons, and a worn gauze mask hanging just below his double chin. A short, stout middle-aged resident of a single-room-occupancy hotel in Uptown, Mickey waddles into B.L.U.E.S. several times a week to take up his usual spot at a bar table close to the stage. From this perch he places himself in a prime position to greet his fellow regulars as they make their rounds through the club, and all stop to offer their greetings, from longtime fans to local blues legends: "Hey, Mickey!" "How's it going, Mickey!" A local celebrity in his own right, he responds with his characteristic, "Hey! Hey!"

Persistent as well as gregarious, Mickey is often impossible to avoid, and over the years he has cultivated a reputation for being somewhat of a pest. Clutching a collection of worn, filthy bags and the occasional cheap tabloid newspaper, he flutters around the club to joke with local musicians, mooch sodas and popcorn off the bartenders, and chatter endlessly throughout the night with audience members who regard him with either good humor or trepidation. Often, he relentlessly tries the patience of the staff with his requests for current gossip until threatened by Jack or Big Time Sarah.[9] And on a good night, Mickey tries his best to impress as he shimmies up to unsuspecting female patrons on the dance floor.

But in spite of his wild antics, Mickey's routine appearances at clubs like B.L.U.E.S. offer a reassuring sense of continuity in a social world packed with transient audiences. The staff and regulars of the club admire his dedication to its community of regulars, and they warmly reciprocate with their kindness and patience. They look out for Mickey by offering him free admission and complimentary soft drinks and snacks, and on slow evenings they occasionally invite Mickey up to the stage to sing his wildly interpretive rendition of a B.B. King number: "Rock me, baby!! Rock me all night long!!!" In return, he watches over his family of regulars with a vigilant eye. After one Wednesday night at B.L.U.E.S. Etcetera, he stops me on my way out to warn me about the evening's weather: "Hey, are you driving? No? Oh, 'cause you know, it's raining pretty hard out there, yeah . . . What are you going to do? Do you have an umbrella?" Likewise, in the local press a human-interest story on Mickey reported that, according to one bartender, "Whenever a musician is sick or in the hospital, he goes to see them. He goes to all the funerals, and if there is a benefit, you can be sure that he'll tell everybody in town." [10]

In addition, the pseudo-familial ties that characterize Mickey's friendships with other members of the local blues scene greatly contribute to his self-esteem. For patrons like Mickey, the blues club serves as a comfortable haven where participants can develop attractive nocturnal identities as bar regulars and local heroes. It is often difficult for men and women who are marginalized because of their declining health, mental illness, substance abuse, or relative poverty to establish a sense of personal worth in conventional arenas of social life, and so the blues club provides them with an alternative means of developing a positive self-image. Since regulars like Mickey sometimes face difficulties gaining recognition as social beings in the world existing *outside* local clubs, they are all the more appreciative and protective of their group membership *inside* places like B.L.U.E.S. and B.L.U.E.S. Etcetera, where club participation provides them with an affirmative social self that they enjoy displaying to newcomers at the club. [11] One evening after a lengthy Friday night show at B.L.U.E.S. Etcetera, I stop over at Mickey's corner by the pay phones near the front door, where Guy, a local blues guitarist, introduces him as "Mr. Blues." Mickey shakes my extended hand and asks:

> Oh, hey, so do you live in Chicago? What neighborhood? . . . I live up there around Clark and Broadway, by the Green Mill—Do you know the Green Mill? Oh, yeah . . . Hey, did you see that guy over there, with the guitar? Yeah, that's Lurrie Bell, he's one of Chicago's best blues guitarists, yeah . . . And his father is a famous bluesman, too, yeah . . . You know,

Carey Bell? . . . Oh, yes . . . Hey, did you say you play the saxophone? Do you, umm . . . do you know the Mighty Blue Kings? Yeah, I know one of those guys, yeah, we've been friends for about five years now . . . Yeah, I'll see you on Wednesday . . . I'll be here, yeah.

Bartenders and the Moral Order of the Club.   Just as customers like Mickey demonstrate their identification with B.L.U.E.S. and the sense of camaraderie and belonging it inspires, the club's bartenders characterize the social universe of B.L.U.E.S. as a social and moral haven as well as a workplace. By defining the club as a place that promotes racial tolerance, an anti-commercial ideology, and a strong sense of community, they fashion themselves within its social world not merely as employees, but as full-fledged members of the club's larger community of regulars.[12]

For example, one evening in mid-February I arrive at B.L.U.E.S. shortly after midnight for a nightcap and begin chatting with Aimee, one of the regular Tuesday night bartenders. She offers to buy me a shot of tequila, but not before she grabs my beer bottle straight out of my hand, pours a gulpful into a glass, and downs it after clinking it against my returned bottle. She begins describing her evening by noting how, although the crowd seems to be thinning out, "the personalities have lingered."

> So this [white] guy comes in, and I serve him a drink, and it's obvious that this drink is the one that puts him over the limit—he's really drunk, falling over himself—and I'm at the cash register, talking aloud to myself about how this guy has had too much and needs to be cut off, and maybe I should get Jack to escort him out, and this [white] couple overhears me and one of them says to me, "I saw he was hanging out with those three 'mooks'—I'll bet he's a 'wannabe,'" and I'm just freaking out now because I'm thinking to myself how clueless these people are—this is a *blues* bar, for god sakes, I mean, of *all* the places—and so I tell them that they should really keep their racist comments to themselves, because that sort of thing is not cool with me here. And I know the three guys, too: they're my friends from across the street. So it's been a crazy night.

In her discussion of this encounter, Aimee depicts the moral order of the blues club as ideally tolerant of racial difference by countering her customers' remarks against what she believes to be the normative moral fabric of B.L.U.E.S. And by doing so, she simultaneously establishes an identity for *herself* on the basis of her defense of racial harmony and integration.

In a similar manner, Robin, another bartender, ties the club's moral order to an anti-business ideology when she recalls her relationship with Suzanne, a former coworker who waited tables at the club two nights a week before she was fired:

> You know, I would say that Suzanne was a really selfish person, just a really self-centered person. She used to try stupid stuff like pretend she didn't know she had to work, and she would refuse to help clean up after closing. And when she was working, she would treat the customers based on how well they tipped. I mean, it was really bad: she would coax big tippers from the bar to the tables and send the bad ones back to the bar. She was just really selfish, and really fake— if you tipped big, she was nice to you, and if not, she would just ignore you.
>
> Now, my feeling is, what matters is if you're a nice person, you know? Not everybody can afford to give me a twenty-dollar tip. And so I try to treat people nice if they are nice, right? So one night a guy who works in the service industry was in here, and she was serving him, and he doesn't tip until the end of the night, and so she literally ignored him the whole night. She was just so rude to him, and later he came to the bar and told me that he had never been so insulted at a bar before. So one night she refused to clean up: she had washed her hands and didn't want to get dirty, and we had just had it and told her to just get the hell out. You know, all of us—me, Jack, Marci, the whole bunch of us—we had just had enough of her shit.[13]

Robin targets Suzanne for failing to represent the idealized image of authenticity that regulars and staff associate with the club, a place where presumably "everybody knows your name" because of its collective aura of comfort and friendly familiarity, rather than its coarser desire for financial profitability. And like Aimee, by characterizing the club in this image, Robin helps to fashion her own personal identification with its social world as well.[14]

Interestingly enough, I found that in my own conversations with Suzanne, she *also* had the ability to display a subtle yet tender affection for the cast of nocturnal characters that frequent the club. Before opening the bar for business one Monday night, she explains:

I've been working here for a year now, and I still can't get my friends to come out here. They call this place "Blues-Mart," you know, like Kmart? It's because they think of the club as really commercial. And it's true, and the T-shirts on the wall definitely detract from the "soul" of the place, and the tourists here can be annoying at times, but I just love how this place attracts such a great mix of so many different kinds of people between the tourists, the musicians, the regulars, and the locals, and we get so many characters in here. And I really feel like this is my family here. I don't have family in Chicago, but this is my family. And, of course, when you work at this job, you have to put on a smile for the customers, because that's part of your job. But as the night wears on, if the music is good, I get into it, and I actually find myself starting to feel good, and soon the smile that I've plastered on my face for the job becomes real.

On the one hand, Suzanne emphasizes many of the commercialized aspects of working at B.L.U.E.S., including the commodification of local culture through souvenir kitsch, the ubiquity of out-of-towners, and, most of all, the emotional labor required of female waitresses and bartenders. While women like Marci do serve in high-ranking managerial capacities at the club, gendered norms characterize behavior among service staff.[15] Unlike the burly male bouncers employed by B.L.U.E.S., who are permitted to be forthright and antagonistic when provoked, female employees have less leeway when treating customers, and the emotional labor required of them extends to handling rude and suggestive comments from drunk male patrons with grace and aplomb, laughing at jokes that aren't particularly funny, and even bouncing and clapping to the music in time while working behind the bar. As Suzanne asserts, "When you work at this job, you have to put on a smile for the customers, because that's part of your job."[16]

But in spite of these criticisms, Suzanne accentuates the ambiguous relationship between work and leisure in a place like B.L.U.E.S., where musicians and staff often blur distinctions between their job responsibilities and their social lives. While she clearly dislikes the more coercive elements of working at B.L.U.E.S. (and, unlike Marci, does not spend her nights off there as a customer), Suzanne nevertheless finds intimacy and a sense of belonging in the club's social milieu. In fact, my own relationship with Suzanne demonstrated this ambiguity. During her last months of employment at B.L.U.E.S., many of our conversations shifted from small talk to personal matters, from her boyfriend troubles to our shared frustrations balancing work and school; as our relationship developed, she began bringing me complimentary drinks with frequency and eventually began refusing my tips. Our friendship was indicative of many of the relationships shared between staff members and regulars. Like her fellow bartenders and the musicians they serve, Suzanne sought out the authenticity represented by the signs of community suggested by the club's friendly social world, and in doing so, she balanced the occupational pressures of work with her needs for sociability and a local family to call her own.[17]

The Jam Session and the Search for an Authentic Self.

In Chicago, New York, and other urban areas, jazz and blues musicians traditionally frequented certain after-hours clubs for intense jam sessions where they could practice their craft by improvising with fellow artists in settings removed from the more commercial world of public performance. Held in the back rooms and basements of private clubs, secret speakeasies, or other invitation-only gatherings, musicians and their hangers-on would congregate and play at the jam after their paid gigs in order to experiment with new ideas, learn about possible jobs, network and talk shop with fellow performers, and compete for in-group status among their peers. In this manner, the jam session provided them with an alternative space of leisure and work, a place where they could socialize with colleagues and rivals until the wee hours and simultaneously fulfill a set of professional needs and responsibilities.[18]

Because late-night jam sessions typically excluded nonmusicians, jazz and blues aficionados tended to regard these clandestine meetings as far more authentic than the concerts, dances, and other public appearances where music was performed. As a result, cultural entrepreneurs began staging commercial jam sessions in the late 1930s during which audiences would be permitted to witness these formerly private moments of improvisation. Of course, opening up these jam sessions to paying outsiders diminished their capacity to symbolize the same authenticity they once did in an earlier, less constraining environment.[19]

Today many blues jam sessions in Chicago operate as little more than open-mike nights where amateur and up-and-coming musicians are permitted to sit in with established house bands and take improvised solos for paying audiences on typically slow weeknights. However, in spite of the commercialized aspects of these latter-day jams, they continue to serve as an emotional outlet for young musicians and other bar regulars in search of community. At the former weekly jam session held every Wednesday night at B.L.U.E.S. Etcetera, Adam, a guitarist in his mid-twenties, emphasizes the scene's impact on his overall sense of well-being:

> Yeah, I can't wait for the Wednesday night jam. It's like I need my fix. I remember a year ago I had been playing in a bunch of rock and metal bands, and suddenly I got really into blues and started playing it alone in my apartment, and it was great, but I wanted to jam with other guys, and no one else I knew was into playing blues. Then I showed up at the jam, and it was like so great, you know? And now, I get really depressed if I miss it. It's like therapy.

Of course, like their more traditional counterparts, contemporary jam sessions also offer an alternative world for musicians to develop professionally by providing exposure and experience for new arrivals and amateurs, a meeting place for aspiring musicians to find potential band mates and accompanists, and a forum where they can learn about local employment opportunities. In fact, Adam met the members of his current band at a series of jam sessions throughout town, while Elliot, the aforementioned singer and guitarist from chapter 1, credits a local jam session for introducing him to the city's blues scene.[20] He owes much of his reputation to a contest held at the prestigious jam session at Buddy Guy's Legends, at which he garnered the top prize:

> Well, the jam sessions are really the places where you get your start if you're new . . . That's where you go to get known . . . I got my start at the jams, just going to the weekly jam session . . . making connections, networking . . . Music is just like a business in that way . . . And that helped open doors for us.

In addition, jam sessions provide a fertile ground for blues artists seeking to develop their artistic talents and professional skills. During encounters between musicians, advanced players often befriend their novice counterparts to teach them various techniques and tricks of the trade. In my own experiences at B.L.U.E.S. Etcetera's Wednesday night jam session, Jeffrey, a fellow saxophonist, would frequently take me aside to teach me basic playing techniques, such as using the blues scale to improvise while playing solos. (The blues scale consists of the root, ♭3rd, 4th, ♯4th, 5th, and ♭7th intervals of the major scale: for example, the blues scale in the key of C major [C-D-E-F-G-A-B-C] would be: C-E♭-F-F♯-G-B♭-C. By raising or lowering the notes of the major scale by half-intervals, thereby making them sharp or flat, musicians deliberately play "out-of-tune" to produce the "blue" notes indicative of blues and jazz melodies.) For many of the jam session participants, mentoring involves showing inexperienced players how to take solos and harmonize using these scales. These lessons often expand into general lectures on practicing, instrument maintenance, and artistic development: where to take private lessons and shop for equipment accessories, the importance of listening to old records and attempting to replicate solos at home, the merits of metallic and rubber mouthpieces over plastic ones, and so forth.

While some advanced musicians hold these impromptu lessons in their private encounters with less experienced players, others turn their onstage interactions into pedagogical opportunities. At B.L.U.E.S. Etcetera participation in the horn section offers such an opportunity. Sequestered at bar stools near the right side of the stage, brass and woodwind horn players congregate, harmonize softly to accompany the band, and switch off taking solos at the horn microphone. Their interactions provide opportunities for the passage of advice among musicians of varying degrees of ability.

I experience such an encounter one night when I assist James, a black semiprofessional trumpet player and regular at the jam, by helping provide harmonic accompaniment to the band's performance. At the stage James asks me to follow his lead and begins to play off the major third, which I simply imitate until the song's completion. Although we have grown acquainted through our interactions at the microphone for the past few months, we tend to confine our conversations to topics of music performance. On break between songs, James turns to me and remarks: "Yeah, I haven't seen you here for a couple of weeks, so I know you've been practicing. And it sounds good, man, it sounds real good. I can tell you've been practicing, man."

We begin chatting about music and harmony, and he suggests that we play the same rhythmic part to lend a strong accompanying base to the musicians onstage. He then runs down a chromatic scale of successive notes on his horn. (A typical chromatic scale consists of twelve tones played at half-step intervals in ascending or descending order. For example, the chromatic scale in C major includes the following notes: C-C♯-D-E♭-E-F-F♯-G-G♯-A-B♭-B.) As I echo James's trumpet by singing the notes aloud, he continues the impromptu lesson: "See, that's your best teacher, right there. You've got to sing it to yourself, and then you play it . . ." We begin playing to the music, and suddenly he stops to implore: "Here, see, follow me. Listen!" and he holds the root note of the first chord of the progression, and then continues, "Then we just play down the chromatic scale, like this . . . Yeah, that's it . . . you've got it."

While James offers his impromptu lesson to facilitate the performance at hand, he also uses the opportunity to perform the role of the seasoned musician and mentor by displaying his knowledge of music theory and offering encouragement to a younger protégé. Meanwhile, younger players seek out the kind of instruction offered by James because it helps them to develop their craft in a supportive environment. In the end, these moments give blues musicians (amateurs as well as their more advanced counterparts) the pleasure associated with a distinctive nocturnal identity in the club's community of regulars.

In fact, while contemporary jam sessions bear scant resemblance to their celebrated Prohibition-era counterparts, they still provide an alternative forum for young performers to develop a highly stylized nocturnal self. By offering amateur musicians the opportunity to perform before paying audiences and chat with fellow players in a public world of strangers, jam sessions enable would-be superstars lacking in subcultural status the ability to act out roles compatible with their pursuit of an authentic sense of self. In this manner, the symbol-rich setting of the blues club provides the necessary dramaturgical backdrop for such persons to actually *become* blues artists.[21]

Of course, this art of "becoming" is much simpler to accomplish in musical settings than other established professional fields—after all, one can at least *claim* to be a blues or jazz player (although not necessarily a very good one) with a minimal degree of musical knowledge and experience more easily than one can appropriate the professional title of doctor or lawyer without proper training and public legitimacy. While institutions of higher learning and certification regulate the process by which such careerists become professionals, similar organizational structures rarely exist for urban musicians or their subcultures.[22]

On the way to becoming blues artists, young musicians sometimes create personae based on the fantasies provided by the myths of the stage. In their bombastic acts, musicians play characters familiar to the world of blues and jazz, and vocalists possess the expressive resources to use this strategy to the fullest extent. While men belt out their best "Sweet Home Chicago" or "Born Under a Bad Sign," their female counterparts enact highly stylized performances of torch songs like "Call It Stormy Monday." Adorned in sequined dresses and high heels, such singers whisper and coo into their microphones as they attempt to embody a sultry sensuality on the stage. By incorporating these dramatic strategies into their performances, they employ the theatrical resources of the club to great effect.

These strategies complement the more subtle performances maintained by amateur musicians during their *offstage* breaks from playing music. Some young players attempt to heighten their performance of authenticity by appropriating the timeworn role of the urban hipster and subcultural insider through fashion, slang, and other affectations of countercultural style.[23] Likewise, amateur performers try to exaggerate their insider credentials by directing liberal amounts of criticism at audience members and fellow musicians. At the same time, these players exude enthusiastic optimism regarding their *own* careers as they fix their sights on future stardom, imagining themselves as young mavericks and starlets on the verge of fame and inevitable professional success.

On Wednesday evenings at B.L.U.E.S. Etcetera, amateur musicians flaunt these roles in their attempts to impress peers, audiences, and skeptical professionals. Bill, a young but highly talented saxophonist, offers a case in point. A sophomore at a local college, his participation at B.L.U.E.S. Etcetera's jam session allows him the ability to act out a heavily affected urban identity. Augmented by gestures, demeanor, and a Black English speaking style, his self-conscious performance overemphasizes his struggle for subcultural status and urban authenticity: "Yeah, my man, well, you know how it is . . . Now I ain't gonna bullshit you, but I'm trying to get together a horn section . . . I'm in school now, but the minute I get that diploma—*Bam*, I am outta there, and this is gonna be it, know what I'm saying? Shit . . ."

Like Bill, Greg, a young white musician in his early twenties, appropriates the jam session as a backdrop for his expressive on- and offstage performance of a nocturnal identity. On most Wednesday nights, Greg, a singer, harmonica player, and bandleader, can be found in the back room of B.L.U.E.S. Etcetera shooting pool and slapping palms with his fellow band mates, buying rounds of beer for his friends, and watching the evening's basketball game on the overhead television set with a scattered assortment of the club's older black regulars and hired professional musicians. Greg moved from Washington, D.C., to Chicago in search of its blues scene after graduating from college and found a place where he could develop a new life as an artist. One evening over a game of pool, he leans on his cue stick, strokes his goatee, and explains his decision to move to the city:

Yeah, well, when I was sixteen, I had a job working as a clerk in the Senate, and after that I decided that I didn't want that kind of life. So, after college I just decided that this was what I always wanted to do . . . Ever since I was a kid, I've wanted to play the blues. So I just came out here, and I've been going to clubs, and hanging out with the best musicians, and sitting in, and getting them to teach me something, anything . . . and it's been the best. I've learned more in the past four months then I ever thought I could. It's just the best.

As a newcomer to the Chicago scene, Greg idolizes the city's blues musicians and the clubs where they perform and incorporates their world into his own by forging a nocturnal identity for himself as a subcultural participant and by dreaming of stardom aloud, literally. Pointing to me, and then to himself and two of his fellow mates, he predicts: "Someday, like five years from now, I have no doubt that all of us, the four of us, are going to be running the whole show, and that's going to be *us* up there." He points to the stage and smiles.

In actuality, Greg recognizes the hardscrabble difficulties inherent in pursuing a career in music and realizes that, in all likelihood, he will eventually have to seek out an occupational life elsewhere. After sharing his dreams about achieving status as a bluesman, he acknowledges that he lacks alternative career goals and fears the uncertainty of his future. Meanwhile, Greg finds the financial instability of the musician's life unsatisfying and frightening, and he clearly dislikes his present blue-collar job working for the city. However, in spite of these realizations, Greg maintains his guise as a subcultural member and up-and-coming artist, insofar as it provides him with an affirmative self-image and the means to smoothly interact with his peers and role models at the club.

Although they possess status on account of their seniority and long-standing presence at the club, older nonprofessional musicians often rely on strategies of nocturnal role-playing as much as their younger counterparts. For instance, Donny, a middle-aged black gentleman, enjoys plopping himself in the middle of the "action" at the club, invited or otherwise. He generally plays a proactive if obtrusive role at weekly jam sessions at B.L.U.E.S. Etcetera by approaching musicians on their break and imploring them to approach the stage by pointing and shouting: "Go on up! Play! Play!" As an "armchair" blues artist, he runs around to each of the musicians, offering his running commentary on their performances, and frequently attempts to "conduct" the horn section from a couch near the stage. At one Wednesday night jam session, Donny approaches me from his seat and signals me to follow his lead, belting out "Bop! Bop!" while furiously motioning with his hands. Later that same evening he tries to convince me to participate in another jam session in Rogers Park, where one of his acquaintances will be performing, and takes my phone number down as he runs back and forth between groups of established musicians at the club. When I mention this to Jeffrey, he warns: "Yeah, I've seen him around. He talks a lot and tries to tell you how many people he knows, but I just ignore him." Sure enough, I later overhear him listing all the local musicians he knows to a session bass player. The next week I run into Donny at B.L.U.E.S., and after reaching for a hug, he asks me if I have been to Kingston Mines, the club across the street.

"You should get a gold card, man—just tell them you play with a band. Now, *I* got one from my cousin, you know, *my cousin*, now *he* played until he was eighty-eight, and he died when he was eighty-eight. That was Sunnyland Slim, he played until the day he died . . . Hey, I'll show you his picture, it's up on the wall here . . ."[24]

If regulars like Donny attempt to accentuate their nocturnal status by playing up their strong (if embellished) connections to the club's subcultural elite, other musicians do so by cultivating more of an artistically elitist sense of self. An alto saxophonist in his mid-thirties, Jeffrey moved to the Chicago area several years ago from Germany and performs regularly at a number of local jam sessions on a weekly basis. One Wednesday evening in April, I spot him at B.L.U.E.S. Etcetera enjoying a beer along with any number of Marlboro cigarettes. I approach him, and after chatting for a few minutes about the jam, he leans over and pulls me close to holler into my ear above the clamor of the club. Barely audible, Jeffrey shouts:

"You know, you just have to play for yourself, that's the most important thing"—as he gestures toward the audience—"because these people don't care at all, and most of them hardly even listen. And it's really frustrating, because you play a solo, and they don't respond, and so you think it sucked . . . Now, I want to get to the point where I'm good enough so I can get gigs, and people will know who am I, and that way at least if you suck, you know. But now, they don't listen and they don't even know what a good solo is." As he points out two trumpet players, he continues: "Like, take these guys. These guys aren't that great, and what they are playing isn't very interesting, but the audience doesn't even notice! That's why you have to play for yourself, because most of these people can't tell a really great solo from just an OK solo . . ."

In other conversations Jeffrey develops his future plans by imagining a career trajectory before him, and months later he affirms: "See, what I want to do is spend the rest of the year really practicing until I'm really great, and then I want to put together a band. But I don't want to go out there until I'm ready." But unfortunately, as the owner of a suburban video rental store, his day job prevents him from touring with fellow musicians or establishing regular gigs on his own; consequently, his amateur status renders him unable to develop a truly professional identity. To compensate, he forges an artistic self at the club by criticizing not only the audience, but his fellow musicians as well.[25] In fact, Jeffrey often refuses to perform on especially slow evenings at the club when he does not approve of its lineup of amateur players. On one such occasion he even refuses to open his saxophone case, and instead of joining the performance, we chat in a corner of the club as he pokes fun at the predictability of the featured band's repertoire. As the evening passes on, he challenges me to a contest: "I'll bet you that the next song will be in concert G, and it will be . . . hmmm, let's see . . . 'Stormy Monday.' If I'm wrong, I will buy you a beer." He is correct.

The Staging of Subcultural Cool.   While local musicians obviously stress the importance of skill and technique when evaluating themselves and their fellow players, they develop their nocturnal identities as bar regulars by emphasizing more emotional faculties, such as an aggressive self-confidence and a heightened sense of subcultural cool. But although they may naturalize their own use of such affectations in the club's theatrical setting, musicians still remain highly aware of the performative aspects of artistic identity. At the club experienced players and club regulars try to socialize their novice counterparts into the social world of the blues by stressing the maintenance of self-confidence and subcultural style as integral to one's successful presentation of a nocturnal self. Accordingly, neophytes gradually become seasoned regulars through this process of acculturation.[26]

This socialization process became evident on my first night of performing at the B.L.U.E.S. Etcetera jam session. On a Wednesday evening I timidly walk from my apartment to the club at around 10 P.M. with my alto saxophone case in hand, nervous about confronting the club's community of regulars as an out-of-practice player. As Jack nods me into the club without asking for the nominal dollar charge expected of amateur jam participants, the sight of the relatively anonymous crowd of out-of-towners, as opposed to the usual gang of insiders, only slightly eases my fears. I sit at the bar and order a Budweiser from Robin (who, like Jack, works at both B.L.U.E.S. and B.L.U.E.S. Etcetera) while listening to Louis and his band play their obligatory first set before the jam begins. Near the end of the set, I finally gain the courage to head toward the stage, where I sit next to a guitar player, and we slowly nod to one another while watching the music together in silence. Meanwhile, other musicians casually chat over discounted $1.50 bottles of Leinenkugel's beer and lively billiard matches in the back room of the club.

After the set ends Louis grabs his clipboard and sign-up sheet and calls a handful of participants to the stage for the jam's first set.[27] The club seems fairly packed for a Wednesday evening, without a single empty table in sight. I head toward a group of musicians assembling and tuning their instruments at the side of the stage and slowly take out my saxophone, turning around to see if anyone is watching me. I try to feign confidence, but upon scanning the large audience, my stage fright only deepens, leaving me to wonder what possessed me to attempt this foolish endeavor in the first place.

Then suddenly, only moments later, Louis introduces the first jam, with *me* as the entire Wednesday night horn section. As the music begins, I stay fixed on my bar stool, unable to turn toward the microphone. Instead, I hunt around for the correct key, and at some point I actually duck into a corner of the club behind the video game machines to pull out the cheat sheet I've drawn up of the twelve major blues scales, just in case I get even more desperate than I already am. To my surprise, I stumble across a number of fellow players back there in the corner, including an elderly black gentleman toying with a harmonica. Caught red-handed, I show him my cheat sheet, but he denies that this consultation actually constitutes "cheating."

I eventually find myself heading out to the stage as the next song comes on, and I timidly approach the microphone to play along with the song, making up a riff until the next verse when the singer shouts "Saxophone!" and points to me. Taking my cue, I hesitate, take a deep breath, and plunge into a feeble attempt at improvisation, faltering with panic through each insecure beat. Nevertheless, I'm off, rushing through a blur of notes in the wrong key, and I'm so shaky that I'm really all over the map, jumping octaves at a squeaky pitch, then hitting a barrage of flat notes, and I polish it all off with an obese, sonic burp.

Meanwhile, as Ari, another young saxophonist, approaches the microphone, I return to my bar stool to gape in awe as he performs an impressive improvised solo with confidence and style. I spot Louis looking on, and I point to Ari and exclaim, "He's smokin' me!" but the bandleader quickly retorts, "Hey, that's *not* what it's all about. It's all about coming down and just playing, no matter *who* you are." As he walks away, I begin honking away at my seat, just trying to practice by playing along with the band, but at some point Ari turns to me and suggests that I should play into the microphone so the audience can actually hear me.[28]

The set ends as Louis reaches the stage to implore to the crowd, "Hey, if you like what you hear, please drop a ducat in our bucket and help keep the blues jam alive," and I take this as a cue to duck into the men's rest room, only to be accosted by the patron at the next urinal.[29] An audience member from Canada, he starts hammering away.

"How often do you guys jam? Is it open to everybody? Are there any callbacks?"—and after I briefly explain the organization of the jam, *he* offers me feedback on my playing: "You're shy," he tells me. "And now, you *are* good, but you are, well, a little *wobbly*. You have to just play through it and not worry if you hit a wrong note, just keep on with it." Frazzled, and even more embarrassed than earlier, I attempt to regain composure, when *another* customer turns to make a similar suggestion as we all exit the small rest room together.

At the jam session, brief encounters with musicians and audiences teach the uninitiated performer basic rules for handling oneself in the club and on the stage, and many of these lessons emphasize the importance of attitude and style, rather than musicianship and technical skill. This socialization process, through which advanced musicians attempt to transform "shy," "wobbly" newcomers into more assertive players, continues when amateurs accompany more established musicians during their gigs.

At half-past two in the morning at B.L.U.E.S., Jack, who leads his own local band in addition to his other many responsibilities at the club, invites me up to the stage with my saxophone to take a solo during the last song of his final set. I timidly approach the bandstand while Jack points to me and whispers, "Dave, just play off a shuffle in F major." But, as he awaits my improvised solo, I suddenly freeze. Most blues instruments are tuned to the key of C, but the alto saxophone is always tuned to the key of E♭. Consequently, when a bandleader requests a solo in a particular key, I always have to mentally transpose that key into the appropriate equivalent for the saxophone, which in this case would be D major. Most professional musicians either have the formula for this transposition committed to memory, or the talent and experience to enable them to figure it out immediately, playing by ear after listening for a few seconds. But for someone who possesses *neither* of these abilities, that process takes a little bit longer. And so, amidst all the excitement I forget the notes, and after running through the possible combinations in my head for what must seem like an eternity, I begin slowly fumbling through *all* the keys on my horn, evading the microphone as I hunt in vain for the appropriate sound.

Jack's face reveals concern as he mistakes my technical incompetence for stage fright—as does Jason, his guitarist, who leaves his post to lower the microphone into the bell of my horn. So, not wanting to disappoint, I start honking and squeaking out random notes as I search in noisy, out-of-tune desperation for the correct key. After another half a minute of poking around, I eventually stumble upon the appropriate blues scale and finish out the solo barely in tune. Surprisingly, the audience generously proffers its enthusiastic applause as prompted by Jack—"Let's hear it for Dave!" As I leave the bandstand for my bar stool, the German tourists at my cocktail table shake my hand and seem, astonishingly, impressed.

And then, just as my spirits begin to lift, Jack takes me aside.

"OK, time for a lecture."

I begin to shake.

"Dave, you play really good, man—you've got some chops." What? "You've obviously been playing for a while, and you've got some jazz influences that I heard in there, am I right?" Confused, I offer an uneasy nod when suddenly I realize that Jack has somehow mistaken my out-of-tune improvisation as an intentional use of complex harmonic structures suggestive of more avant-garde musical styles, like hard bop and free jazz.

"But, Dave, you've got to play into that microphone, man, you can't be afraid of it. I see you at the jam session, and you're always hiding in the corner. Man, you got to step up to the microphone, man, and just play, because that's the only way you'll get better. I mean, you play much better than most of those sax players they got there, man. You've got to just do it."

While musicians often assume the technical competence of their fellow players in spite of all evidence to the contrary, they tend to attribute their onstage foibles to more psychological barriers, such as stage fright. Since professional musicians are highly aware of these and other performative aspects of nocturnal identity, they try to socialize their novice counterparts into their social world by teaching them to manage their self-confidence while performing. From this constructive criticism, advice, and encouragement, amateurs gradually learn how to appropriately present themselves with a relaxed self-assurance and a seemingly natural kind of cool during their performances. As Willy, a tenor saxophonist and longtime regular at the jam, advises me one evening at B.L.U.E.S., "Well, the important thing about the jam is to just play, and feel good about it and get an emotional response from it. But sometimes, some guy who thinks he's a badass will show up and try to show up everybody and lay down a trip, but that's not what the jam is about, you know. It's all about emotion."

Experienced musicians also transfer these lessons in self-evaluation and impression management to less advanced players by recalling their own experiences as newcomers to the club and the advice their mentors gave them during their own amateur years. On the evening of my first jam session described above, I reveal my onstage fears to Jeffrey, but he takes me aside to reassure me.

"Oh, but you shouldn't feel intimidated at all. I mean, *that's not what this is about*, you know? We all play at different levels, and you've just got to do what you can. Like when I played at my first one of these things four years ago, my friend Lincoln took me here, and I played, and I hadn't been playing very long, and I sucked! And I was so frustrated that as I was leaving, I said I would not come back for a whole year, and Lincoln just shook his head and said, 'Oh no, you're coming back in two weeks!' And so I did, and I still wasn't good, but you play what you can, and you learn from the others, and that's how you get better. And now, there are still guys, you know, who are just like *here* compared to me," he says as he raises his hand above his head, "but you always have to learn, and you get better."

Community and Commerce as a Way of Life.   I have argued that tourist-oriented blues clubs often sustain a community of regulars who socialize alongside their out-of-town counterparts. Thus far, the discussion has characterized these two coexisting groups as discrete entities because audience members and club regulars generally internalize and enact different sets of roles in local clubs. Indeed, after crossing the line that separates outsider from insider, one seldom finds a comfortable road leading back to the other side.

However, the synergy between local urban cultures and commercial change often creates its own internal logic with surprising consequences for the individuals who participate in such subcultures. This becomes clear during a Tuesday night encounter with Philip, the Japanese guitarist discussed earlier, shortly after midnight during a Mardi Gras celebration at B.L.U.E.S. Just after I give away my necklace of plastic beads in exchange for a free drink from a local reveler, Philip and I stumble upon one another at the bar. As we shake hands in mutual recognition, I remember that his band has a regular Tuesday night gig at Kingston Mines across the street, and so I ask him if he isn't supposed to be there. As Philip slowly sips his bottle of beer, he casually replies, "Yeah, we're playing tonight. We get an hour break between sets. You know, they charge us three dollars for a beer over there? Even on nights when we're playing. So I come here, man, it's just a dollar." Still confused, I ask him, "But don't you get tired of this scene? Wouldn't you rather take your break someplace else?" But he insists, however, on his comfort at the club: "No, man, it's cool here . . . I can sit down, drink a beer, see some great band, hear some music . . ." Philip then turns to greet some friends and eventually strolls to the back of the bar to chat with the band, making his rounds as would any other regular.

While a club like B.L.U.E.S. functions as a place of labor for working musicians, it also provides them with a comfortable zone of leisure, a safe refuge from the demands of the stage. In this context it may seem ironic that performers working in tourist-oriented blues clubs would seek refuge in *other* tourist-oriented venues, but in fact musicians welcome the familiarity and camaraderie of places like B.L.U.E.S. during their breaks. While the club occasionally serves as their place of work, the rest of the time it remains someone *else's* workplace, and they enjoy the leisure and escape it provides.

One evening in July Betty, a local blues singer, settles into B.L.U.E.S. for an hour break from her regular weekly gig at Kingston Mines. Accompanied by her drummer, she takes a bar stool from a corner of the bar and relaxes until Lindsay Alexander, the evening's headliner, announces her presence "in the house" and suggests to his audience that their encouragement might coax her onto the stage for a song. As the crowd eggs her on with Alexander's help, Betty attempts to ignore their cheers, but he persists. After an agonizing five minutes, she finally capitulates, but not before protesting: "I've been singing for the past hour and a half!" While the audience of the club and the performing band acknowledge her presence as a local entertainer, Betty's protests suggest that she would rather be invisible at B.L.U.E.S., where, for the moment,

at least, she seeks sanctuary away from her workplace at Kingston Mines. (Of course, by now Betty probably recognizes the difficulty of actually achieving this invisibility, and the possibility exists that her protests are disingenuous and intentionally employed in the service of heightening her desirability.)

While B.L.U.E.S. serves as a place of leisure for working musicians on most weeknights, its regular crowd often crosses the street after its two o'clock closing time en masse to Kingston Mines, which remains open for business until four in the morning. To facilitate their frequent late-night socializing at the club, regulars and their hangers-on solicit Doc Pellegrino, the bar's owner, for coveted "gold cards," or VIP passes, which offer free admission to holders and their guests.[30]

According to Farrell, "anybody" can obtain a gold card. To prove it one night, he proposes to me, "I'll bet we can get *you* a gold card in the next five, ten minutes." I am skeptical, but when Doc eventually stops by our perch at the back bar of the club, Farrell introduces me as a graduate student working on a dissertation on Chicago blues clubs. Doc turns to me, asks me my name, and, sure enough, pulls out a batch of business cards, finds a gold card, and after scrawling out my name in misspelled chicken-scratch, hands it over for my complimentary use during the upcoming year.

Of course, Farrell overstates the case: while I may be the exception that proves the rule, in reality not just *anybody* can solicit Doc for a card, but only those with close connections to the club's social network of local musicians and regulars, knowledge of the card's existence, and the chutzpah to inquire about it. Not surprisingly, celebrities and other beautiful people routinely receive complimentary gold cards from the club as well. On the same night in question, another musician explains how Doc offered the late comedian Chris Farley a pass upon his arrival to the bar.

The proliferation of these passes suggests the strange relationship that exists between commerce and community at Kingston Mines. While gold cards confer a certain kind of status upon their fortunate bearers by offering them entrance to the club anytime without having to pay the door charges expected of most patrons, Kingston Mines still remains a tourist attraction until the wee hours of the night and hardly affords the exclusivity promised by the VIP areas of more elite Chicago nightclubs.[31] For this reason, musicians and other regulars commonly fraternize in back bar areas away from the club's stages and the out-of-towners they attract. These tactics highlight the multifunctionality of blues clubs like

B.L.U.E.S. and Kingston Mines that serve as places of entertainment and labor, sociability and socialization, professional networking and refuge from the world of work.

But while various sets of participants may rely on the blues club for different purposes, regulars frequently blur the boundaries that might otherwise distinguish them from more mainstream audience members. First, they often appropriate the commodified wares of tourist-oriented blues bars as a means of strengthening their association with the local music scene. For example, Ken, the regular who imagines B.L.U.E.S. as his Cheers, makes a tradition out of purchasing the club's annual summer T-shirt every August for his collection and proudly wears it out to events. While the club targets out-of-towners for its merchandising efforts, he and other regulars often wear club shirts and jackets as a means of increasing their identification with B.L.U.E.S. Likewise, professional musicians regularly collect similar articles from various clubs throughout the city and incorporate them into the outfits they wear during their shows. While some performers dress in more stylized get-ups as would-be cowboys, swingers, beatniks, or soul-stirrers, many often reject these seemingly authenticated fashions in favor of logo-bearing souvenir apparel instead. Rather than distance themselves from these representations of tourism and commodification, regulars often uncritically embrace such products as symbols of who they are and where they want to be.[32]

Consider Nina: a professional writer and bar regular who approaches each performance at B.L.U.E.S. with a more critical eye than most patrons, she nevertheless makes a habit of seeking out blues artists at the club to autograph her copies of their compact discs. At first I found this strange. After all, she and her husband visit B.L.U.E.S. about three times a week to see these same musicians perform and socialize night after night—wouldn't their aura have worn off by now? But one summer evening she explains the necessity for collecting these autographs "while they're still with us." As a writer, Nina sees autograph requesting as the "best compliment" one can give an artist, and at the same time, she enjoys the comfort provided by these mementos because they represent her proud association with B.L.U.E.S. She explains how "thirty or forty years from now I can flip through my old CDs" and fondly reflect on her time spent at the club. By participating in these and other highly consumer-oriented activities, Nina and her fellow regulars blur the distinction between subcultural insider and outsider.[33]

Regulars take on roles normally assumed by more mainstream audiences in other ways as well. Generally, regulars make highly noncommittal audience members. During performances they socialize, tell dirty jokes, critique the performers, shoot pool, and isolate themselves in small groups outside or in hidden corners inside the bar. If they applaud, sing along, or engage in call-and-response interactions with the performer, they generally do so with less enthusiasm than other audience members. Given their familiarity with the performances of local bands, perhaps this lack of enthusiasm makes sense. As Philip suggests in an earlier chapter, musicians themselves often tire of the standards predictably repeated on Chicago stages night after night.[34]

But however rarely, regulars still find instances when they get caught off-guard during the performance of a favorite song. In these moments even the most jaded of barflies turn their attention toward the stage and swoon to the music along with the rest of the crowd. On one particular weeknight Big Time Sarah and I fixate on a female vocalist performing a rendition of Leroy Carr and Scrapper Blackwell's classic yet seldom heard "How Long, How Long Blues," and as I turn to her at the bar in surprise, her eyes remain glued to the stage as the usually cantankerous singer whispers the chorus softly and gently to herself, "How long? How long? Baby, how long?"

Earlier that same month, as Farrell and I enjoy a performance by Jimmy Burns, Farrell explains to me his affection for Burns's music, whom he considers among the finest blues guitarists in the entire city: "Hey, here's something you can put in your book. I'll never forget the night I went to this show, and Jimmy Burns was playing with James Cotton for some kind of benefit, and, one by one, these famous guys come up to jam with them—oh, Junior Wells, Buddy Guy, you name it. And by the end of the night, the only one who smoked them all was Jimmy Burns."

And so, a sometimes surly Farrell takes to the night with the joyful enthusiasm of a star-struck fan by singing along to Burns's rendition of Major Lance's rarely performed song "The Monkey Time," coaxing his neighbors at the bar to join along with him on the chorus: "Oh, hey, come on . . . 'Are you ready? *Are you ready* . . . for the Monkey Time?!' " Later in the evening Burns launches into a slow blues progression, and as Farrell enjoys what he calls a "Poor Man's Speedball"—a Bud Light chased down with a glass of hot coffee—he turns to me and remarks in an uncharacteristically mellow voice, "The threshold has just been crossed. Now *this* is the blues."

On these occasional moments professional musicians appropriate the role of the audience member, and the club becomes more than merely a functional and convenient meeting place, but a world of entertainment—*their* entertainment. At B.L.U.E.S. this world becomes even more pronounced on special occasions like birthday bashes, Halloween masquerades, Christmas parties, and 1970s nostalgia nights. During such events the club evolves into a stomping ground where regulars take over the bar, pal around drunk, and jump and sing along to familiar standards as if hearing them for the very first time.

Saving the Last Dance.   Of course, even as regulars allow themselves to be overtaken by the beauty of the blues in their moments of leisure at the club, they can deftly shift into more professional roles when deemed necessary. Generally, a share of the regulars at B.L.U.E.S. on any given night will be friends or associates of the headliner and may be invited onstage over the course of the evening as a guest performer for a song or an improvised solo. These patrons often arrive at the club with their instruments in anticipation of such an invitation, and established performers sometimes earn a small fee for their efforts.[35]

However, on some evenings these regulars are asked to take on an even larger responsibility. Although shows tend to run quite smoothly at B.L.U.E.S., every once in a while a crisis develops onstage that prevents the show from continuing in a normal fashion. Since tourist-oriented clubs are generally reluctant to hire unproven or unreliable artists, these kinds of crises rarely occur. However, on the unusual occasions when they do, the club owner may decide that his hired bandleader is incapable of finishing out a performance without relief. On such occasions, the cast of regulars will spring into action in a last-ditch effort to save the performance from devolving into a disastrous mess. Musicians, audience members, and even bartenders will emerge from "the bench," rise to the occasion, and perform on the spot for the sake of the club and its paying patrons. By volunteering to substitute for hired band members as they play out the final songs of the evening, these regulars blur the boundaries between work and leisure, performer and spectator.

One winter evening I arrive at the club just a few minutes after 11 P.M., and Aimee presents me with my usual beer by the time I find my nightly bar stool. After chatting about graduate school and the bartending business, I sit back to watch the band, a Chicago outfit just back from a fifteen-hour drive from a gig in Canada. Looking around the club, it feels like business as usual for a Sunday night at the club: Rob Hecko, the bar's owner, sits in the back sipping coffee; Daniel, a guitarist and bandleader, shares his relationship problems at the bar with his friend Karen, the photojournalist; a group of international tourists crowd into the back of the club; two young women discuss purchasing Chicago souvenirs at the bar.

As the night wears on, Aimee grows more aggravated with the band, both onstage and off. Over the course of the evening, a number of patrons have bought Hank, the lead singer, drinks, including double shots of vodka. According to Aimee, Hank is also a regular who frequents the club on Monday nights, tips like a miser in spite of his standard musician discount, and lives up to his reputation as a notorious alcoholic. Months later I would learn from Marci that he regularly hounds the club's unsuspecting customers until they buy him drinks and has been frequently reprimanded for doing so by the club's bartenders. Because of this reputation, he hasn't been hired in the years since Aimee has tended bar at the club. As for tonight, in spite of any of his inherent musical abilities, Hank's wild drunkenness renders him nearly incoherent, and so the bartenders cut him off.

As the night wears on, Hank's stupor drives the performance into the ground. Onstage, in his wide-brimmed black hat, he hollers and whines about how he has been unfairly treated at the bar, refers to his liquor moratorium as "bullshit," and insists upon his sobriety even as he stumbles back and forth before his audience. He moans that he needs a drink, and he desperately begs anyone in his audience to procure him a shot. He appears livid when the crowd doesn't respond as enthusiastically as he would like, and when he asks them to clap in time to the music, they misunderstand and applaud, which infuriates him even further. As Aimee and I exchange concerned glances, she remarks, "I just hope the people feel sorry for him."

And then, suddenly, the show takes a turn. In a daze, Hank defers the stage to a singer he invites up from the audience to perform a medley of the Isley Brothers' "It's Your Thing" and the Muddy Waters standard "I Just Want to Make Love to You." Later, as the audience members smile and bop their heads to the music, Hank eventually relinquishes his guitar to Daniel, nearly dropping it before handing it off to him and heading offstage for the remainder of the night. Daniel begins to play a sober and competent set of Delta-inspired blues, as Karen, sipping a Coke, claps and bounces on her bar stool in time to the music.

Shortly thereafter, Debbie steps from behind the bar, where she has served drinks all evening, and approaches the stage. Standing in her work clothes—jeans and a B.L.U.E.S. tee pulled over a long-sleeved shirt—she belts out Aretha Franklin's "Dr. Feelgood" with all her might, as if she were singing for her blessed life. The song closes to a thunderous audience response as the "Applause!" sign lights up behind the bar. Impressed with her strong voice, the two women at the bar share their awe with Aimee and declare her performance to be the best of the evening. Next, Jack abandons his post at the door, approaches the stage, and whips out his harmonica for an impromptu solo as a series of musicians from the audience join the band.

By the end of the evening, Hank has invited nearly every capable musician in the club to the stage to perform. Meanwhile, Debbie has left the stage to continue clearing empty beer bottles from the dirty cocktail tables of dispersed patrons, the staff gathers to head out to Kingston Mines after closing, and although Aimee swears that next evening's performance promises to be better, there seems to be little need for improvement.

Keepin' It Real

Chicago Blues Musicians
and the Search for Authenticity

> These men, who had to renounce the blues to be sanctified, who often
> sneered at the preachers in their songs, were the ones who really believed
> in the devil; they feared the devil most because they knew him best. They
> understood, far better than the preachers, why sex was man's original sin,
> and they sang about little else. . . . The blues singers accepted the dread but
> refused the piety; they sang as if their understanding of the devil was strong
> enough to force a belief in God out of their lives. They lived man's fear of life,
> and they became artists of the fear. —Greil Marcus, *Mystery Train*

All That Glitters Is Gold.   It's a cold Thursday night in February, and I arrive at B.L.U.E.S. Etcetera at about a quarter to eleven. After
I shake hands with Jack and he invites me into the club, I saddle up
to the bar and order my usual beer from Hannah, one of the regular
bartenders. Looking around, I take note of just how dead it is—only a
handful of regulars shoot pool in the back room while a table of out-of-
towners chat across from the bar among a scattering of the band's friends.
Still a newcomer to the blues scene, I decide to keep to myself, and so,
following the lead of the other bartender, I thumb through the music
section of the *Chicago Reader*, waiting for the band to begin their set.

Although the club is practically empty, one would never know it from
watching a falling-down drunk Quintus McCormick and his band enthusiastically stumble to the stage and shout, "Are y'all ready for the
blues, or *what*?!" He receives no response from the lonely room, and so
he asks again, but even louder, "*I said, 'Are y'all ready for the blues!!!!'*"

The band breaks into a blaring set of blues standards, à la guitar rock—"Let the Good Times Roll," "Every Day I Have the Blues," "I Play the Blues for You"—and four songs later the out-of-towners walk out, leaving behind a bare bones crowd of two bartenders, the pool shooters, the band's buddies, and, of course, me at the side bar, newspaper in hand. Yet the crescendo of the bass and drums never ceases, and the volume peaks at full tilt as Quintus roars away at his thinning audience. I mean, this music is LOUD, very LOUD.

When the number of pool players remaining at the club drops to near zero, I suddenly get very excited. What do blues musicians play when the lights go off and there's no audience left to appease? Do they continue to draw on the familiar set list of standards, or do they hang it all, and just play what they *really* want to play? In other words, if authenticity is merely a performance, then how do blues musicians perform authenticity for *themselves*? How do *they* define authenticity in the blues? Do Robert Johnson's songs exemplify their sense of the authentic? Or perhaps Blind Lemon Jefferson's? What about Howlin' Wolf's? Suddenly, two of Quintus's cronies hit the stage, and they start up an impromptu chord progression—and then they begin to *rap*.

"How about one more time for my boys?" the drummer asks of the three or four of us still at the club. "Yeah, you know, all this music, it's all derivative, it all comes from the blues, it all comes from gospel, and from jazz, and from the fields—you know, it's all this and that, that and this . . ."

And then, perhaps in the spirit of this musical boundary spanning, Quintus McCormick, about two shots over the line, begins to croon, "There's a lady who's sure all that glitters is gold—And she's buying a stairway to heaven . . ." I burst out laughing. Of course, if Led Zeppelin can cover Robert Johnson's "Traveling Riverside Blues," I suppose Quintus McCormick can cover "Stairway to Heaven," right? But the next thing I know, McCormick starts tearing through the Jimmy Page guitar solo at top speed, and just as the amplifiers begin to crackle, he launches into a high-pitched falsetto for the song's grand finale: "And as we wind on down the road!! Our shadows taller than our souls!!" And he lifts up his hand for the final words of the night, "To be a rock, and not to roooooooll . . ."

In some ways, the idea of a black blues singer from Detroit not merely singing, but downright *imitating* Led Zeppelin's "Stairway to Heaven" in a Chicago blues bar seems just plain bizarre, especially since Led Zeppelin is a British white rock band who spent the greater portion of their career attempting to capture the sound of the Mississippi Delta blues. On the other hand, by doing so, Quintus McCormick truly demonstrates the malleability of authenticity, which I only began to appreciate during my initial stint at clubs like B.L.U.E.S. Etcetera. When I first started my fieldwork, I wondered what blues musicians considered to be authentic blues; I suppose I had figured that if *anyone* maintained a privileged understanding of this music, it would be them. I was therefore surprised to discover that, in fact, musicians themselves not only disagree about what is authentic, but also whether authenticity is even useful as an organizing principle for evaluating and understanding the blues. While some performers hold steadfast to traditional ways of thinking about "authentic" blues music (and the musicians who perform it), others maintain more flexible definitions of authenticity, while many musicians actively resist the very notion of authenticity altogether. In fact, this battle over authenticity lends shape to a range of orientations and interpersonal relations, a world around which Chicago blues musicians organize themselves into a subculture.[1]

The Subcultural World of the Chicago Blues.   Blues musicians are often characterized by towering myths and legendary folktales: they are mournful saints and unabashed sinners, wise sages and innocent fools. In their moments of passion and rage, blues players tear up guitars like lightning and are thought desperate enough to sell their very souls to the devil in exchange for that talent. Authentic blues musicians are sexual conquerors, nomads who wander from town to town singing for their supper. As rock music critic Greil Marcus asserts in his vivid description of the myths surrounding Robert Johnson and his fellow country-blues songsters, "they feared the devil most because they knew him best."[2]

But while local musicians may benefit from the proliferation of these tall tales, such stories can sometimes prevent us from understanding these performers as real human beings who work in relatively established occupational environments. Alas, while Robert Johnson may have famously cried in "Me and the Devil Blues": "You may bury my body, oooh, down by the highway side—So my old evil spirit can catch a Greyhound bus and ride," contemporary blues musicians in Chicago can be a relatively mild bunch. During the day they work as schoolteachers, mechanics, computer programmers, video store managers, and graduate students. Most of them forgo signing pacts with the devil so they can practice eight hours a day, and even *they* have off nights during their performances. By abandoning our romanticized notions of what it actually takes to play the blues, we can better examine the social and economic reality that blues musicians inhabit as participants in what the sociologist Howard S. Becker would call an "art world," a series of interlocking networks through which artistic and expressive culture "happens."[5]

Within this art world, blues musicians demonstrate signs of solidarity in their strong friendship ties, common strategies of interaction, and buoyant musical passions. But unlike other kinds of urban artists, musicians do not exactly forge subcultural selves out of this solidarity. Rather, they develop identities in *contradistinction* to their fellow performers on the basis of their experience in the city's entertainment market. As a result, the world of the Chicago blues reveals an internal social structure consisting of collective interests and competitive differences among local musicians. At B.L.U.E.S. and other local clubs, a grounded typology of blues musicians reveals four separate peer groups loosely organized on the basis of race, professional status, career stage, and orientation toward commercialization: *players, old-timers, lions,* and *survivors.*[4]

The majority of successful bluesmen in Chicago are young black musicians. Ranging in age from their early thirties to late fifties, these musicians—whom I call *players*—secure the most prestigious weekend gigs at tourist-oriented clubs like B.L.U.E.S. and Kingston Mines. These musicians include active bandleaders as well as their band mates, with whom they tour around the country, lead local jam sessions, and offer employment to up-and-coming performers. Like their early predecessors, such as Muddy Waters and Big Bill Broonzy, some players migrated to Chicago from the rural South: for example, Shawn, a bass guitarist, migrated to Chicago from Mississippi in the early 1960s to take a job with blues legend Howlin' Wolf. In contrast, many others have spent their entire lives in and around Chicago, and some enjoyed their teenage years frequenting the city's South and West Side clubs. Tiger's recollection of those formative years growing up in the Chicago blues scene provides a familiar background:

> Well, my dad was a musician, and when I was real young, like fourteen, I started going out to all the clubs in Chicago—South Side, West Side, North Side. You know, I was so young, I don't know even know how I got in! And I used to see everybody, you know: Buddy Guy, James Cotton, Junior Wells,

Otis Clay. And I would get up there and they would let me play, and I'd try to cut 'em, you know, because you got to if you're gonna try and make it, especially with *these* guys.

Tiger's story is a familiar one among local players. Of course, while many of Chicago's young black musicians may have studied their craft in the hard-edged clubs of the West Side, some players also increased their proficiency while attending local colleges and universities; for example, Fruteland Jackson studied at Columbia College and Roosevelt University, while Billy Branch discovered the blues while a student at the University of Illinois.

In contrast to the charismatic bravado displayed by these younger players, black *old-timers* like Dizzy often find themselves relegated to the sidelines of the club. When their experience of exile (self-imposed or otherwise) turns to grumpy indignation, such musicians get extremely defensive about their age and its impact on their image as capable performers. In a desperate attempt to make conversation one evening, I ask Dizzy to recall his memories of soul legend James Brown, whom, it is said, he has performed with earlier in his career. Sending me on my way, he grumbles:

> I'm gonna try to save my voice before I sing again . . . You know, people will say, "Aw, his voice is shot 'cause he's old," when it's because I've been talking all night about somebody else! Well, I don't want to lose my voice wasting time talking 'bout somebody else—why can't I talk about *me*?! What the hell do I want to talk about somebody else for? It makes no sense, just a waste of time . . .

Meanwhile, old-timers like Tommy McCracken, the ebullient singer whose rendition of "How Blue Can You Get?" I introduced in the prologue, ignore the constraints of old age altogether when they perform for their adoring, if somewhat bewildered, audiences. McCracken's own stage show, which largely consists of a surprisingly energetic James Brown imitation replete with jumps, kicks, and side-to-sides, is as self-mocking as it is impressive—and no one is more hip to the joke than McCracken himself. Of course, as he twists a mélange of previously discussed minstrel stock characters (including the down-on-his luck loser, the happy-go-lucky man about town, and the virile sex machine) into an over-the-top theatrical production, bemused audiences and jovial hecklers demonstrate their own disbelief with his act. Nina, the professional writer who frequents B.L.U.E.S. as a regular, emphasizes the self-parody suggested by McCracken's performance:

> What's so striking is that if you turn around and don't look at the stage and just listen, the music just sounds great. But when you watch him perform, it's like a pastiche, you know, it's like a parody, with his toupee, trying to act like James Brown, and Elvis in the seventies. It's like a pastiche—a parody of the blues.

Of course, if these gentlemen are occasionally mocked for their outlandish theatrics, it is certainly the case that their younger white counterparts, seduced by their venerable charms, rich experience, and the authenticity suggested by their old age, seek out such men for technical advice, emotional support, tall tales, and words of wisdom. Daniel, a former sideman of old-timer Tail Dragger, remarks on his colleague's highly theatrical performances as if kneeling before the footsteps of greatness:

> I want Tail Dragger, 'cause it's drama, it's something that'll never be no more once it's gone. Tail Dragger, he's a movie star; it's an event, it's theater, and that appeals to me, man . . . Because when you hear it live . . . when you see him, and you're hearing his speeches and stuff, you know, it's a dramatic event.

In fact, many of these old-timers found success years ago, including Tail Dragger, who earned his nickname by arriving late to gigs run by his former boss, the great Howlin' Wolf. Meanwhile, Dave Myers has performed with a rich and storied collection of blues legends, including Sonny Boy Williamson, Memphis Minnie, Big Bill Broonzy, Muddy Waters, and the Four Aces, a successful combo whose members included Junior Wells, Little Walter Jacobs, and Myers's brother Louis; for a brief spell during the 1950s and 1960s, Malcolm "Little Mack" Simmons, a recently deceased bandleader and harmonica player from the West Side, garnered a number of respectable blues hits; and before his untimely passing (following a bout with pancreatic cancer), Dizzy had been entertaining audiences in Mississippi, East St. Louis, Detroit, and Chicago for over fifty years.

Some old-timers, like Myers, still enjoy vibrant careers playing regional music festivals in Europe and South America. However, in spite of their successes outside Chicago, many of these Delta bluesmen remain underappreciated by local club owners and booking agents and are often forced to play for small audiences at ill-attended neighborhood clubs around the city. In fact, in the last years of his career, seventy-year-old Dizzy had to settle for gigs at B.L.U.E.S. on slow weeknights, and even less lucrative weekend jobs at Smoke Daddy.

While Tail Dragger, McCracken, and Dizzy share the status of the elderly old-timer, Daniel and his contemporaries represent a much younger peer group of white musicians in their twenties and early thirties. For the most part, these musicians—whom I call *lions*—grew up outside the city; they either moved to Chicago to attend one of the local universities or migrated to the city soon after college to pursue music careers.[5] In terms of formal education, most have attended college, many have graduated from elite institutions (a small sample would include Northwestern, Georgetown, and the University of Chicago), and some have pursued advanced graduate degrees.[6]

As relative newcomers to the field, these musicians often suffer the trials expected by new artists in any local entertainment field, namely, low-paying, sporadic gigs at second- and third-tier venues. However, the small proportion of those who do manage to find success often attract a large local following of young white blues fans like themselves. For example, Daniel and his sidemen boast one of the largest local followings of any blues band in the city—white *or* black—and their gigs at local clubs like B.L.U.E.S. and Smoke Daddy regularly attract the same steady pack of young admirers.

However, since these younger musicians remain in a relatively transitional stage in their lives, many are less committed overall to the music profession as a permanent career choice.[7] Many lions hold so-called "straight" jobs elsewhere in the city as software programmers, private music teachers, and bartenders.[8] Meanwhile, those who have committed themselves to full-time careers in the field rarely lose sight of the opportunities available to them in the nonartistic job market. For instance, Guy has played guitar for a number of elderly black bandleaders in the city, including Tail Dragger and Jimmy Burns. Born on the South Side, Guy grew up in the Chicago suburb of Flossmor and eventually attended the University of Arizona to study English. But despite his educational background, he opted for a mercurial career in the blues instead of a more stable professional life. With his long brown hair and pierced tongue, at twenty-five Guy finds deep satisfaction with his aggressively artistic lifestyle while remaining fully aware of the options available to him in the world existing outside the blues club. He explains:

Yeah, man . . . like, I could probably get a job making sixty thousand dollars a year or something like that, but man, this is the life, you know? . . . Just being around all these guys, to hear these guys play, and to play with these guys, I mean, it's awesome, man, you know? That's what I'm talking about, man . . . Sometimes, my girlfriend and I talk . . . I think sometimes she wishes that I had a more respectable job, you know, instead of being a musician.

Although he enjoys the pleasures associated with maintaining an artistic lifestyle, Guy does not doubt that he "could probably get a job making sixty thousand dollars a year" working in a more "respectable" field. Likewise, as an educated musician in his late twenties, Daniel demonstrates a similar kind of self-awareness regarding his opportunities in the wider labor market: "Some people don't really have any other options . . . I mean, I could do whatever, you know, I've got a degree from the University of Chicago . . . But some people don't have any other options, I mean, they'd be selling dope, or working at McDonald's . . ."

In contrast to these young lions, older white musicians in their late thirties and forties, like Farrell and Jack, make up the group that I call *survivors*. Unlike their younger counterparts, survivors exhibit strong differences with regard to socioeconomic class and educational background. While some survivors grew up in middle-class households and graduated from elite universities, many others dropped out of high school to pursue music careers and a lifestyle to match.[9] Regardless, most of these men grew up in the Chicago area and spent their formative years in local blues hangouts during the 1970s, just prior to its insurgent popularity among mainstream audiences in the following decade. Jack's description of his own introduction to the city's blues scene echoes the recollections of other working-class Chicago natives who still "survive" in its social world:

Well, I guess you could say that my life as a bluesman began when I was born. Even when I was four, my parents would play Muddy Waters records at home, and I just always felt the blues inside me. Now, I grew up in the Bridgeport area, and then Beverly Hills, and when I was old enough to start heading out by myself, I began coming downtown to Chicago, and I'd head to Maxwell Street to listen to all the local musicians play, and by the time I was fourteen, I was hanging out with some of the greatest legends in the blues—in all of music history, in fact: Big Walter Horton, Jimmy Rogers, Eddie Taylor, Sunnyland Slim. So, in 1977, when I turned sixteen, I told my parents I was leaving school, and they asked me what I planned to do for work, and I told them that I was going to tour around with these guys, and I moved out of my folks house to the South Side, near Thirty-first Street, Thirty-fifth Street, Indiana Avenue. And I began traveling with these guys, and I eventually started playing with Muddy Waters, and he got me started with my singing. And when we weren't traveling, we were hanging out at Kingston Mines . . .

As I have discussed in chapter 1, white musicians who lack the symbolic authenticity typically conferred upon their black counterparts face difficulties finding steady gigs in the city. But while young lions expect to face such obstacles on account of their novice status and lack of professional experience, survivors have generally grown frustrated by these difficulties by the time they have entered their forties, and often lack the fashion-conscious, stylistic prowess (or the desire to accumulate it) that lions like Daniel and Guy use to attract young, predominantly female, fans. While these survivors do include some active professional musicians who accompany black bandleaders, many fall into semiretirement to pursue other ventures after succumbing to the double-edged curse of whiteness and middle age.[10] Perhaps for this reason, survivors remain the most critical of all musicians in the field with regard to the increased commercialization and popularity of blues music in the city. As Farrell mutters one night to me at B.L.U.E.S., "I'd say blues in Chicago has really been a lot of bullshit. It's all about promotion, and entrepreneurship, and kissing the asses of club owners, and far from being anything like the real blues, or whatever—and it's really been that way for the past twenty years."

Mapping the Social World of the Club.   Local musicians do not actually refer to each other as lions, survivors, players, or old-timers, nor do they really employ any other shared vocabulary to define one another in terms of these peer groups. By the same token, I should warn the reader that some musicians do not fit neatly into any of these categories, and not all of the members within a given category necessarily conform to the exact same styles of behavior or ways of thinking; rather, my typology suggests a set of broad generalizations about the world of the blues club and emphasizes certain tendencies among its participants. For example, musicians do frequently organize their social interaction around the racial and generational differences suggested by this typology. When socializing, musicians carve out small spaces within local blues clubs and give visible expression to the latent distinctions of race and age that structure their social milieu.[11] At B.L.U.E.S. Jack and his pals fraternize by his bouncer's perch near the door and regularly move their conversation to the sidewalk in front of the entrance to the club. As subcultural insiders, they can afford to physically distance themselves from the performance, as their aloofness and self-imposed exile from the inside of the club emphasize their status as seasoned regulars and nonpaying customers.[12]

Meanwhile, on any given night, groups of players—professionally employed black musicians—and their cronies socialize near the stage, drink cocktails at the bar, and chat in the back room as they watch their friends perform and await the chance to sit in with them onstage. Like survivors, their subcultural status precludes the necessity for them to demonstrate any enthusiasm for the performance; however, maintaining an eye on the stage allows them to keep tabs on the styles and shticks of their colleagues and friends. While survivors can afford to emphasize their aloofness as spectators during performances, their marginalized position within the subculture relative to players actually diminishes their ability to cut loose in public, even when they want to; in contrast, the high status of players accords them free reign to cheer, jeer, or jump and shout to their comrades on- and offstage with impunity if they wish.[13] Meanwhile, old-timers often sit quietly alone near the back room of the bar during these same performances.

If players, survivors, and old-timers socialize in different corners at B.L.U.E.S., lions hardly frequent the club at all. With the exception of a smattering of musicians who work across the street at Kingston Mines as sidemen or bouncers, or who perform in bands with regulars at B.L.U.E.S., lions tend to patronize more remote clubs like Smoke Daddy. As entry-level professionals lacking the racial and generational markers of authenticity, out-of-the-way places like Smoke Daddy provide a stomping ground for young hip musicians and regulars to stake out club territory as an alternative to the player- and survivor-dominated worlds of B.L.U.E.S., B.L.U.E.S. Etcetera, and Kingston Mines. At these bars lions like Daniel, Guy, and Chad have a chance to reign over a smaller subcultural pond, and their groupies prefer its trendy edginess, fashionably young clientele, and symbolic authenticity to more market-oriented tourist attractions like B.L.U.E.S. Smoke Daddy's proximity to freshly gentrified residential areas where many lions and other artistically inclined enthusiasts live adds to the popularity of the club among young white musicians and their friends and fans.

To be sure, distinctions of race and age merely provide a broad template for socializing in local clubs, and much peer-group overlapping exists.[14] Black and white musicians always take time to socialize together at the club. As discussed in the previous chapter, lions, players, survivors, and old-timers often cross racial and generational boundaries to greet one another, joke around, and catch up on the current gossip circulating the scene on a nightly basis in the back rooms of clubs like B.L.U.E.S. and B.L.U.E.S. Etcetera. Out of respect for his legendary status, talents, and good-natured temperament, Daniel, Darryl, and their respective band mates long ago adopted Dave Myers as an intimate peer, and he them. Likewise, Guy and other white sidemen enjoy the company of their elders like Jimmy Burns and constantly gush about the sense of privilege and honor they experience while performing for them and studying their every move. Interracial and intergenerational friendships often emerge between fellow band mates, mentors and students, and barroom regulars on the basis of common backgrounds, shared life experiences, and the need for sociability among familiar faces.[15]

My relationship with Farrell offers a case in point. While he is twenty years my senior, our common educational backgrounds provide a basis for our often lively discussions over beers at B.L.U.E.S. Likewise, young white musicians often take on the responsibility of caring for their older black counterparts when they face financial, health, and drug problems. Dizzy often counted on Jack to drive him to gigs on the North Side, just as Big Time Sarah relies on the kindness of club bartenders and regulars for transportation. A few years ago Dustin, a white blues guitarist in his forties, frequently helped an older blues musician through his methadone treatments for his chronic heroin addiction by offering him rides to and from gigs and occasionally invited him to his second-floor flat for home-cooked meals. A semiprofessional guitarist, Steve spent a period of time caring for Robert, a local blues guitarist diagnosed with clinical schizophrenia, living with him in addition to assisting him with his medication. Likewise, both black and white musicians enjoy organizing benefits for old-timers when they fall on hard times. This emotional attachment sometimes extends to the sweet hereafter, as when Jack took up a collection a few years back to raise money for the funeral of an elderly black musician.[16] Of course, these types of relationships develop *within* peer groups as well; for example, Big Time Sarah constantly looks after Robert at the club and gives him bus fare to go home for his medication when he forgets to take it—often in spite of his protests.[17]

White Blues Musicians and the Problem of Authenticity.

However, in spite of the intimacy and sociability shared among the members of different peer groups within the local blues scene, musicians constantly compete with one another for subcultural status and professional success. In some ways, the struggle over the symbolic and material rewards available to blues musicians is largely dictated by the politics of race and authenticity surrounding local clubs. The popularity of black performers to the frequent exclusion of their white counterparts puts the latter at a disadvantage when it comes to finding gigs in the city, and this serves as a perpetual source of thinly veiled resentment and subtle, if unintentional, racism among white lions as well as survivors.

These musicians subtly express this frustration in their private criticisms of *all* their fellow performers, but particularly when evaluating the artistic abilities of local black players and old-timers. In such moments, lions like Daniel often turn on their predecessors:

I think a lot of them are really jaded . . . A lot of the black performers are really jaded. Not all of them—I don't want to put people down. But I think a lot of the black people who are playing for the white tourist crowd are pretty jaded.

I don't know . . . maybe because they're doing it all the time, they've been doing the exact same thing for years . . . A lot of them are just, you know, in a sort of artistic stasis. They're doing the same thing for, like, this endless sea of white faces . . . But I don't know. Some of them just have drug problems, you know, and like they're just waiting to get paid so they can go score . . .

And maybe after twenty years or so they just lose their drive to do it. Their career has reached the point where it just doesn't seem to be going any higher. I mean, if their career was on the up-and-up, then they might be more enthusiastic, but some people, they're just working at, you know, wherever, and just going around and around, and nothing's really happening for them. And it's not just black performers, but white performers too . . . Well, you know, some people, they're stuck doing the same thing, and it's just kind of a grind, I mean, you know, trying to make it in the music business can be kind of a grind.

A fellow lion, Michael, takes similar jabs at local players and old-timers:

> The blues scene in Chicago is probably better here than anywhere else . . .
> But in so many of the clubs in the city, the guys they got playing are
> these poseurs who don't really know how to play, who only know like three
> chords . . . I guess my other pet peeve is how people want to come out to
> hear some old guy playing the blues . . . Most of these old guys didn't know
> how to play in the fifties and don't know how to play now.

This sort of deprecating criticism contrasts the more defensive measures taken by white musicians who, when denouncing the racially charged typecasting common in local clubs, draw on the same explanations that *black* workers frequently use to describe the formidable hardships they regularly face in more normative occupational worlds. According to Elliot, "The truth is, if you're white you have to go out there and prove yourself even more . . . I have to work twice as hard, play twice as good, because I'm *white*. In the world of blues, *I* am affirmative action."

Meanwhile, survivors express their resentment at the hiring practices of local club owners who have prevented them from securing steady gigs in the city for decades. Although Jack has recorded multiple albums and tours extensively around the world with several renowned artists, his local career has waned in recent years, and he bitterly attributes that failure to the pervasive power of racial typecasting in the blues:

> Honestly, I get more support on the road than I do at the clubs in Chicago,
> due to the local reverse discriminatory practices. For example, Kingston
> Mines never hires white headliners, and neither does Blue Chicago. And
> at B.L.U.E.S., I'm practically the *only* white artist that ever gets hired here.
> I mean, just look at this month's schedule: the only other white blues artist
> on the calendar is a white woman, and she is a novelty act, kind of a female
> Johnny Winter . . . The problem is that most people don't have the slightest
> comprehension about what it takes to be a good bluesman—they don't get
> that it doesn't matter if you're black, white, red, green, orange . . . That's
> why Doc at Kingston Mines doesn't hire white guys. That's why Gino at
> Blue Chicago doesn't hire white guys. People coming in the door expect to
> see an old black guy on the stage . . . I play some of the biggest venues on
> the planet—why can't I get a gig in my own hometown?[18]

Survivors like Jack attribute these "reverse discriminatory practices" to the knee-jerk demands of mainstream audiences and the club owners who serve them. Similarly, Darryl, a white harmonica player and twenty-year veteran of the Chicago blues scene, expresses contempt for what he discerns to be an amateurish and underdeveloped set of aesthetic tastes and expectations among such audiences:

> The people who come to these shows don't know anything about what blues really is and wouldn't really appreciate the real thing anyway . . . They're mostly clueless middle-aged people for whom the punk clubs are probably too outré, and these aren't people who would want to go to the symphony, so they wind up at these North Side clubs . . . I really think a study of these clubs is sort of like dissecting a turd . . . The music is shit, and the people who go are Philistines. I mean, the music is really, really awful, it's crass . . . And the audiences don't notice the difference and don't really care.

This type of criticism extends to the songs that audiences demand to hear in local clubs. As it has been suggested earlier, musicians tire of performing the same standards night after night, those catchy numbers that make up what Daniel mischievously refers to as his own private "Set List from Hell":

> What happens on Friday and Saturday night when it's like, you know, packed full of tourists who really don't know anything? . . . You know, they want to hear, I mean, I can just list for you the "Set List from Hell": "Every Day I Have the Blues," "Sweet Home Chicago," "Mustang Sally" . . . and, you know, those other fucking songs, you know, "Kansas City," and fuckin', you know, "Johnny B. Goode" and shit. You know, how are you supposed to play those songs for ten years, twenty years? . . . But *that* is what these people wanna hear! Like, go to B.L.U.E.S. or Kingston Mines, or wherever . . . The two blues songs everybody knows are "The Thrill Is Gone" and "Sweet Home Chicago." And what does everybody sing along to? "Mustang Sally."[19]

In their private moments, white musicians can take on a fairly dismissive tone when describing the audiences who patronize clubs like B.L.U.E.S. This appears to be a potentially common approach among low-paid service workers in general and professional musicians in particular.[20] In his classic study of Chicago jazz musicians, the aforementioned sociologist Howard S. Becker discovered that the marginalized performers he interviewed often characterized their audiences in similarly derisive terms. According to one of his informants, a commercial saxophonist:

It doesn't make any difference what we play, the way we do it. It's so simple that anyone who's been playing longer than a month could handle it. Jack plays a chorus on piano or something, then saxes or something, all unison. It's very easy. But the people don't care. As long as they can hear the drum they're all right. They hear the drum, then they know to put their right foot in front of their left foot and their left foot in front of their right foot. Then if they can hear the melody to whistle to, they're happy. What more could they want?[21]

According to Becker, because these musicians are often persuaded by the dictates of the marketplace to forgo the pleasures of complex jazz improvisation for rumbas, polkas, and assorted pop favorites when they perform at weddings and dances, they experience their professional careers as a kind of self-sacrifice they are forced to endure when they "go commercial." As a result, they tend to distance themselves from the musical tastes of their audiences and nonmusicians in general, whom they ridicule for being, in the somewhat dated argot of the 1950s beat scene, "square."[22] According to another one of Becker's informants:

They've got a nice class of people out here, too. Of course, they're squares, I'm not trying to deny that. Sure, they're a bunch of fucking squares, but who the fuck pays the bills? They pay 'em, so you gotta play what they want. I mean, what the shit, you can't make a living if you don't play for the squares . . . They're the ones that pay the bills, and you gotta play for them. A good musician can't get a fucking job. You gotta play a bunch of shit. But what the fuck, let's face it. I want to live good. I want to make some money; I want a car, you know. How long can you fight it? . . . Don't get me wrong. If you can make money playing jazz, great. But how many guys can do it? . . . If you can play jazz, great, like I said. But if you're on a bad fucking job, there's no sense fighting it, you gotta be commercial. I mean, the squares are paying your salary, so you might as well get used to it, they're the ones you gotta please.[23]

In some ways, the remarks made by these jazz musicians seem eerily similar to the descriptions provided by lions and survivors about their own audiences and their expectations of the blues scene. And yet, in spite of their overwhelming distaste for what Daniel posits as a perpetual "Set List from Hell," young white blues musicians are complicated men (alas, they are mostly men) who wrestle with the tension between their somewhat contradictory roles as both appropriately sensitive artists *and* popular entertainers. While these musicians agonize at the sound of what must seem like ear-splitting melodies the thousandth time around ("Come on, baby, don't you want to go . . ."), they still revel in the challenge of satisfying a cheering crowd of listeners—as well as gaining the subcultural status that comes from succeeding at such a feat. On playing for what he refers to as a club "packed full of tourists who really don't know anything," Daniel acknowledges its seductive quality:

> When I get up in front of a crowd like that, I have to overcompensate. I have to be better, because I'm white . . . I have to really bring it on, you know? But I appreciate any circumstances that'll make me do that . . . I enjoy having to win an audience over, no matter who they are, and I can look at an audience and see what I have to do and try to do that. I mean, that's the total challenge . . . I'm into that shit, you know, that's what it's all about . . . You know, I enjoy performing, period—no matter *who* they are, and I do like the variety . . . I play all kinds of situations, and I enjoy the variety . . .

Surprised, I ask, "So, you don't seem to find any fault with the audience . . . ?"

> They don't know any better . . . I mean, they saw *The Blues Brothers* and they want to hear songs they know . . . I mean, audiences are paying your salary, period—you can't just say "You're wrong," you know? Maybe you can educate them a little bit—maybe, maybe not . . . and there are times you can, and times you can't.

Of course, as evidenced by Daniel's own ambivalence about the crowd, even the most empathetic musicians still tease their most "square" patrons, if only among themselves. According to Michael, a tenor saxophonist and bandleader in his mid-twenties:

> Well, I guess I've played for a lot of tourists at the House of Blues, and they're all right. I have no problem playing for tourists . . . Like that night at the House of Blues, they enjoyed the music and had a good time, and as long as they like my music, that's the most important thing to me. Now, some of these tourists *can* be a little ridiculous . . . Like that night at B.L.U.E.S., when we played with Daniel? I don't know if you noticed, but there were these five tourists all sitting together and wearing Blues Brothers baseball

caps, and they just looked ridiculous, you know? And some of these guys, you know, everything they know about the blues is from *The Blues Brothers*.

In such moments of private ridicule, musicians typically joke around in a good-natured manner. However, professional blues players demonstrate much less patience when faced with an aggressive audience, especially when they threaten their authenticity and self-respect. According to Sonny, a folk-blues guitarist and singer:

Yeah, it used to really bother me when students that I'd give lessons to would ask me to teach them rock songs by guys like Tom Petty and Lynyrd Skynyrd, but I used to do it when I had no money. Ha! One night I was playing . . . and this drunk woman comes up to me and hands me a napkin and says, "Now, we want you to play these songs, but start from the bottom, because *that* one's mine." And the songs were like "Cat's in the Cradle," "Margaritaville" . . . I think "Alice's Restaurant" by Arlo Guthrie was another one, and I told her that I don't really know those songs, and so she says, "What's the matter, don't you know any *folk* music?!"[24]

So then I went to do a gig at Whole Foods, and it's around Easter time, and the woman who hired me takes me around and tells the guys at the counter, "Today Sonny's going to play some happy, springtime music—none of that *blues* or anything."

It is hardly surprising that musicians take issue with their patrons and employers during these uncomfortable kinds of encounters. But interestingly enough, if and when they are eventually accorded with the respect they feel they deserve from those same audiences, they are generally willing to demonstrate their appreciation in kind. Chad, a blues and rockabilly player, describes an altercation that took place during one of his gigs at Smoke Daddy between himself and some of the crowd's rowdier members:

Well, they're all nice people, you know? Yeah, they're cool . . . Now, some of them do need to learn how to respect the music, not talk so much when somebody is playing . . . It's not really their fault—they just don't know any better. Like last night, I was playing here, and these people were talking really loud and laughing, and then I realized that they were making fun of me and my "country" music . . . So, right into the middle of a song, I just stopped and shouted, "Shut the fuck up!" and they seemed shocked, like no one had ever told them off like that before, and after the set a couple of them actually stopped me and apologized, and said they were sorry and hadn't realized they were being rude, and I thought that was pretty cool. For me, as soon as they had apologized, the whole situation had ended, right then and there. And for the rest of the night, everything was cool.

Certainly, no one appreciates being publicly ridiculed; Chad is no exception, and so he defends himself in a clear and aggressive manner. But like his fellow lions, he gives his audience the benefit of the doubt because he assumes "they just don't know any better" and reconciles his artistic autonomy with his responsibilities as a performing showman. As Sonny asserts, "The audience is there to be entertained, and it's your job as a musician to entertain them, no matter what—*that's your job*. If they don't get into it, if you can't win them over, then it's your own fault, man."

For this reason, musicians offer complimentary praise to their audiences when they react enthusiastically to their performances, because it is during these moments that their subcultural status and artistic authenticity actually express themselves in the world of the blues club. Even Farrell has been known to speak glowingly of his audience after his performances; he remarks to me on one such occasion, "Yeah, I was pretty happy about the crowd . . . By the time I came up to play, the crowd was really great . . . In fact, they were probably at their best when we played. They *responded*."[25]

Whiteness and the Performance of Authenticity.

While the remarks of white lions and survivors suggest a certain amount of resistance toward the commercialization of the blues in Chicago and the ways in which audiences evaluate their authenticity as blues performers, these same musicians frequently find themselves catering to those very expectations as a means of attaining gigs and establishing subcultural status for themselves. As I suggested in chapter 3, some white musicians attempt to compensate for their whiteness by appropriating styles commonly associated with black urban culture. Likewise, lions and survivors often pay tribute to the stock characters conventionally played by black blues singers in their onstage performances. Before introducing Tommy McCracken to the stage, his sideman Andy, a survivor, growls out Rufus Thomas's "Walking the Dog" in heavily accentuated fits and starts. Meanwhile, Keefe, a younger lion who sits in as a keyboardist for a more established black performer, howls away like a hound dog as he sings and successfully encourages his audience to follow suit. These on-stage moments often thrill audience members, who remark on the novelty provided by watching whites take on roles ordinarily performed by black entertainers.

Like black blues musicians, lions and survivors are highly aware of the demands of their audiences and strive to produce authenticated roles for themselves. But unlike the musicians discussed in these examples, most correctly assume that if they begin their shows by throwing up signs, preaching to their audiences, and playing their guitars with their tongues, their audience will find the performance contrived at best and, at worst, offensive and racist. This puts white performers in a difficult position. If they conform to the ideal types suggested by local expectations, their patrons will accuse them of impersonating black performers; however, if they avoid those conventions by employing more original styles of performance, audiences will reject them on the basis of their inability to conform to their expectations of an authentic blues player.[26]

White musicians attempt to solve this dilemma by constructing authenticated roles for themselves based on a different set of criteria than those governing the credibility of black blues musicians. Through creative uses of style and a staged script, musicians like Daniel forgo the privileged authenticity suggested by stock characters such as the preacher and the sexual stud for less valued roles that they can confidently pull off. By borrowing from a pool of *white* stock characters in their onstage performances—such as rock stars and folklorists—these musicians attempt to fashion themselves as convincingly authentic to audiences.

Some manage by playing the role of the rock star. During his gigs Chad swings his guitar over his head between songs as he struts and swaggers about the stage. As his band performs covers of blues-rock songs by the Allman Brothers, Eric jumps atop amplifiers while screaming into his microphone, while Jack introduces his "Shake, Rattle & Roll/Hound Dog" medley with a rousing "How many rock 'n' roll music fans do we have in the house tonight?" Likewise, white musicians appropriate countercultural styles of dress and adornment indicative of wider cultural trends among postwar youth that capitalize on the contemporary coolness of nostalgic kitsch and proletarian chic.[27] For instance, Jack appropriates the image of the 1960s motorcycle-riding outlaw with celebrated gusto, sporting long dirty blond hair, black pants (worn typically with a red or blue bandana in the back pocket), and a leather vest that reveals the "Ace of Harps" tattoo on his right bicep.[28] Chad smokes and drinks at Smoke Daddy in his secondhand, blue-collar work jacket worn along with a silver-spiked black belt and an extra long key chain dangling from his left pants pocket; his sideburns and tattoos complement his gritty outfit. In keeping with current "retro" styles, Daniel performs in horn-rimmed glasses, slicked-back hair, sideburns, pointed shoes, and a leather jacket; in contrast, Eric wears beads and loose-fitting clothing while sporting a goatee. By dressing up as caricatures representative of mythologized postwar subcultures—the beat, greaser, outlaw, hippie, punk, and slacker—white blues performers are able to offer their audiences a truncated yet credible display of manufactured authenticity.

If these musicians appropriate the pose of the rock 'n' roller, other white players eschew the provocative roles commonly performed by black musicians and instead adopt the persona of the traditional folklorist, storyteller, or academic. In his relatively conservative dress—a buttoned-down gray shirt tucked into his dress slacks, black polished shoes, and long hair tied back into a ponytail—Sonny teaches his audience about the heritage of the American blues between performing acoustic numbers such as Elizabeth Cotton's "Freight Train" and Blind Boy Fuller's "Too Many Women Blues" on his steel guitar, harmonica, and kazoo:

> It's great to be playing tribute to one of my favorite blues players. I got to hear Brownie McGhee perform shortly before he died, at the Chicago Blues Festival in 1996. This is a song by him that I haven't played in a while. It's one of my favorites . . . Since this is a tribute to Brownie McGhee, I thought I'd also pay tribute to Sonny Terry. This is an old blues tune . . . Another East Coast guitar player who heavily influenced Brownie McGhee was one of my favorite blues performers, Rev. Gary Davis . . . This is "Buck Dance" . . . A lot of people don't know this, but when Brownie McGhee was young he had polio, and one of his legs was five, six inches shorter than the other one . . . and it wasn't until later in his life that he eventually got his leg fixed and they were of equal length. I've always imagined that it was after this that he decided to write this song. This is probably my favorite Brownie McGhee tune—this is "Walk On."

By playing the part of the storyteller and folklorist, white performers like Sonny may forgo the authenticity accorded black blues musicians, but at least gain *some* credibility and status as middle-class curators of the traditional working-class blues heritage of American blacks.

Black Blues Musicians and the Commercialization of Culture.

As demonstrated above, white musicians take serious issue with the expectations of their audiences and the black musicians and club owners who attempt to satisfy those expectations. For their own part, black musicians also exhibit feelings of resentment toward club owners by stressing how the enforcement of their demands frequently rises to the level of either exploitation or exclusion, and ultimately denies them the autonomy to perform the blues on their own terms. According to Louis, the aforementioned black bandleader who once ran the jam session at B.L.U.E.S. Etcetera, cultural entrepreneurs such as club owners have disproportionately gained from the rising popularity of the Chicago blues, especially when compared to their dutiful employees:

> Well, it's true . . . the blues scene in Chicago has become more commercial . . . Today people who have money are spending it on blues, and so it has become very profitable. Musicians have had nothing to do with that—blues has just become profitable, and in fact while musicians are making a little more money, those profits have mostly gone to club owners, record companies, and other people.

Louis suggests that the economic imperative inherent in the increased commodification of the blues ultimately diminishes his ability to perform with a real sense of creative autonomy:

> Today the quality of the music is not the bottom line at these clubs . . . bringing in money, that's the bottom line. I mean, it don't matter who you are . . . If you're a garage band, and you can bring people in the club and make them money, you'll be hired. You're in this to make money. Now, when I first started out, I initially did it for the love of the money. But now, I want to do my *own* thing, I want to be that band that when people come to hear you, they know you're doing something original, something that's all your own . . .

In fact, according to many of the black musicians with whom I met over the course of my fieldwork, local club owners force players and old-timers to tailor their performances according to prevailing assumptions about what *they* think their customers will regard as authentic, as opposed to how the musicians themselves actually want to perform. One evening at B.L.U.E.S. Etcetera, I accompany Tiger across the street so

we can move his car, a brand-new gold Cadillac. On our way back to the club, he explains:

> I don't like a lot of the bands they got playing at the Kingston Mines . . . Over there, they're not really singing what they feel . . . They're just doing it for the audience—doing the same old thing, you know? When I hear a band, I want some variety, I want to see something new. But it's the *owners*, see? They tell these bands what to play, what to wear . . . even what kind of hat to wear. And after playing the same tunes, you get tired . . . but even I know you have to play them.

According to Tiger, the demands that club owners and audiences place on musicians ultimately deny them the autonomy to play "what they feel," just as within the context of hip-hop music and style, artists are often accused of not "keepin' it real" when they respond to the pressures of the marketplace.[29] Likewise, Tiger is critical of how such demands ultimately hinder the ability of the musician to move the genre forward in a progressive manner.

> I'm trying to get away from that old "lumpty-lump" style of playing . . . I'm trying instead to develop a new style, my *own* style. I don't want to play that same old thing, that "lumpty-lump, lumpty-lump"—I want to play a new style, something more funky, more danceable . . . I'm not into that sad type of blues, you know? "Lumpty-lump" is killing me . . . A song like "Sweet Home Chicago"? Man, I'm bored with it . . . I've just played it so many times.[30]

In fact, because they view the expectations of audiences and club owners as an affront to their creative autonomy as self-reliant performers, many black musicians ardently criticize their employers for blackballing local *white* musicians. According to Shawn, a bass player:

> I've always been treated OK, but a lot of times the owners will try to break up your band if you have too many white guys. Like, if a band has three black guys, the owners sometimes let them have two white guys, but a lot of times they'll say there's too many white guys on the stage, because, well, you know, the blues is supposed to be the music of blacks, and they're doing it for the tourists, and it's all about business.
> But if you can play the blues, it doesn't matter who you are—anyone can

play the blues. It doesn't take a certain kind of person to play the blues . . . Everybody *gets* the blues, right? So, either you can play the blues or you can't, and it doesn't matter if you're white or black or whatever . . . But the owners, they'll try to break up your band if you've got too many whites.

Meanwhile, rather than capitulate to the expectations of local owners, old-timers often resist the demands of their employers by purposefully refusing to play the blues and R&B standards generally expected of them. According to one old-timer who sings, plays guitar, and leads his own band, "Some guys, they want to put the blues in a straitjacket. But not me—I'm not a purist. You see, the blues is evolutionary . . . If you keep the blues stagnant, it can't grow." Billy, another old-timer who leads his own band, remarks, "I won't play any of those songs, you know, like 'Stormy Monday,' 'Sweet Home Chicago,' 'Got My Mojo Working' . . . They're all washed up, been played to death, I'm sick of them . . . Now if a player wants to do one, and he is sincere about it, and he's gonna do it right, then I'll play it with him."

For all their differences, black and white musicians tend to agree that market demands place a set of constraints on their autonomy as blues performers. However, it is nevertheless the case that players and old-timers generally find greater popularity among mainstream audiences than their white counterparts, due to the prevailing politics of race and authenticity in the Chicago blues scene. Perhaps it is for this reason that black musicians tend to identify with their mainstream audiences more than the lions and survivors discussed above who privately tease those audiences because "they don't know any better." One night before a jam session at B.L.U.E.S. Etcetera, Louis and I lean against the stage and chat as I attempt to fix the wristband of his watch. When I ask him what kinds of crowds he most prefers performing for, he remarks that it makes almost no difference to him. "As long as they enjoy the music, as long as I'm satisfying the audience, that's all right with me."

Getting more and more frustrated trying to undo the clasp on his watch, I press Louis on this point a little further. "Then which is more important, satisfying the audience or fulfilling your creative needs as a musician?"

"Well, one isn't secondary to the other . . . Satisfying the audience is just as important as satisfying myself—the audience is just as important as me. I have to satisfy us both . . . and so I become part of the audience. So I'll do [a] request, but I'll do it in my own way, and then I'll like it, and they'll like it, too."

I ask Louis if it matters more when the request is for a perennial blues standard such as "Sweet Home Chicago."

> Well, you definitely have audiences that ask for that . . . and the musicians, we get tired of playing it. But if I get a request, then normally, if I know it, I'll do it . . . You can do other people's music, but that's all right, because you take their ideas and you make them your own. If you work the circuit, you gotta do those standards, but you make them your own . . . Because for me, I like to be on the stage, and I'll play anything . . . And in the end, you do put your own mark on it. You can't help but put your own mark on it.

In our conversations Tiger expresses a similar sentiment, remarking, "I *love* the audience, 'cause I'll get to them sooner or later. And when I'm a sideman, I play what the leader wants me to play, I'll do whatever they want, and I'll do it the best that I can, and *get paid*. Of course, I'll try to add something to it . . . and it doesn't matter for me, because I'll get to them, regardless." As Tiger's remarks suggest, in a context of commercialized culture, "getting paid" is as much a sign of subcultural status as any other marker of authenticity. If for some musicians the art is in the performance, then for many others the pleasure is in the profit. As Dizzy cackles one evening at B.L.U.E.S., "Having fun? Shit, man . . . It's not about havin' fun. It's about *makin' money*—now *that's* what it's all about! Having fun? Naw, making money, man, that's what *I'm* talking about . . . Hell, then you can go out and *buy* your own fun! Ha-ha!!"

And in some ways, "getting paid" is the most significant hurdle that black blues musicians face, insofar as the stumbling blocks placed before players and old-timers in the local employment market still provide a formidable challenge to their professional careers. While earlier remarks made by lions and survivors might suggest otherwise, the truth is that black musicians are generally forced to "overcompensate" even more than whites in their professional dealings with club owners, booking agents, and bartenders. When players arrive late to their gigs on account of car trouble, owners often call their reliability and professionalism into question, whereas a white band might receive the benefit of the doubt. Likewise, bartenders often accuse old-timers of shamelessly panhandling when they tease audience members in their search for complimentary drinks, but when white musicians engage in similar interactions, they usually occur without incident.

As frequent targets of exploitation through low wages, unfair treatment, and regularly meted disrespect from white club owners, black musicians articulate their resentment in their private moments during the set breaks of their performances. During one set break at B.L.U.E.S., Billy complains to a group of us in the back room about how white businessmen have historically exploited black music for profit, and he draws on the marketing of blues-oriented rock 'n' roll as a prime example. After recalling with disgust how Ed Sullivan hailed the Rolling Stones' performance of Howlin' Wolf's "The Red Rooster" as "new" music, he jabs, "Meanwhile, I'm a goddamn American and I can't even get my records played on the radio! I played at Blues Fest—I was the last act on a Friday night—and they . . . made me stop, because folks living in those tall buildings complained. Man, if I was the Stones, or Frank Sinatra, if *I* had blue eyes and blond hair, they would have let me play all night."

Billy's lament raises an important point about the relationship between race and the professional success of the blues musician. While white performers make a reasonable case against their own unfair treatment by local club owners, it is also undeniable that among those who employ blues styles in their performances, the highest-paid, most successful artists have been white, including Elvis Presley, Bob Dylan, Jimmy Page, Eric Clapton, Janis Joplin, Bonnie Raitt, Mick Jagger, Keith Richards, and the Grateful Dead. In some ways, the public attribution of authenticity to these performers as rock stars has trumped any social costs that being a white musician might have inflicted on their artistic credibility. While black musicians may be admired for their authenticity in the local context of the Chicago blues scene, they simply cannot compete with these moneymakers in the global marketplace, and even top-selling players and old-timers of the past and present—Muddy Waters, John Lee Hooker, Bobby "Blue" Bland, B.B. King, Buddy Guy, Koko Taylor, Robert Cray—have often been forced to play second fiddle to those white performers they have inspired and, in some cases, legitimated through brief guest appearances in the studio and on the stage. My point here is not to suggest that these white musicians are any less deserving of success than their black counterparts, but simply to observe that for all of the lions' and survivors' talk about reverse discrimination and the need for affirmative action in the blues, whites have traditionally fared much better than most black players and old-timers in terms of financial reward, artistic autonomy, and professional respect in the highest levels of the popular music and entertainment industry. As Billy's remark demonstrates, this fact has not been lost on the city's black blues musicians.

Of course, among those performers, few are treated as badly as the city's small minority of black female singers, as revealed by a 1998 interview with Big Time Sarah for a small local music fanzine:

> Obstacles were abundant for her in the beginning of her career. "The men have always been there. The clubs, the booking agents, the record companies, always seemed to give the men the breaks." When asked if she felt that it was different today, she said that things have changed, but only a little. "We do have a lot of clubs that are starting to book a lot of lady singers." She still believes though that "when it comes to club owners, booking agents are going to always grab a male entertainer." Her biggest complaint is that the agents want to take 20–25% of the money "when you ain't making it."
>
> Sarah will be the first to tell you that the life of the blues singer is not as glamorous as it may seem. Has the blues paid the rent handsomely for her? "Sometimes—sometimes it doesn't pay when my shows are slow and laid-back. I'm not getting any work." . . . As a struggling woman in the blues Sarah felt it hard to earn the respect of her male peers. "Yeah, it was very hard because any way a man's gonna always think he's the boss."[31]

Meanwhile, old-timers contrast the frequent abandonment they face from club owners to the favoritism enjoyed by younger players, including Sarah. From a corner bar stool at B.L.U.E.S., Dizzy watches in frustration while Sarah sells her compact disc to the remaining patrons at the club and eventually protests, "I don't know, man . . . What I want to know is, why *she* can sell her CD here, but they won't let me sell *mine*? Why can't I sell *my* CD, man? What about *me*?"

The Authenticity of the Musician.   The present discussion reveals how players, old-timers, lions, and survivors all think about authenticity in the context of their professional careers, and how they shape their identity as blues musicians around issues of race and respect in the face of market pressure and cultural commodification. This search for self-respect demonstrates how musicians may not desire to *find* authenticity as much as they want to *be* authentic themselves. After one of his band's Sunday night sets, one player expresses this yearning for authenticity in the aforementioned language of hip-hop: "We try to do our *own* thing, you know, keepin' it *real*. Yeah, we do our own thing, we try to keep it real."

But while most musicians strive for an authentic sense of self, they tend to disagree with regard to exactly how one goes about "keepin' it real," particularly when it comes to determining what authentic blues music actually sounds like. Indeed, is Quintus McCormick "keepin' it real" when he performs "Stairway to Heaven"? As I discovered in my conversations with a wide variety of Chicago blues musicians, it all depends on whom you ask.

I think it is safe to assume where Darryl stands on the matter. On a cold December morning, he and I meet at Valois "See Your Food" Cafeteria in the racially mixed South Side neighborhood of Hyde Park, and the place is packed with the midday crowd of local diners, including L.V. Banks, a black blues singer who lives in the area.[32] Darryl introduces us, and as he bids farewell, we begin chatting about the blues music performed in contemporary clubs in Chicago.

"You know," Darryl begins, "the lead bluesmen probably know how to play it right, but their backing sidemen don't really follow in the tradition of blues, and the audiences don't either, so it's all very showy—a lot of posturing, and the new sounds are so exaggerated—a really loud wail, and then a shift to an extremely low note, and then back up again, and it's ridiculous and totally inauthentic . . . especially when compared to what blues is really about, where emotion is produced through a subtle shift in tone." He sings a few bars to demonstrate his point.

As we eat and talk, a lively backdrop of local interaction colors our conversation. At one point a middle-aged black woman begins to holler and causes a stir, which attracts a member of the cafeteria's staff. Apparently, she had left her bags and coat on a seat at a side table, and a young black girl moved them aside and took over her table. She gets very upset at this, and when the manager/owner tries to explain that he really cannot ask his younger customer to move, the woman demands her money back. When he denies her request, she begins shouting loudly: "Now I've been in cafeterias before, and if I can't get my money back here, then this place is low-class! Do you hear what I am saying to you? This place is *low-class*! It's cheap, it's *ignorant*!" The owner eventually capitulates and gives the lady her money back.

Meanwhile, Darryl continues:

> I think part of the problem is that a lot of these musicians aren't playing within the blues tradition . . . I mean, the really great masters in the fifties—Muddy Waters, Jimmy Rogers—they definitely sounded different from the earlier blues of the thirties, but it was still authentic, because they were following a tradition. That tradition ruptured in the 1960s when blues

began sounding more like gospel, really. And the difference between gospel and blues is the emotion and feeling of the music—gospel tries to shake you up, it's very powerful because it's so loud and emotional, while blues is more detached and simple. This style became popular among blacks in the 1960s, when the older, traditional music seemed so dated and old-fashioned.

Remember when that woman caused the scene in here before, she said this place was "low-class," "ignorant"? Well, that's how blacks felt about blues back then, it was considered low-class and backward, like a southern sharecropper. So the music was already changing to meet the new tastes of audiences who wanted something different.

As I discussed in chapter 1, during the late 1950s and 1960s, blues performers like Muddy Waters and Howlin' Wolf fell out of favor among black audiences, who rejected their style as "gutbucket," "lowdown," "dirty"—and, most of all, "low-class." In the wake of this shift away from the traditional blues idiom, soul stirrers like Bobby "Blue" Bland, Buddy Guy, Johnnie Taylor, and B.B. King popularized a more contemporary style of urban blues that replaced the southern twang of the blues harmonica with a jazzy saxophone section, and straight-ahead vocals with a looser, gospel-inflected style of singing.[33] The sound of this music marked a stylistic departure from the blues recordings of the early 1950s, and in Chicago rivalries formed between "down-home" South Side players and more modern-styled West Side performers.

In some ways, Darryl's criticisms of the contemporary blues scene represent an extension of that rivalry that continues to mobilize other survivors as well, like his band mate Jay, a drummer. In the back room of B.L.U.E.S., Jay explains:

Most guys nowadays, their playing is much too flamboyant . . . It's like Darryl says—you know how on an amplifier, you can only turn up the volume so much, and after it reaches a certain point, it just becomes noise? That's how a guitar string sounds when you bend it. If you do it gently, you can make some great music, but you can bend it too far, and it just sounds like garbage—and that's how most of the guitarists now play. And it's the same thing with drums . . . only a few guys can play it right.

Many of Darryl and Jay's fellow survivors would agree. According to Dustin, a white guitarist in his forties, " 'Down-home' blues is the way they used to play on the South Side. Back in the fifties, there were blues joints just all over the South Side, and the guys who played there were

locals who played simple music and weren't afraid to play out of tune . . .
More authentic, you might say." Likewise, as a self-proclaimed "traditionalist," Jack passionately explains his frustration with what he deni-
grates as the "watered-down" state of the blues.

> Nowadays, the blues scene is really getting away from the influences of the
> Chicago blues tradition. Before, the music performed in the city followed
> the singular path of traditional blues styles. But today most of the players
> have broken away from those roots . . . and so what used to be the essence
> of the blues has been lost. Of course, another factor is that most of the guys
> who could play well have all died . . . Twenty years ago this city had about
> fifty really outstanding guitar players . . . today there are maybe eight.
>
> The problem is, ninety percent of these people can't really play the blues,
> and most of the younger black kids don't play all that well either, because
> they try to sound like Jimi Hendrix instead of traditional Chicago blues.
> And so the people that come down here to listen to the blues get a watered-
> down version of it. For example, take [a local band]. Now, they can't play the
> blues at all, they flip-flop between blues progressions and R&B styles . . .
>
> Now, I think of myself as a hard-core traditionalist: I play a modern
> sound, but it's an evolution of the Chicago blues tradition. But most of these
> other guys, they listen to a couple of Buddy Guy and Jimi Hendrix albums,
> and learn like three or four clichéd licks . . . and if that's how you play, then
> you're not doing the *real* shit, you're just playing *bullshit*. And so at Kingston
> Mines, they hardly ever have a real blues band. Like, look at this band here
> tonight. This is a cover band—and not an especially *good* cover band. They
> don't understand the subtle nuances of the blues performance; they just turn
> up the volume and play some R&B mixed with rock . . . It's all "show" and
> no "go."
>
> But blues is a language, it's not about gimmicks. Most of these bands
> today, they're not real blues artists . . . And this band—we book 'em because
> he's a good singer, and he shows up on time, so who the hell else are we going
> to hire?

Jack makes a number of strong assertions in these remarks. First, he argues that the fundamental problem with his fellow musicians is that
they have "broken away" from the roots of the Chicago blues tradition,
an assertion that assumes that the Chicago blues actually has a "sin-
gular" and authentic musical tradition, as opposed to one marked by
change and contestation; the music commonly played by contemporary

blues performers represents an attempt to evade this tradition; and this evasion constitutes a loss in the authenticity of the current Chicago blues scene. On this basis, Jack identifies the reasons why local musicians have abandoned this tradition, and thus their own authenticity: namely, they lack (1) the necessary *knowledge* about the Chicago blues tradition, (2) the *competence* to employ this knowledge successfully in the context of their stage performances, and (3) the *desire* to carry on this legacy as defined by Jack and other cultural authorities supportive of this interpretation of musical history and aesthetic judgment. He contrasts their behavior and attitudes with his own, and in doing so, he portrays his personal musical style—and by extension, *himself*—as the very representation of authenticity in the blues.

How can Jack's remarks be explained? This is a highly problematic question: after all, sociologists can rarely identify the causes of individual human behavior with the same reliability as those who operate in more positivist fields such as biochemistry or physics. And so, instead of trying to deconstruct Jack's personal motivations in this particular instance, let us try to understand why someone *like* Jack might describe the current state of the Chicago blues in the manner suggested by his remarks. First, it is clear that unlike their black counterparts, who are generally assumed to be authentic on the basis of their racial characteristics, white musicians need to justify their claims of authenticity to their audiences (as well as each other), and while they cannot do so on racial grounds, an ideological orientation rooted in aesthetic exclusivity may provide a handy self-defense in the absence of other symbolic markers of authenticity. Second, white musicians—and particular older white musicians—frequently face the steady fate of diminishing returns in the local hiring market, and therefore may require an effective means of explaining away their occupational marginality while keeping their claims to authenticity intact. For many survivors, the hope of "keepin' it real" can presumably compensate for a lack of professional success among musicians and other kinds of artistic workers. Finally, it is important to keep in mind that the producers of music are often among its most enthusiastic consumers as well, and that the search for authenticity among these white musicians may simply represent how extremely knowledgeable and selective consumers attempt to experience the same kinds of authenticity as more mainstream audiences—a quest for meaning that may distinguish such musicians from their audiences in degree, but not necessarily in kind.[34]

The Resistance against Authenticity.   Of course, by deny-
ing the authenticity of their fellow performers, the efforts of these survivors run counter to the strategies of those musicians whose repertoires
include traditional *and* modern Chicago blues styles, as well as funk,
reggae, disco, gospel, and pop. Since these latter musicians rely on dominant definitions of authenticity to give them access to its symbolic *and*
economic rewards, they defend their artistic mettle against the attacks
of their survivor counterparts by espousing a more inclusive and flexible definition of authenticity.[35] For example, Daniel enthusiastically explains his band's attempts to move *beyond* the styles indicative of "classic" Chicago blues music:

> Well, it's like Chicago blues, but it's a little bit later . . . like, there's the clas-
> sic Chicago blues, like Muddy, Jimmy Rogers, and Howlin' Wolf, there's
> that, and then . . . a little bit after that there was like the Magic Sam thing,
> and I'm sort of into the Magic Sam and later thing . . . It's like the clas-
> sic Chicago blues, but it's slightly more modern. It's more modern . . . I'm
> slowly learning some jazz tunes, and I'm playing some ballads like Lonnie
> Johnson, ballads and shit, so I'm into that . . . It's not straight classic Chicago
> blues . . .

Likewise, his discussion of the shift from traditional to modern styles
in the performance of urban blues is brimming with enthusiasm and
celebration:

> There's still a gigantic black blues audience, but they listen to blues that
> white people don't listen to. They listen to Bobby Bland and Little Mil-
> ton . . . If black people voted, Bobby Bland could be president of the United
> States, because he's just so popular . . . and it's *blues*, and it sounds *good* . . .
> It has a different feel, it doesn't really have a rock feel, and the vocals are
> much more fun . . . Little Milton is great, he's really great. Now, he was a
> contemporary of B.B. King, and so was Bobby Bland . . . Clarence Carter's
> another guy: you know, it's more R&B stuff . . . and it's kind of racy, sexy . . .
> like sort of soap opera shit, you know, like the way old blues *always* has been
> soap opera-y.

In contrast to their more "traditionalist" counterparts, lions and players maintain an inclusive and flexible definition of the genre that recognizes a diverse and multivalent vision of the blues as an evolving work

in progress. In asserting their autonomy as musicians in an already sti-
fling commercial atmosphere, these musicians characterize the postwar
shift from blues to soul as a *continuation* of an evolutionary chain in
the history of blues music, instead of a rupture or break with tradition.
By doing so, lions and players fashion their artistic authenticity on the
basis of their creativity as innovators, rather than as traditionalists.[36] For
example, Louis's repertoire emphasizes a fusion of blues, jazz, pop, and
funk. In his band's performances, they present a diverse range of familiar songs—including blues standards like Muddy Waters's "I'm Ready"
and "Every Day I Have the Blues," jazz fusion hits such as Herbie Han-
cock's "Chameleon," and even long-forgotten 1980s pop hits like Lionel
Richie's "Hello"—in unusual arrangements that synthesize a rainbow
of musical styles.[37] Louis explains:

> Well, I'm not interested in playing traditional music—I'm more interested
> in creating my own style. Like what I do now, it's not really blues, jazz, or
> R&B, but I call it "blusion," and it's my *own* thing, see? Music is all about
> metamorphosis and change. You know, it's like if you listen to Charlie Parker
> or Miles . . . These guys created a new style, and some people said to them
> in the beginning, "Hey, what the hell are you doing?" And I get that, I
> get bad feedback sometimes from owners because I don't play in a tradi-
> tional way . . . And you know, I don't have a problem with that, because it's
> business . . . but then I deal with the audience, and I try to win them over
> with it.

"How has the music changed in Chicago over the past twenty or thirty
years?" I ask.

"Well, nowadays so much of it is technological, you know . . . We've
got synthesizers, computers, newer amplifiers. But music is constantly
metamorphosing; it's always changing."

"Some musicians and critics suggest that the blues today is getting
away from its roots," I respond.

> You know what? I just see it like a cycle. Blues is the root of all American
> music, whether it be rap, jazz, rock, soul, R&B . . . and today all that shit
> is becoming attached to blues . . . I hear it in the clubs. Dixieland, gospel,
> zydeco—blues is the root of *all* of that music, all that comes from the blues,
> so it's just coming back to it, back to the roots . . . You look at Ray Charles.
> He played every kind of music his whole life, it was *always* changing . . .
> but it was always *him*, you always knew it was Ray singing and playing.

Like the traditionalists, Louis accepts an evolutionary model of musical change. However, while musicians like Darryl and Jack legitimate a single historical trajectory from which contemporary performers have "broken away," Louis rejects a linear view of cultural change in favor of a cyclical one in which multiple visions of the blues tradition can be revisited for reinterpretation. As a player who admittedly draws on an eclectic mix of black music styles, the authenticity of Louis's performance relies on the credibility of a broad and inclusive definition of the blues, and his success as an admired artist *and* commercially savvy entertainer depends on the acceptance of that ideology within the blues community.

Likewise, since Elliot incorporates blues-rock and funk rhythms into his self-penned compositions, he maintains not only a sizable symbolic stake in the promotion of an inclusive and flexible definition of authenticity in the blues, but a reasonably large financial stake as well. During a set break at the Green Room at Macaw's, a small downtown bar, he argues that in spite of its inherent traditionalism, the vitality of the blues depends upon a willingness among practitioners to deviate from earlier recording and performing styles: "I would say the state of the blues is healthy—and funky. Chicago's new blues sound is very funky. In the late 1960s Junior Wells started throwing some James Brown influences in his music, more funk and R&B. All cities have different blues: Texas blues is very rock, and Chicago is very urban funk."

I reply, "I think many musicians would agree with you, but some might not regard this shift away from tradition as necessarily 'healthy.'"

Let me ask you this—do these musicians play electric instruments? If so, then doesn't *that* break with tradition? Among a lot of white musicians, blues is very studied, very written, very academic . . . so they struggle to play every note just like the masters did before. Now, I believe blues should have one foot in the Delta—but it should also have one foot in the present. You know, when Muddy Waters had his debut, he had broken with tradition. He was playing something entirely new, something deeply influenced by the present. Blues is not an island. Its rhythms are affected by the present, by the everyday rhythms in people's lives. What's wrong with blues changing? Blues has always influenced rock—why can't rock influence blues?

Insofar as he also infuses his performances with a blues-rock sensibility, Tiger levies a similar attack when he admonishes his critics in the local media. I ask, "You've been criticized in the local press for diverting from the blues tradition. Is that a fair criticism?"

You know, the blues is a lot of different things, there's not just one type of blues . . . there's all types of blues, everybody's got a different idea of what the blues is, and everybody plays the blues with a different type of feeling. For example, you take B.B. King, right—now, when he's singing about how he lost his woman, you know something happened to him, right? You know *something* happened to *somebody*, right? And it's the same thing with Albert King . . . these guys take their own feelings, and they make different types of blues with them. Johnnie Taylor, now his blues is more like soul . . . so it's a different *type* of blues.

Tiger's inclusive definition of the blues offers a kind of cultural relativism necessary for recognizing the contested nature of all formal genre definitions; indeed, as I discovered in my barroom conversations with Tiger and others, "everybody's got a different idea of what the blues is."[38] Shawn, a fellow player, agrees:

Well, back then guys would play more laid-back, and some of the old-timers still do, but a lot of the younger players play much more up-tempo, more like rock, you know? But it's still the blues; it's the blues. Now, when I play down on the South Side, they like to hear more soul and R&B, you know, but it's all blues . . . it's different, but it's the blues. See, you got blues and gospel, and then jazz, like somebody like Billie Holiday? Now, in jazz they might take the basic three chords and make it an eight-bar instead of a twelve-bar, and move some notes around and change the syncopation—but it's still the blues.

Meanwhile, other black musicians express genuine outrage toward the traditionalist critique and the musicians who espouse it, and ultimately reject the very notion of authenticity altogether. For a player like Louis, the entire debate over authenticity only serves to hinder what little remains of the autonomy of the local blues performer and the solidarity of the subculture:

I'm not interested in all that petty shit, musicians criticizing what other guys are doing. I pay no attention, it don't affect me—I'm not jealous of anybody. I need jobs, but I'd never knock another band. I'm just doing my own thing, and other guys, if they like what they're doing, *they* should play it.

The truth is, if you play something for an audience, and they like it, then it must be right . . . I don't like these purists, these critics who say this isn't right. They say, "Well, the audience liked it, but it still wasn't good . . ." I mean, if the audience likes what you're doing, then who the hell are you? If the people like the music you're making, who cares? Hey, if you're onstage, and the audience likes it, and they're paying you, then something must be right.

Because for me, I like to be on the stage, and I'll play anything. You adapt . . . everybody adapts. Miles adapted, James Brown, Ray Charles . . . So for me, if I'm on the stage, and the audience is happy, and I'm making money, then that's what it's all about.

Other musicians, particularly young white lions and the occasional survivor, even go so far as to reject the criticisms of "these purists" by denouncing them as "Blues Nazis." On a late Monday night in a Mexican taqueria a few blocks away from B.L.U.E.S., Farrell explains the term to me over warm plates of chicken tacos and salsa:

You know how these "Blues Nazis" are . . . [In a bad German accent] "*You love zee blues . . . Vee have ways of making you love zee blues.*" You know, if they had their way, if a guy doesn't sound like Big Bill Broonzy and record in the twenties or thirties, then it's not blues. So can you imagine if these people were around when something like, I don't know, Jimmy Reed came out? "*Oh, this isn't blues, it's R&B, it's soul music, it's not the blues . . .*" I mean, let's have some fun, let's think about what other classic blues would be dismissed by the "Blues Nazis" . . . OK, how about, I don't know, "Stormy Monday"? "*Oh, no, sorry, this isn't blues, it's jazz . . .*"[39]

Meanwhile, Sonny, a young, white folk-blues singer who *does* perform Big Bill Broonzy songs in his act, agrees with Farrell's criticisms. Like Tiger and Louis, he respects an inclusive and flexible definition of the genre that clearly embraces a wide range of styles (including his own) under the rubric of "blues."[40] He expands upon Farrell's definition of the "Blues Nazi":

"Blues Nazis" . . . Yeah, I definitely hear that term used around some. These guys, these "Blues Nazis," they all seem to be guys who really love blues, and they have a real emotional attachment to it, and really want to be a part of it, but for whatever reason can't play an instrument, or they can't make it performing, and so they tend to be really critical and obsessive about blues. I think part of it comes the fact that we can really communicate with these blues musicians, and they're jealous because they can't, and they would like to. And so they talk about how blues artists don't understand their own music or the traditions.

For me, when I think of guys like Ray Charles and Al Green, I see them as blues singers. Maybe not all R&B, but definitely most of that music—soul, funk—it all comes from blues and gospel, it's all the same thing. I even know a guy who doesn't think blues music recorded before the 1970s is real blues! But to me, it's all blues. Like, Ray Charles is the quintessential blues singer. It's just all blues, even though a lot of these "Blues Nazis" will tell you differently.

Weeks later Sonny and his occasional band mate and fellow lion Jon continue the discussion after an alternative-country music show at the Hideout, a secluded honky-tonk bar located in a light industrial zone off the interstate. After meeting Jon at the bar and telling him about some of my interviews and barroom conversations with local survivors like Darryl and Jack, he shakes his head in disapproval. "You know what we call those guys? *'Blues Nazis.'* These guys, they sit in the back of the club and whisper about the bands, and how they think this or that musician sucks because he doesn't play exactly the way they heard it on the record. Those guys are so fuckin' rude . . . And [a local white musician], he's a good player as long as he's copying a Little Walter song note for fuckin' note, but that's it . . ."

Sonny nods in agreement and reiterates his resistant stance in this subcultural battle over authenticity. "Yeah, it's like what I always say about [a local critic] . . . One night somebody asked him if a show he had seen was any good, and he went off on it, saying how they were trying to do this-or-that, and that it wasn't 'real,' and I'm like thinking, 'Who the hell cares? Did it sound good? Did you like it? Did they look like they were having a good time?' You know, who *cares*? What *difference* does it make?"

Chicago Confidential
The Rise of the Blues Club
as a Tourist Attraction

One of the topics most frequently addressed in blues songs is the blues itself. Personification being a technique frequently employed by blues singers,
regardless of whether they recognize it as a literary concept, the blues is also
a familiar *character* in their songs—walking like a man, thumbing a ride, bid-
ding the singer good morning, and implying that it's going to be around for
a good long spell no matter what the singer does to chase it away. Those
who write about the blues also tend to grant it human characteristics. It's
born in Mississippi before the turn of the century, wanders around the South
a little bit, spends a considerable amount of time in Texas, then turns up in
Chicago just in time to father rock 'n' roll. It dies a natural death around 1960,
but—stubborn old cuss that it is—rises up like Lazarus every ten years or so.

Of course, nothing is that simple. . . . Let's just say the blues has a large
extended family and bears a strong resemblance to many of its relatives. Especially in its younger years, it was frequently sighted in places it may or may
not have been, and mistaken for blood relatives long since forgotten.

—Francis Davis, *The History of the Blues*

The Commercialization of the Blues.   In some ways, there
seems to be nothing unusual about the current commercialized nature
of the Chicago blues, especially in light of the recent popularity of hip-
hop and other music genres identified with African American expressive
culture and style.[1] Black music artists appear in countless entertainment
forums, including commercials, and the blues in particular has been employed in television advertisements to sell everything from McDonald's

hamburgers to All laundry detergent. Of course, if John Lee Hooker's appearance in a Pepsi commercial angered his most beloved fans, at least he agreed to participate in the ad campaign while he was still alive—which is more than one can say for Howlin' Wolf, who posthumously appeared on a recent Gap billboard for, apparently, wearing khakis.[2]

Nevertheless, while the Chicago blues has always found an audience among a diverse array of consumers, its contemporary visibility and commercial appeal on the global cultural stage are surely impressive by any measure of media popularity and success. How might we account for its cultural ascendancy in recent decades among mainstream audiences? It is an interesting question, given that the most common explanations tend to emphasize either the set of sweeping social and political changes in this country and abroad brought about by the modern-day civil rights movement, or the appropriation and revival of the blues idiom by American and British rock 'n' roll stars in the 1950s and 1960s.

However, I would argue that while both of these events certainly played a role as formative influences, it is difficult to fully understand this cultural history without also exploring the local urban processes that gave rise to the popularity of the blues club as a tourist attraction in Chicago. While broadly defined national movements frequently lend themselves to convincing stories about cultural change, such explanations alone tend to provide facile and simplistic solutions to complex historical questions. Rather, in this chapter I would like to explore how this historical shift occurred as a result of a specific set of local urban processes that took place within this larger macro-level context of commodification and global cultural change, including the gentrification of a handful of artist-friendly neighborhoods on Chicago's North Side during the 1960s, the increased promotion of racially charged cultural consumption in the city's alternative press, and the development of the international tourism industry in Chicago. In doing so, I would like to argue that the search for authenticity among the city's countercultural and more mainstream audiences, in addition to a well-timed response from cultural authorities and local boosters interested in mining its persuasive powers for their own benefit, all encouraged the eventual rise of the blues club as a tourist attraction.

Northbound Blues and the Chicago Counterculture.
Postwar Chicago's segregated Black Belt provided a cultural space where blues and jazz could flourish as an expressive urban subculture. In the

city's South Side and West Side neighborhoods, musicians from Muddy Waters to Jimmy Rogers to Buddy Guy performed blues music nightly in taverns, jukes, barrelhouses, nickel-a-drink dance halls, and house parties. In working-class haunts with colorful names—the Purple Cat, Theresa's Tavern, Cadillac Baby's Show Lounge, and the Cosy Inn—the subcultural world of the black ghetto could be experienced through long evenings of blues intertwined with usual bar brawls and abuses of gin.[3] At this time the city's "race" recording industry was among the strongest in the nation, as evidenced by the dominance of local South Side labels such as Bluebird, Decca, Vocalion, and Chess, and West Side record companies like Profile, Chief, Abco, Artistic, and Cobra. And on Maxwell Street, blues guitarists and singers executed their art among the immigrant merchants and shoppers of that West Side neighborhood's bustling marketplace.[4]

But during this same period, a seemingly different type of entertainment milieu emerged on the city's North Side as middle-class artists, bohemians, students, journalists, and other young singles began moving into Lincoln Park's ethnic enclaves and working-class neighborhoods. Attracted by low land values and affordable rents, these young newcomers participated in the widespread renovation of residential homes and storefronts in the area's Old Town district. By the early 1960s these residents began to view themselves as a bohemian community in cultural opposition to the so-called "square" world of the city. Writing in 1961, Ed Morris describes this sense of community in the *Old Town Holiday Booklet*, a locally distributed pamphlet:

> Old Towners are no different than any other cross section of any community, except that there is an especially good melting together of disparate races, creeds and colors which, in more than usual fashion, have learned to live together in peace and enjoyment of each others' quality. We believe that Old Town epitomizes all of the best aspects of Brotherhood at work. This is the life of Old Town.[5]

As Old Town's middle-class population grew and slowly began pricing out the area's poorer residents, local entrepreneurs developed an entertainment zone to take advantage of the aesthetic desires of the neighborhood's burgeoning artistic presence. While individual gentrifiers and professional developers found Old Town's inexpensive properties ideal for remodeling into extremely palatable middle-income housing, affordable commercial space made buildings in the area attractive for artist studios, music venues, drinking pubs, and specialty shops. Antique stores, coffeehouses, ethnic restaurants, art galleries, and folk music clubs soon lined up along Wells Street, the area's central commercial strip; meanwhile, the Old Town Triangle Association, a neighborhood "improvement" organization, sponsored countless street fairs and outdoor square dances, as well as the annual Old Town Holiday Arts and Crafts Fair.[6]

By the mid-1960s many local residents fancied themselves as countercultural bohemians representative of the nation's burgeoning youth culture. A respondent from Margaret Warner's unpublished dissertation on the renovation of Lincoln Park remarks:

> [Old Town's] Meyer Court was like something out of a play with a mixture of hippies and Old European Catholics. Younger people tended to live in carriage houses because they were cheap. There was a lot of painted windows, parties, free love, experimentation.[7]

As demonstrated by countless guidebooks published on the area during the 1960s, this countercultural milieu developed as entertainment and drinking establishments catering to this community proliferated throughout the commercial area surrounding Wells Street.[8] By 1962 the Rising Moon was a "showcase for some of the best of the early Chicago folk singers."[9] By 1964 the Rising Moon was demolished and replaced by Mother Blues, another folk music club offering hootenannies every Monday night. Just down the street from Mother Blues, the Hungry Eye featured modern and progressive jazz, El Grifton offered Spanish and Cuban music, and the Earl of Old Town emerged as a popular, progressive folk tavern. Meanwhile, the Crazy Horse and the Abbey offered ragtime music and other styles indicative of the American folk tradition. By 1965 Old Town's prominent night music spots grew to include Bulls, which featured flamenco, and the Yellow Bird and Old Town Gate, which offered folk and Dixieland jazz entertainment.

As demonstrated by the proliferation of these new coffeehouses, clubs, and drinking pubs, as well as the growth of strong local institutions like the Old Town School of Folk Music, by the mid-1960s the neighborhood surrounding Wells Street and North Avenue had emerged as the entertainment hub of Chicago's politically charged folk music revival.[10] These spaces offered live performances by folkies as renowned as Bob Dylan and Joan Baez, and in keeping with this roots-oriented aesthetic, local clubs such as Earl of Old Town and Mother Blues began booking local blues artists on a semifrequent basis.

In a way, these two clubs represented two opposite ends of the American countercultural spectrum during the 1960s. While the Earl of Old Town attracted progressive academics, hippies, and other assorted characters associated with the New Left and the folk revival, Mother Blues was more of a working-class biker bar where patrons enjoyed the more amplified sounds of blues-rock bands. But if these two subcultural groups were frequently at odds with one another, they found a common joy in listening to Chicago blues players and old-timers like Muddy Waters, Otis Rush, and Junior Wells at Mother Blues.[11] Considered the "Chicago Blues Center," the bar became the first of the Old Town clubs to offer blues seven nights a week. Well-known throughout the city, Jory Graham's 1967 guidebook *Chicago: An Extraordinary Guide* describes Mother Blues as "the only place other than the South Side or West Side Negro ghettos to hear Howlin' Wolf, chief linguist of 'dirty, down-and-out' back country blues."[12] Another local guide would later describe the music performed at the club as "basic, wild, gutsy blues, served up the way it should be, with Muddy Waters on hand most of the time."[13]

As the 1960s wore on, Old Town's reputation as a hotbed of radical politics and creative mayhem grew enormously. In the final years of that decade, Old Town and the adjacent Lincoln Park (the park for which the entire neighborhood area is named) served as an arena for massive political protest and police rioting, a cacophonous mix of anti–Vietnam War demonstrations, countercultural theatrics, and extreme state-supported violence. During the 1968 Democratic National Convention, Lincoln Park provided the base of operations for Abbie Hoffman and Jerry Rubin's media-savvy Yippies, as well as the site where squads of Chicago police officers attacked middle-class leftists, working-class "greasers," and freelance militants like the New York–based Motherfuckers with billy clubs, nightsticks, and exploding tear-gas canisters, all while beat poet laureate Allen Ginsberg attempted to quell the civil unrest by chanting Eastern mantras in the park. On October 8, 1969, the Weathermen, a radical offshoot of Students for a Democratic Society (SDS), began their Four Days of Rage, an antiwar demonstration that, like the 1968 police riots, also ended in tragedy. According to the cultural sociologist Todd Gitlin:

> The two or three hundred people who showed up in Lincoln Park to "bring the war home" were almost all students and ex-students, equipped with helmets, goggles, cushioned jackets, and medical kits, armed with chains, pipes, and clubs, the men outfitted with jockstraps and cups. They had convinced

themselves, and aimed to convince everyone else, that the movement was precisely the nightmare which the police had fabricated a year before. . . . They psyched themselves up with *Battle of Algiers* war whoops and chants of "Ho Chi Minh," and to the astonishment of more than two thousand police—who must have known that the vast majority of the demonstrators of August 1968 had been peaceful until roused—they charged onto the upper crust Gold Coast, trashing cars and windows, smashing into police lines. "Within a minute or two," Shin'ya Ono wrote, "right in front of my eyes, I saw and felt the transformation of the mob into a battalion of three hundred revolutionary fighters." The police fought back in kind, shooting six of the Weather soldiers, arresting two hundred fifty (including forty on felony charges), beating most of them, sticking them with $2.3 million worth of bail bonds requiring $234,000 in cash bail. The fighters injured enough cops (seventy-five), damaged enough property, precipitated enough arrests and headlines ("SDS WOMEN FIGHT COPS," "RADICALS GO ON RAMPAGE"), and outlasted enough fear to talk themselves into a fevered sense of victory.[14]

Perhaps not surprisingly, as the neighborhood's countercultural reputation spread to Chicago's growing suburban population and beyond, tourists and traveling hippies descended upon the Wells Street area in crowds to purchase incense and psychedelic posters as well as listen to the Chicago blues music repopularized and made "safe" by Old Town's middle-class gentrifiers.[15] As a result, the owners of local entertainment venues inflated their prices to take advantage of these new consumers who craved the swirling buzz of Old Town. As Warner explains:

> A few established artistic activities—notably folk music at the Earl of Old Town and satiric revues at Second City—remained in Old Town Triangle in spite of drastic increases in land values. Those which remained were forced to charge higher prices, however. The Earl of Old Town went from charging a .50 cover charge in 1967 to charging $2.00 with a two-drink minimum in 1972; Second City admission rose from $3.00 to 4.25 in that time period.[16]

Along with rising cover charges, both residential and commercial land values increased dramatically as the 1960s wore on into the next decade.[17] As the neighborhood became more widely known to visitors, Old Town began to attract more conventional singles, and rents became too high for Old Town's less affluent residents.[18] As a result, music venues were forced to compete for a newer market of consumers: a more main-stream middle- and upper-class audience expecting the "authentic" fla-vor of a bohemian enclave, which, ironically, had been economically priced out of Old Town. Brian, a local music fan from those days, explains this shift toward greater commercialization during a barroom conversa-tion at the Green Room at Macaw's:

> Back then I used to sneak into the Earl of Old Town because I was underage, and they had great live music. There was blues, but it was mostly folk, like Arlo Guthrie, and those shows were free. Yeah, back then Old Town was a really happening place—people were wearing tie-dyes and everything . . . Then, toward the late 1960s, those places all changed. They started charging covers and got expensive.

Meanwhile, initial stages of renovation in the DePaul section of Lin-coln Park just north of Old Town began in the late 1960s and early 1970s. Following the same trajectory as Old Town, the area developed its own countercultural entertainment district as grassroots commercial ventures such as the Book Store, which sold handmade clothing pro-duced in-house, proliferated along Fullerton and Lincoln Avenues and the nearby DePaul University campus.[19] According to Warner, "often these early ventures had a certain informality and friendliness to them, a pride in the craziness of it all."[20] These commercial enterprises in-cluded experimental music clubs indicative of Old Town's 1960s counter-cultural milieu. John Barleycorn became the first of these clubs, followed by the opening of the Wise Fools Pub in 1969. By 1972 the Kingston Mines Company Store, No Exit Cafe, Alice's Revisited, and Ratso's had gained prominence among patrons attuned to Lincoln Park's bohemian nightlife. Extraordinarily eclectic and in constant flux, these cut-up es-tablishments featured a diverse array of entertainment offerings includ-ing, in addition to Chicago blues music, bluegrass, country, ragtime, pro-gressive jazz, anarchist shtick, and guerrilla theater.[21]

Although there were no clubs offering blues music exclusively, by the early 1970s Lincoln Park had reestablished itself as the prime location to hear urban blues on the city's North Side. *Serendipity City*, a guidebook to Lincoln Park, could boast of this reputation as early as 1971:

> Any Chicago blues fan knows already that what's happening now at the Wise Fools, Alice's, and the Quiet Knight is really as good as what used to happen

at Big John's, or Mother Blues, or even in a few of the South Side clubs. . . . The Wise Fools is about the hottest thing going for Chicago-style blues and other music.[22]

Like their predecessors in Old Town, these newer venues booked blues artists who had previously performed only in South Side and West Side clubs, including Howlin' Wolf, Muddy Waters, Otis Rush, and Junior Wells. In a 1972 interview for *Living Blues* magazine, Chicago harmonica player Shakey Jake compared this period to the 1950s: "Now, more Negro musicians are playing in these white clubs—like on Rush Street and Wells Street, and all over pretty near—and they've got better opportunities now than they had in those days."[23]

As land values in Lincoln Park increased steadily, the DePaul area continued to maintain its reputation as a countercultural entertainment zone by attracting young college students, musicians, artists, and hangers-on to the area. The area of Lincoln Avenue near the Fullerton intersection managed to cling to the cultural affectations of its earlier stages of gentrification by hosting inexpensive eateries, cafés, arts and crafts stores, and various left-wing political groups, including the *Seed*, an underground newspaper and the former local proxy of the New York–based Yippies.[24] Later in the decade some of the city's first post-Stonewall era gay bars, such as the Grapevine and Carol's Coming Out Pub, opened on Halsted Street just north of Fullerton.

By the mid-1970s the popularity of the blues music consumed by Lincoln Park's bohemian element in the late 1960s had begun to trickle down to some of the city's young professionals and an assortment of their suburban counterparts. As *Sweet Home Chicago*, an alternative Chicago guidebook, reported on the neighborhood's local bars in 1974: "By now, even the Lincoln Avenue and Rush Street types have begun to comprehend that Chicago is even more famous for blues than for political corruption; so they're starting to book blues bands from time to time."[25] Still, the neighborhood was in its early stages of commercial development. While land values continued to rise, the area's entertainment venues—including blues clubs like Elsewhere on Lincoln, the Kingston Mines, and the Wise Fools Pub—still failed to attract large numbers of affluent consumers. During a weeknight conversation at B.L.U.E.S., Jim, a longtime patron and employee of the nearby Kingston Mines, recalls the urban danger represented by the street-level conditions of Lincoln Avenue and the strip's relationship to the Mines at that time:

Back then the neighborhood was completely different . . . It was a real scary place. I used to have to walk down the street with an eight-inch bowie knife . . . I used to take the Red Line to Lincoln Park, and I'd be the only white guy on the street, everybody else would be black . . . Back then they had poetry and theater in the front, blues in the back . . . There were no tourists, and if any showed up, they would just turn around and walk right out . . . There used to be, maybe, twenty people there, tops, and like five or six by the end of the night . . .

As a teenager, Jack regularly snuck into Kingston Mines during the late 1970s, and he echoes Jim's recollections:

Well, it wasn't the kind of neighborhood it is today, I can tell you that much. You know all those nice row houses on the next block east of here? Well, none of those houses were here, and the street was filled with drug addicts and winos . . . It wasn't the upscale neighborhood that it is now.

Many local musicians reveled in the informality and urban authenticity suggested by the rough-and-tumble conditions of the neighborhood and continue to share their fond recollections of the subcultural lives they cultivated in neighborhood clubs like Kingston Mines and Elsewhere on Lincoln, another popular hangout. According to Darryl:

I remember in 1976, when I first started going to the first Elsewhere on Lincoln, it was very informal, you know, it was a small place—it was just a little neighborhood bar . . . It had a real folk feel to it, a kind of bohemian atmosphere where they would pass a hat around for contributions for the musicians. And there were always all these old-timers who would play there, you know, people like Homesick James, Floyd Jones . . .

Similarly, in his reporting on Kingston Mines in the *Chicago Reader* in March 1976, James Steck characterizes this "bohemian atmosphere" indicative of Lincoln Park's cultural milieu during the mid-1970s:

When I started working at the Mines there were on the staff a lawyer, a doctor, and a nurse, all trying to find themselves. I asked the nurse if she'd ever tried working stoned and she said, "Ever try working here straight?" . . . Why did we all persevere in this burning skyscraper of a club? There was the music, of course: bluegrass players nearly from Kentucky, blues players drowsing on the stage, folkies of the quality of Tom Rush down to Hank

Mush. (I heard "The Train They Call the City of New Orleans" nearly a hundred times while I cooked there.) The nurse waitress, however, gave our principal motive when she noted the "characteristic air." The Mines was an unplanned club. You couldn't foresee the package you would get, as you can, say on a Club Mediterranee tour. You couldn't foresee that the guy from an art studio down the street would show up in a white lab coat and lie on the stage, or that a motorcycle gang would try to close the place down, or that the emcee would put a Dutch apple pie in a performer's face.

Monday nights, which were supposed to be unplanned, were uncontrollable. There was an open mike, and many of the musicians were immune to ordinary audience cues. They would, for instance, take loud obscenities as affection. In addition, I don't think anyone was hired as a doorman or waitress who didn't have under his bushel a hidden lamp like imitating Elvis Presley or playing a single bongo drum. . . . The unplanned quality was no doubt what attracted us young highly-planned bourgeois trying to find ourselves. It being the Age of Aquarius, we were looking to refresh ourselves from the real world.[26]

The Gentrification of the Chicago Blues.   Drawing on the success of this cultural environment among local consumers, Rob Hecko and Bill Gilmore opened up B.L.U.E.S. on Halsted Street in April 1979. True to the cultural ecology of the neighborhood's entertainment district, the club initially offered a communal social space where local musicians and die-hard blues fans could congregate and socialize. In fact, the ritualized commercial practices of the club's management reveal the delicate balance they achieved by fostering this subcultural cohesion while simultaneously attempting to generate revenue. Over breakfast in a Lincoln Park diner, Hecko explains:

> There was no cover charge . . . and we'd pass the troll around . . . Have you ever seen the troll? David, Bill Gilmore's life-long friend, made it out of papier-mâché, so we had this troll, a blue troll with a great big tail, and a great big hole in its head that you'd walk around and gather money for the band, and that's how we'd "pass the hat." The only days we had a cover charge was Friday and Saturday, for which we had a dollar cover charge . . .

But as in Old Town, the opportunities for economic growth and profit in Lincoln Park eventually reached a tipping point, and by the 1980s the area had been infiltrated by pricey restaurants, chic boutiques, and other businesses oriented toward the young affluent set. Many of the neighborhood's countercultural enterprises folded during this time, and those that managed to stay open for business became transformed into upscale haunts for more mainstream audiences. Music clubs began to feature top local and nationally recognized performers, rather than amateur talent, and they quickly replaced their free admission policies with cover charges and drink minimums.

The entertainment district's popularity unexpectedly grew even further when Kingston Mines moved to its present location across the street from B.L.U.E.S. in the early 1980s.[27] At first, Hecko was concerned that competition from the club would drive him out of business, but today he agrees that the synergy generated by their close proximity to one another allowed B.L.U.E.S.'s business to *triple* shortly thereafter:

> The Kingston Mines wasn't making enough on Clark Street, and they proceeded to close up, and two days later Doc had bought Redford's [a local jazz club] and moved right across the street . . . which was very good for both of us, *very* good for both of us, because it was the best move he could have done, and what initially seemed like not a very good thing for us turned out to be a very good thing for us . . . It was the only place where there were really two clubs—probably, it was the only place in the city where there was music happening every night of the week, you know, especially the same *type* of music in the entire city of Chicago . . . When you're bringing so many people there, I mean, if one club would fill up, then the other club would fill up, and you would get a certain amount of people who would go back and forth between the two . . .

The spatial clustering of the two clubs transformed the Halsted Street area into an identifiable entertainment zone that successfully drew consumers away from the downtown area. In fact, Hecko singles out the development of this North Side blues corridor as a turning point for his club's growth in popularity among mainstream audiences because it helped B.L.U.E.S. generate recognition among suburbanites, international travelers, conventioneers, and local cultural authorities. On his club's continued success through the mid-1980s, Hecko recalls:

> Pretty much '84, '85—I would say it was pretty much then, 'cause that's pretty much when we starting forming the record company, which meant that we had been making too much money . . . We had started developing much more of a convention crowd . . . I think the longevity, and the

Europeans realizing we were there . . . we were developing a reputation overseas . . . the conventioneers, the tourists, the hotel concierges downtown realizing we were there . . . I think that was the big hoop to get over . . . Also, at some point in time we were getting a lot of suburbanites . . . especially on the weekends.[28]

As B.L.U.E.S. began to pull in greater numbers of affluent consumers and out-of-towners, the club gradually became transformed into a tourist attraction, and this diminished the sense of attachment that many local musicians and regulars felt toward the club. For example, Darryl's recollections suggest how this heightened commercialization dampened his impression of the club's more countercultural atmosphere:

Back in those days, B.L.U.E.S. just had more authentic bands, you know, guys who were really big in the fifties would play there like Sunnyland Slim, Smokey Smothers, Big Walter Horton, Floyd Jones, Big Leon, and I just remember the music was really great . . . Of course, the audience was basically white, because it was a North Side club, but for some reason, the crowds never seemed as shallow or loudish as they do today . . .

Then one day I came to this realization that the audiences at these clubs had changed; they were really shallow now . . . It had become a kind of culture for fraternity guys and tourists . . . At B.L.U.E.S. they had become much more concerned with maintaining a glossy image . . . Like one night I remember we found Good Rockin' Charles a few blocks away from the club, and he was really drunk and had hit his head and was just bleeding everywhere, and we realized that we had to get him inside and we wanted to call an ambulance, and so we thought we could bring him into B.L.U.E.S. and take him into the back room, and the bouncer knew us, and he gave us a really hard time and he almost didn't let us in, and it was just terrible, because Charlie's head was really bleeding badly, and the bouncer just stood there arguing with us, and after that he *finally* let us in.

Darryl links the intensified commercialization of B.L.U.E.S. to a greater set of changes affecting other blues bars in the DePaul entertainment district. Regarding Kingston Mines, Darryl remembers:

As I recall, Kingston Mines used to be a really seedy place, you know . . . it was an after-hours hangout for local musicians, and prostitutes would hang out there late at night; there were rumors that the management was selling drugs . . . But now, the Mines has turned into a big operation, and the staff all have headsets, and the place is packed with lots of tourists . . .

Darryl's recollections suggest that shifts in the cultural commerce of the area not only had consequences for the social worlds within these blues clubs, but the meanings that local participants attached to these places. This transformation seems most pronounced for survivors like Darryl who regret the current mainstream popularity of Lincoln Park and its deleterious effect on the area's subcultural milieu.

Interestingly, neighborhood bohemians had been mourning this sense of loss since at least the mid-1970s. According to Steck:

> The Mines was a fairly authentic bohemian club then, but about subsequent clientele Iberus Hacker, the preacher turned folk singer, was prophetic. He said, "Old Town was sold out, New Town lasted six months, and now Lincoln Avenue is starting to go." What he meant was that bohemians were dying. . . . The sinking feeling, the loose gravel underfoot, that preceded the fall of the bohemians was the emergence of the hipeoisie. I must take a minute to explain who the hipeoisie are. Cheerful beaded people on bare mattresses are hip, worried people on quilted four-posters are bourgeoisie, and smirking people on $200 mahogany-paneled waterbeds are hipeoisie. People whose apartments are stuffed with boutique-bought trinkets to stare at when you're wasted, man, on Venezuelan hashish are also hipeoisie. In their music clubs, the hipeoisie wanted managers with pre-faded jeans, fake green coloring on Irish coffees, and musicians who claimed their music would help you get laid. Half of Lincoln Avenue was going in this direction, and the culmination of the threat of the Mines was the rumor that the owner of Ratso's wanted to buy it out and set up a more commercial, rhinestone-studded cabaret.[29]

In both the Old Town and DePaul areas of Lincoln Park, business entrepreneurs developed entertainment zones where musicians and die-hard blues fans could build nocturnal worlds for themselves. These commercial districts remain emblazoned in their memories as deeply authentic, in part because they nostalgically remember them—idealistically or otherwise—as bulwarks of community solidarity and bohemian creativity, all while surrounded by the romantic lure of urban danger.[30] But eventually their favorite clubs were transformed along with their enveloping entertainment zones, and the reputations of these places increased among suburbanites and foreign travelers while consequently diminishing among local scene-makers. Indeed, Lincoln Park blues clubs began losing their authentic cache among bohemians *because* their commercial popularity among mainstream consumers began to soar.

Authenticity and the Racial Politics of Urban Space.

Even as blues gained popularity in Lincoln Park during the 1960s, musicians continued to perform in local theaters and bars in the city's black ghetto neighborhoods. In their never-ending search for authenticity, small numbers of die-hard white blues fans frequented clubs like Theresa's Tavern, Pepper's Lounge, and the Blue Flame during that decade. Nick Gravenites describes how fans like himself traveled all over the city during the mid-1960s in search of musicians who might be "blue enough" for their tastes:

> I spent most of my waking hours listening to blues, talking blues, hanging with bluespeople in bluesbars, going from one blues scene to another, reeferin', pillin' and drinkin', partying and jamming my way to blues oblivion. I remember sitting with friends on bleak, hungover afternoons, trying to figure out what blues band to hear that night, who could it be that could possibly excite us, be blue enough to reach us, to get us up and out and alive again. Should we go see Walter? No, we saw Walter two nights ago. How about the Wolf at Silvio's? No, he's coming to Big John's tomorrow. How about Muddy at Pepper's? No, it's always Muddy, lots of Muddy. Detroit Junior on South State? Junior Wells or Earl Hooker at Theresa's? Magic Sam on Sixty-third Street? Cotton on Cottage Groove? Smokey Smothers at the Blue Flame? Otis Rush on the West Side? Maxwell Street sidewalk blues?[31]

Gravenites's romantic portrait of the period reveals the extent to which Old Towners continued to patronize South and West Side blues clubs even after taverns located in more accessible North Side neighborhoods began hiring local bands away from those venues. During the 1970s Lincoln Park's community of die-hard blues fans continued to frequent clubs in the city's black neighborhoods: in Englewood, Florence's; in Greater Grand Crossing, the Sweet Queen Bee Lounge; in Washington Park, the Burning Spear; on the Near South Side, Pepper's Lounge; and in Grand Boulevard, Theresa's Tavern, Turner's Blue Lounge, and, of course, the Checkerboard Lounge. In large part, the popularity of these clubs among North Siders can be explained by the critical acclaim of their talent pool: indeed, such clubs frequently booked artists as renowned as Junior Wells, Big Walter Horton, Otis Clay, Tyrone Davis, Sunnyland Slim, David "Honeyboy" Edwards, J.B. Hutto, James Cotton, Lefty Dizz, Hound Dog Taylor, Carey Bell, L.V. Banks, Son Seals, and Howlin' Wolf. Also, the convenient proximity of many of these clubs to the Loop as well as Hyde Park's University of Chicago community likely served as a pull factor for many slumming white artists, graduate students, and self-proclaimed progressives and hipsters.

But more importantly, clubs located in the Black Belt offered bohemian music fans access to what they regarded as a community-based and exotic populist culture to compensate for their increased disenchantment with Old Town. Not surprisingly, city guidebooks published in the late 1960s and early 1970s evoked common racial stereotypes to depict these clubs as decidedly more authentic than their North Side counterparts. In the aforementioned *Chicago: An Extraordinary Guide*, author Jory Graham celebrates the history of the black migration to Chicago's ghettos, where the blues articulated "hard, driving sounds of inner-city pressures"; she argues that this tradition continues in surviving clubs on the contemporary South Side, where "soul—the raw emotion, the pain of being black—is not withheld." Graham relies on arcane, pseudo-anthropological notions of racial difference to promote such clubs: "Since 'soul' is the one inalienable possession of the Negro, the one thing whites may comprehend but never possess, it's perfectly natural that the places to hear the blues nightly are in the Negro ghettos of the city."[32]

Like Graham, *Living Blues* magazine editor and local critic Jim O'Neal relies on stereotypical characterizations of blackness to promote the relative authenticity of the Black Belt in comparison to Lincoln Park's blues clubs. In his 1973 *Chicago Reader* review of the city's blues clubs, O'Neal writes:

Most of Chicago's live blues activity is concentrated in black neighborhoods on the South Side between 39th and 79th Streets and on the West Side not far from either Roosevelt Road or Madison Street. A few North Side coffeehouses, cafes and clubs frequently book blues acts as well, and these are the places that seem to get all the newspaper publicity. Several North Side spots such as the Wise Fools Pub, the Attic and Ratso's sponsor regular blues nights, featuring either bands or solo artists. Such places have provided a valuable service in bringing blues to white audiences either too young, too unaware or too afraid to go to the South and West Side clubs.

. . . [But] really, nothing can compare with a night of blues in a real blues club. The atmosphere, the crowd, the way the band sounds, everything is just—bluesier. At most South and West Side blues lounges, the door charge (if there is one) is $1.00; I.D.'s are checked irregularly. Beer is usually 75¢ a bottle. Big Duke's two clubs, Pepper's and others serve ribs, chicken, and other soul food from their own kitchens as well. The accommodations aren't deluxe, and the washrooms may be smelly, but it doesn't matter. . . . The dancing, drinking, talking and laughing of the crowds may be loud in comparison to the polite attention and applause the artists receive on the North Side, but the music is loud too. And funky.[33]

O'Neal privileges the experience of visiting a "real" South Side or West Side blues club for its "soul food," cheap beer, "funky" music, and "bluesier" authenticity. Indeed, although he claims otherwise, the fact that at such clubs the "accommodations aren't deluxe, and the washrooms may be smelly" *does* matter to North Siders who regard such things as the true markers of urban authenticity. O'Neal's consequent reviews for the *Reader* reveal a similar racially tinged bias even in his defense of *North* Side blues bars:

There are more reasons for hearing blues in a black tavern than just the quality of the music. For one, the natural ambience of the crowds adds a dimension to the blues experience that's missing in more formal settings. . . . The North Side clubs have brought a lot of blues to audiences who never would have heard it otherwise, and the bands earn more up north than at most black taverns; however, it came as quite a shock to read—in a guidebook to black America, no less—that the hottest, most authentic blues spot in Chicago was the Wise Fools. Certainly the Fools offers lots of good blues, but if you have the urge for a little authentic blues atmosphere on the North Side, try a black bar in Uptown, like Otis' Playroom.[34]

Throughout the 1970s other mainstream publications would characterize these racial and spatial distinctions in equally essentialist ways. In an article for the *Chicago Tribune* in 1976, local journalist Herb Nolan writes:

In recent years blues have become popular entertainment on the North Side, especially along Lincoln Avenue, notably at the Wise Fools Pub, Kingston

Mines, and Elsewhere on Lincoln; but the distance between the music on Lincoln Avenue and experiencing it at, say, the Checker Board Lounge on East 43rd Street is far greater than the number of blocks separating them.[35]

But except for the same small group of die-hard blues fans, musicians, and their bohemian counterparts who split their evenings between North Side and South Side venues, this "distance" and the fear it generated—particularly in light of conventional if exaggerated assumptions regarding the safety of the city's black neighborhoods—discouraged potential white audiences from trekking down to bars like the Checkerboard. As a reaction to these apprehensions, critics in the local alternative press wisely tried to disabuse their most timid readers of their suspicions regarding the safety of these areas of the city. A review of O'Neal's writing for the *Reader* throughout the 1970s provides several cases in point. For example, in a September 1974 article, he reminds his readers: "It is not necessary to carry shotguns or machetes with you when you go into a black neighborhood; you do not need to travel by armored car; a white face does not single you out for snipers' target practice; there is no blues bar called 'The Bucket of Blood.' "[36] In his same column the next year, he writes:

And it's sad that more people from outside the neighborhoods don't get to hear the many fine blues musicians this city has. The perennial question asked by those who might like to hear a blues band on 43rd Street or Roosevelt Road is, "Is it safe? I heard . . ." And unfortunately the answers probably come from someone who's never been on 43rd Street unless he got off the Dan Ryan at the wrong exit—"You're not serious, are you?" or "Sure it's safe—if you take a machine gun and a battalion of Marines with you." A few years ago I tried to interest the Chicago *Tribune* in an article on Theresa's Lounge at 48th and Indiana. No, was the department editor's reply, he wouldn't want to lead readers astray by even suggesting that they venture into "that neighborhood." Civilization, however, does not cease to exist outside of Lincoln Park, Hyde Park, the suburbs, and the Tribune Building.[37]

But while writers like O'Neal attempted to quell the fears of their readers, other cultural critics and promoters actually *drew* on these anxieties as a means of heightening the thrill of entering racially segregated neighborhoods in the city. Guidebooks aimed at the countercultural market frequently exoticized the Black Belt as a dark, dangerous place where only the most daring and adventurous of middle-class whites might venture. For example, the 1974 edition of *Sweet Home Chicago: The Real City Guide*—a book described in a later guide as "a hip, savvy, politicized guide, mostly for young people who still live, or still remember, the counter-culture and the underground" with "a heavy focus on community activities and alternative life styles"—wholeheartedly promotes evening trips to the South Side *on the basis* of its perceived risks.[38] Its authors remark:

> Contrary to the impression fostered by most Chicago media, there is good live music to be heard all across the city, not just in the "nightlife" districts of Old Town, New Town, Lincoln Avenue and Rush Street. In fact, it's usually more rewarding to venture to the South Side for blues and jazz. . . . The neighborhood bars tend to be more modest, of course, and often more rough and tumble: but I've usually found that getting there, and staying in one piece once you've gotten there, is often half the fun.[39]

Throughout the volume, the authors incorporate fantasies of risk and danger into an overall promotion of the authenticity of the social worlds surrounding these clubs. By depicting a trip to Chicago's South Side as an adventure through the dark underworld of the nocturnal metropolis, these writers rely on the same tactics of "extreme" tourism marketing that send affluent Westerners to formerly war-ravaged cities in Vietnam and Cambodia, and underage sex palaces in Bangkok.[40] Of course, this strategy of associating authenticity with stereotypical images of race and urban danger also parallels the attempts by neighborhood survivors like Jim and Jack to glamorize 1970s Lincoln Park as a "real scary place" where clubbers "used to have to walk down the street with an eight-inch bowie knife" for protection against "drug addicts and winos."

The Decline of the Blues in Black Metropolis. Despite attempts by the city's alternative media to promote South Side and West Side blues clubs as more authentic than their more mainstream counterparts, such venues would eventually lose their dominance as Chicago's premier blues venues. In large part, this shift can be explained by the growing popularity and accessibility of blues establishments in neighborhoods like Old Town and DePaul in Lincoln Park. As the number of clubs increased in North Side areas of the city during the 1970s and 1980s, they provided convenient alternatives for die-hard blues fans; and as such clubs gained in popularity, they began paying local musicians more money, which attracted the city's most celebrated performers away from less lucrative gigs in the Black Belt.

Meanwhile, during this same period the urban communities where blues clubs had once thrived, including Grand Boulevard, Englewood, and Washington Park, all experienced decreases in population, employment, and real income.[41] These neighborhood changes were related to larger socioeconomic forces that facilitated the decay of several of Chicago's black working-class communities, including the wholesale disappearance of blue-collar jobs across the Midwest, which employed and paid reliable wages to a significant proportion of inner-city residents in those neighborhoods. Since the 1960s, structural changes in the national and local economy have initiated a decrease in opportunities for industrial work among the residents of these areas: for example, Chicago lost 326,000, or 60 percent, of its manufacturing jobs between 1967 and 1987. The relocation of manufacturing industries to suburban areas (as well as abroad), along with the recent institutional and economic divestment, continued residential segregation, and depopulation of Chicago's inner-city neighborhoods all contributed to drastic increases in concentrated joblessness, poverty, and community instability in Black Metropolis during the past thirty years.[42]

As these neighborhoods fell into decline, it became increasingly difficult for their blues taverns to remain in operation, and today those clubs that have not already closed down face severe difficulties attracting enough customers to support the booking of a band. For instance, while the Cuddle Inn remains open to serve whiskey and cheap beer to a dwindling group of local residents, its deteriorating walls, lack of live entertainment, and large supply of empty bar stools on a Friday night attest to the decline of a once-prosperous blues culture on the South Side.[43]

Still, clubs continued to offer blues and soul music on a regular basis in black neighborhoods on the city's West Side and South Side throughout the 1990s: in Austin, the 5105 Club and Mr. Lee's Chateau; in McKinley Park, Red's; in Calumet Heights, the Dating Game; in Greater Grand Crossing, Lee's Unleaded Blues and Moonlight; in West Pullman, Nightlife; in Roseland, the Easy Living Lounge; and of course, in Grand Boulevard, the Checkerboard Lounge. These clubs serve as a launching pad for up-and-coming talent and, somewhat ironically, provide an available source of low-paying jobs to *white* blues musicians unable to procure gigs in the city's more upscale downtown clubs on account of their race. At the 5105 Club Daniel used to perform with Tail Dragger on a weekly basis, while old-timers like Dave Myers always offer young white lions advice on their guitar playing during jam sessions at the Checkerboard.

But while clubs in these neighborhoods once hosted artists as renowned as Junior Wells, Big Walter Horton, James Cotton, and Howlin' Wolf, these venues now have a very difficult time attracting big-name talent. In fact, many of the city's local blues artists *only* perform at clubs located in Lincoln Park and elsewhere on the North Side. According to Dustin, a survivor and guitar player, the South Side and West Side clubs pay very little, if at all. While he would actually prefer to play at such venues, the wage differential forces him to perform at North Side clubs exclusively: "If we can't get at least seventy dollars a guy for a gig, at this point it's not really worth our while."[44] According to Ed Williams, a local bandleader:

> On the West Side, it's very difficult. Not like the North Side: that's easy and smooth. For one thing there's no money on the West Side and for another the proprietors don't provide any of the advantages you get in the North Side clubs. No free drinks, nothing like that.[45]

As I suggested in an earlier chapter, musicians attempting to eke out a career in entertainment generally tend to abandon the quest for symbolic authenticity in order to pursue more material ends, such as lucrative wages and the availability of amenities like complimentary food and drinks. According to Louis, the comforts of a well-endowed club far outweigh the pleasures of playing exclusively for audiences from a particular neighborhood: "If you're playing in a club that's comfortable, with a really good sound system, monitors, there's a dressing room backstage, then those kinds of places are the most enjoyable for me . . . As far as the audiences, it doesn't matter if they are from the suburbs or the inner city."

And so an unintended consequence of the increased success of the North Side clubs during the 1970s and 1980s was the wholesale abandonment of the South Side by local musicians as well as patrons. The marketability of blues in up-and-coming neighborhoods like Lincoln Park made their clubs attractive to the city's top musicians and local bandleaders, and this pull drained the Black Belt of its most prominent performers. In short time, most of the die-hard fans and tourists followed, leaving many of Chicago's blues clubs isolated from the commercial networks that direct the city's flow of valued entertainers and affluent audiences.

Still, as I argue in chapter 1, the Checkerboard Lounge continues to succeed as a tourist attraction and magnet for local talent, drawing conventioneers and their post-adolescent counterparts to its dank fixtures and dilapidated stage. Likewise, a handful of South Side clubs continue to attract a sizable and vibrant pool of local residents. In the area of Greater Grand Crossing, regulars at Lee's Unleaded Blues enjoy the pleasures of lively companionship engendered by the club's popularity among neighborhood residents. In the small yet festive interior of the club, overhead lights cast a red glow over the room and its leatherbound bar stools, brown carpeted walls, and wooded bar decorated with red tinsel and a photograph of Harold Washington, the former black mayor of Chicago. Meanwhile, Junkyard Dog, the house singer, leans on his crutches as he belts out a repertoire of rhythm-and-blues standards like "Fever" and "Money (That's What I Want)" to lively and appreciative crowds on the weekends. On one occasion a young black woman visiting from Mississippi, where she sings in her church choir, parades across the club with a microphone to shower the audience with a lively rendition of Albert King's "Feel Like Breaking Up Somebody's Home," and after she finishes her song, strangers run up to offer hugs and money for her efforts.

Due to its increased visibility in the local press, Lee's Unleaded Blues has begun to attract more and more neighborhood outsiders in recent years, audiences for whom the Checkerboard no longer fulfills its promise as a bastion of symbolic authenticity. But ironically, clubs like Lee's Unleaded Blues that have managed to persist in spite of surrounding ghetto conditions are increasingly finding themselves on the chopping block by the city itself. In the name of "urban renewal" and economic development, the city recently shut down the famous Geri's Palm Tavern to make way for what some hope will be a new blues-oriented entertainment zone made up of gentrified tourist attractions along Forty-seventh Street.

Also on the chopping block for the past few years has been the glorious Maxwell Street Market, a recently retired open-street bazaar in what used to be Chicago's old Jewish neighborhood, where blues musicians in the 1940s would plug their electric guitars into portable generators and perform the blues alongside Hasidic merchants selling everything from kosher chickens to used vacuum cleaners. Sadly, the city, along with the nearby University of Illinois at Chicago, shut down the long-standing market in 1994 and in recent years began bulldozing over the very concrete where great blues legends once played. According to Steve Balkin of the Maxwell Street Historic Preservation Coalition, after razing the entire area (including the Heritage Blues Bus Music shop, the Juketown Community Bandstand, and the Blues Wall of Fame), the university and the city plan on replacing this once-thriving street market with college dormitories, retail stores, and high-priced condominiums. But of course, with a touch of bitter irony, the university does have plans to erect a series of old facades from a handful of demolished buildings on the exterior of an on-site parking garage to commemorate the rich history of the area, in a city where the icons of an authentic past trump all surviving terrains of urban cultural life—icons so irresistibly charming they almost seem invented from scratch, a point that, while not entirely true, is not exactly false, either.

The Blues Capital of the World. Although the moniker seems fitting and commonsense enough to contemporary mainstream consumers, Chicago's self-identification as America's so-called "Home of the Blues" or "Blues Capital of the World" is actually a relatively recent invention. While musicians have performed the blues in Chicago's Bronzeville district since the 1920s, it was not until such artists began playing in up-and-coming North Side entertainment zones in the late 1960s and early 1970s that local boosters chose to incorporate its blues legacy into the city's overall presentation of self.[46] In fact, travel guides published during the 1950s—supposedly the heyday of the city's thriving blues culture—hardly even acknowledge the presence of Chicago's black residents at all, much less the blues clubs in their neighborhoods. Indeed, the depictions of black working- and middle-class culture in Chicago that *are* presented in local guidebooks published during that time seem shockingly racist by contemporary standards. For instance, in his 1953 guidebook *Chicago the Pagan*, Weimar Port writes:

47th and South Parkway, the 42nd and Broadway of the colored district. Here Negroes are in their heyday. They chatter, laugh loudly, look at all that is happening, and strut in gay clothes. They love life. They keep enuf of Africa's superstitions to serve as a bulwark against Chicago's woes of living. Down the street a negress laughs in repeated high musical tones like a mocking bird and is to be envied for her lustiness. The Negro has votes, aldermen . . . he has newspapers and magazines; he has big bands and orchestras, jazz steppers and blues singers . . .

Politically the Negroes rule the Democratic party and without finesse, kick the lily-faced politicians around. Unfortunately Negroes vote as Negroes rather than as unprejudiced Americans. It would be better if they split their votes between the parties but Negro politicians are wilier than their white counterparts.

Postscript: Maxwell Street area has been invaded by Negro residents; night bazaars are no longer. Only the daytime buzz is to be seen and heard.[47]

In his depiction of the city's black life, Port describes the Black Belt as an exotic place where "negress" sirens promise decadence, and yet while the text romanticizes the alleged "underworld" of the city's ghetto life as a slice of authentic local color, it hardly embraces this image of the city as a glorification of Chicago's ethnic identity, much less a tourist attraction. Thus, he bemoans the presence of black culture on Maxwell Street as an invasion, rather than a cultural celebration that tourists might be encouraged to experience firsthand. Port's depiction mirrors similar 1950s characterizations of Chicago's black residents. Jack Lait and Lee Mortimer's *Chicago Confidential*—a 1950 guide described by its authors as "a cheeky, impudent, uncensored, shocking account of the fast, fabulous, fascinating city"—offers the following in a chapter on Bronzeville entitled "Black Paradise":

> Purse-snatching takes place almost by the minute. Whoring in every phase and form is prevalent. Mugging (attacking a victim from behind by strangling with a bent arm about the neck) is a typical form of robbery, executed by women as well as men. Crimes are so customary that there is no attempt at concealment and they are pulled off without embarrassment before the eyes of passing throngs. . . . It is not the purpose here to impugn or condone. But those who knew these neighborhoods twenty years ago are appalled at the change. Filth and overcrowding, a general spirit of roughhouse, a superfluity of saloons and pool-halls and dance-halls, garbage in the streets and in the alleys, the unmistakable odor of marijuana, are surface indications of the terrific transformation. When you venture beyond these you find dingy dens, depraved homosexual exhibitionism, lumber-camp licentiousness, drunkenness, dope, and every sinister sign of virtually uncontrolled abandon. . . . On 47th Street you can buy anything: reefers, "hard" dope, policy slips, guns, brass knuckles, knockout drops, trick knives, and women. In Harlem the price of a good-looking high-yaller is now $20. Older and darker ones wouldn't spit at you for less than $10. But in Bronzeville they solicit you for $2.[48]

In stark contrast to these maligned representations of the city's Black Metropolis, local newspapers and guidebooks began to incorporate Chicago's blues legacy into their affirmative depictions of the city in the late 1960s and early 1970s, just as blues clubs on the North Side began growing in popularity among white audiences. The following passage, taken from a 1972 issue of the *Chicago Reader*, perfectly exemplifies this new characterization of the Chicago blues:

> Ever since the first blues 78's were recorded in the early 1920s, Chicago has been a major center of blues activity. A number of excellent blues artists worked out of Chicago in the '20s, '30s, and '40s, but the city really established its musical dominance after World War II, when mass black migrations brought with them the earthy blues traditions of Mississippi, Arkansas, Tennessee and other southern states. Boasting artists such as Muddy Waters, Howlin' Wolf, Elmore James, Jimmy Reed, Little Walter and Sonny Boy Williamson, and successful independent record companies like Chess, Vee-Jay and J.O.B., Chicago was the undisputed blues capital of the world—and it still is. . . . [O]nly Chicago has been able to support any kind of substantial blues scene over the years, and there's no better place in the world for blues.[49]

Chicago newspapers published after the 1960s commonly draw on historical accounts of the city's blues legacy. With regard to newspapers in particular, music critics and other cultural authorities rely on its popularity because it increases their professional value and cultural influence; editors use its salience to fill column inches on slow weeks; press owners rely on its sexiness to sell daily newspapers. And in the long run, the marketing of any popular form of entertainment in the city not only encourages cultural consumption and local tourism, but can also help stimulate commercial activity and residential population growth, all of which can eventually lead to increased circulation rates, advertising revenues, and larger readerships. For this reason, civic boosters and print media often promote their city's cultural heritage when it serves to support currently viable commercial enterprises.[50]

These kinds of historical legacies gain traction, or "stickiness," in the public imagination as memorable stories when they are appropriated by trusted messengers and diffused throughout the body politic in compelling, if somewhat misleading, ways.[51] The preceding passage from the *Reader* appropriates a four-part narrative structure common to such accounts. First, it begins with an introductory *assumption of authenticity* suggesting that Chicago has been "a major center of blues activity" for most of the century. Next, the passage attempts to portray the 1950s as a *legendary reality*, a historically reasonable, yet unusually glorified, age of supposed authenticity when blues legends like Muddy Waters and Howlin' Wolf made the city "the undisputed blues capital of the world." Then, in an attempt to surround this claim with an *aura of inevitability*, this blues legacy is linked to the postwar black migration, hearkening back to the "earthy blues traditions" of the authentic rural South. Finally, it concludes by evoking a *myth of continuity* as a rhetorical device, an assertion that the success of contemporary blues clubs in Chicago thrives as an everlasting survival from the past, rather than the commercialized revival of a cultural heritage ignored by the city's cultural elite until the late 1960s.

These same rhetorical strategies operate in later newspaper reports of the local blues scene. According to a 1976 article that appeared in the *Chicago Tribune*:

> Of the major northern industrial centers, Chicago was one of the most accessible—thanks to the Illinois Central Gulf Railroad; and as blacks migrated from the Mississippi Delta they brought with them a rural music that would be nurtured here and evolve into the urban blues found in Chicago today. At first the blues were played at house parties, in alleys, in whisky joints, and later in clubs. . . . During the 1950s blues in Chicago boomed. People like Little Walter, Jimmy Reed, Sonny Boy Williamson, Howlin' Wolf, James Cotton, Otis Rush, Junior Wells, and Muddy Waters were on their way to becoming legends. Although its commercial popularity faded, the music didn't . . . with the (current) vast blues activity surging through the city, it could go on for the next 200 years.[52]

Not surprisingly, local presses oriented toward the city's black community commonly evoke these same types of heritage-based narratives, as demonstrated by an article published in the nationally renowned *Chicago Defender* in the mid-1990s:

> During the great migration northward, African Americans brought their idioms with them and Chess Records later documented the many blues singers and instrumentalists, enabling Chicago to become a center for the blues. And tonight, Bossman Productions is presenting A Chicago Blues Blowout at 7 P.M. at Mr. Ricky's Note. . . . In the early years of development of the blues, they became the outcry and expressed joys of those who were not Christians. People who were serious members of the church wouldn't have anything to

do with blues people. During the decades of the late '40s through the '60s, however, there developed the urban blues styles and it flourished, particularly in Chicago. When the blues are performed at Mr. Ricky's, it promises to be a social travelogue in music of the African American experience in the big city.[53]

By employing a narrative of the past as a means of representing the present, these rhetorical strategies serve the purpose of attracting tourists in search of an authentic Chicago adventure, and, for this reason, celebrations of the city's blues legacy in recent Chicago travel guides have become quite commonplace as well.[54] Consider the introductory passage from *The Best of Chicago*, a guidebook that pays homage to Chicago's legendary reality as it connects that heritage to the contemporary blues scene:

> In the early part of this century, as the steel mills of Gary and Hammond and East Chicago began smoking in earnest, Chicago began to attract its now-majority black population, many from the Mississippi Delta. It's a community that has contributed greatly to the city's special flavor . . . and the creation of the urban electric blues by Muddy, Little Walter . . . music that provided rock 'n roll with its heartbeat. . . . And the blues is still alive and well in Chicago.[55]

Of course, as exemplified by *Sweet Home Chicago: The Real City Guide*, this appropriation of the city's blues legacy among local travel guidebooks continued into the 1990s:

> As jazz flourished and faded on "The Stroll," blues pianists came into their own at the South Side rent parties—Pine Top Smith, who popularized the term *boogie woogie*, Little Brother Montgomery, and the legendary, indestructible Sunnyland Slim. Then came the bluesmen, scuffling for small change in the once colorful but now doomed Maxwell Street Market. Then they took over the South and later the West Side taverns, and here the moody, introspective rural sound became brash and urban—the classic Chicago Style with harmonica, electric guitars, drum set, and a loud driving beat. Chicago blues and the recording companies were inextricably connected, from Paramount in the 1920s to Chess in the 1950s and now to Alligator, whose set Living Chicago Blues is a good primer. The history-making men have been legion: Big Bill Broonzy, the Sonny Boy Williamsons I and

II, Little Walter, Willie Dixon, Magic Sam, Buddy Guy, Junior Wells, and the star names of Howlin' Wolf and Muddy Waters.

. . . Chicago blues is now big and international. . . . The atmosphere varies from club to club, but the artists are great and tend to do a circuit. There is no end of talent: Billy Branch, Son Seals, the Kinsey Report, Willie Kent, Magic Slim, Otis Clay, Lonnie Brooks, Dion Payton, Koko Taylor, Sugar Blue, Valerie Wellington, and lots more.[56]

Inventing the Chicago Blues.   As I have suggested in earlier chapters, traditions and legacies are always the product of narrative manipulation and are therefore ideological arguments about history, rather than unmediated historical facts.[57] But in spite of this, Chicago's claim to its blues legacy must seem remarkably credible even to the most skeptical of readers. After all, many of the twentieth century's most celebrated blues and jazz figures resided, performed, and recorded in the city, including Louis Armstrong, Jelly Roll Morton, Muddy Waters, Howlin' Wolf, Sonny Boy Williamson, Jimmy Rogers, Junior Wells, Bo Diddley, Jimmy Reed, Willie Dixon, and countless others.[58] In fact, cultural entrepreneurs have been able to draw on the biographies of these artists to make all sorts of convincing claims regarding the inevitability of the city's cultural status.[59] How can the ideological retention of Chicago's blues legacy be explained?

As suggested above, one strategy employed by local boosters relies on the assumption that southern blacks who migrated to Chicago from the Mississippi Delta region at the turn of the century and through the postwar era simply brought their blues traditions with them. The years immediately following 1890 began what would be a tremendous northern exodus of rural sharecroppers in search of higher-paying work and improved lives. Chicago was a principal destination of the Great Migration, due in large part to its prominence at the head of two major southern railroad lines, its dominant steel and meat-packing industries, and an established black community. Traveling on the Illinois Central Railroad's route from New Orleans to Chicago throughout the first half of the century, the vast number of black migrants from the east south-central states (Mississippi, Alabama, Kentucky, and Tennessee) settled in the northern Midwest states of Illinois, Michigan, Ohio, Indiana, and Wisconsin; of these migrants, many chose to seek their fortunes in Chicago.[60] Between 1890 and 1915, Chicago's black population increased from less than fifteen thousand to over fifty thousand; and between 1915 and 1920, this new population more than doubled.[61]

The black population in Chicago would increase even further in subsequent decades. During the 1930s widespread unemployment in the southern states due to the depression brought blacks to the North in search of work. Later, the largest influx of southern blacks to Chicago and other industrial urban centers would come in the 1940s, when labor shortages during World War II pulled migrants northbound in droves.[62]

Since these migratory movements suggest a set of strong social and demographic links between the Mississippi Delta and the city of Chicago, local boosters frequently draw on the Great Migration as a means of heightening the aura of inevitability surrounding the city's blues legacy. According to a recent report from the *Defender*:

> Blues have been a part of the Chicago community since the first part of the 20th century, when African Americans migrated to Chicago searching for a new lease on life and freedom from the oppression, hatred and prejudices experienced throughout the South. As they changed their depraved conditions in the South, they brought with them the melodies and wisdom which is called the blues.[63]

Likewise, according to the same *Chicago Tribune* article reviewed above:

> There are other cities like San Francisco and St. Louis where the blues thrive, but nothing compares with Chicago. . . . Why Chicago? "In a nutshell, it's simply that a lot of black people came here from Mississippi, the center of blues in the South, and they brought the music with them," says Bob Koester, owner of Delmark Records, as well as the two Jazz Record Mart Stores. . . . [64]

Rhetorically, the migration hypothesis works so well because it elevates Chicago's prominence as the "Blues Capital of the World" to a level of inevitability, as if its reputation were the consequence of historical destiny instead of the efforts of cultural entrepreneurs and local boosters.[65] However, relying on the Great Migration to accurately explain Chicago's blues legacy presents a number of problems. First, it reduces blues music from a complex artistic form to some kind of cultural baggage "naturally" possessed by *all* black migrants, instead of musicians and songsters in particular. In other words, Koester's assertion that black migrants "brought the music with them" suggests that the blues, like idiomatic speech, represents a common "folk" culture in which all stereotypically "countrified" blacks not only could, but actually *did* engage, regardless of trade, talent, or temperament. This explanation relies on a vulgar reflection theory of culture that suggests that social and psychological conditions alone produce cultural expression independently of any institutions of cultural production, whether commercial, ideological, professional, or otherwise—to say nothing of human agency, imagination, and creativity.[66] In their discussions of the blues, musicologists frequently employ this kind of old-fashioned reasoning, as exemplified by the introduction to Paul Oliver's classic study *Blues Fell This Morning*:

> Yet the apparent fact remains that only the American black whether purple-black or so light-skinned as to be indistinguishable from his sun-tanned white neighbor, can sing the blues. If there is a conclusion to be drawn from this it is that the blues has grown with the development of black society on American soil; that it has evolved from the peculiar dilemma of a particular group, isolated by skin pigmentation or that of its ancestors, which was required to conform to a society and yet refused its full integration within it. This enforced partial isolation produced, in spite of black desires to be accepted on wholly equal terms within the social pattern of American life, a certain cultural separation which bore fruit in, amongst other things, the blues.[67]

Later in the same introduction, Oliver writes:

> In the blues were reflected the effects of the economic stress on the depleted plantations and the urban centres, where conditions of living still did not improve. In the blues were to be found the major catastrophes both personal and national, the triumphs and miseries that were shared by all, yet private to one. In the blues were reflected the family disputes, the violence and bitterness, the tears and the upheavals caused by poverty and migration.[68]

Needless to say, while the blues certainly emerged in a context of rural poverty and racial oppression, it is nevertheless the case that, as blues critic and historian Francis Davis reminds us, the early blues pioneers were very protective of their status as musicians and certainly "wouldn't have taken kindly to the implication that any black field hand with a guitar could have sung the blues," as the migration hypothesis (and Oliver's rhetoric) seems to suggest.[69]

In addition, such a hypothesis assumes that musicians in the Delta labored at their craft in a cultural vacuum outside of a multicultural and technologically sophisticated society. The preceding passages suggest that southern blacks introduced "their" country-blues to the North, when in fact rural musicians developed their musical styles in part by listening to live and studio recordings produced in Chicago and other cities. In the 1920s urban vaudeville performers like Bessie Smith and Ma Rainey were highly influential among rural blues artists in the southern states, and vice versa.[70] Likewise, plenty of blues musicians from the South traveled back and forth between Chicago and the Delta to record, and musicians in both regions listened to each other's styles of performances on radio shows transmitted across state and regional boundaries.[71] To suggest that Chicago owes its blues legacy to the migration process itself ignores the presence of long-standing cultural exchanges between the city and the Mississippi countryside—to say nothing of the fact that similar conversations and collaborations also took place between the South and a host of other cities that, like Chicago, could (and, in many cases, do) incorporate their *own* blues legacies into their overall presentations of self, including New York, St. Louis, Kansas City, Memphis, Atlanta, Los Angeles, Detroit, San Antonio, and Dallas.[72]

But in addition to the migration hypothesis, local boosters also rely on the mythical power of the city's so-called "essence" in their attempts to explain the persistence of the city's blues legacy. In the case of Chicago, the imagery suggested by its blues clubs mirrors the city's most idealized characterizations, or what one could think of as its *landscape of authenticity*. Indeed, one cross section of its accumulated iconography— Al Capone, the Union Stockyards, frigid winters, political corruption— naturalizes the so-called essence of Chicago as a cold, industrial metropolis of crime and danger, the gangster-ridden "Crime Capital" of days past.[73] As exemplified in the introductory text of *Going to Chicago: A Year on the Chicago Blues Scene*, a popular coffee-table souvenir book sold at many of the bookshops in Chicago's downtown tourism district, Chicago's blues legacy blends smoothly into this mythical landscape:

> Bruce Iglauer, president of Alligator Records, calls Chicago Blues, "the toughest, hardest, rawest form of electric Blues. Partly because it grew out of the toughest, rawest form of acoustic Blues which was being played in the Delta, and partly because Chicago is very hard-edged, very unrelaxed, a very loud city where you've got to play hard-edged, unrelaxed, loud music to fight it. Chicago Blues is the music of an industrial city, and it has an

industrial sense about it. It's also a cold city, and Chicago Blues has a sense of fighting the cold, and it's an angry city, and the Chicago Blues has Chicago's anger in it."[74]

In this passage the personification of Chicago blues music as "hard-edged" and "tough" easily coalesces with the gritty image of an "industrial" working-class city wrought with Chicago's so-called "anger," as if local blues musicians developed their urban styles of performance through osmosis rather than artistic diligence. In fact, the attempt here to associate the authenticity of blues with the cold winters of Chicago is especially ironic given that the blues actually developed in the hot and humid climate of the Deep South.

Still, this Rust Belt depiction of the Chicago blues succeeds because it resonates with a common set of agreed-upon characterizations of the city's landscape of authenticity, a seedy Back-of-the-Yards alleyway that bleeds with the edgy coarseness of Upton Sinclair's industrial dystopia; the 1919 Black Sox; the St. Valentine's Day Massacre; the rough edges of Carl Sandburg, Nelson Algren, and Boss Daley; and, of course, the red-hot jazz and blues music of Louis Armstrong, Jelly Roll Morton, Muddy Waters, and Howlin' Wolf. However, as the next chapter demonstrates, even the most celebrated myths of the past require the cultural and financial resources of the present if they are to be reborn as memory.

Sweet Home Chicago

Selling Authenticity in the Urban Metropolis

Historic preservations and retro urban designs are literal representations of
the past. They too are designed for inattentive viewers, for the tourist or city
traveler who browses through these real-life stage-sets scarcely aware of
how the relics of the past have been indexed, framed, and scaled. . . . These
tableaux separate pleasure from necessity, escape from reality. They widen
the gap between the city on display and the city beyond our view. And in
doing so they sever any connection they might have had to the art of building
real cities, for, after all, these city tableaux only claim to be special places
for fun and entertainment, areas of the city to explore during periods of play,
which promise not to burden the spectator with the seriousness of reality.

—M. Christine Boyer, "Cities for Sale"

Cultural Chicago and the Authenticity of the Blues.
In the last chapter I offered examples of how private local boosters, like
newspapers, appropriate Chicago's blues legacy and the authenticity it
represents as a means of serving a variety of self-interests. City governments depend on these kinds of promotional strategies as well, especially in post-industrial cities where manufacturing production has been
replaced by cultural consumption, and specifically entertainment, as a
dominant engine of local economic growth.[1] This shift forces cities to
make themselves attractive to increasingly mobile investors, land developers, corporations, conventioneers, leisure travelers, and high-income
workers who might add revenues to their local economies. As cities and
their metropolitan areas compete with one another for capital in a post-

industrial economy, the need for promoting desirable images of place grows even stronger. As a result, many cities exploit their local cultural movements as potential resources for attracting out-of-town recreational and business travelers. By marketing the presence of artists and musicians in local ethnic communities and bohemian enclaves, cities can benefit from the symbolic power that their authenticity represents to cultural consumers.[2] At the same time, city governments reap the political rewards generated by their attempts to stimulate local growth by shielding their efforts behind the rhetoric of multiculturalism and progressive politics.

To this end, in April 1997 the city announced a three-year "Cultural Chicago" campaign to help market itself to foreign and domestic tourists.[3] At a cost of $6 million, the program was designed to draw on the previous successes of Chicago's cultural attractions in order to increase the city's status in the global tourism economy. Armed with $3.4 million supplied by the state of Illinois as well as additional funds provided by a host of corporate sponsors, including travel-oriented businesses such as United Airlines and Budget Rent a Car, the city implemented a series of cultural programs to promote its image nationally as well as abroad; such programs included a variety of free downtown concerts, public birthday celebrations, and local photography exhibits.

Significantly, this marketing strategy relied heavily on the city's reputation as a blues and jazz capital. On weekdays the city invited musicians to perform free concerts at the Chicago Cultural Center in commemoration of the birthdays of jazz and blues legends such as Duke Ellington, Ella Fitzgerald, Lionel Hampton, and Muddy Waters.[4] In promotional print campaigns, portraits of local music personalities like Buddy Guy ran alongside the tag line "Chicago . . . Heart, Soul, Rhythm and Blues."[5]

However, while marketing campaigns like Cultural Chicago often prove successful in attracting increased local attention and press coverage, such projects often run the risk of alienating visitors in search of the authenticity promised by the images of the city described in the last chapter. For example, performances held in the food court of the Chicago Cultural Center can suggest the sanitized aura of a museum exhibit. Ornately decorated with marble walls and tables, vaulted ceilings, track lighting, carpeting, and quilts from a local school arts project, the decor of the center's Randolph Cafe stands in sharp contrast to the raw grittiness of the Checkerboard Lounge. Likewise, the center's lunchtime crowd of elderly diners and city employees often demonstrates a lack of enthusiasm during these performances. In November 1998 the city hired Sonny, the folk-blues singer and guitarist introduced in an earlier chapter, for a concert to commemorate the classic bluesman Brownie McGhee on the anniversary of his birth. (I alluded to this performance in chapter 4.) As he strums his steel guitar and sings numbers by country-blues singers like Blind Boy Fuller and Rev. Gary Davis, the members of his audience display their attentiveness to varying degrees: one elderly gentleman fumbles with a newspaper; another reads the center's brochures; two ladies chatter loudly during one of Sonny's explanations of a McGhee song. When another elderly gentleman turns to the couple to firmly request, "Excuse me, can you please be quiet?" his attentiveness toward Sonny seems somewhat surprising among his fellow lunchtime diners. Meanwhile, even Sonny feels out of place performing in this rarefied setting; as he explains afterward, "I don't usually play concerts like this, you know . . . I'm not really used to talking up onstage. I'm used to playing in rowdy bars—*that's* more my milieu."

Authenticity and the Commodification of Neighborhood Life.　　In order to meet tourists' demands for more authentic encounters with urban life, in May 1997 the city began running Chicago Neighborhood Tours (CNT), an enterprise intended to provide alternatives to the entertainment options offered in the central downtown district. Sponsored by the Chicago Office of Tourism and the Department of Cultural Affairs, the CNT project offers what promotional materials advertise as an "urban odyssey" for affluent local travelers and out-of-towners wishing to experience an up-close-and-personal view of the city's cultural and ethnic diversity. Such sojourns promote Chicago through the romanticized authenticity promised by nine local neighborhood areas: South Shore, Bronzeville, Chinatown/Pilsen, West Side, Near South Side, Wicker Park/Humboldt Park, Uptown, Andersonville/Lincoln Square, and Devon Avenue. According to the program's 1998 brochure:

> Join us on an urban odyssey. Discover the best way to enjoy the feel and flavor of Chicago's exciting and diverse communities through the Chicago Neighborhood Tours. These half-day bus excursions, generously sponsored by Sears, Roebuck and Co., take an in-depth look at the traditions, stories and people of this great American city, with tours departing from the Chicago Cultural Center every Saturday.

Each week, the spotlight shines on a different neighborhood, so you'll want to come along for a new adventure every time you explore Chicago! Seek out artistic havens, learn the history of local landmarks, roam through unique shopping areas, and join in the sights and tastes of ethnic celebrations. Most importantly, experience every community firsthand, as the people who live in the neighborhoods become your tour guides, sharing their stories with you. Enjoy our city![6]

For a twenty-six-dollar ticket price, tour buses escort guests from the Chicago Cultural Center to the ethnic enclave of their choice. Upon arrival, such travelers "explore" the urban terrain of the city as they consume the Indian, Russian, and Jewish commercial areas of Devon Avenue; Mexican shopping strips in Pilsen; Puerto Rican neighborhoods in Humboldt Park; Vietnamese quarters in Uptown; bohemian art galleries in Wicker Park; and the blues heritage of the South Side's Bronzeville district.[7] By capitalizing on exoticized notions of ethnicity, community, and urban space, these "motorcoach excursions" transform local communities and their landscapes of everyday social interaction into commodified tourist attractions. The program models itself after privately run neighborhood heritage bus and walking tours conducted in Bronzeville as well as in New York City's Harlem and Memphis's Beale Street areas.[8]

According to Sarah, a program coordinator for the CNT project, the tours target a wide variety of consumers: local Chicagoans, domestic and international tourists, and weekend visitors traveling by car from the Chicagoland area and elsewhere in the Midwest.[9] In addition, the program serves conventioneers, business travelers, and touring groups, who pay extra fees for custom-made neighborhood tours of the city. According to Sarah, tourists enjoy the tours because they allow them to "explore a new neighborhood, an area which they have been enthusiastic about, while enjoying the comfort and safety of being in a group."

Typically, the city schedules a visit to a different neighborhood every Saturday, and the average tour takes about four hours to complete from start to finish. Upon arrival at the Cultural Center, all passengers are offered a laminated bus pass for the ride. After boarding, a representative from the Office of Tourism welcomes their out-of-town guests to Chicago and proceeds to spin a scripted set of tales about the city's storied past, pointing out landmark sites as the bus rolls farther and farther away from the familiar spaces of the downtown area. Once the bus arrives at its specified neighborhood destination, a local "expert" from the community takes the helm and leads the tour while the representative from the office steps back to make sure everything runs smoothly, troubleshooting along the way. The local guides are always current or former residents from the neighborhood and are selected by CNT on the basis of the legitimacy that the city claims they bring to the tour. According to Sarah, these guides are paid twenty-five dollars per hour to provide the authenticity necessary for tourists to fully experience the communities they visit. In our interview she asserts:

> Someone like me could give the tour, and I could point out this and that sight, but it would be "all surface" because it's not my place to show people around these neighborhoods and talk about them as if it is. The local guides live in the communities and can tell their personal stories about their experiences there. And the tourists really enjoy meeting and having conversations with the people who actually live there, who can talk about these places from their own personal experiences. This way, it's not me talking *for* them, but the locals themselves, describing their communities casually, in their own words, rather than with a formatted script.
>
> On one occasion during our tour of the Swedish community in Andersonville, the guide accidentally ran into a friend of hers from the neighborhood who had just happened to be passing by. So, the friend starts telling stories to the group and produces a photograph of their guide dressed in a traditional Swedish outfit, and everyone had a nice laugh about that . . .

According to Sarah (who is white), these local guides are the lifeblood of the CNT program. As an example, she describes the efforts of Mandie, a guide for the South Side tours of the historic Bronzeville district and its blues and jazz landmarks:

> Mandie grew up in Bronzeville, and she is very outgoing, has a great personality, so she can share personal stories to the tour groups about the impact of the neighborhood on her own life growing up there. On one tour she pointed out the church where her father used to take her family. And as the bus passed the University of Chicago, she told this funny story of how she slept late on her graduation day, and how her mother had to wake her as the ceremony began . . .

Of course, just in case such guides cannot recall any personal stories about their local community, the Office of Tourism provides them with suggested formatted scripts and a supplementary training manual. Nevertheless, the city eagerly promotes its neighborhood tours on the basis of their authenticity as intimate and thus valuable cultural experiences. In fact, tour guides incorporate this personal aura of authenticity into the tours themselves. At the conclusion of her Bronzeville tour, Mandie (who is black) turns to her microphone and reiterates Sarah's point:

> We like to have people like myself, who are from these neighborhoods, give the tours ourselves, as opposed to a company, who would just collect information about the place and then bring people in . . . We'd much rather prefer to introduce these neighborhoods to you in the first person, as a firsthand account, sort of a tour of the people, for the people, and by the people.

Like many of the musicians who perform in the city's tourist-oriented blues clubs, the personal identities of guides like Mandie enhance Chicago's image as a city of ethnic authenticity, but at the cost of transforming themselves into commodities. Still, Sarah suggests that the program's most popular tours owe their success to these morally ambiguous efforts. She explains how tourists on the Chinatown tour enjoy the "real community feel" suggested by their interactions with local community members and their traditions, in spite of the fact that such encounters often inconvenience and offend neighborhood residents and business owners:

> During the Chinatown walking tour, we take our group to Maxim's, a tea house on Wentworth, and here the group can find old Chinese men chatting as they sip tea on their Saturday mornings, and the tourists really enjoy the real community feel of a place like this, and we order interesting Chinese pastries for them, and pork buns, and they just love it. Occasionally, every once in a while someone from the group complains about this or that—like once, the bathrooms there were really dirty, and so we asked them to have them clean for us for the next time. Of course, there is always a communication gap, since the owner doesn't speak English, and only knows a dialect of Chinese unknown by our interpreter, but we try not to overstay our welcome.

A Stroll through the Ghetto. These encounters with the present-day realities of Chinatown during these tours contrast the virtual absence of any discussion of the economic deprivation that plagues nearby neighborhoods. In fact, local guides often ignore contemporary neighborhood conditions in their attempts to promote Chicago's image as an authentic yet attractive city. In these moments, the experiences of tourist passengers must border on the surreal. When her tour bus passes the South Side's infamous Checkerboard Lounge while slowly creeping down Forty-third Street (officially dubbed "Muddy Waters Drive" by the city) during a Saturday afternoon tour of Bronzeville, Mandie enthusiastically describes how the neighborhood once provided its residents with a real sense of community solidarity. Meanwhile, her script ignores what the view *outside* the bus reveals: torn-up sidewalks, abandoned businesses, deteriorating storefront churches, vacant lots, and the residual markers of an otherwise hollowed-out ghost town, a decaying symbol of urban poverty and civic neglect.

A drive down State Street provides an equally torturous mismatch of romanticized history with political and economic reality. As Mandie describes in glowing detail the glory days of 1920s Bronzeville and the jazz greats who performed in the many nightclubs that lined the once-famous street aptly nicknamed "The Stroll," passengers press their noses to the windows of the bus to stare as they pass the Stateway Gardens low-income housing development. The bus continues to slowly creep down the street as some of the development's black residents turn to stare at the bus in bewilderment, presumably confused by the lingering presence of a chartered bus in front of their homes. Meanwhile, as the bus passengers continue to point and gawk at the residents and their surrounding neighborhood, Mandie persistently delivers her speech on the Stroll's hot jazz cabarets, the local celebrity of Jelly Roll Morton and Louis Armstrong, and the vitality of the area's once-heralded Black Metropolis, conveniently ignoring the surrounding blight. As the bus heads back to the Loop, Frank Sinatra's "My Kind of Town" along with the familiar 1950s refrain of "Sweet Home Chicago" blare from the intercom as passengers ask one another, "Has welfare to work been successful at all?" As they disembark from the bus, one of them approaches Mandie to ask a question she felt went unanswered during the tour: "As we went through all those projects, I couldn't help but notice that there weren't any supermarkets anywhere. There must be thousands of people living down there—what do they do for food?"[10]

While the CNT succeeds by commodifying the cultural resources that local neighborhoods supply, the Office of Tourism defends the program on the basis of its ability to provide what it calls "economic development" to the neighborhoods it visits. According to Sarah, this "development" takes three primary forms. First, the program brings visitors to frequently depressed neighborhoods where they might spend money shopping for souvenirs or dining on local cuisine. Secondly, the tours provide promotional introductions to these communities where visitors might make return trips. As Mandie announces near the conclusion of her Bronzeville tour, "We like to think of these tours as a means of bringing economic development to these communities in the hopes that our guests will make return visits to the neighborhoods." Finally, the Office of Tourism provides funding to community-based cultural centers that serve as destinations for their tours. On the Bronzeville tour, these centers include the DuSable Museum of African American History, the art galleries of the neighborhood-led Little Black Pearl Workshop, and Willie Dixon's Blues Heaven Foundation.[11] Headquartered in the former studios and offices of Chess Records, the Blues Heaven Foundation walks visitors through the hallowed rooms where Muddy Waters recorded, the basement where former Chess employee Chuck Berry slept while in town, and a video documentary detailing how record companies and music publishers regularly exploited the talents of local blues musicians throughout the twentieth century by withholding their deserved royalty checks.[12] Afterward they are directed toward a gift boutique and souvenir shop, where they might purchase compact discs, coffee table books on blues music, T-shirts, and so forth. The Office of Tourism helps to support cultural centers like the Blues Heaven Foundation and the DuSable Museum by donating the finances necessary to build gift shops and other tourist-oriented services in their spaces.[13]

The assertions made by Sarah and Mandie regarding the "economic development" spawned by the neighborhood tours program echo the arguments made by their office in its press materials and promotional buzz. According to a news release generated by the Chicago Department of Cultural Affairs (DCA), " 'Not only is this a remarkable opportunity for people to experience the history and character that has evolved in Chicago's neighborhoods,' said Commissioner Lois Weisberg, 'it is also a way to extend the reach of tourism's economic impact into the many communities that make up this city.' "[14]

Participants involved with the CNT program—including founder Juana Guzman, director of community cultural development at the DCA—frequently promote this angle in interviews with local reporters. According to a September 1997 article that appeared in *Crain's Chicago Business*:

Hoping to spark economic development within and beyond its walls, six cultural arts centers in Chicago are building retail stores with the help of government and foundation grant money. . . . The potential for economic development fed into the grant-making decision, says Susan Duchak, community relations manager for corporate contributions at the Hoffman Estates–based retailer. "We're not able to quantify it, but logically, if you bring in tourists, they'll spend money," Ms. Duchak says. That appears to be the case at the Mexican Fine Arts Center in Pilsen and the DuSable Museum of African-American History on the South Side. Ms. [Juana] Guzman says these locations ring up as much as $1,000 in sales during a single [bus stop]. . . . Community development officials applaud the retail sites. "It makes sense to have a retail component. Tourists like to shop, to have souvenirs indigenous to an area," says Martin Berg, a community development director at the Chicago Assn. of Neighborhood Development Organizations.[15]

However, there are several reasons to be skeptical of the program's abilities to actually benefit these neighborhoods in a substantive manner. First, it is unclear how effectively the CNT project can bring tourism dollars to these communities or spark job growth, since the tours only come to each neighborhood six times a year. Since so many of their customers are international and domestic travelers, it is hard to predict how many will come back to Chicago at all, much less revisit these neighborhoods. As the CNT organizers themselves suggest, their patrons enjoy the comforts provided by a reliable tour bus, the "comfort and safety of being in a group," and a personable "authentic" guide, all of which make these neighborhoods physically and psychologically accessible to out-of-towners (as well as the program's largest market, the elderly), and it is unlikely that a privately initiated visit would offer the same sorts of conveniences. Moreover, the tours take them to tourist attractions (i.e., cultural centers, churches, etc.), instead of homegrown businesses that might invite return trips by their customers. Finally, the CNT project may be too small-scale to generate much change in these neighborhoods, and by its own admission, few permanent jobs are expected to come out of its gift shop creation and expansion programs.[16] In fact, the "development" promised by the CNT does little more than maintain the tourism infrastructure necessary for the program to successfully persist in these neighborhoods.[17]

But if the CNT cannot pull areas like Bronzeville out of their stagnant economic state, the *city* benefits disproportionately from the program's efforts. The tours serve as a potential attraction for domestic and international tourists visiting the city, as well as visitors from neighboring midwestern states traveling by car who might choose to spend the night in Chicago instead of driving back home in the evening. According to Sarah, the city prioritizes cultural and entertainment offerings that offer incentives for day-trippers to stay overnight in Chicago, so that they might help decrease vacancy rates at local hotels and spend money on nocturnal leisure activities from dining to nightclubbing.

More significantly, the program effectively and inexpensively promotes Chicago as a "city of neighborhoods," a multicultural image of place that heightens the city's authenticity among travelers.[18] This kind of image marketing draws on the same urban fantasies beheld by tourists who target authenticated blues clubs located outside the downtown area for the high level of nocturnal capital they confer. In a sense, the image of Chicago as a city of neighborhoods works so well because it contrasts with more mainstream urban attractions that cater to local tourists, including its shopping malls, deep-dish pizzerias and steakhouses, downtown architectural tours, chartered boat cruises, skyscraper observation decks, and the themed entertainment of Navy Pier and the Near North district. But in addition, Chicago's emphasis on neighborhood populism and community life allows the city to successfully compete against other world-class American cities on the basis of its local cultural resources, rather than its shortage of national monuments, ocean-side beaches, or temperate weather relative to challengers in the domestic tourist economy such as Washington, D.C., Miami, Los Angeles, or San Francisco. In fact, since cultural entrepreneurs in places like New York City use their *own* local neighborhood resources to enhance their cities' attractiveness among travelers, Chicago must offer comparable entertainment options for its visitors in order to remain competitive as a travel destination.[19]

Finally, the CNT project benefits the city because it offers a low-cost means of promoting Chicago's image as a bastion of ethnic diversity and social liberalism *as well as* an entertainment center without investing in the same kinds of large-scale rehabilitation efforts that often characterize actual economic development in the city. While urban governments generally support costly development projects because they placate local pro-growth coalitions and booster organizations while increasing the power of the city center and its elite, these enterprises frequently lack the diverse interest-group support necessary to get such projects off the ground.[20] On the other hand, programs like the Chicago Neighborhood Tours are relatively inexpensive to implement, placate local ethnic communities, and generate widespread political support and celebratory press coverage for Mayor Richard M. Daley and his administration, all while helping Chicago to market itself as an authentic "city of neighborhoods" attractive to foreign and domestic travelers alike. Thus, such programs allow the city to use public funds to promote its urban image and local identity in the global tourism economy under the guise of neighborhood development and civic philanthropy.

Pepsi Pop Culture and the Chicago Blues Festival. In their implementation of the Chicago Neighborhood Tours project, the Department of Cultural Affairs and Office of Tourism use the city's ethnic communities to market the city by transporting tourists from the downtown area to the neighborhoods where they reside. In contrast, the Chicago Blues Festival, a four-day live musical event held annually in Grant Park, exemplifies a more conventional approach to civic promotion by bringing the cultural resources of its local communities to the city center. This strategy mirrors past as well as recent attempts by the city to centralize a sanitized version of its local populist culture for worldwide public consumption, including its celebrated 1893 Columbian Exposition and the postmodern rehabilitation of Navy Pier.

Like the organizers responsible for the CNT program, festival planners are very conscious about the political and economic rewards that come from successfully exploiting the artistic production of the city's neighborhoods and their creative sectors. According to Barry Dolins, the Blues Festival coordinator and deputy director of the Mayor's Office of Special Events, one of the major purposes of the event is to increase the popularity and attractiveness of the city in the global imagination as a means of promoting tourism:

> The Blues Fest is one of many enterprises which markets the city to visitors . . . We have moved from a city of manufacturing to a service-based city where tourism has become increasingly important, where catering to leisure travelers is as important to the city as big business . . . The festival helps to foster an image of Chicago as a world-class city, as a mecca for free outdoor cultural events like no other city in the country.

The festival, which began as an annual event in 1984 under Harold Washington's reign as mayor, seems to serve this purpose quite well. In

1998 the *Chicago Tribune* reported that the Office of Special Events estimated the attendance for that summer's Blues Fest at a record-breaking 660,000 over the four-day period.[21] Dolins estimates that close to 40 percent of the festival's attendees represent out-of-town travelers. He reinforces this point by suggesting how quickly the city's hotels fill up for the event, describing the extent to which potential visitors from all over the country call his office in desperate and often vain attempts to secure accommodations during that weekend, asserting that "the festival creates a demand for hotel rooms, and the hotels have been picking up on that." Dolins's intern tells of a group from Ohio who slept in the park because they were unable to procure lodging for the event.

In contrast to the neighborhood tours program that shuttles visitors to the geographic as well as figurative margins of the city, the Chicago Blues Festival takes place within the hypercommercialized world of the downtown area. Once visitors arrive at the festival gates, they are bombarded on all sides by the promotional advances of the festival's corporate sponsors, which, in recent years, have included tourist-oriented transit vendors and hotels; local boosters, including newspapers, television outlets, and radio stations; music hardware and software vendors; and the beverage manufacturers who provide refreshment for the event.[22] Brand-name mascots dressed as Best Buy tickets and Vienna Beef hot dogs dance among reveling crowds throughout the park, while a giant inflatable Miller Genuine Draft beer can towers over their heads. Nearby, representatives from pharmaceutical companies promoting products ranging from Zyrtec to Pepto-Bismol pass out free antacid caplets and squeeze bottles.[23] Other sponsors invite passersby to play "Pepsi Pop Culture," order a central air-conditioning tune-up from Peoples Gas for only seventy-nine dollars, win a brand-new Gibson guitar, and receive free samples of SPF 15 sunscreen from the Sony Corporation.

Like all of the summer festivals held in Grant Park, "fun" food serves as a source of entertainment for visitors and revenue for local businesses as well as the city. At ticket booths centrally located at the Jackson/Columbus intersection in the middle of the park, partygoers pay six dollars for five dollars' worth of nonrefundable food coupons redeemable at nearby vendors; the city collects the extra dollar to cover the cost of amenities. Armed with sheets of coupons, patrons choose among three types of cuisine, each suggestive of a different brand of manufactured authenticity: southern "soul" food (smoked ribs, barbecued turkey drumsticks, red beans and rice, corn-on-the-cob), Pan-Asian dishes (grilled chicken satay with peanut sauce, vegetable tempura, pad thai, chicken egg rolls), and classic "Chicago" fare (Polish and Italian sausage, pizza, Billy Goat Tavern cheeseburgers, Vienna Beef hot dogs).[24] They wash down such culinary delights with beer, fluorescent mai-tais, mass-produced mudslides and margaritas, and the soft drinks of their choice, as long as those soft drinks are produced by Pepsi.

Of course, in spite of the fact that the city insists on producing its own currency for each of its Grant Park summer festivals, visitors have plenty of opportunities to spend cash as well. At the center of the festival, presenting sponsor Best Buy sells blues and jazz compact discs and box sets in a pavilion equipped with a small stage for bands who perform loud blues songs to attract customers. Blue Chicago, Buddy Guy's Legends, and Kingston Mines all share a Chicago Blues Club booth, where they collectively sell souvenir T-shirts, tank tops, tie-dyes, baseball caps, and athletic jerseys. Meanwhile, the city grants a single vendor the privilege of selling the festival's only "official" merchandise. In 1997 that vendor estimated that it would sell close to seventy thousand T-shirts throughout the weekend and would sell out all ten thousand of its most popular product, a black shirt emblazoned with a "Chicago Blues Festival" fluorescent logo. Strategically placed cash machines provide visitors easy access to their bank accounts for the occasion.

The Disneyland of the Blues.   There are four primary stages at the festival where musicians perform.[25] At the northeastern section of Grant Park stands the Petrillo Music Shell, the festival's main stage. While audiences fortunate enough to garner free seats at the front of the stage benefit from a state-of-the-art sound system and a spectacular view, most spectators fill the vast lawn extending north to Monroe Street and east to Lake Shore Drive.[26] On popular nights they pack the lawn with picnic blankets and illegal beverage coolers to watch the festival's most celebrated performers; in past years those who have played in this venue on opening night have included Ray Charles, Bobby "Blue" Bland, Chuck Berry, and Buddy Guy.

On opening night of the 1997 Blues Fest, WBBM-TV anchorperson Lester Holt welcomes a crowd of screaming blues fans in anticipation of a free Buddy Guy performance at the Shell. After bantering about a recent Chicago Bulls victory over the Utah Jazz (and suggesting that, in light of their defeat, perhaps it would be more fitting to dub *Utah* as the new "Home of the Blues"), he introduces WXRT-FM disc jockey Tom

Marker, who, in turn, introduces headliner Buddy Guy by invoking the three most essential components of the city's presentation of self during the 1990s: buildings, basketball, and the blues.[27]

> We're here at Blues Fest, we're talking about Chicago, we're talking about the Chicago world-class downtown skyline, we're talking about world-class architects like Louis Sullivan and Frank Lloyd Wright, we're talking about world-class sports, we're talking about the world-champion Chicago Bulls, we're talking about the World Capital of the Blues, and when we're talking about the blues, we're talking about the real deal himself, we're talking about Buddy Guy!!!

All three of these elements represent a 1990s urban cosmopolitanism that can easily be integrated into a storied biography of the city, stocked with celebrated legends from Frank Lloyd Wright to Michael Jordan to Muddy Waters. Unlike the relative irretrievability and difficult marketability of more dour images of the city—the Great Chicago Fire, the Haymarket Affair, the St. Valentine's Day Massacre, the Weathermen's 1969 Four Days of Rage—they are all accessible components of a kinder and gentler present-day Chicago insofar as tourists can actually peruse the city skyline, watch the post-Jordan Bulls play at the United Center, and patronize a local blues club all in the course of a single evening.

In addition to the Petrillo Music Shell, the festival boasts three smaller stages, and the city designates each one according to a certain theme or image associated with American blues music.[28] At the far end of Jackson Boulevard, musicians entertain crowds with modern electric blues performances at the Gibson USA Guitar–sponsored Crossroads stage. In the festival's promotional materials, an attempt is made to mythologize the music performed there:

> The Crossroads Stage was named for the famous Robert Johnson song, "Cross Road Blues." The crossroads—that lonely outpost where two country roads intersect—is an image rife with portent and mystery in blues lore. Here, it's been said, is where a young musician might go at midnight to make a pact with the devil. Go to the crossroads and play your guitar; a mysterious-looking man will emerge from the shadows, take your guitar and tune it, play a piece, and hand the instrument back to you. You'll walk away with newfound talent—and the devil will have claim to your soul. Although the music emanating from the Crossroads Stage at the Chicago

Blues Festival is some of the most joyful to be heard anywhere, if you listen closely you can hear echoes of Robert Johnson: "I went down to the crossroad, fell down on my knees / Asked the Lord above, 'Have mercy—save poor Bob, if you please.' "[29]

Where legend has it, a young musician could sell his soul to the devil in exchange for becoming a great blues player. This stage gives you more of a nightclub feel, where you can shake your moneymaker to some of the hottest contemporary blues artists today. Bring your appetite for pumped-up blues and don't forget your dancing shoes![30]

At the Crossroads area, Chicago blues entertainers perform the same stage shows they offer in the city's tourist-oriented clubs. In contrast, the staged authenticity of the festival's Juke Joint stage tries to provide an alternative to the music popularized in local venues by attempting to re-create a hole-in-the-wall blues joint in the center of Grant Park. According to the festival's official programs:

A "Juke Joint" is a neighborhood club where the gettin' down is serious and they play the blues like they mean it, because the blues is life—you'll find one on a backstreet corner of the city under the elevated train line, or out across the cotton fields under the cypress trees; maybe it's right across town, on the funky side of the tracks. It's where the aroma of cigar smoke, whiskey, and perfume hit you like a sweet punch when you walk in the door; where the laughter is loud, the jokes are raucous, and the blues are as raw as a dirt road and as exhilarating as a shot of rock & rye. At the 1998 Chicago Blues Festival we've got a Juke Joint stage of our own, along with musicians with enough jubilation and power to fill it to capacity.[31]

Recently sponsored by Southern Comfort and the House of Blues, the stage backdrop of the festival's Juke Joint has been rudimentarily rendered in paint to depict peeling wallpaper, blue stars, and exposed piping. Against this background, hand-painted signs read: "The Stars Love Dem"; "No Bad Language, No Sitting, No Laying"; "Be Nice or Leave." An announcement on the door reads, "Open Time: Thur 20c, Fr 120c, Sat 110c, Sun 110c—PARTY TIME!"; "Fine Music—Live Blues"; "No Gambling; No Fighting; No Beer Sold after 12 o'clock—House Rules, No exceptions." An American flag stands at the side of the stage, and in some years an obtrusive House of Blues sign announces itself to festival audiences. In a Rolling Stones T-shirt and Cleveland Indians baseball cap, one reveler utters, "Gee, you think people are getting the message?"

At the Juke Joint stage, audiences sit on blue benches during the day to listen to solo artists and small ensembles perform Delta-inspired blues numbers in an intimate setting. Some years folk-blues legend David "Honeyboy" Edwards plays Robert Johnson covers on his bright red acoustic guitar with a slide, and old-timer Homesick James plays from a set list of traditional classics. In his black suit, gray hat, and shades, James hollers blues standards ranging from "Shake Your Moneymaker" to "I Believe I'll Dust My Broom." During a slow, grinding number, he pleads, "Juanita . . . What do you want me to do? . . . I did all I could, child . . . But I just can't get along with you."

Since the Juke Joint features traditional and revivalist blues performances, the stage attracts some of the festival's more inquisitive audience members. Barry, a part-time student enrolled in an adult education course on Chicago music at a local university, happily attends the festival as a class project assigned by his teacher. He notices me writing in my field notebook during the show, and so he approaches me after the performance to ask if I will chat with him for a few minutes. In his Blues Fest T-shirt, his curiosity pours out before us both: "Is it true that Homesick James was an original player on Maxwell Street? Was he singing traditional songs and covers, or were those his original songs?"[32]

Meanwhile, the festival's Aiwa-sponsored Front Porch stage depicts a countrified setting where audiences lie about on a sweeping lawn to listen to southern blues and folk music. According to the event's official programs:

> The Front Porch Stage, decorated to evoke a country front porch where musicians sit and play, is the showcase for acoustic blues. Here the traditionalists hold forth, with occasional contributions from more high-energy, electrified acts. This is the kind of atmosphere that used to prevail in Handy Park in Memphis, where the Memphis Jug Band and others used to play impromptu outdoor concerts.[33]

> On a cool summer evening, down a dusty dirt road, on a wood plank porch, musicians would break out the acoustics and jam. This stage recreates that "front porch" feel. You'll find plenty of great acoustic and stripped-down blues sets here. The fingers will be picking and the toes will be tapping for a rollicking good time.[34]

At the Front Porch stage, folk bluesman Fruteland Jackson plays a southern country-blues set on an electric steel guitar. In blue overalls, he executes some prison songs, a rendition of Robert Johnson's old standard "Walking Blues," and a song commemorating the sinking of the *Titanic*: "How many of you saw the movie *Titanic*? Well, I saw the movie *Titanic* three times, and here's my spin on it . . ." On another occasion he performs a folk-blues set to honor Johnson's legacy; in typical brooding fashion, he sings: "Gimme that old-time religion . . . It's good enough for me."

Along with the Juke Joint stage, the Front Porch offers a rare opportunity for old-timers to showcase themselves to mainstream audiences in Chicago. As suggested in earlier chapters, old-timers who play the rural blues indicative of the music from the Mississippi Delta region in the 1930s and 1940s generally do not perform in the city's more popular blues clubs; in contrast, the exploitation of tactical niche-marketing at the festival allows these musicians the opportunity to perform in a local setting. At the Front Porch, old-timers Dave Myers and Robert Jr. Lockwood perform a set list of traditional blues standards: Leroy Carr and Scrapper Blackwell's "How Long, How Long Blues," Jimmy Rogers's "That's All Right," Robert Johnson's "Ramblin' on My Mind" and "Stop Breakin' Down Blues," Brownie McGhee's "Key to the Highway 70," Big Joe Turner's "Shake, Rattle & Roll," and Lowell Fulson's "Reconsider Baby": "Well, so long, you know I hate to see you go . . . The way that I will miss you, I guess you'll never know." During his performance of his "Elevate Me Baby," Myers implores the crowd to purchase his newest compact disc, *You Can't Do That*, shouting, "I'm so poor, I'm used to it!" In between songs Lockwood teases Myers about his age, which generates big laughs from the crowd.

Likewise, the Front Porch area offers festival attendees the only grass-lined venue outside of the main stage, and during the day they rent lawn chairs, enjoy picnics, and surreptitiously drink their cans of beer before security guards confiscate their coolers. The expanse of the lawn and the size of its crowd allow revelers the opportunity to leave their inhibitions back at their hotel rooms. During one set of performances, a blond woman dances in cut-off jeans shorts and a star-spangled bikini top while an older gentleman shows off his ponytail, bare chest, and extensive tattoo work; another enjoys his music in a loud Hawaiian shirt, spandex shorts, shades, and rainbow-streaked umbrella hat. Nearby, one reveler wears a beer glass around his neck and puffs on a skinny cigar while making out with his female companion under a shady tree; another thrusts his hand down the back of his girlfriend's purple biker shorts. Further in the crowd, shirtless boys form a circle and kick around a hacky-sack.

The Reversal of Roles.   At the Front Porch stage, musicians and other regulars from the local blues scene, especially those without day jobs, share the open lawn with their leisurely out-of-town counterparts. In these settings musicians share a certain kind of freedom from the world of labor suggested by the blues club, and yet their subcultural status within the local blues scene allows them the comfort of enjoying the festival among friends. On the outskirts of the performance area, Daniel chats with an older gentleman beneath a shady tree as Guy, a fellow lion, parties closer to the stage with a group of regulars from Smoke Daddy. As we shake hands, Guy asks, "Hey, how's that book comin' along? You 'bout finished yet?" Likewise, the variety of countrified blues styles represented at both the Front Porch and the Juke Joint stages provides even the most contrary of survivors with an alternative to the standards commonly performed in local clubs. During the Myers and Lockwood set, I spot Darryl lurking about the crowd, and after waving him down, he joins me on the lawn. As one of Myers's longtime protégés, he listens attentively to the performance and attempts to convince a group of tourists sitting nearby to attend the old-timer's show later that night at a downtown club. When I ask Darryl if he had managed to catch Bobby "Blue" Bland's more soul-oriented show the night before, he just rolls his eyes and offers a look of disgust, and then quietly turns back toward the stage and his hero. By rearranging the sociospatial relations common to local blues clubs, the setting of the festival affords musicians the opportunity to become audience members.

By the same token, the decentralization of the park's social world affords all audience members the ability to experience the festival's offerings in all their variety. In doing so, tourists feel as if they possess a greater sense of control over their leisure than they might at local clubs. At the Front Porch stage, I encounter Barbara, a Hungarian immigrant currently residing in Iowa whom I had met a month earlier at B.L.U.E.S. Between snapping photographs of the stage, she inquires about where to go next: "So, who would be good to see at the festival? Where should we go later—who is playing?" Moreover, the festival provides her with the symbolic resources necessary for her to appropriate a city-oriented sense of self. Standing on Columbus Drive, she scans the park, turns to look up at the skyline behind her, and, in a thick eastern European accent, announces: "I long to be in the city . . . I want to live here . . . you know, the buzz . . . the event? Back in Iowa, they are all farmers, and they're nice people, but I am not like them. We are very different kinds of people, you know?" As a reveler at the festival, Barbara imagines what it would be like to live in the city and incorporates an image of the city into her overall self-identity. Just as the social context of the festival allows *musicians* to imagine themselves as audience *members,* the cosmopolitanism suggested by the heightened activity of the festival allows *tourists* to temporarily imagine themselves as *locals,* as urban dwellers who might feel at home in Chicago long after the weekend crowds dissipate.

But clearly, the festival's most impressive, if unintentional, feat is its ability to incorporate a cross section of the city's more marginalized citizens into its universe of public life. While the city employs an army of police officers to patrol the festival grounds, the synergistic activity that emerges when 660,000 people converge upon a central location over four days provides a formidable challenge to the enforcement of local law. As a result, the antics of homeless people and other so-called undesirables easily elude their gaze in the park. In their exuberant liberation from social norms frequently enforced by a sober public and a vigilant police force, these men and women take pleasure in the carnivalesque atmosphere provided by the festival.[35]

In this manner, stigmatized social *outsiders* are permitted to become full-fledged *participants* in the ritual of the festival. A black gentleman in a straw hat cruises around the festival in his automated wheelchair inviting passersby to pluck the strings of his old guitar; later he tools around the park while Aretha Franklin's "Respect" blasts from a cheap radio resting in the basket of his chair: "R-E-S-P-E-C-T . . . Find out what it means to me . . ." At the Juke Joint stage, another black gentleman struts back and forth by the stage, screaming, "Do it! . . . Do it to him!" to Homesick James as he tries to sing; after a while an exasperated James finally pleads to the crowd, "Stop him!" in a half-kidding, half-serious tone of voice. At the Front Porch stage, Robert, a black blues player and chronic schizophrenic, dances on the lawn in ninety-one-degree heat in his long, hot overcoat while attempting to keep time with his harmonica. During a Jimmy Reed tribute a few hours later, a drunken black woman wearing a denim jacket, red sweatshirt, white sneakers, and a baseball cap stumbles over, stares me down, shakes her finger at me, and begins massaging the shoulders of a complete stranger before falling onto his blanket and nearly crushing his date.

Meanwhile, the outrageous antics displayed during the Myers and Lockwood set by Mickey, the B.L.U.E.S. regular introduced in chapter 3, speak for themselves. Wearing the widest smile in an unusually colorful outfit—blue shirt with pens in pocket, shorts, cap covered with buttons, and rainbow side pouch—Mickey maintains his perch near stage right by strutting, snapping, clapping, hula dancing, playing air guitar, singing, and yelping, "That's the blues! . . . That's the blues, yeah! Yeah!! Yeah!!" Myers sees him from the stage and, in the middle of his set, yells, "Hello, Mickey!" "I'm all right . . . How are you doing?" As Myers hocks his compact disc between songs, Mickey turns toward the crowd and yells: "Hey, show your appreciation . . . *Buy something*!" As a blond photographer snaps Myers's photograph, Mickey rushes over and, without invitation, begins caressing her shoulders. Finally, Myers has had enough and pleads: "Shut up, Mickey!" Suddenly, a gentleman from the crowd approaches the stage, but instead of offering praise to Myers or Lockwood, he asks Mickey for *his* autograph.

Music on the Margins.   If these encounters blur commonly enforced social boundaries between the city's privileged and marginalized citizens, then the spatial layout of the festival reinforces the distinctions that exist between city-sanctioned musicians and peripheral bluesmen excluded from the event. While official performances literally and figuratively take center stage inside the park, the event relegates musicians who lack city sponsorship to the physical margins of the festival area. While celebrities like Buddy Guy take to the Petrillo Music Shell on opening night, lesser-known performers play for spare change on the outskirts of the park, where a complex social world emerges as marginalized musicians and their groupies entertain tourists entering and exiting the festival grounds.

I discovered this world on opening night of the 1997 Chicago Blues Festival, when my friend Jim and I met a little after 6 P.M. in front of the Art Institute of Chicago. As we stroll down Michigan Avenue near the Jackson Boulevard entrance on our way to the park, we spot Little Mack Simmons and Mojo Kings just outside the festival gates, performing a sidewalk rendition of Little Walter's "You Better Watch Yourself," a familiar song in the band's repertoire. A diverse crowd of nearly 150 tourists and office workers has surrounded the band as onlookers tap their feet and bounce to the rhythm of the song in the middle of the street. To the side, a gentleman attempts to sell the band's compact discs while volunteers collect money from passersby in two small barrels. According to Dustin, the band's lead guitarist and manager, "We'll take in four hundred dollars tonight—a hundred bucks apiece. Not bad for four hours of work. And it will be even bigger on the weekend, when the crowds are bigger."

But as our conversation continues, I discover that in spite of his band's immediate windfall, Dustin still remains pensive about the perils associated with street performing. He explains that because they have opted to play illegally on what is technically the property of the Art Institute, the museum and/or the police could make them leave at a moment's notice. On the sidewalks outside the festival, bands must stake out prime performance areas in the morning and wait until the crowds come—there are no reservations, no schedules, and no guaranteed paychecks. Although the next day's first official festival act wouldn't perform until 1 P.M., Dustin and his gang would have to arrive much earlier to claim their spot off the park.[36] Also, every member of the band must always abide by city regulations concerning street musicians. For example, unlike those performing on stages sponsored by the city inside the park, all must wear permit badges, which cost fifty dollars apiece.

While lingering on the margins of the festival that night, I observed the extent to which sidewalk performances provide a nonthreatening environment where street-corner men can socialize with tourists, who then experience those moments as highly authentic urban encounters. Whereas the city attempts to feign authenticity in the context of the Juke Joint and Front Porch stages, tourists often respond more strongly to the authenticity suggested by the marginalized culture of street musicians, their cronies, and the photo ops they apparently provide. In this manner, the periphery of the sidewalk fulfills the same function for these thrill-seekers as the Checkerboard Lounge and other off-the-beaten-path bars do for their nocturnal patrons.

And so, during Little Mack's streetwise performance, an elderly black gentleman in a wheelchair smokes a marijuana joint and smiles as he surveys the crowd, while to the side, an onlooker films the whole scene on a small video camcorder. Meanwhile, three older black gentlemen take turns dancing along the pavement with a cheerful selection of younger white female spectators who switch from partner to partner. One of these male dancers is C.J., a fairly tipsy Chicago Housing Authority employee who resides on Thirty-fifth Street on the city's South Side. In his black baseball cap, blue zippered sweatshirt, and Walkman headphones, he clutches a can of Old Style beer in one hand while dancing with one of these spectators, a white blond woman, with the other. Looking on, her boyfriend smiles and eagerly photographs the happy couple.

After listening to C.J. dubiously explain how his brother plays bass and once wrote music for the Jackson Five, I ask him how he convinces these spectators to dance with him. In a drunken drawl he explains, "Well, I go up to them, and I say, 'You know how people used to dance before? You know, back then, years ago? Let's dance like that right now.' " And off they go. I ask him, "So, what do their boyfriends say when you steal away their sweethearts?" C.J. looks at me, squares off, and smiles. "Man, they don't say shit. What are they going to say?"

During the 1998 Chicago Blues Festival held the following year, I decided to explore this social world in greater detail, and so I spent the duration of that weekend moving between the center and the margins of the festival. As I approached the empty intersection of Michigan Avenue and Jackson Boulevard at about 4:30 P.M. on Friday afternoon, I spot Little Mack and Dustin once again leaning against the Art Institute extension on Michigan Avenue, and I stop to chat with Dustin. Between bites of his sandwich, he explains that he continues to hold a straight job canvassing for an environmental group, and that he has been recently playing on a regular basis with Sharon Lewis, a local blueswoman, since Mack was having trouble retaining gigs on account of how "people are sick of his shit."

As in most years, he and Mack found that the festival provided a way for musicians to turn initiative into fast money, and so they worked out an arrangement with Tony Mangiullo, the owner of Rosa's, a blues club located in Logan Square where Dustin used to perform with Mack, but now plays every other week with Lewis: Tony would play the drums for free and supply the portable generator necessary to run the amplifiers, and in return the band would let him display his club's placard and pass out handbills in between sets. According to Dustin, the relationship works out nicely, especially since his gigs often go unattended during the week at Rosa's and he could always use the free advertising.[37] Still, he complains that Tony constantly bothers him by announcing his every move, including his trips to the bathroom.

After chatting with Dustin, I decide to follow the crowd through the festival gates to compare the desolation of the street to the noisier epicenter of the park, and so I head toward the Gibson USA–sponsored Crossroads stage in the hopes of catching Tiger, at the time a recently made acquaintance, perform before a sizable afternoon crowd. As he progresses through his usual set list of energetic songs, I actually spot Franz, the

German tourist introduced in chapter 1, standing by the stage with his friend Peter, and so I make my way through the crowd to catch up with them. Peter tells me that on my advice they had gone to Smoke Daddy on Monday night to catch Daniel's band perform, and that they had a great time, but he then explains how disappointed he was at the short length of Ray Charles's performance at the festival the night before: "I flew six thousand miles to hear Ray Charles play for fifty minutes!"[38] I ask him if he views his trip to the festival as a kind of pilgrimage, and he nods in agreement, although he doesn't have much more to add, as the music (and perhaps a cocktail or two) seems to overwhelm his sensibilities. Dancing and bouncing about, he turns to me and smiles, remarking: "This sounds a bit like reggae!" and continues to groove in syncopated rhythm to Tiger's guitar playing. Scanning the crowd for more familiar faces, I later spot Franz flirting with a younger female spectator, and while watching him bring plastic cups of beer to her friends, I briefly lock eyes and exchange hellos with Karen, the photojournalist, as she lingers around the press pit with her camera bag.

On my way out of the park at 6:30 P.M., I decided to check back with Dustin and the gang on the margins of the festival. Still armed with their instruments at the intersection just off the museum, Tony complains of feeling chilly in the cool evening wind without a jacket. Dustin explains that they collected thirty-seven dollars in total during their previous set, but that during the approaching weekend they hope to earn around four hundred dollars per day. During our conversation I hear a number of panhandlers yelling at the band to resume performing—not only do they enjoy listening and dancing to the free music, but they also rely on bands like Dustin's to attract unwitting crowds of onlookers who might be receptive to their solicitations.

Spotting Farrell off to the side with his bass, I head toward his perch alongside the wall and we begin chatting, but Dustin breaks up our conversation by announcing to his band mates, "Come on, let's make another twenty bucks," and they all suddenly jump into motion, ready to play. As I depart for a dinner party on the North Side, Dustin suggests that I bring along my saxophone over the weekend and accompany the band on a couple of songs. When I explain that I don't have a street performer's license, he just brushes it off, explaining that no officer would arrest me for sitting in on a few songs with an established street band. Excited and flattered, I agree to meet them on Sunday afternoon.[39]

And so two days later I arrive at the intersection to peruse my new temporary work environment along a stretch of sidewalk of Jackson

Boulevard. For sure, our makeshift performance area and its acoustics seem less than state of the art, especially when compared to the themed stages inside the park and their hi-fidelity sound systems. The band's amplifiers straddle the wall that buttresses the grounds of the Art Institute, with our instrument cases and jackets strewn about the pavement. As we begin the set, Tony bangs on a small drum kit atop a filthy white carpet laid across the sidewalk for shock absorption; meanwhile, Ruby, a fiddler and frequent participant in Dustin's performances, struggles at "stage left" in his attempts to quiet the roaring portable generator during a performance of Sonny Boy Williamson's "Don't Start Me to Talkin'." Farrell points out that the eight hours of playing can be a real grind, and when performing outside, the elements (wind, sunburn, extreme changes in temperature) that accompany all outdoor work can exhaust even the heartiest musicians. Meanwhile, Dustin feels compelled to mollify the police officers lurking across the street by announcing to the crowd: "If everybody could just come in a little closer . . . we need to keep the far lane open for police cars to pass through. So if everybody could move north of the yellow dotted line, that would be great."[40]

Of course, street bands outside the park depend on the kindness of strangers for their pay, and as our emcee, Dustin hardly seems shy about requesting it; as he implores the crowd, "We have to pay our rent, and unlike the folks inside, we're not getting paid, so please drop some money in the bucket . . . You will be supporting your local blues artists, and that's a very good thing." Thankfully, a crowd of nearly two hundred people appears before us mesmerized, listening attentively without talking, then responding, making the effort to drop their dollars into our white pail and inverted copper drum. Leaning against a lamppost bearing a sign reading "NO ALCOHOL MAY BE BROUGHT INTO THE PARK," Mack sings standards like Bo Diddley's "I'm a Man," Muddy Waters's "I'm Your Hoochie Coochie Man," and Otis Redding's "(Sitting on) The Dock of the Bay" with limited range but great enthusiasm in his Rosa's T-shirt, torn blue jeans, sneakers, and a red headband tightly wound about his skull. Meanwhile, Ruby offers his accompaniment in exchange for a five-dollar bill that Mack plucks from the bucket to hand him in the middle of the set.

As our band picks up steam, spectators begin dancing in the semicircle surrounding us. A young black man wearing a baseball cap and athletic warm-up suit struts alongside an older black gentleman in a knit cap and white pants with shoes to match. To our side, a well-dressed white gentleman taps his complimentary Zyrtec squeeze bottle to his palm in time to our rendition of Muddy Waters's "I'm Ready": "I'm drinkin' TNT! I'm smokin' dynamite! I hope some screwball start a fight 'cause I'm ready, ready as anybody can be—I'm ready for you, I hope you're ready for me." Nearby, a mother rocks and sways in place while holding her baby. A black woman begins dancing close to the band, and soon a white woman with long dirty blond hair in a black motorcycle T-shirt struts beside her. In keeping with the strange mix of spectators who linger on the margins on the festival, a reveler dressed as Jesus Christ, replete with crucifix, passes by the band and heads up Jackson on his way into the park. Meanwhile, armed with my saxophone but stuck between an amplifier and a stone wall, I try my best to simply keep up with the rest of the band. As we wind down, Calvin, the blues guitarist introduced in chapter 3, strolls past the band and points his finger at me and my horn as he smiles and teases, "Oh! Oh! I have all your albums!"

Suddenly, right in the middle of his rendition of the soulful classic "For Your Precious Love," Mack breaks into a sermon and begins to preach: "Now, I want to know, how many of y'all believe in God?! Do you believe in God?! Because you *must* believe in him . . . He is *always* there for you, in whatever you do . . . Michael Jordan is the best basketball player in the world and *he* believes in the Lord . . ." and then wails on his harmonica and continues to preach to his band's performance of the slow gospel song. Holding hands and swaying to the music in time, three black spectators stand together and nod in response to his pleas. As Mack concludes, a black gentleman approaches him and tries to embrace him while others approach the makeshift bandstand to purchase his compact discs and ask for his autograph.

Shortly after the set, I ask Farrell for his impressions of the performance and the response of the audience. Nodding, he remarks on what he regards as an important distinction between the experience of performing inside versus outside the festival grounds: "In a way, people sort of see us as an alternative to the tyranny of the blues in the bigger venues. You know—'*Do you want to hear the blues? I can't hear you! Louder! We can make you like the blues!!*' . . . Meanwhile, most times the crowd is so isolated and removed from the stage, the musicians, and, ultimately, the music . . . It seems as though the bigger the venue, the more removed the audience is going to be from the performance."

As the crowd dissipates, Dustin counts the money collected during the performance. He reports to me that a bystander dropped a fifty-dollar bill into their bucket during the previous set and hopes to match Saturday's all-day take of somewhere between seventy and eighty dollars a person. Handing Farrell a ten-dollar bill, he asks him if it is counterfeit. After I confirm that it is, Mack immediately begins attempting to figure out how they can parlay it into real money. Meanwhile, Farrell seems content with the weekend's earnings: "Oh yeah, for us it's great. The crowds flow down to us, watch a set, give us money, and then they leave, and more people come by to replace them, and it's the same thing all day long. We get a very high turnover, if you know what I mean." Meanwhile, although tempted, I do not take the opportunity to ask Dustin, Mack, or Farrell to financially compensate me for participating in their street gig, nor do they offer me a "taste" from the bucket after our set. Looking back on my performance, they were robbed.

After taking leave of the band, I head back into the park with my saxophone to try to catch a show at one of the smaller stages. Relaxing on the lawn in front of the Petrillo Music Shell, I watch the carnivalesque crowd pass over me: the rogue vendor selling handmade macramé bracelets in rainbows of bright color; the couples attempting to sear their dinners on portable grills; the young woman passing out Phish handbills. Still, the contrasting behaviors of individual audience members remain striking. I spot a frustrated gentleman attempting to block the music from his ears with his hands while conversing on his cellular phone, and I cannot help but chuckle to myself and smile.

And as I wander through the park, I encounter Russ, a street guitarist; sitting at the edge of the Front Porch lawn, he asks me to pull out my horn so we can jam together. I explain to him that I don't have a permit, but he brushes off my concern: "Hey, man, neither do I!" Russ explains that he has endured no fewer than six arrests in recent years for performing in public without a license but has never been convicted. His strategy this weekend has been to find spots in the park that are out of sight of patrolling police officers, but close enough to festival visitors that he can still earn money. A young musician who resides in suburban Hoffman Estates but spends his weekends in Chicago, Russ echoes Farrell's sentiments concerning the vitality of street music in contradistinction to the official culture provides by the festival's main stages: "Man, they can't get rid of us, because the street musician represents the heart of the city . . . We *are* the culture of the city." And I nod and chuckle, and I smile.

Insult to Injury.   The physical layout of the park reinforces the differentiation that exists between city-sponsored performers like Buddy

Guy and the excluded bluesmen who play at the festival edges like Russ, Farrell, Dustin, and Mack. But as I suggested earlier, tourists may respond more favorably to the authenticity symbolized by the marginalized culture of these street musicians than to the staged authenticity displayed by the festival's more renowned headliners. In fact, their enthusiasm during impromptu street performances expresses the same attitudes that the tourists discussed in earlier chapters articulate in their remarks at small neighborhood clubs like B.L.U.E.S. and the Checkerboard Lounge. Likewise, the street musicians who compensate for their marginality by deriding the festival's "tyranny of the blues" display the same kinds of sentiments as their fellow survivors like Darryl and Sebastian, who prefer casual blues bars to more upscale venues. Finally, the remarks made by Russ concerning the "culture of the city" echo the opinions expressed by Chad and other lions who enjoy bars like Smoke Daddy because they "make up the lifeblood of the city."

Of course, the Mayor's Office of Special Events may not necessarily agree with Russ's and Farrell's assertions regarding the importance of unofficial street performance in the urban metropolis. In preparation for the 1999 Chicago Blues Festival the following year, the city enacted a special set of rules and regulations for street performer's on June 1, two days before the start of the event. The tenor of these rules expresses the city's position on street music and its performers quite unambiguously. They include the following regulations:

> Rule 2. During special events, performances in the vicinity of the event shall be limited to designated areas, which are indicated in the maps attached in Exhibit B.[41]

> Rule 3. Performers shall be limited to a two-hour performance in a given area per day. Performers are required to check in with MOSE (Mayor's Office of Special Events) at a check-in area located at the northeast corner of Jackson Street and Columbus Avenue. Performers shall be assigned time slots on a first-come, first-served basis. Time slots will be assigned to performing groups, where applicable; by ordinance, each performer must have an individual street performer's permit. To increase the number of performers who have access to performance areas, there shall be separate spots available for performers generating sound above an average conversation level and for those performers with less loud types of performances.[42]

> Rule 4. Performers may not generate any sound by any means that is louder than an average conversational level at a distance of 100 feet from the point

of generation. Any amplifiers must be battery or solar power; shore-power (or plug-in) electricity and generators are prohibited.

Rule 5. Performances shall be permitted only during the official hours of the special event.

Rule 6. Due to the extreme pedestrian congestion during the last two hours of a special event, during that time period, street performers are prohibited from performing on the public way on both Monroe Street and Jackson Street, between the west side of Lake Shore Drive and the east side of Michigan Avenue.

Rule 7. Performers may not engage in vending unless they have a speech peddler permit.

Rule 8. No structures or signs are permitted, and no equipment or other materials used by performers may be left or stored in a designated area.

While the actions of Dustin, Farrell, and Mack during the 1998 Chicago Blues Festival would have violated each of these ordinances had they been entered into law at the time, their band successfully abided by every one of them during the festival in June 1999. They did not perform at all.

Conclusion

The Search for Authenticity

This was really the way my whole road experience began, and the things that were to come are too fantastic not to tell.

Yes, and it wasn't only because I was a writer and needed new experiences that I wanted to know Dean more, and because my life hanging around the campus had reached the completion of its cycle and was stultified. . . . [I]n his excited way of speaking I heard again the voices of old companions and brothers under the bridge, among the motorcycles, along the wash-lined neighborhood and drowsy doorsteps of afternoon where they played guitars while their older brothers worked in the mills. All my other current friends were "intellectuals"—Chad the Nietzschean anthropologist, Carlo Marx and his nutty surrealist low-voiced serious staring talk, Old Bull Lee and his critical anti-everything drawl. . . . But Dean's intelligence was every bit as formal and shining and complete, without the tedious intellectualness. . . . Besides all my New York friends were in the negative, nightmare position of putting down society and giving their tired bookish or political or psychoanalytical reasons, but Dean just raced in society, eager for bread and love. . . . A western kinsman under the sun, Dean. Although my aunt warned me that he would get me in trouble, I could hear a new call and see a new horizon, and believe it at my young age; and a little bit of trouble or even Dean's eventual rejection of me as a buddy, putting me down, as he would later, on starving sidewalks and sickbeds—what did it matter? I was a young writer and I wanted to take off.

Somewhere along the line I knew there'd be girls, visions, everything; somewhere along the line the pearl would be handed to me.

—Jack Kerouac, *On the Road*

The Authenticity of Urban Culture.   While I have dedicated the bulk of this book to my research on the commercialized character of Chicago's blues clubs and the search for authenticity that propels consumers through them, I want to conclude by exploring how this discussion could also be used to explain how authenticity is produced and consumed in other kinds of cultural contexts. First, I will discuss the rise of tourism and cultural commerce in the post-industrial metropolis, with particular emphasis on the consumption of nightlife and nouveau cuisine that blurs the boundaries between authenticity and fantasy, local tradition and a global future. I will then explore the relationship between commercialization and the struggle over authenticity in three urban music scenes: independent rock, hip-hop, and the contemporary rave subculture. I will finally conclude with a brief set of observations concerning the search for authenticity within academia in general and sociology in particular.

To begin, the last chapter demonstrates the extent to which cities rely on idealized representations of themselves in order to increase their prestige and cultural capital in the global tourism economy. A look at other American cities provides an opportunity to explore appropriate comparative cases, particularly since the symbolic economy of authenticity found in the world of the Chicago blues parallels similar networks of signification and local promotion elsewhere. For example, Memphis markets itself on the basis of its musical legacy that draws travelers to a variety of tourist attractions, including the former recording studios of Sun Records and Stax Records, the popular voyeuristic tours of Elvis Presley's Graceland, and the dozen-or-so blues clubs that line that city's famous Beale Street.[1] While in town, tourists linger around the lobby of the Peabody Hotel for a chance to catch the twice-daily parade of mallards and drakes that waddle through the lobby accompanied by the music of John Philip Sousa—which, as New York *Times* reporter Rick Bragg notes, "is worth $200 a night if someone else is paying."[2] Memphis was the hometown of W.C. Handy, "Father of the Blues," and the city has erected his statue in Handy Park just in case visitors forget while en route to the Rum Boogie Café or B.B. King's Blues Club.

Likewise, Nashville draws on its cultural heritage as the nation's capital of country music production to attract tourists and increase local revenues to the city. It has succeeded in this regard not only by relying on countless tributes among members of the music community, but also through the development of cultural attractions such as the Grand Ole Opry, the record companies along Music Row, celebrity-owned music clubs like (Mickey) Gilley's, and, until recently, the roller coasters and waterslides of Opryland, the city's former country music theme park. Like Chicago, Nashville attracts international travelers in search of the authenticity represented by tourist spots like the Country Music Hall of Fame and the Bourbon Street Blues and Boogie Bar, and also by its small neighborhood taverns and whiskey bars, which may connote an even greater sense of authenticity. Regarding the former, one would have to imagine that at least some of the city's local musicians have grown tired of wearing cowboy boots and affecting a southern drawl while performing "Stand by Your Man" for the weekend crowd.

While Memphis and Nashville rely on the authenticity suggested by the countrified sounds of the South as a strategy of promoting tourism and cultural consumption, it is not uncommon for cultural entrepreneurs in other world-class cities to exploit the cultural resources of their local communities to enhance their city's attractiveness among travelers. In New York, Big Apple Greeters offers a program in which residents from local communities lead visitors on private tours of their neighborhoods, while Harlem Spirituals, Inc., conducts special gospel, jazz, and "soul food" tours of Harlem's storied districts.[3] In Toronto tourists attend walking and biking tours of Old Chinatown, the taverna-lined Greek area of East End, and the recently gentrified Irish neighborhood dubbed Cabbagetown by locals.[4] By directing tourists toward consumer activities outside their downtown districts, local boosters and cultural entrepreneurs heighten the images of their cities by emphasizing their community and ethnic traditions alongside more metropolitan depictions of contemporary urbanism.

Meanwhile, other cities blend distinct vestiges of their authentic pasts with images of an imagined future.[5] While San Francisco continues to exploit its 1960s acid-rock music legacy to draw tourist to its commercialized Haight-Ashbury district, "Summer of Love" tours, and the Flower Child Room of the Red Victorian Peace Center Bed & Breakfast, it simultaneously sells itself as the very embodiment of the new technological age, as evidenced by its promotion of the locally based *Wired* magazine offices, the rise of its web development corridor, and the city's much-touted proximity to the high-tech campuses and engineering labs of Silicon Valley thirty miles to the south.[6] In Paris tourists shift between the twelfth-century Gothic authenticity of the Cathedral of Notre-Dame and the boldly postmodern Pompidou Center, adorned with steel and glass corridors reminiscent of the space-age modules depicted in the *Jetsons* and *2001: A Space Odyssey*. Across the Chunnel in

London, visitors hunt down age-old landmarks like Westminster Abbey and St. Paul's Cathedral, the staged authenticity of Shakespeare's Globe Theatre, and more up-to-the-minute temples to the global age, from the super-slick, international noodle-shop chain Wagamama, to Itsu, a trendy Soho sushi parlor where diners select Japanese dishes from a futuristic conveyer belt. In these cities contradictory images of place are the norm and seem to be broadly indicative of a postmodern world, where local authenticity and global newness have become ironic commentaries on one another.

These contradictions extend to the nocturnal lives of urban thrill-seekers as well, as evidenced by the increasing popularity of cultural pursuits that draw on simultaneous desires for authenticity and fantasy, hyperreality and make-believe. In Chicago the rage over swing dancing provides a case in point. The revival of swing and its various incarnations represents a pointed nostalgia for the romanticized life and times of the Swing Era (1935–45) and its glamorous affectations—dry martinis and cigars, checkered three-piece suits and smooth cocktail dresses, black-and-white saddle shoes and sharp wing tips. As a result of its retro-friendly myopia, this rather woeful period in American history—an era marked by depression-era poverty, intense racism and bigotry, the rise of fascism abroad, and the onslaught of World War II—reemerges from the national psyche as an age of fun, codified in a series of dance steps that reinsert normative gender roles and stylized conformity into the public world of urban nightlife. On swing dance nights at local bars and lounges in the city, the artificial staging of authenticity as a performance is self-conscious, and perhaps it is an attempt to compensate for a loss of authenticity in the present by reproducing what all participants recognize as the decadent pageantry of the past. Whether they dance the Charleston, the Madison, the Shag, or the Jitterbug Stroll, participants can step out into the nocturnal city and follow the fashion of their dreams as characters in a well-costumed period film set to what has become (just like in the blues) a standardized soundtrack, featuring Glenn Miller's "In the Mood," Benny Goodman's "Sing, Sing, Sing (With a Swing)," and Louis Prima's "Jump, Jive, an' Wail," a jump-blues number whose inclusion in a 1998 Gap commercial may have single-handedly launched the neo-swing revival itself.[7]

Certainly, the attempt to mix local authenticity, cinematic fantasy, and global invention extends well beyond the revivalism of popular music and might suggest suitable comparisons with other kinds of urban entertainment, such as the current move among city restaurateurs to sell haute cuisine as a theatrical experience. In Philadelphia Stephen Starr has carved a culinary empire out of his high-concept dining establishments like Tangerine, Buddakan, and Morimoto, where customers are swept through luxuriously appointed dining rooms and served by gorgeous actresses and models looking for steady creative work. The chefs of these establishments excel at preparing eclectic fusion entrées that balance regional ethnic flavors with traditional Continental fare, thus making a mockery of the authenticity once celebrated by the nineteenth-century French gastronome elite.[8] At Tangerine, which specializes in nouvelle Moroccan, Mediterranean, and French dishes, diners ogle over multicultural selections that include chickpea crepes with chanterelle mushrooms, and harissa gnocchi served with dates and creamy celery root. A similarly global dreamscape flutters through Buddakan, where customers admire a ten-foot gilded statue of the great god himself while feasting on Old and New World flavors such as seared Kobe beef carpaccio and truffle-scented edamame ravioli.

But the centerpiece of Starr's restaurant dominion is Morimoto, named for its head cook, the Iron Chef of cult television fame. The interior decor features a undulating ceiling of compressed bamboo rods, smiling psychedelic holograms, and illuminated dining booths that change colors throughout the evening. Like its local counterparts, the menu celebrates the international fusion of Japanese and European ingredients, such as tempura served with Gorgonzola cheese sauce and chocolate mousse with fresh grated wasabi. As for Morimoto himself, a cover story in a special restaurant issue of *Philadelphia Magazine* revealed that the Iron Chef simultaneously rejects and glorifies notions about authenticity and Japanese cuisine:

> Today, he's a chef attempting something few others would dare, something very hard to label. "No fusion! Fusion is *con*fusion," says Morimoto angrily. "No nouveau! They call my food nouveau Japanese, everybody tries to copy. Junk nouveau. They say to me, 'Your food is not Japanese.' I say, 'I don't give a shit!' I cook, I am Japanese. I have Japanese techniques. I see lots of different foods, French food. I say, mmm, good idea. I don't copy it. I take from every cuisine—Greek, Spanish, Turkish . . .
>
> "I will pull back my cuisine. Do things the traditional way. Restaurants use powdered wasabi—I will grate my own from the root, like the grandmothers did. Restaurants buy plastic bags of bonito shavings for katsuobushi"—a dried tuna-like fish used as a condiment. "I will grate my own in the traditional katsuobushi chef's tool. I get Starr to buy me a rice machine.

I take the hull off here in the restaurant. I will reintroduce the tradition. Then I make hop, skip, jump sideways into a newer new cuisine—Morimoto cuisine!"[9]

Commercialized Music and the Battle over Authenticity. If cities beyond Chicago demonstrate the cultural usefulness of authenticity as a strategic tool for the promotion of place, certainly other kinds of art worlds rely on internal debates over definitions of authenticity as a means of negotiating the pervasive forces of commercialization. In the world of American independent, or indie, rock music, battles over commodification and creative autonomy characterize the artistic landscape inhabited by consumers as well as musicians. Broadly defined, indie rock refers to a wide variety of styles of popular music recorded and performed by bands on small, independently owned record labels, all without the benefit of a distribution deal with one of the five mass-media conglomerates that own and control the nation's major record companies: Sony (Columbia, Epic, Legacy, Sony Classical), Bertelsmann (Arista, RCA, Jive, J, V2, Windham Hill, BMG Classics), AOL Time Warner (Atlantic, Elektra, London-Sire, Rhino, Warner Bros.), Vivendi Universal (Interscope, Geffen, A&M, Island, Def Jam, MCA, Mercury, Motown, Universal), and EMI (Capitol, Virgin).[10] While a small number of indie post-punk bands, such as Black Flag, Sonic Youth, and Fugazi, rose to subcultural notoriety during the 1980s despite their near-total exclusion from mainstream networks of promotion and distribution—including record store chains, major concert venues, FM radio, MTV, and industry boosters like *Rolling Stone*—the overwhelming majority of these acts performed for diminutive audiences until they eventually faded into obscurity.[11]

In some ways, 1980s indie rock and the Chicago blues went through similar cycles of exclusion and subsequent commercialization and mass marketing. The 1991 commercial success of the Seattle-based band Nirvana and their multiplatinum selling album *Nevermind* led record companies and their buying public on a frenzied search for the authenticity represented by gritty images of angst-ridden youth, a curious brew of bourgeois alienation and heroin chic. Like the blues, at that time indie rock suggested a romanticized image of the *real* to its fans and, as such, a welcome antidote to the bubble-gum pop of late 1980s acts like Michael Jackson and Duran Duran, while the culture industries recognized this young audience as a relatively untapped market ripe for exploitation.

Soon, major record labels began scouting the national periphery for the very same independent bands they had vilified and subsequently ignored during the previous decade. Just as Chicago's blues revival grew when local boosters recognized the moneymaking potential of the city's blues legacy, a suddenly "alternative" rock was born, a repackaging of a variety of resurrected styles from the 1980s underground indie rock scene, including the straightedge hardcore of Minor Threat, iconoclastic feminist rage of the Slits, and the post-punk of Hüsker Dü and the Replacements. Perhaps no band represented the staged authenticity necessary for this enterprise better than Pearl Jam, a Seattle "grunge" band whose lead singer Eddie Vedder appeared on the cover of *Time* magazine in 1993 for not only lending his voice to songs about extreme depression and high school revenge fantasies, but for achieving such a performative state of alienated rage that, according to one reporter, he "reminded fans of an animal trying to escape from a leash."[12]

The industry's misadventures in selling this corporately modified bohemia to disaffected American youth led to a number of highly visible moneymaking enterprises, including the nearly total reprogramming of MTV's video music format, a three-day concert to mark the twenty-fifth anniversary of the 1969 Woodstock festival, and Lollapalooza, a multiband tour where middle- and upper-class teenagers could defy conformity by slam dancing in unison to bands like Jane's Addiction and Primus after getting their tongues and navels pierced and having the same dragonfly tattoo etched onto their backs on site. The irony here is that just as alternative rock mesmerized a generation of adolescents in search of the authenticity represented by images of rebellion and anti-capitalist purity, the commercialization of punk led to a fierce backlash among the members of numerous bands against the mass-media establishment—including, interestingly enough, Pearl Jam, who stopped filming videos after their first album, drastically cut down on their touring and availability to the press, and testified to Congress against Ticketmaster's monopolistic business practices.

Many of these musicians eulogize the authenticity once symbolized by underground bands like Big Black and Mission of Burma while bemoaning the current commercial promotion of multiplatinum selling pop acts like Blink-182 as little more than easy money for record company executives and their A&R personnel. In a scatological tract on "The Problem with Music," Big Black frontman and indie producer Steve Albini warns would-be rock superstars about the perils of the mainstream recording industry:

Whenever I talk to a band who are about to sign with a major label, I always end up thinking of them in a particular context. I imagine a trench, about four feet wide and five feet deep, maybe sixty yards long, filled with runny, decaying shit. I imagine these people, some of them good friends, some of them barely acquaintances, at one end of this trench. I also imagine a faceless industry lackey at the other end, holding a fountain pen and a contract waiting to be signed.

Nobody can see what's printed on the contract. It's too far away, and besides, the shit stench is making everybody's eyes water. The lackey shouts to everybody that the first one to swim the trench gets to sign the contract. Everybody dives in the trench and they struggle furiously to get to the other end. Two people arrive simultaneously and begin wrestling furiously, clawing each other and dunking each other under the shit. Eventually, one of them capitulates, and there's only one contestant left. He reaches for the pen, but the lackey says, "Actually, I think you need a little more development. Swim it again, please. Backstroke."

And he does, of course.[13]

Like independent rock, hip-hop experienced a similar transformation in meaning in the wake of its mainstream acceptance. With its hyperkinetic rhythms, complex sampling, dubbing techniques, and freestyle vocals with lyrical allusions to street violence, sexual gamesmanship, and political resistance, early hip-hop as black urban style represented an authentic alternative to more prominent popular music genres for many of its fans. But when hip-hop gained visibility on commercially central outlets like MTV in the 1990s and rose in popularity among white audiences, a struggle emerged among rap artists over whether one could remain authentic and thus "keep it real" in an age of widespread fandom and financial profitability. In this context, authenticity refers to a number of related values considered paramount to the maintenance of an urban subcultural identity, including artistic individualism and self-expression, adherence to "old school" traditions, street credibility, creative autonomy from the demands of commerce and mass popularity, and the promotion of blackness as a valued racial and cultural identity.[14] In other words, the symbols of authenticity and "selling out" within the hip-hop nation share a common set of themes with their counterparts in the Chicago blues.

The public display of this orientation bears itself out in interviews with professional and amateur rap artists that Kembrew McLeod conducted and documented in an article on "Authenticity within Hip-Hop and Other Cultures Threatened with Assimilation." According to Wu-Tang Clan member and solo performer Method Man, authenticity connotes self-expression: "Basically, I make music that represents me. Who I am. I'm not gonna calculate my music to entertain the masses. I gotta keep it real for me."[15] Rapper Rass Kass suggests an adherence to prevailing depictions of the authenticity of the black ghetto: "For me, the most important thing is the street. That's what I make my shit for and to do anything else would be fake."[16] Meanwhile, MC Eiht draws on multiple catchphrases that express authenticity in his explanation of what "keepin' it real" means in rap:

> Real, underground hip-hop is staying true to what you have always done and not trying to go mainstream or Top-40 or Top-20 on the radio just to sell records or get your face on MTV or be on the Lollapalooza Tour. I think being underground is just making records that the people on the street appeal to. Not to win an award on the American Music Awards or a Grammy or a Billboard Music Award. It's just a fact that you make the music that people on the street want to listen to.[17]

The relationship between cultural commerce and the social construction of authenticity in the contemporary rave underworld follows a similar pattern, which is ironic because unlike hip-hop and the blues, mainstream music fans have disparaged electronic dance music as plastic and artificial since its rise to prominence in disco clubs and other sites of gay urban culture. In a thinly veiled fury of homophobia and racism, anti-disco sentiment reached a feverish pitch in the late 1970s, perhaps most famously demonstrated on Disco Demolition Night, a public relations event gone awry at Comiskey Park on July 12, 1979, during a double-header between the hometown Chicago White Sox and the Detroit Tigers. The brainchild of Steve Dahl and Garry Meier, two local radio disc jockeys, the evening culminated in a near-riot as rock fans tossed and burned vinyl records throughout the night and eventually stormed the field, shouting "Disco Sucks!!" until Chicago's forfeiture of the second game.

Since that tumultuous evening, electronic dance music and its many contemporary variants—such as deep house, techno, drum 'n' bass, trance, and happy hardcore—has symbolized authenticity to its fans largely through its association with representations of rebelliousness, particularly the aesthetics of black ghetto culture, semi-illegal warehouse parties, and the use of designer drugs like ecstasy, crystal meth, and Special K. By infusing everyday objects with shared alternative meanings, participants in the rave underworld collectively produce a consumer playground with its own symbolic economy of authenticity. Within this subcultural universe, elements of style, including up-to-the-date slang, dance moves, fashion, and drug paraphernalia serve as markers of status and authenticity that can be employed to stratify participants and exclude outsiders altogether on the basis of their nocturnal capital. As just one example, by appropriating the ritualistic accessories valued by adolescents and college students for their utility as drug enhancers—candy bracelets, glow sticks, pacifiers, menthol nasal inhalers, surgical gauze masks, Vicks VapoRub, and so forth—young consumers differentiate themselves not only from a law-abiding public but also from adult drug users who forgo such rituals when getting their rocks off.[18]

However, as the rave subculture rose in popularity, it became more financially viable for event promoters to host commercial raves where suburban kids could pay upward of forty dollars for admission to parties housed in venues ranging from elite nightclubs to rented parking lots. Electronica music gained even more visibility in the public arena as artists like Moby, the Orb, and the Propellerheads began licensing their CD tracks for use in television commercials advertising multinationals like American Express, Volkswagen, and Apple. Meanwhile, in a wave of moral hypocrisy and fierce competition over ratings and ad revenue, raves became the subject of countless tabloid television "news" programs eager to capitalize on wildly exaggerated stories of teenage sex, drugs, and death.[19]

And in a now strangely familiar twist, the increased commercialization, popularity, and visibility of rave culture have encouraged a battle over the authenticity of the current state of electronica among consumers. According to Sarah Thornton's study of the British club scene, the desire for subcultural status grows even more intense as established party hounds mock newcomers to the scene. Many criticize these novice thrill-seekers for exhibiting what they consider a rather doltish lack of knowledge and hip sensibility regarding both current music and style, and refer to the mainstream clubs that cater to them as "drunken cattle markets" where "tacky men drinking pints of best bitter pull girls in white high heels," and clueless amateurs named "Sharon and Tracy dance around their handbags."[20]

But in spite of this increased concern over authenticity in popular music arenas among die-hard fans who bemoan the increased commercialization that pervades all aspects of contemporary public culture, many indie rock, hip-hop, and electronica artists face the same dilemma as Chicago blues musicians—namely, how do they negotiate their way through the set of competing demands and desires for artistic autonomy *and* popular mainstream acceptance, local appreciation *and* global visibility, financial profits *and* subcultural credibility? By recognizing the manufactured quality of authenticity, some performers express their own critique of commonly held assumptions about the nature of producing music as simultaneously art, entertainment, and commerce.

For instance, in a March 2001 *New York Times Magazine* feature story, "For Rock Bands, Selling Out Isn't What It Used to Be," John Leland reports that while pop giants like Bruce Springsteen and Neil Young can afford to turn their noses up at licensing their recordings for use in television commercials, this kind of advertising actually provides one of the few outlets available to indie rock artists in search of audience exposure, particularly in the risk-averse climate of contemporary radio and video music programming. As a result, musicians of all genres are tempering their older, punk-oriented definitions of authenticity in light of their inconsistencies with present-day market realities, especially since past fears of selling out could hinder their ability to record and perform music for their fans without being relegated to a life of professional marginality. According to Robert Schneider, lead singer and guitarist for the indie rock band the Apples in Stereo, at a certain point in one's music career the price of purity becomes an albatross too heavy to bear. "You understand it better as you get older. Our band might not be able to keep going if we couldn't do this."[21]

Many rappers maintain a similar ambivalence about prevailing definitions of authenticity within the hip-hop nation. This sometimes comes through in song lyrics, as in the late Tupac Shakur's "I Ain't Mad at Cha," in which he vents, "So many questions, and they ask me if I'm still down / I moved up out of the ghetto, so I ain't real now?"[22] In fact, at times contradictory representations of authenticity come to a head for these performers. In a *New York Times* feature story, "Guarding the Borders of the Hip-Hop Nation," Dog and Trife, two aspiring rappers, refute the notion that whites can consume hip-hop in a truly authentic manner, but do so primarily because they are suspicious of whites who fetishize the authenticity represented by images of black ghetto life:

Dog found it curious that whites—suburban mall rats, college backpackers—bought most rap records. "White people can listen to rap, but I know they can't relate," he said. "I hear rap and I'm saying, 'Here's another guy who's had it unfair.' They're taking, 'This guy is cool, he's a drug dealer, he's got all the girls, he's a big person, he killed people.' That is moronic."

Later, Dog said: "Hip-hop is bringing the races together, but on false pretenses to make money. Look at Trife. He's got two felonies. That means he's finished in society. But he can rap. His two felonies, in rap, man, that's a plus."

"It's messed up," Trife said. "In hip-hop I'm valid when I'm disrespected."[23]

Meanwhile, DJ Muggs, an Italian rapper in the interracial hip-hop outfit Cypress Hill, rejects the criticisms that his group's success among white suburban fans should diminish his credibility within the subculture: "Yeah. Keepin' it real. I hate that fuckin', um, yeah. I just try to be who I am. People be too worried about how many records I sold and that I was on fuckin' MTV."[24]

Sociology and the Search for Authenticity.   Like many sociologists, I did not originally seek out a life in the academy or gravitate toward its abstract texts during what some might call my misspent youth. In my early twenties, my heroes were a familiar set of American writers who described the mysterious subcultural worlds of the nocturnal metropolis. Worn, used paperback copies of their books filled my shelves: Ernest Hemingway's *The Sun Also Rises*, Jack Kerouac's *On the Road*, Tom Wolfe's *The Electric Kool-Aid Acid Test*, Hunter S. Thompson's *Fear and Loathing in Las Vegas*. In each of those books, a protagonist finds himself lost in the city, dumbstruck by the brilliant lights of downtown; and in the midst of their confusion, they try to explain to the reader how the helter-skelter world of the city feels to the human touch. Admittedly, in hindsight I find my adolescent reverence for their authorial grandiloquence slightly embarrassing. Still, their literary flights of fancy, if sometimes pretentious, infused their descriptions with a textured sensibility often missing from much academic prose, and I remain bedazzled by their ethnographic eye, the tireless energy of their writing, and, of course, their unrelenting search for authenticity in the heart of the city.

As I have hopefully demonstrated in the preceding chapters, the search for authenticity is never ending, but always expresses a fantasy that the experience of an idealized reality might render our lives more meaningful. And having said that, I find it quite striking that in my encounters at both collegiate seminars and cocktail parties, I am constantly reminded of the pervasiveness of this desire for authenticity among highly educated, affluent professionals in general and university academics in particular. "So, where are the authentic blues clubs in Chicago? Where should we go?" I have given hour-long talks on the social construction of authenticity at university colloquia, only to be taken aside by faculty members afterward to be asked a request along these lines: "Well, I completely agree with your argument. But now that the talk is over, and there's nobody around, please tell me—What do *you* think the most authentic clubs are in the city? Come on, it will be just between us! I promise I won't tell a soul!!" It is said that when the French philosopher Jacques Derrida gave a lecture at the University of Chicago during the 1990s, the one local tourist attraction he insisted on visiting was the Checkerboard Lounge, and it hardly surprises me.

And among academics, sociologists may yearn for the authenticity suggested by the urban milieu more than most. In 1999 I was invited by a very prominent cultural sociologist (an ethnographer whose work I greatly admire) to organize and lead a bus tour of local blues and jazz clubs for the upcoming annual conference of the American Sociological Association (ASA), as it was to be held in Chicago later that year. Naturally, I suggested that I take the group to B.L.U.E.S. After all, I was familiar with the bands that performed there on the weekends, and I knew enough of the staff and regulars that I was sure we could get a good rate, or at least a warm welcome—besides, I sort of wanted to help the club out by throwing some business its way. But my proposal was immediately rejected because it was thought that a busload of sociologists in search of the Chicago blues would demand to see a more *authentic* club, and not some tourist attraction in Lincoln Park. And so I wound up bringing the group to the Green Mill, for its historic value as a Capone-run speakeasy, and—where else?—the Checkerboard Lounge, which they just *loved*. By the evening's end, I caught a glimpse of one of my passengers—a renowned past president of the ASA—smiling down in the front row, drinking a bottle of Budweiser, and tapping his feet to the music. When I finally had to send the bus back to the hotel, I practically had to drag the whole gang out of the club.

In fact, the practice of sociology is inextricably bound up with this search for authenticity, not only for its positivist traditions as a social science, but also because its ethnographers have historically been attracted to the edges of the city where they might explore worlds of poverty, crime, and social marginality. While this work reflects some of sociology's most important contributions to the understanding of the causes and consequences of urban desperation and abandonment, it is equally clear that ethnographers who study these pockets of the city are aware of how their *own* sense of authenticity as urban sociologists will be viewed by their readers, particularly in the moments when they invite crack dealers into their home, witness acts of violent crime, fraternize with homeless men, and, yes, when they hang out with blues musicians in Chicago. If the search for authenticity is a stumbling block that must be overcome if one is to see the world as it is, rather than how one would like it to be, then it is something that we *all* must get over—not just the readers of urban fiction, journalism, and sociology, but writers as well, even this one.

As I remarked in the introduction, Duke Ellington's "Black and Tan Fantasy" offers a critique of race relations in the context of urban nightlife and the consumption of jazz and blues, but it is also a prayer, a symbol of hope in an imperfect world. I hope that I have successfully presented a similar examination of the Chicago blues and the search for authenticity in all its complexity, warts and all. While the authenticity found in the city's blues clubs may, in fact, be little more than a mirage, the ever-increasing popularity of the blues among audiences suggests that even myths disguised as reality can be all too real in their consequences for those who chase after the bright lights of their urban fantasies, black-and-tan or otherwise. And certainly, few understand this better than the black and white blues musicians of Chicago, who struggle to entertain those audiences with the most heavenly music, even as they are asked to play songs from a Set List from Hell.

NOTES

Introduction

1. I identify all the blues clubs in this book by their real names, in order to invite readers to reanalyze and propose alternative interpretations of their social and cultural environments, should they feel compelled to do so. However, in the interests of protecting the identity of my informants, I have changed the names of all the individuals I interviewed, with the exception of a small number of major public officials and club owners. I have also retained the real names (or stage names where applicable) of all the musicians I observed or discussed in public during the course of my study but was unable to interview or otherwise make use of their statements in the book. All pseudonyms should be identifiable by my sole use of first names in such cases, such as "Jack." Also, the reader should be aware that since parts of this book are written in the ethnographic present to reflect my field experience during the late 1990s, certain attributes of place, notably the staff employed by the local clubs featured in the study, have changed. On the use of the ethnographic present in sociology, see John A. Keiser, *The Vice Lords: Warriors of the Street* (New York: Holt, Rinehart and Winston, 1969), 11; for a critique, see James Clifford, *The Predicament of Culture: Twentieth-Century Ethnography, Literature and Art* (Cambridge: Harvard University Press, 1988).

2. According to the 1990 U.S. Census, Lincoln Park boasted an annual median family income of $75,113, with 67 percent of its residents making over $50,000 a year, while the median value of an owner-occupied housing unit reached $330,556. Meanwhile, the census tract where B.L.U.E.S. operates displayed an even greater degree of affluence, with a median family income of $81,292, 73 percent of its residents making over $50,000 annually, and a median value of $372,700 for an owner-occupied housing unit. For additional data on Lincoln Park, see Chicago Fact Book Consortium, *Local Community Fact Book: Chicago Metropolitan Area 1990* (Chicago: Academy Chicago, 1995), 54–56.

3. Carl Sandburg, "Chicago," in *Chicago Poems* (New York: Henry Holt, 1916). On the recent loss of manufacturing jobs in Chicago's inner city areas, see William Julius Wilson, *When Work Disappears: The World of the New Urban Poor* (Chicago: University of Chicago Press, 1996).

4. On the impact of these post-industrial shifts on the cultural landscapes of urban down-

town areas, see Saskia Sassen, *The Mobility of Labor and Capital: A Study in International Investment and Labor Flow* (Cambridge: Cambridge University Press, 1988), and *The Global City: New York, London, Tokyo* (Princeton: Princeton University Press, 1991); David Harvey, *The Condition of Postmodernity* (Cambridge, Mass.: Blackwell, 1990); Edward W. Soja, *Postmodern Geographies: The Reassertion of Space in Critical Social Theory* (London: Verso, 1989); Sharon Zukin, *Landscapes of Power: From Detroit to Disney World* (Berkeley: University of California Press, 1991), and *The Cultures of Cities* (Cambridge: Blackwell, 1995); M. Christine Boyer, "Cities for Sale: Merchandising History at South Street Seaport," in *Variations on a Theme Park: The New American City and the End of Public Space*, ed. Michael Sorkin (New York: Hill and Wang, 1992); and John Hannigan, *Fantasy City: Pleasure and Profit in the Postmodern Metropolis* (London: Routledge, 1998). The restructuring of Chicago's economy from manufacturing production to business services and entertainment can be observed in the rise of the city's convention industry. According to the Chicago Convention and Tourism Bureau, Chicago attracted 25 of the 200 largest conventions in the nation in 1996. In that year the city hosted 1,135 conventions, 140 trade shows, and 37,062 corporate meetings, for a total of 38,337 events. Attendance at these events totaled 4,244,121 participants: for conventions, 874,712; trade shows, 2,122,422; corporate meetings, 1,246,987. In January 1997 *Trade Show Week* anointed Chicago as a "Top Trade Show Destination"; part of the city's draw lies in the popularity of its newly expanded McCormick Place complex, the largest exhibition and meeting facility in North America. Furthermore, the financial impact of the city's convention business on the local economy has been astounding: in 1996 conventioneers spent over $1 billion during their stays in Chicago, and attendees of trade shows and corporate meetings spent $3.2 billion and $515 million, respectively. On the convention business in Chicago, see *Chicago Tourism Fact Book* (City of Chicago, 1997); and Katharine A. Diaz, "Chicago: Your Kind of Town," *Corporate & Incentive Travel* (August 1997): 62–65.

5. It should also be noted that by fusing together disparate song fragments into these musical collages, this game of mix-and-match parallels the improvisational work of early swing and bebop jazz musicians, the use of medleys in traditional R&B and soul performances, and the sampling and mixing techniques employed by disc jockeys in current hip-hop and electronic dance music. Similarly, in *Subculture: The Meaning of Style* (London: Routledge, 1979), Dick Hebdige applies the concept of bricolage to the production of subcultural identity and its representation in fashion and popular culture. On the development of lyrical sampling in jazz, see Eric Nisenson, *Blue: The Murder of Jazz* (New York: Da Capo Press, 2000). Meanwhile, Paul Gilroy, *"There Ain't No Black in the Union Jack": The Cultural Politics of Race and Nation* (Chicago: University of Chicago Press, 1991); and Tricia Rose, *Black Noise: Rap Music and Black Culture in Contemporary America* (Hanover, N.H.: Wesleyan University Press, 1994), both discuss how urban rappers and other hip-hop artists incorporate the latter into their craft; on electronic dance music, see Sarah Thornton, *Club Cultures: Music, Media and Subcultural Capital* (Hanover, N.H.: Wesleyan University Press, 1996); Matthew Collin and John Godfrey, *Altered State: The Story of Ecstasy Culture and Acid House* (London: Serpent's Tail, 1997); and Simon Reynolds, *Generation Ecstasy: Into the World of Techno and Rave Culture* (New York: Routledge, 1999).

6. For a discussion of the uses of call-and-response styles in black church culture, see Charles V. Hamilton, *The Black Preacher in America* (New York: William Morrow and Company, 1972), 28–32; and Lawrence Levine, *Black Culture and Black Consciousness: Afro-American Thought from Slavery to Freedom* (Oxford: Oxford University Press, 1977). According to Mary Pattillo-McCoy, "Church Culture as a Strategy of Action in the Black Community," *American Sociolog-*

ical Review 63 (1998): 767–84, practices borrowed from black church culture are often used in secular settings to encourage social solidarity and incite collective action. For discussions of its uses in popular music performance as a symbol and strategy, also see Amiri Baraka (as Leroi Jones), *Blues People: Negro Music in White America* (New York: William and Morrow, 1963); and Charles Keil, *Urban Blues* (Chicago: University of Chicago Press, 1966).

7. For example, see Arjun Appadurai, "Disjuncture and Difference in the Global Cultural Economy," *Public Culture* 2 (1990): 1–24.

8. Bill Dahl, "Stale Home Chicago," *Chicago Tribune* (March 15, 1996), sec. 5, p. 1.

9. Hugh Merrill, *The Blues Route* (New York: William Morrow, 1990), 11; emphasis in original. In addition, Merrill writes of his travels to New Orleans, Memphis, and, perhaps fittingly, Chicago.

10. I would argue that today these processes all occur simultaneously in the everyday operations of this entertainment-oriented art world. To this end, I submit that the structural forces that encourage the growing commodification and globalization of local urban culture both influence *and are influenced by* the cultural needs and desires of the individual social actors who participate in this process of authenticity production and consumption. This theoretical approach resonates with the social scientific paradigm known as *structuration*, as put forth by Anthony Giddens, *The Constitution of Society: Outline of the Theory of Structuration* (Cambridge: Polity, 1984); William H. Sewell Jr., "A Theory of Structure: Duality, Agency, and Transformation," *American Journal of Sociology* 98 (1992): 1–29; and others, which begins with the assumption that humans beings are not only constituted by larger social structures (such as stratification systems organized on the basis of class, gender, or racial distinctions), but also have the ability to change those structures in the process of negotiating their way through them in the course of their everyday lives.

11. Erving Goffman, *The Presentation of Self in Everyday Life* (Garden City, N.Y.: Anchor Books, 1959); for Lord Jacques's "All the world's a stage" soliloquy, see William Shakespeare, *As You Like It* act 2, scene 7, lines 139–67.

12. In fact, in *The Tourist: A New Theory of the Leisure Class* (New York: Schocken, 1976), Dean MacCannell relies on Goffman's dramaturgical approach to inform his reading of tourist attractions and suggests that the back regions of cultural attractions—like VIP lounges—are often staged for the benefit of curious consumers.

13. Richard A. Peterson, *Creating Country Music: Fabricating Authenticity* (Chicago: University of Chicago Press, 1997); Eric Hobsbawm and Terence Ranger, eds., *The Invention of Tradition* (Cambridge: Cambridge University Press, 1983); MacCannell, *The Tourist*.

14. Peterson, *Creating Country Music*, 195–96.

15. Michael Kennedy, *The Concise Oxford Dictionary of Music* (London: Oxford University Press, 1980), 79.

16. Don Michael Randel, *Harvard Concise Dictionary of Music* (Cambridge: Belknap, 1978), 55–56.

17. W. I. Thomas and Dorothy Swaine Thomas, *The Child in America: Behavior Problems and Programs* (New York: Knopf, 1928), 572; for a historiography of the diffusion of this often-misattributed scientific maxim, see Robert K. Merton, "The Thomas Theorem and the Matthew Effect," *Social Forces* 74 (1995): 379–422.

18. I thank Robert Petrin for his suggestion that I examine the world of the blues club as a symbolic economy of signs and social relations.

19. In recent years a number of urban sociologists have argued for the necessity of collecting systematic observational data through the use of audio and video technologies as a means of

generating an accurate record from the field, including William H. Whyte, *City: Rediscovering the Center* (New York: Doubleday, 1988); Mitchell Duneier, *Sidewalk* (New York: Farrar, Straus and Giroux, 1999); Jack Katz, *How Emotions Work* (Chicago: University of Chicago Press, 1999); and Robert J. Sampson and Stephen W. Raudenbush, "Systematic Social Observation of Public Spaces: A New Look at Disorder in Urban Neighborhoods," *American Journal of Sociology* 105 (1999): 603–51. In fact, while I initially attempted to employ a cassette recorder when conducting fieldwork at B.L.U.E.S. and other clubs, I soon abandoned that strategy for a number of reasons. First, I was observing settings where the combination of loud music and chattering customers made the level of background noise extremely high, and thus a recording device would have proven useless. Second, ethnographers who rely on such devices in the field often require a trial period before their informants are able to freely interact without reacting (either positively or negatively) to the presence of the recorder. Since my encounters with strangers at these clubs were often fleeting, I feared that we would not have the usual requisite period after which the presence of the recorder would be unremarkable and consequently ignored by my informants. Third, sociologists generally need to obtain informed consent from their subjects in order to record them, and I feared that in many cases I simply would not be able to develop a sense of rapport strong enough to withstand a request to tape their barroom chats and howls after only a few minutes. In addition, these participants were often quite drunk, which would obviously make obtaining truly "informed" consent to record them a problem. Finally, there are further legal and ethical implications for recording musical acts during their performances.

20. For this supplementary fieldwork, I selected thirty-six bars, nightclubs, cafés, and restaurants that at least occasionally offered blues music and/or its jazz and folk variants. In the city's downtown entertainment districts, these establishments include the following: in the Loop, Buddy Guy's Legends, Hothouse, the Green Room at Macaw's, and Koko Taylor's Chicago Blues; in the Near North Side district, Blue Chicago, Blue Chicago on Clark, Dick's Last Resort, Famous Dave's, House of Blues, Jazz Showcase, Joe's Be-Bop Cafe and Jazz Emporium, and Redfish. In the following North Side neighborhoods in the city, they include the following: in Lincoln Park, B.L.U.E.S., Kingston Mines, Lilly's, and U.S. Beer Co.; in Lakeview, B.L.U.E.S. Etcetera, Java Jo's, Lunar Cabaret, and the Townhall Pub; in Uptown, the Green Mill; in Lincoln Square, Winner's; in Rogers Park, the No Exit Cafe. On the South Side of Chicago: in Grand Boulevard, the Checkerboard Lounge; in Greater Grand Crossing, Lee's Unleaded Blues and the New Apartment Lounge; in the Near South Side, the Velvet Lounge. Finally, on the West Side: in Irving Park, the Peek Inn; in West Town, Smoke Daddy, the Hideout, Nick's Beer Garden, and the Note; in Logan Square, Rosa's Lounge, the Charleston, Gallery Cabaret, and Lula Café.

21. See Michael Haralambos, *Right On: From Blues to Soul in Black America* (New York: Drake, 1975); Robert Palmer, *Deep Blues* (New York: Penguin Books, 1981); Rose, *Black Noise*; Francis Davis, *The History of the Blues* (New York: Hyperion, 1995); Robert Cantwell, *When We Were Good: The Folk Revival* (Cambridge: Harvard University Press, 1996); and Giles Oakley, *The Devil's Music: A History of the Blues* (London: Da Capo, 1997).

22. See Walter C. Reckless, *Vice in Chicago* (Chicago: University of Chicago Press, 1933); and William Howland Kenney, *Chicago Jazz: A Cultural History, 1904–1930* (New York: Oxford University Press, 1993).

23. Of course, there is nothing unusual about this process of meaning-making: after all, Bronislaw Malinowski, *Argonauts of the Western Pacific* (New York: E. P. Dutton, [1922] 1961); and Marcel Mauss, *The Gift: Forms and Functions of Exchange in Archaic Societies* (New York: W. W. Norton, 1967), demonstrate that shells and yams possessed great social value as gifts

among traditional premodern tribes, just as inexpensive, mass-produced greeting cards can embody rich significance in our own world.

24. Stanley Fish, *Is There a Text in This Class? The Authority of Interpretive Communities* (Cambridge: Harvard University Press, 1980). Although certain kinds of mass culture are consumed by a wide range of consumers, such as commercial films, paperback novels, and pop music, it has become generally accepted among contemporary sociologists of culture that various publics frequently consume the same cultural productions (whether texts, objects, or events) in different ways and, in doing so, may attribute divergent meanings or values to those productions and their experiences consuming them. On the consumption and interpretation of film among various and multiple audiences, see Chandra Mukerji, "Artwork: Collection and Contemporary Culture," *American Journal of Sociology* 84 (1978): 348–65; Shyon Baumann, "Intellectualization and Art World Development: Film in the United States," *American Sociological Review* 66 (2001): 404–26; and Jo Ellen Shively, "Cowboys and Indians: Perceptions of Western Films among American Indians and Anglos," *American Sociological Review* 57 (1992): 725–34; on literary fiction, see Janice Radway, *Reading the Romance: Women, Patriarchy, and Popular Literature* (Chapel Hill: University of North Carolina Press, 1984); Wendy Griswold, "The Fabrication of Meaning: Literary Interpretation in the United States, Great Britain, and the West Indies," *American Journal of Sociology* 92 (March 1987): 1077–117; Wendy Griswold, *Bearing Witness: Readers, Writers, and the Novel in Nigeria* (Princeton: Princeton University Press, 2000); Marjorie L. DeVault, "Novel Readings: The Social Organization of Interpretation," *American Journal of Sociology* 95 (1990): 887–921; and Sarah M. Corse, "Nations and Novels: Cultural Politics and Literary Use," *Social Forces* 73 (1995): 1279–308; on popular music, see Amy Binder, "Constructing Racial Rhetoric: Media Depictions of Harm in Heavy Metal and Rap Music," *American Sociological Review* 58 (1993): 753–67; Paul DiMaggio, "Cultural Entrepreneurship in 19th Century Boston," in *Rethinking Popular Culture*, ed. Chandra Mukerji and Michael Schudson (Berkeley: University of California Press, 1991); and Richard A. Peterson, "Understanding Audience Segmentation: From Elite and Mass to Omnivore and Univore," *Poetics* 21 (1992): 243–58; on the visual arts, see Howard S. Becker, *Art Worlds* (Berkeley: University of California Press, 1982); Nicola Beisel, "Class, Culture, and Campaigns Against Vice in Three American Cities, 1872–1892," *American Sociological Review* 55 (1990): 44–62; Vera L. Zolberg, "Barrier or Leveler? The Case of the Art Museum," in *Cultivating Differences: Symbolic Boundaries and the Making of Inequality*, ed. Michele Lamont and Marcel Fournier (Chicago: University of Chicago Press, 1992); and David Halle, *Inside Culture: Art and Class in the American Home* (Chicago: University of Chicago Press, 1993); on food, Pierre Bourdieu, *Distinction: A Social Critique of the Judgment of Taste*, trans. Richard Nice (Cambridge: Harvard University Press, 1984); Gary Alan Fine, "The Culture of Production: Aesthetic Choices and Constraints in Culinary Work," *American Journal of Sociology* 97 (1992): 1268–94; and Priscilla Parkhurst Ferguson, "A Cultural Field in the Making: Gastronomy in 19th-Century France," *American Journal of Sociology* 104 (1998): 597–641.

25. There is actually a funny explanation for how Budweiser, a brand of beer I dislike and almost never drink in any other context, became my "usual" at B.L.U.E.S. On one of my first nights of fieldwork, I mistakenly ordered a Pete's Wicked Ale, which was then served to me in a decorative twenty-two-ounce glass, hardly the beverage of choice for an ethnographer attempting to inconspicuously pass as a local barfly. I quickly shifted to the least expensive beer on the menu (along with Rolling Rock, a beer that I have not been able to enjoy since college, even after moving to Pennsylvania after graduate school), and after ordering it a few times, the bartenders simply assumed it was my favorite and began referring to it as my "usual." As I was

flattered by the fact that I had gained this familiarity with the staff, and I was too embarrassed to explain the story to them, I stuck with Budweiser for the duration of my fieldwork.

26. On the history and legacy of the Chicago school of urban sociology, see Martin Bulmer, *The Chicago School of Sociology: Institutionalization, Diversity, and the Rise of Sociological Research* (Chicago: University of Chicago Press, 1984); Dennis Smith, *The Chicago School: A Liberal Critique of Capitalism* (New York: St. Martin's, 1988); Ulf Hannerz, *Exploring the City: Inquiries toward an Urban Anthropology* (New York: Columbia University Press, 1980); James S. Coleman, "A Vision for Sociology," *Society* 32 (1994): 29–34; Gary Alan Fine, ed., *A Second Chicago School? The Development of a Postwar American Sociology* (Chicago: University of Chicago Press, 1995); Andrew Abbott, "Of Time and Space: The Contemporary Relevance of the Chicago School," *Social Forces* 75 (1997): 1149–82; Andrew Abbott, *Department and Discipline: Chicago Sociology at One Hundred* (Chicago: University of Chicago Press, 1999); Andrew Abbott, "Los Angeles and the Chicago School: A Comment on Michael Dear," *City and Community* 1 (2002): 33–38; Michael Dear, "Los Angeles and the Chicago School: Invitation to a Debate," *City and Community* 1 (2002): 5–32; and Robert J. Sampson, "Studying Modern Chicago," *City and Community* 1 (2002): 45–48.

27. Robert E. Park, "The Natural History of the Newspaper," in *The City*, ed. Robert E. Park, Ernest W. Burgess, and Roderick D. McKenzie (Chicago: University of Chicago Press, 1925), 80.

28. Harvey Warren Zorbaugh, *The Gold Coast and the Slum* (Chicago: University of Chicago Press, [1929] 1976); Paul G. Cressey, *The Taxi-Dance Hall* (Chicago: University of Chicago Press, 1932); and Reckless, *Vice in Chicago*. On the city as a process of accumulation, also see Gerald D. Suttles, "The Cumulative Texture of Local Urban Culture," *American Journal of Sociology* 90 (1984): 283–304; and Harvey Molotch, William Freudenburg, and Krista E. Paulsen, "History Repeats Itself, but How? City Character, Urban Tradition, and the Accomplishment of Place," *American Sociological Review* 65 (2000): 791–823.

29. On the marketing of local artistic movements as a strategy of city boosterism, see Sharon Zukin, *Loft Living: Culture and Capital in Urban Change* (Baltimore: Johns Hopkins University Press, 1982), and *The Cultures of Cities*.

30. On the history of Chicago and New York's black and tan cabarets, see Reckless, *Vice in Chicago*; Lewis A. Erenberg, *Steppin' Out: New York Nightlife and the Transformation of American Culture, 1890–1930* (Chicago: University of Chicago Press, 1981); David Levering Lewis, *When Harlem Was in Vogue* (New York: Oxford University Press, 1981); Kenney, *Chicago Jazz*; and George Chauncey, *Gay New York: Gender, Urban Culture, and the Making of the Gay Male World, 1880–1940* (New York: Basic Books, 1994); on Ellington's recording of "Black and Tan Fantasy," see Barry Ulanov, *Duke Ellington* (New York: Da Capo, 1975); John Edward Hasse, *Beyond Category: The Life and Genius of Duke Ellington* (New York: Da Capo, 1995); Gary Giddins, *Visions of Jazz: The First Century* (New York: Oxford University Press, 1998); and A. H. Lawrence, *Duke Ellington and His World: A Biography* (New York: Routledge, 2001).

31. As the Harlem Renaissance poet Langston Hughes explains in "Minstrel Man," in *The New Negro: Voices of the Harlem Renaissance*, ed. Alain Locke (New York: Atheneum [1925] 1992), these hardworking entertainers had to interact with whites as dictated by a racist and sometimes violent set of social norms and expectations, and thus had to sublimate their own personal needs and desires during these interracial encounters:

> Because my mouth
> Is wide with laughter
> And my throat

Is deep with song,
You do not think
I suffer after
I have held my pain
So long.

Because my mouth
Is wide with laughter
You do not hear
My inner cry,
Because my feet
Are gay with dancing,
You do not know
I die.

32. Baraka, *Blues People*; Samuel Charters, *The Roots of the Blues: An African Search* (New York: Da Capo Press, 1981); Palmer, *Deep Blues*.

33. Barry Ulanov, *A History of Jazz in America* (New York: Viking, 1952), 178.

Chapter 1

1. Houston A. Baker, *Blues, Ideology and Afro-American Literature: A Vernacular Theory* (Chicago: University of Chicago Press, 1984). In elite cultural fields such as contemporary jazz music, authenticity is often measured in terms of artistic innovation and originality as opposed to more populist-oriented standards; see Irving Louis Horowitz, "Authenticity and Originality in Jazz: Toward a Paradigm in the Sociology of Music," *Journal of Jazz Studies* 1 (1973): 57–63.

2. On the Great Migration and the formation of Chicago's segregated black neighborhoods, see St. Clair Drake and Horace R. Cayton, *Black Metropolis: A Study of Negro Life in a Northern City* (New York: Harper and Row, 1945); Allan Spear, *Black Chicago: The Making of a Negro Ghetto, 1890–1920* (Chicago: University of Chicago Press, 1967); William Julius Wilson, *The Declining Significance of Race: Blacks and Changing American Institutions* (Chicago: University of Chicago Press, 1978); Arnold R. Hirsch, *Making the Second Ghetto: Race and Housing in Chicago, 1940–1960* (Cambridge: Cambridge University Press, 1983); and Douglas S. Massey and Nancy A. Denton, *American Apartheid: Segregation and the Making of the Underclass* (Cambridge: Harvard University Press, 1993).

3. The historian Michael Kammen, *American Culture, American Tastes: Social Change and the 20th Century* (New York: Knopf, 1999), celebrates the participatory and interactive quality of the nation's popular cultural pursuits during this period. Similarly, Lewis, *When Harlem Was in Vogue*; Erenberg, *Steppin' Out* and *Swingin' the Dream. Big Band Jazz and the Rebirth of American Culture* (Chicago: University of Chicago Press, 1998); Kenney, *Chicago Jazz*; and Scott DeVeaux, *The Birth of Bebop: A Social and Musical History* (Berkeley: University of California Press, 1997), emphasize the populism suggested by the locally based production and consumption of jazz music in Chicago and New York during this period.

4. Erenberg, *Steppin' Out*; William Barlow, *Looking Up at Down: The Emergence of Blues Culture* (Philadelphia: Temple University Press, 1989); and Kenney, *Chicago Jazz*.

5. Palmer, *Deep Blues*, 155–69.

6. See Paul Oliver, *Blues Fell This Morning: Meaning in the Blues* (Cambridge: Cambridge University Press, 1960); Keil, *Urban Blues*, Jeff Todd Titon, *Early Downhome Blues* (Chapel

Hill: University of North Carolina Press, 1977); David Evans, *Big Road Blues* (New York: Da Capo, 1987).

7. See Keil, *Urban Blues*; Haralambos, *Right On*; and Sandra B. Tooze, *Muddy Waters: The Mojo Man* (Toronto: ECW Press, 1997).

8. Haralambos, *Right On*; and Tooze, *Muddy Waters*.

9. Cantwell, *When We Were Good*; and Greil Marcus, *The Old, Weird America: The World of Bob Dylan's Basement Tapes* (New York: Henry Holt, 2001).

10. Raeburn Flerlage, *Chicago Blues* (Toronto: ECW Press, 2000).

11. It should be noted that not all audiences who frequent the city's blues clubs rely on these kinds of distinctions to the same extent. In fact, while conducting this study, I observed that a good number of my respondents displayed an extraordinarily complex understanding of the history of blues music and characterized the performances they attended in highly sophisticated terms. My attempt here is merely to report on the general tastes and prejudices of the majority of the audience members I interviewed during the course of my fieldwork.

12. Ironically, American blues and jazz music have remained popular cultural staples in Japan since the 1920s, where anxieties and ambivalences over issues of authenticity serve as a constant source of discussion among musicians and critics: see E. Taylor Atkins, "Can Japanese Sing the Blues?: 'Japanese Jazz' and the Problem of Authenticity," in *Japan Pop! Inside the World of Japanese Popular Culture*, ed. Timothy J. Craig (Armonk, N.Y.: M. E. Sharpe, 2000).

13. Joel Rudinow, "Race, Ethnicity, Expressive Authenticity: Can White People Sing the Blues?" *Journal of Aesthetics and Art Criticism* 52 (1994): 127–37.

14. Amiri Baraka, "The Great Music Robbery," in *The Music: Reflections on Jazz and Blues* (New York: William and Morrow, 1987), 330–31.

15. Baraka, *Blues People*, 147–48.

16. Ralph J. Gleason, "Can the White Man Sing the Blues?" *Jazz and Pop* (1968): 28–29.

17. Oliver, *Blues Fell This Morning*, 4.

18. Paul Garon, *Blues and the Poetic Spirit* (New York: Da Capo, 1978), 61.

19. Appadurai, "Disjuncture and Difference in the Global Cultural Economy."

20. W. E. B. Du Bois, *The Philadelphia Negro: A Social Study* (Philadelphia: University of Pennsylvania Press, [1899] 1996); Drake and Cayton, *Black Metropolis*; and Tukufu Zuberi, *Thicker than Blood: How Racial Statistics Lie* (Minneapolis: University of Minnesota Press, 2001). The anti-black racism and general absurdity of claims of racial authenticity reveal themselves even further when we move from black/white distinctions to black-on-black comparisons; indeed, is the blues sensibility of a light-skinned black musician of racially mixed parentage only a fraction of that of his darker counterpart?

21. Stephen Steinberg, *The Ethnic Myth: Race, Ethnicity, and Class in America* (Boston: Beacon Press, 1989); Noel Ignatiev, *How the Irish Became White* (New York: Routledge, 1995); and Matthew Frye Jacobson, *Whiteness of a Different Color: European Immigration and the Alchemy of Race* (Cambridge: Harvard University Press, 1998).

22. Jeffrey Melnick, *A Right to Sing the Blues: African Americans, Jews, and American Popular Song* (Cambridge: Harvard University Press, 1999); also see Michael Rogin, *Blackface, White Noise: Jewish Immigrants in the Hollywood Melting Pot* (Berkeley: University of California Press, 1996).

23. Zuberi, *Thicker than Blood*. For a critique of the so-called causal "effects" of decontextualized sociological variables, see Andrew Abbott, "What Do Cases Do?" in *What Is a Case?*, ed. Charles Ragin and Howard Becker (Cambridge: Cambridge University Press, 1992).

24. On race as a "master status-determining trait," see Everett Cherrington Hughes,

"Dilemmas and Contradictions of Status," *American Journal of Sociology* 50 (1945): 357. Unfortunately, even contemporary exceptions to this rule exist in all too great a number; for example, see Richard J. Herrnstein and Charles Murray, *The Bell Curve: Intelligence and Class in American Life* (New York: Free Press, 1994).

25. Frantz Fanon, *Black Skin, White Masks*, trans. Charles Lam Markmann (New York: Grove, 1967); and bell hooks, "Marketing Blackness: Class and Commodification," in *Killing Rage: Ending Racism* (New York: Henry Holt, 1995), 175.

26. Fanon, *Black Skin, White Masks*; also see bell hooks, "Eating the Other: Desire and Resistance," and "Selling Hot Pussy: Representations of Black Female Sexuality in the Cultural Marketplace," in *Black Looks: Race and Representation* (Boston: South End Press, 1992). In "The White Negro: Superficial Reflections on the Hipster" (San Francisco: City Lights, 1957), 2, Norman Mailer's writing exemplifies the employment of this racial stereotype in American intellectual thought:

> Knowing in the cells of his existence that life was war, nothing but war, the Negro (all exceptions admitted) could rarely afford the sophisticated inhibitions of civilization, and so he kept for his survival the art of the primitive, he lived in the enormous present, he subsisted for his Saturday night kicks, relinquishing the pleasures of the mind for the more obligatory pleasures of the body, and in his music he gave voice to the character and quality of his existence, to his rage and the infinite variations of joy, lust, languor, growl, cramp, pinch, scream and despair of his orgasm.

27. Amiri Baraka as Leroi Jones, "Jazz and the White Critic," in *Black Music* (New York: Da Capo, 1968), 13–14.

28. Quoted in Gene Lees, *Cats of Any Color: Jazz, Black and White* (New York: Oxford University Press, 1994), 189. Moreover, while individual black composers and performers invented the blues genre, it seems rather strange to assume that *all* black musicians should then have more of a legitimate claim to this music than whites by virtue of their racial identity. Few would argue that Russian ballets and Italian cuisine can only be rightfully performed or prepared by the citizens and ethnic descendants of such cultures as a consequence of having been developed in particular social and historical contexts, oppressive or otherwise. Similarly, as argued by Rudinow, "Race, Ethnicity, Expressive Authenticity," 134, the experiential access argument proposed by Baraka and others relies on a relatively unsophisticated view of cultural transmission. Even if the blues *did* represent some kind of cultural code embedded in the African American experience, then such a code would presumably be possible for whites to learn, just as contemporary black musicians have developed an understanding of how late-nineteenth-century blues metaphors and musical themes operate stylistically.

29. hooks, "Eating the Other," 21.

30. Ibid., 23; also see hooks, "Selling Hot Pussy."

31. Jon Cruz, *Culture on the Margins* (Princeton: Princeton University Press, 1999).

32. Of course, these same anthropologists were simultaneously interested in discovering a similarly primitive world among *white* musicians in the Appalachian region; on the hunt for this "old, weird America," see Cantwell, *When We Were Good*; and Marcus, *The Old, Weird America*.

33. For example, Ray Pratt, *Rhythm and Resistance: Explorations in the Political Uses of Popular Music* (New York: Praeger, 1990), argues that white listeners interpreted the blues as a revolutionary, rebellious, and highly political form of cultural expression.

34. See Hannigan, *Fantasy City*; and Naomi Klein, *No Logo: Taking Aim at the Brand Bullies* (New York: Picador, 1999). Kammen, *American Culture, American Tastes*, 182, argues that

the post-1950s rise of American mass culture and "a national standardization of taste and desirability" was encouraged in part by the proliferation of corporate-managed franchise outlets throughout the country. Certainly, a similar argument could be made that the blues has been drastically transformed by the efforts of the mass media and entertainment industry and its by-products (i.e., *The Blues Brothers* films and soundtracks, the House of Blues franchise) to popularize the blues for a mass audience.

35. A blues club in its own right, the Blue Chicago Store hosts early evening performances by local bands.

36. Eric Lott, *Love and Theft: Blackface Minstrelsy and the American Working Class* (New York: Oxford University Press, 1993).

37. Barlow, *Looking Up at Down*.

38. Titon, *Early Downhome Blues*.

39. Barlow, *Looking Up at Down*; and Titon, *Early Downhome Blues*, 196, 210. Likewise, according to Peterson, *Creating Country Music*, particular institutional arrangements in the country music recording industry promoted the use of stock characters as a marketing tool: these cartoonish images included the "old-timer," the "hillbilly," and the American cowboy.

40. The mythical "Staggerlee" character of countless folk-blues songs exemplifies the aggressively masculine black stock character often found in the lyrics of blues songs as well as other American popular music styles; see Greil Marcus, *Mystery Train: Images of America in Rock 'n' Roll Music* (New York: Plume, 1975). On images of black men in rap, see Binder, "Constructing Racial Rhetoric"; also see Rose, *Black Noise*.

41. This appropriation of heterosexist rhetoric as a means of developing a hypermasculine role resonates deeply with accounts detailing the intensification of homophobia during the 1930s on the part of working-class men attempting to negotiate their own sense of marginality in the wake of disruptions in the sexual division of labor during the Great Depression; see Chauncey, *Gay New York*.

42. While persons of all sexual persuasions regularly attend local blues clubs, gay couples (unlike their straight counterparts) rarely express their intimacy in an overtly conspicuous manner at B.L.U.E.S.

43. From verbal banter between songs to forays into the crowd between sets, musicians perform during nearly *every* moment of their public interaction with their audience. However, even though their strategies of interaction are scripted and the performer's "authentic" self is often patterned as a stage character, onstage chatter between songs during musical performances is often regarded as outside the song frame by audience members. Unlike staged plays, audiences frequently interpret role-playing in music performances as natural and uncontrived. In *Frame Analysis: An Essay on the Organization of Experience* (Boston: Northeastern University Press, 1974), Erving Goffman discusses these issues in his chapter "The Theatrical Frame."

44. Feminist camp represents a cultural style and strategy that utilizes theatricality, irony, humor, and burlesque in order to emphasize the artifice of social norms and conventional gender roles; see Susan Sontag, "Notes on Camp," in *A Susan Sontag Reader* (New York: Farrar, Straus and Giroux, [1964] 1982); Richard Dyer, *Heavenly Bodies: Film Stars and Society* (New York: St. Martin's, 1986); Chauncey, *Gay New York*; and Pamela Robertson, *Guilty Pleasures: Feminist Camp from Mae West to Madonna* (Durham, N.C.: Duke University Press, 1996). On the subversiveness of classic blueswomen like Rainey and Smith, see Angela Y. Davis, *Blues Legacies and Black Feminism* (New York: Pantheon, 1998).

45. The lyrics to Bessie Smith's "Hateful Blues" are transcribed by Davis, *Blues Legacies and Black Feminism*, 286–87, in which she describes the progressive political implications of

the work of the early female blues pioneers and places particular emphasis on the potential of the blues as a means of raising and expressing feminist consciousness. On the self-reliant and sexually emancipatory nature of the performances of the early female blues singers, also see Bryan D. Palmer, *Cultures of Darkness: Night Travels in the Histories of Transgression* (New York: Monthly Review Press, 2000), 355.

46. As transcribed by Davis, *Blues Legacies and Black Feminism*, 356–57.

47. At the time this book went to press, some of the abandoned structures along Forty-third Street across from the Checkerboard Lounge had been torn down and replaced by a Catholic Charities–run food center, which provides a range of social services to poor families who reside in the surrounding neighborhoods. However, in the 1950s a number of blues bars thrived along Forty-third Street, including the Cosy Inn, Don's Den, and Pepper's Lounge; see Mike Rowe, *Chicago Blues: The City and the Music* (London: Da Capo, 1975). While Buddy Guy gave up the Checkerboard a few years after the club's opening, he currently owns Buddy Guy's Legends, a tourist spot located in the downtown South Loop area.

48. From 1960 to 1990, the U.S. Census has consistently reported the racial composition of the community area of Grand Boulevard at 99 percent; see Chicago Fact Book Consortium, *Local Community Fact Book: Chicago Metropolitan Area 1990*, 130.

49. In addition, Rajiv's comparison of the Checkerboard Lounge and the Green Mill emphasizes how audiences measure the quality and authenticity of blues clubs according to a different set of criteria than they normally use to evaluate jazz venues.

50. As argued throughout MacCannell, *The Tourist*, this anti-tourist position is common among modern travelers.

51. In ibid., MacCannell defines "tourists" in terms of their motivations to consume cultural attractions, regardless of their residential status as locals or otherwise.

52. Reuben A. Buford May, *Talking at Trena's: Everyday Conversations at an African American Tavern* (New York: New York University Press, 2001), 82–83. In addition to the impact of residential housing segregation among blacks of all socioeconomic classes (e.g., Massey and Denton, *American Apartheid*; and Mary Pattillo-McCoy, *Black Picket Fences: Privilege and Peril among the Black Middle Class* [Chicago: University of Chicago Press, 1999]), this division may be correlated with the fact that blacks and whites often display different patterns of cultural consumption and taste, specifically with regard to music and the arts; see Paul DiMaggio and Francie Ostrower, "Participation in the Arts by Black and White Americans," *Social Forces* 63 (1990): 753–78; and Richard A. Peterson and Albert Simkus, "Musical Tastes Mark Occupational Status Groups," in *Cultivating Differences: Symbolic Boundaries and the Making of Inequality*, ed. Michele Lamont and Marcel Fournier (Chicago: University of Chicago Press, 1992).

53. Elijah Anderson, *A Place on the Corner* (Chicago: University of Chicago Press, 1976); and May, *Talking at Trena's*.

54. For this reason, the racially diverse Checkerboard has much in common with a handful of South Side jazz clubs, including the New Apartment Lounge and the Velvet Lounge. Besides Chicago's blues and jazz clubs, other places of leisure in the city that attract a racially mixed clientele include a set of dance clubs located in the River West downtown area, a handful of North Side reggae venues, and the gay bars and nightclubs located in the Lakeview entertainment zone of Boystown. In addition, a number of bars, restaurants, and cafés located in the racially mixed neighborhood of Hyde Park attract an interracial patronage as well, including Jimmy's Woodlawn Tap and Valois "See Your Food" Cafeteria; on the latter establishment, see

Mitchell Duneier, *Slim's Table: Race, Respectability and Masculinity* (Chicago: University of Chicago Press, 1992).

55. By the same token, elderly black men often initiate encounters with younger white women on the dance floors of local blues bars; these moments shared between strangers allow the participants to playfully challenge normative racial boundaries by drawing on generational differences to produce desexualized and therefore "safe" roles within the context of social interaction.

56. See Erving Goffman, "Where the Action Is," in *Interaction Ritual: Essays on Face-to-Face Behavior* (New York: Pantheon, 1967), for his analysis of risk taking in everyday life; and Harold Garfinkel, *Studies in Ethnomethodology* (Cambridge: Polity, 1967), for a discussion of norm breaching as ethnographic practice.

57. The inflated cover charge can be explained by the expense of the evening's booking. For his two performances on Saturday and Sunday, Rush was paid six thousand dollars by the Checkerboard, and as a barmaid pointed out to me that night, although the club would probably do great business, it is unlikely that they would make back their investment over the course of the weekend. But the strategy makes sense as a publicity stunt, and conversations with local club owners suggest that tactics such as these are quite common. In an interview, B.L.U.E.S. owner Rob Hecko remarked that every once in a while he likes to book a band he cannot afford, just to get the publicity and press coverage—a little excitement to stir up local business.

58. On white slumming in Chicago during the Jazz Age of the 1920s, see Kenney, *Chicago Jazz*, and Reckless, *Vice in Chicago*; on Harlem, see Erenberg, *Steppin' Out*; and Lewis, *When Harlem Was in Vogue*.

59. In *American Apartheid*, 74–78, Massey and Denton argue that in 1980 Chicago was one of sixteen "hypersegregated" metropolitan areas in the country; the remaining cities include Atlanta, Baltimore, Buffalo, Cleveland, Dallas, Detroit, Gary, Indianapolis, Kansas City, Los Angeles, Milwaukee, New York, Newark, Philadelphia, and St. Louis. On the historical legacy of racial housing segregation in Chicago, see Spear, *Black Chicago*; and Hirsch, *Making the Second Ghetto*.

Chapter 2

1. While other songs in the repertoires of local bands may be just as easy to dance to, audience members prefer dancing to the songs they know best. Ironically, popular crossover R&B hits like "Soul Man" and "Mustang Sally" entice audiences to approach the dance floor more than lesser-known *blues* songs.

2. In this manner, the blues club represents a carnivalesque world similar to other kinds of public spaces and events where certain social norms and rules of decorum are inverted or otherwise abandoned altogether; for example, see Max Gluckman, *Order and Rebellion in Tribal Africa* (New York: Free Press, 1963); Victor Turner, *The Ritual Process: Structure and Anti-Structure* (Ithaca: Cornell University Press, 1969); Mikhail Bakhtin, *Rabelais and His World*, trans. Helene Iswolsky (Bloomington: Indiana University Press, 1984); Mona Ozouf, *Festivals and the French Revolution*, trans. Alan Sheridan (Cambridge: Harvard University Press, 1988); and Bruce Lincoln, *Discourse and the Construction of Society* (New York: Oxford University Press, 1992).

3. Contemporary urban studies of nocturnal culture provide a similar interpretation of how thrill-seekers develop provisional identities while consuming entertainment in the city; for example, Ben Malbon, *Clubbing: Dancing, Ecstasy and Vitality* (New York: Routledge, 1999),

examines how nocturnal consumers appropriate temporary definitions of self while "clubbing" at urban raves and dance parties in London's nightlife districts. Likewise, in her essay "Travel as Performed Art," *American Journal of Sociology* 94 (1989): 1366–91, Judith Adler illustrates the "aesthetic dimension of travel activity" in her exploration of the styles of enacted tropes and conventions commonly utilized by "performing" travelers. On the uses of role-playing and performativity in everyday life, also see Johan Huizinga, *Homo Ludens: A Study of the Play-Element in Culture* (Boston: Beacon Press, 1955); Goffman, *The Presentation of Self in Everyday Life*; Garfinkel, *Studies in Ethnomethodology*; Judith Butler, *Gender Trouble: Feminism and the Subversion of Identity* (New York: Routledge, 1990); and Neil Gabler, *Life the Movie: How Entertainment Conquered Reality* (New York: Vintage, 2000). On the pleasures of specifically nocturnal forms of behavior, see Murray Melbin, "Night as Frontier," *American Sociological Review* 43 (1978): 3–22; and Palmer, *Cultures of Darkness*.

4. On the contemporary nostalgia for popular fashions of the recent past, see Paul Willis, *Common Culture* (Boulder, Colo.: Westview, 1990); David Grazian, "Uniform of the Party: The Impact of Fashion on Collegiate Subcultural Integration," Henry Rutgers Honors Thesis, Department of Sociology, Rutgers University (1994); Angela McRobbie, *British Fashion Design: Rag Trade or Image Industry?* (New York: Routledge, 1998); and Diana Crane, *Fashion and Its Social Agendas: Class, Gender, and Identity in Clothing* (Chicago: University of Chicago Press, 2000).

5. On the culture of nostalgia in earlier times and places, see Raymond Williams, *The Country and the City* (London: Chatto and Windus, 1973); Michael Wood, "Nostalgia or Never: You Can't Go Home Again," *New Society* 7 (1974): 343–46; Fred Davis, *Yearning for Yesterday: A Sociology of Nostalgia* (New York: Free Press, 1979); Hobsbawm and Ranger, *The Invention of Tradition*; and David Lowenthal, *The Past Is a Foreign Country* (Cambridge: Cambridge University Press, 1985).

6. On identity construction within rave subcultures, see Thornton, *Club Cultures*; Collin and Godfrey, *Altered State*; Malbon, *Clubbing*; and Reynolds, *Generation Ecstasy*. On gay drag, see Chauncey, *Gay New York*; and Robertson, *Guilty Pleasures*.

7. However, a core group of regulars who attend the city's blues venues on a nightly basis certainly maintain a more holistic blues-oriented identity, as the next chapter will explore.

8. Contrary to George's remark, Long Beach is actually a major center of blues activity with a number of blues clubs and a renowned blues festival. The fact that George does not mention this point about Long Beach emphasizes the interpretive, rather than objective, quality of local identities of place.

9. Zorbaugh, *The Gold Coast and the Slum*, 98. Insofar as identity construction is an ongoing process of meaning-making, social identities are never entirely fixed, but are malleable, multiple, and sometimes contradictory; see Goffman, *The Presentation of Self in Everyday Life*; Garfinkel, *Studies in Ethnomethodology*; Arlie Russell Hochschild, *The Managed Heart* (Berkeley: University of California Press, 1983); and Andreas Glaeser, *Divided in Unity: Identity, Germany, and the Berlin Police* (Chicago: University of Chicago Press, 2000).

10. Zorbaugh, *The Gold Coast and the Slum*, 98.

11. Although the label seems fitting and commonsensical to contemporary mainstream consumers, Chicago's self-identification as America's so-called "Home of the Blues" is actually a relatively recent development. While the historical record demonstrates that the blues has been a central element of the city's local urban culture since the 1920s, it was not until the late 1960s and early 1970s that local North Side boosters and mainstream publications chose to incorporate its blues legacy into the city's overall presentation of self. Moreover, insofar as

a number of other American cities promote similar kinds of reputations, including Memphis, it is unclear whether such a designation should be merely taken for granted as an undisputed fact, even among die-hard blues fans and Chicago boosters. Indeed, as ideologically mediated representations of reality, the fabrication of local reputations and identities of place parallels the "invention" of national traditions and solidarities; see Hobsbawm and Ranger, *The Invention of Tradition*; Benedict Anderson, *Imagined Communities: Reflections on the Origin and Spread of Nationalism* (London: Verso, 1991); and Ozouf, *Festivals and the French Revolution*.

12. The ideological power of dominant images of place serves as a highly instrumental factor in the development of commercial culture in the urban milieu. In fact, as world-class cities and their local businesses increasingly compete with one another for capital in the global post-industrial economy, the need for constructing attractive local images of place among boosters grows even stronger. On the relationship between city image and the political economy of urban areas, see Suttles, "The Cumulative Texture of Local Urban Culture"; John R. Logan and Harvey L. Molotch, *Urban Fortunes: The Political Economy of Place* (Berkeley: University of California Press, 1987); Zukin, *Landscapes of Power*, and *The Cultures of Cities*.

13. Colleen Dunn Bates, ed., *The Best of Chicago* (New York: Prentice Hall, 1989).

14. Middle- and upper-class audiences show off their cultural capital by exhibiting their knowledge of a multiplicity of elite *and* popular cultural styles and genres. For this reason, Richard A. Peterson, "Understanding Audience Segmentation: From Elite and Mass to Omnivore and Univore," *Poetics* 21 (1992): 243–58, refers to such audiences as cultural *omnivores*, able to code-switch among several different kinds of class-based cultural fields. For further theoretical refinement on the concept of cultural capital, see Pierre Bourdieu, *Outline of a Theory of Practice* (Cambridge: Cambridge University Press, 1977), and *Distinction: A Social Critique of the Judgment of Taste*; Michele Lamont and Annette Lareau, "Cultural Capital: Gaps and Glissandos in Recent Theoretical Developments," *Sociological Theory* 6 (1988): 153–68; Bonnie H. Erickson, "What Is Good Taste Good for?" *Canadian Review of Sociology and Anthropology* 28 (1991): 255–78; Pierre Bourdieu and Loic J. D. Wacquant, *An Invitation to Reflexive Sociology* (Chicago: University of Chicago Press, 1992); and John Hall, "The Capital(s) of Cultures: A Nonholistic Approach to Status Situations, Class, Gender, and Ethnicity," in *Cultivating Differences: Symbolic Boundaries and the Making of Inequality*, ed. Michele Lamont and Marcel Fournier (Chicago: University of Chicago Press, 1992).

15. Of course, Chicago attracts plenty of tourists who lack any desire to visit the city's blues clubs. What is interesting is just how many of those tourists wind up getting dragged to clubs like B.L.U.E.S. by their more eager traveling companions, coworkers, business partners, family members, and local hosts. My own observations from the club demonstrate the varying degrees of patience held by "captive" audience members such as these. Likewise, B.L.U.E.S. often attracts curious yet uncommitted tourists who enjoy "experiencing" the atmosphere of the blues club yet rarely stay for more than a couple of songs.

16. In *Travels in Hyperreality* (San Diego: Harcourt Brace Jovanovich, 1986), Umberto Eco describes how contemporary cultural consumers often enjoy taking part in social events much more than they appreciate the actual content of such moments. Of course, Dave describes his outing to local clubs as just one of several tourist experiences pivotal to his overall evaluation of his trip to the city.

17. In fact, I myself led a convention-sponsored bus tour of local blues and jazz clubs during the ninety-fourth annual meetings of the American Sociological Association when they were held in Chicago in 1999.

18. As has been argued in a number of critiques of MacCannell, *The Tourist*, not all cul-

tural consumers search for authenticity when experiencing tourist attractions; for example, see Michael Schudson, "On Tourism and Modern Culture," *American Journal of Sociology* 84 (1979): 1249–58, and Erik Cohen, "Authenticity and Commoditization in Tourism," *Annals of Tourism Research* 15 (1988): 371–86.

19. On the uses of "frontier" and "pioneer" as metaphors in discourses on the consumption of urban space, see Neil Smith, *The New Urban Frontier: Gentrification and the Revanchist City* (London: Routledge, 1996).

20. For a critique of the idealized nature of the concept of "community," see Joseph Gusfield, *Community: A Critical Response* (New York: Harper and Row, 1978); David Hummon, *Commonplaces: Community Ideology and Identity in American Culture* (Albany: State University of New York Press, 1990); and Wendy Griswold, "The Writing on the Mud Wall: Nigerian Novels and the Imaginary Village," *American Sociological Review* 57 (1992): 709–24.

21. In this manner, West Town's entertainment districts, and Division Street in particular, provide a more contemporary setting for examining the processes of meaning-making that operated in Old Town and DePaul's formerly subaltern zones of cultural commerce, as I discuss in chapter 5.

22. According to the Chicago Fact Book Consortium, *Local Community Fact Book: Chicago Metropolitan Area 1990*, 92–94, by 1990 Latinos made up 61 percent of the West Town's residential population, while at the same time, the overall population of West Town decreased between 1960 and 1990, from 139,657 to 87,703; see Chicago Fact Book Consortium (1995).

23. Loic J. D. Wacquant and William Julius Wilson, "Poverty, Joblessness, and the Social Transformation of the Inner City," in *Welfare Policy for the 1990s*, ed. Phoebe H. Cottingham and David T. Ellwood (Cambridge: Harvard University Press, 1989).

24. Between 1980 and 1990, the number of residents holding white-collar jobs increased from 35 percent to 41 percent while those employed in manufacturing occupations dropped from 42 percent to 31 percent. While the loss of manufacturing jobs throughout the city during the 1980s might help explain this shift, unemployment rates only grew by 2 percent during this period, an increase much lower than in surrounding neighborhoods: for instance, to the west the unemployment rate in Humboldt Park grew from 13 percent to 19 percent; to the south, the Near West Side went from 16 percent to 21 percent; see Chicago Fact Book Consortium, *Local Community Fact Book: Chicago Metropolitan Area 1990*, 89–94, 103–6. I would therefore argue that West Town's low unemployment decrease suggests that manufacturing job losses alone cannot account for occupational shifts in the neighborhood.

25. These figures are adjusted to account for inflation and are given in 1990 U.S. dollar values.

26. Insofar as the consumption of high-concept cuisine requires a substantial level of cultural capital and economic resources, it serves as a strategy of social differentiation for upper-status classes of consumers; see Bourdieu, *Distinction*; Zukin, *Landscapes of Power*, 179–215; and Ferguson, "A Cultural Field in the Making."

27. According to Bob, the restaurant's head chef, the owners opened the spot in April 1998 to attract these very customers:

> We opened this place because we wanted to cater to the fortyish crowd of residents who have bought and own buildings in the neighborhood. We want to provide a fancy place for these people to dine as an alternative to the other establishments in this area which appeal to a much younger crowd . . . This part of the neighborhood is definitely coming into its own as an alternative to the activity up by the intersection, especially with the new stores, restaurants, and clubs on the street.

In hindsight, this decision seems particularly timely insofar as 1990 census data suggests that local residential incomes and property values had risen even higher in the census tracts surrounding the Division Street commercial corridor than in the community area as a whole. In the two tracts that the street borders, the value of an owner-occupied housing unit in West Town more than *quadrupled* between 1980 and 1990 as residents holding white-collar jobs rose in number. In the northern tract (2414), poverty decreased from 39 percent to 27 percent, residents holding white-collar jobs increased from 38 percent to 47 percent, and the value of an owner-occupied housing unit in West Town increased from $55,516 (in 1990 US$) to $244,400. In the southern tract (2422), residents holding white-collar jobs jumped from 35 percent to 44 percent, and the value of an owner-occupied housing unit in West Town increased from $29,820 (in 1990 US$) to $126,000. For additional data on the area, see Chicago Fact Book Consortium, *Local Community Fact Book: Chicago Metropolitan Area 1990*, 92–94.

28. During our conversation Julie also explains how the relatively inexpensive property on Division Street vis-à-vis the more developed Damen and North area made the strip an attractive location for starting a small business. From behind the counter, she recalls:

> We were interested in opening up a coffee bar, and we knew that coffee places don't bring in all that much money, and so we wanted a cheap space for Jinx. So we started looking on Division between Ashland and Damen, and on Damen between North and Chicago, and we just seized on this place when it became available. And I just love this neighborhood . . . To me, this is the best area in the city, because everyone here is so tolerant.

But small-business owners like Julie are in an awkward position. As entrepreneurs, they desire to take advantage of the rent gap (the disparity between a property's actual and potential value; see Smith, *The New Urban Frontier*) by investing in inexpensive areas immediately prior to their rise in popularity and subsequent value, and they know that their business will prosper if the surrounding commercial district develops and can attract a wide range of customers. However, they are also aware that development can lead to rent increases and competition from chain stores like Starbucks and Einstein's Bagels. Frightened by the prospect of displacement, such business owners appropriate the language of gentrification to describe their *own* apprehensions about future commercial development in the neighborhood. After showing me a Polaroid photograph of a local residence that asks, "Have you seen my house? Call 1–800-GENTRIFY . . . Missing house hotline for runaway affordable homes," Julie explains:

> Well, you definitely picked the right neighborhood for a study of gentrification . . . Right now, the Gap is looking to move in down the street, but there is a really strong anti-feeling here among the local businesses toward them moving in . . . With community intervention, we *could* stave off the chains . . . All of the businesses on the street are really supportive of each other right now . . . like I get my haircut at Dynamic, and I'll buy my clothes at the Mystery Spot, and I'll shop at the Kind Store.

The local investments made by business owners like Julie help to increase land values in West Town, make the neighborhood enticing and "safe" for intensified commercial development, and involuntarily assist in the displacement of working-class residents and ethnic-oriented businesses in the area. But because they fear competition from corporate-owned businesses, these same entrepreneurs incorporate an anti-gentrification ideology to defend their existence, even as they enjoy the current benefits of local commercial development.

At the same time, Julie's rhetorical stance against this development parallels the community sentiments of fellow gentrifiers like Henry. For many middle-class residents, the attractiveness of neighborhoods like West Town lies in their authenticity and distinction from the seemingly straight-arrow commercial world of normative upper-class living. Like the University of Chicago graduate students who frequent the Checkerboard Lounge, self-styled bohemian residents fear that the increased presence of affluent whites in the area will devalue the subcultural capital that their residency signifies, and do so without acknowledging that their structural position to the area is in fact *closer* to new gentrifiers than to West Town's recently displaced immigrant residents.

29. Interestingly enough, Chad's recollections of West Town resonate with other blues musicians' memories of B.L.U.E.S. Etcetera's formative years in the gentrifying community of Lakeview. During the club's founding in 1987, the conditions of local street life in the area suggested the neighborhood's transitional quality; according to Willy, a local blues saxophonist who recalls the opening of the club: "Back when they opened this place, you should have seen this block . . . There used to be like three or four crack houses right out here . . . In fact, just across the street here there used to be a market, and that place was 'Crack Central.' " Nevertheless, by that time the neighborhood had developed to the point where local investors such as Rob Hecko were willing to take a chance on Lakeview as an up-and-coming yet still inexpensive neighborhood:

> You want to always be there when you can still afford it, and you see things going in the right direction . . . I knew that I was comfortable with the neighborhood, I knew that the neighborhood was heading in the right direction—I guess all that plays into accounting for the decision one way or the other. We didn't do a demographic study . . . but I guess we kind of did a demographic study subconsciously.

30. The lyrical violence of the Delta blues reveals itself in songs about bloody vengeance, murder, and the electric chair.

Chapter 3

1. Jane Jacobs, *The Death and Life of Great American Cities* (New York: Vintage, 1961), argues that shopkeepers and other "natural proprietors of the street" not only maintain a level of security on neighborhood sidewalks, but also symbolize the presence of community life to strangers and residents alike. On the construction of community as a social process of meaning making, also see William Foote Whyte, *Street Corner Society* (Chicago: University of Chicago Press, 1940); Louis Wirth, *The Ghetto* (Chicago: University of Chicago Press, 1956); Herbert Gans, *The Urban Villagers: Group and Class in the Life of Italian-Americans* (New York: Free Press, 1962); Gerald D. Suttles, *The Social Order of the Slum* (Chicago: University of Chicago Press, 1968), and *The Social Construction of Communities* (Chicago: University of Chicago Press, 1972); Gusfield, *Community*; Hummon, *Commonplaces*; Elijah Anderson, *Streetwise: Race, Class, and Change in an Urban Community* (Chicago: University of Chicago Press, 1990); Griswold, "The Writing on the Mud Wall"; and Ruth Finnegan, *Tales of the City: A Study of Narrative and Urban Life* (Cambridge: Cambridge University Press, 1998). In addition, a number of social scientists continue to explore what kinds of correlations might exist between objective measures, such as violent crime rates, instances of property vandalism or membership in local civic organizations, and the more subjectively based construction of community solidarity and disintegration within identifiable residential areas. These studies include John D. Kasarda and Morris Janowitz, "Community Attachment in Mass Society," *American Sociological Review* 39 (1974): 328–39; Claude Fischer, *To Dwell among Friends: Personal Networks in Town and City* (Chicago: University of Chicago Press, 1982); James Christenson, "Urbanism and Community Sentiment," *Social Science Quarterly* 60 (1979): 387–400; Barry Wellman,

"The Community Question: The Intimate Networks of East New Yorkers," *American Journal of Sociology* 84 (1979): 1201–31; Robert J. Sampson, "Local Friendship Ties and Community Attachment in Mass Society: A Multilevel Systemic Model," *American Sociological Review* 53 (1988): 766–79; Robert J. Sampson, Jeffrey D. Morenoff, and Felton Earls, "Beyond Social Capital: Spatial Dynamics of Collective Efficacy for Children," *American Sociological Review* 64 (1999): 633–660; Robert J. Sampson and Stephen W. Raudenbush, "Systematic Social Observation of Public Spaces: A New Look at Disorder in Urban Neighborhoods," *American Journal of Sociology* 105 (1999): 603–51; and Robert D. Putnam, *Bowling Alone: The Collapse and Revival of American Community* (New York: Simon and Schuster, 2000).

2. These gestures and elements of subcultural style make up the shared cultural repertoire utilized by participants at the club in their moments of interaction; see Hebdige, *Subculture*; Ann Swidler, "Culture in Action: Symbols and Strategies," *American Sociological Review* 51 (1986): 273–86. On the uses of setting as a type of "front" necessary for the performance of self in everyday life, see Goffman, *The Presentation of Self in Everyday Life*, 22–23.

3. As Gary Alan Fine argues in "Popular Culture and Social Interaction: Production, Consumption and Usage," *Journal of Popular Culture* 11, no. 2 (1977): 453–56, the shared collective knowledge of popular culture, including sports, eases social interactions among strangers and persons related through weak ties.

4. See Ray Oldenburg, *The Great Good Place* (New York: Paragon, 1989).

5. Of course, many professionals work long evening hours and routinely travel during the week, like business consultants and attorneys; however, unlike these professionals, the costs borne by musicians and their partners rarely translate into increased income or class status.

6. Howard S. Becker, *Outsiders: Studies in the Sociology of Deviance* (Glencoe, Ill.: Free Press, 1963), 114–19, makes a similar argument about how professional jazz musicians maintain difficulties balancing family and work demands.

7. May, *Talking at Trena's*, examines how collective television viewing can help encourage social interactions among regulars in a bar setting.

8. This "brotherhood of strangers" exemplifies the male-dominated set of social relations existing within many bars, taverns, and neighborhood establishments in Chicago; for example, see Anderson, *A Place on the Corner*; Duneier, *Slim's Table*; and May, *Talking at Trena's*. For examples of the strong sense of community experienced among familiar strangers in urban neighborhoods, see Jacobs, *The Death and Life of Great American Cities*; Suttles, *The Social Order of the Slum*; and Mitchell Duneier, *Sidewalk* (New York: Farrar, Straus and Giroux, 1999).

9. In our own haphazard conversations, Mickey typically offers his handshake, asks me where I live, shares his joy of the music performance of the evening, brags about his friendship with a local blues celebrity, points out an acquaintance in the bar whom he admires, and then, distracted, usually runs off to shake hands with another recognizable regular—all within about a minute.

10. In addition, Mickey is the city's "Number One Blues Fan" and has the award to prove it. In the summer of 1998, the city awarded him the honorary title at the annual Chicago Blues Festival.

11. Anderson, *A Place on the Corner*, 31, 35, makes a similar case for the working-class men who frequent Jelly's, a bar and liquor store located on Chicago's South Side.

12. Of course, by defining the club in terms of its promotion of racial tolerance and integration, anti-commercial disposition, and emphasis on social solidarity, bartenders and regulars ignore the elements of the club's social world that challenge these characterizations, including

the racist and essentialist performances offered by local bluesmen, the commercialized elements of the blues club, and the frequent antisocial behavior of its audience members.

13. I maintained a somewhat friendly and reciprocal relationship with Suzanne; therefore, my own impressions of her are actually quite different from Robin's. Nevertheless, I include the excerpt as a means of analyzing Robin's identification with the club's social world and its presumed moral order.

14. It is interesting that Robin attributes Suzanne's working style to her "self-centered" disposition when, in fact, her real sin may simply lie in her refusal to operate in the efficient and productive, if docile and ultimately self-defeating, manner commonly expected of low-paid service workers; see Leslie Salzinger, "A Maid by Any Other Name: The Transformation of 'Dirty Work' by Central American Immigrants," in *Ethnography Unbound: Power and Resistance in the Modern Metropolis*, ed. Michael Burawoy et al. (Berkeley: University of California Press, 1991); Robin Leidner, *Fast Food, Fast Talk: Service Work and the Routinization of Everyday Life* (Berkeley: University of California Press, 1993); Klein, *No Logo*, 231–45; Katherine S. Newman, *No Shame in My Game: The Working Poor in the Inner City* (New York: Vintage, 2000); and Barbara Ehrenreich, *Nickel and Dimed: On (Not) Getting by in America* (New York: Metropolitan Books, 2001).

15. According to Rob Hecko, the owner, the gendering of these service jobs is intentional:

> Well, if this was a singles bar, I'd hire male bartenders, because it makes the women in the bar feel more comfortable, you know, like they're there to look out for them, like a big brother. But now, this isn't a singles bar, and so I don't hire men as bartenders— and I don't want men as waiters, and that's usually how I get my bartenders: I promote them up from waitressing to the bar. And I don't want to hire male waiters: actually, unless I'm in a fancy restaurant, I don't like to be served by male waiters myself.

16. Hochschild describes the "emotion work" required of service-sector employees during interactions with customers. In *The Managed Heart*, she analyzes how flight attendants perform emotion work in order to appear cheerful, sympathetic, and sociable to their passengers. This kind of labor is commonly expected of female employees in male-dominated drinking establishments such as B.L.U.E.S. In a strange way, Robin's invective against Suzanne's autonomous serving practices exemplifies the extent to which female workers internalize these gender roles. By interpreting what could be regarded as self-reliant behavior as "self-centered," Robin normalizes the expectations within the club that value the comfort of customers over a female worker's need to make material ends meet. On the demand among female employees to expend a high degree of emotional labor in other service-sector occupational settings, see Leidner, *Fast Food, Fast Talk*; and Newman, *No Shame in My Game*, 89–92.

17. In this manner, Suzanne's resistance against the coercive aspects of her occupational position may have eventually diminished over time as she internalized the emotional demands required by the job. On the uncritical internalization of workplace expectations on the part of professional employees, see Leidner, *Fast Food, Fast Talk*.

18. Mezz Mezzrow and Bernard Wolfe, *Really the Blues* (New York: Random House, 1946); and DeVeaux, *The Birth of Bebop*, 202–35.

19. DeVeaux, *The Birth of Bebop*, 277–84. Of course, more clandestine jam sessions continued to attract jazz and blues players throughout the bebop era; see ibid., 202–35.

20. In September 1998 Adam's band invited me to rehearse and perform with them during their second set at a gig held at U.S. Beer Co., a local blues and rock bar. My own relationship with the band began with a series of unplanned encounters at B.L.U.E.S. Etcetera, particularly during its weekly jam session.

21. On the art of "becoming" an occupational self, see Donileen R. Loseke and Spencer E. Cahill, "Actors in Search of a Character: Student Social Workers' Quest for Professional Identity," *Symbolic Interaction* 9, no. 2 (1986): 245–58.

22. On the professionalization of occupational roles, see Andrew Abbott, *The System of Professions: An Essay on the Division of Expert Labor* (Chicago: University of Chicago Press, 1988).

23. On the use of argot and fashion as countercultural style, see Stuart Hall and Tony Jefferson, *Resistance through Rituals: Youth Subcultures in Post-War Britain* (London: Routledge, 1976); Paul Willis, *Learning to Labor* (New York: Columbia University Press, 1977), and *Common Culture*; Hebdige, *Subculture*; Grazian, "Uniform of the Party"; Thornton, *Club Cultures*; and Malbon, *Clubbing*.

24. While I could not ascertain whether or not Sunnyland Slim and Donny were actually cousins, a number of ethnographic accounts suggest that fictive kinship relations are regularly manufactured among friends and colleagues within the context of black neighborhood life. Thus, Donny's use of the term *cousin* to describe his relationship to Sunnyland Slim may, in fact, refer to an invented (but not necessarily less meaningful) relationship; on this practice of "going for cousins," see Elliot Liebow, *Tally's Corner: A Study of Negro Streetcorner Men* (Boston: Little, Brown, 1967), 170–73; and Anderson, *A Place on the Corner*, 17–23.

25. Jeffrey's strategy of constructing identity through boundary work resembles the tactics utilized by the jazz performers in Becker, *Outsiders*; however, while Becker's informants constantly forge distinctions between themselves and their audiences, they rarely extend that hostility to their discussions of fellow musicians.

26. Other urban subcultures acculturate new members in a similar manner; for example, see ibid., 41–58, on socialization within drug subcultures.

27. In Chicago, clubs organize their jam sessions differently according to their own particular rules and norms governing the centrality of the evening's house band, the professional status of the musicians permitted to perform, the scheduling of artists, and so forth. For example, the organizers of B.L.U.E.S. Etcetera's jam session gather random groups of musicians who take to the stage to perform impromptu songs together, while the Green Room at Macaw's, Winner's, and other venues invite players to join the house band one at a time to join in on a song from a predetermined set list. In the first instance, participants maintain a great deal of autonomy over their performances, while the latter jams really just allow participants the chance to perform alongside the club's hired band.

28. Of course, by suggesting the irrelevance of "who you are" at the jam session, Louis obscures the status disparities that exist at the club. Indeed, these same musicians seek individual status by stratifying their world into *unequal* classes of amateurs and professionals, club newcomers and established regulars, beginners and advanced players, organizers and participants, voluntary and paid performers, and mentors and students, to say nothing of the relationship between musicians and their audiences. The mentoring processes of socialization described above integrates new members into the subcultural world of the jam while it simultaneously establishes and reproduces unequal relationships and identities between novices and their more seasoned counterparts. By successfully presenting "expert" selves, experienced musicians naturalize the hierarchical relations existing between themselves and less experienced players. As long as advanced musicians insist that the stratification of the subculture is "not what this is about" by punctuating a moral imperative based on "emotion" rather than experience, status, and subcultural capital, such an ethos masks the material and symbolic distinctions that characterize the stratified social world of the blues club. On mystification as a dramaturgical and ideological tool, see Goffman, *The Presentation of Self in Everyday Life*.

29. While Louis's request suggests that these tips will be paid out to the musicians for offering their free services, in fact, the evening collection—sometimes thirty-five or forty dollars—goes to Louis himself as *his* added compensation for hosting the jam in addition to his fee paid by the club owners. One night before a show, he explains that he uses the collection to pay for the upkeep of the jam session music equipment and shares a portion of the rest with the club's bartenders and waitresses.

30. Gold cards may be used anytime during the week and after midnight on Friday and Saturday night.

31. On the use of VIP passes and nightclub areas as status symbols in other nocturnal settings in Chicago, see Audarshia Townsend, "Playing Hard to Get," *Chicago Tribune* (December 16, 1999), sec. 1, p. 10.

32. On the uses of logos and other types of commodity culture as a means of constructing subcultural identity, see Klein, *No Logo*. In contrast, many theories of subcultural life describe how youth commonly reject or misappropriate the symbols of commodified culture as a means of reinforcing their subcultural identities; for example, see M. Gottdiener, "Hegemony and Mass Culture: A Semiotic Approach," *American Journal of Sociology* 90 (1985): 979–1001; and Willis, *Common Culture*.

33. Nina further exemplifies this boundary spanning in her preparations for B.L.U.E.S.'s New Year's Eve party, for which an advance ticket allows guests to reserve their favorite bar stools at the club.

34. Likewise, such enthusiasm might diminish the abilities of amateur musicians to demonstrate their subcultural coolness in public.

35. Of course, many musicians simply arrive at the club from another gig, and thus with their horn or guitar in tow. Generally speaking, their status, professional role, and relationship to the paid performer determines when they will be invited to approach the stage: low-status guest vocalists often perform during the warm-up with the band before the headliner takes to the stage, while high-status singers and accompanying instrumentalists tend to come up at all times during the performance. Meanwhile, emergent and unknown players may be invited to join the band onstage in the early morning hours, provided they are willing to wait that long. Frequently, musicians plan these guest performances in advance; however, as demonstrated by the preceding incident involving Lindsay Alexander and Betty, impromptu invitations are not uncommon.

Chapter 4

1. These kinds of conflicts regularly occur among the members of art worlds that operate within a commercially based market; see Becker, *Art Worlds*.

2. Marcus, *Mystery Train*, 22–23.

3. Becker, *Art Worlds*, argues that art worlds represent far-reaching collective networks of cultural producers and distributors as well as their audiences and may include individuals (like composers, club owners, booking agents, instrument repair people, blues fans, journalists) as well as large institutions, such as the state. According to this model of art as collective activity, musicians themselves play a vital yet relatively small role within the overall process through which popular music is actually produced and consumed.

4. Musicians do not actually describe themselves as members of these peer groups; likewise, the group names are my invention and have no equivalent among musicians or other subcultural members. The attempt among sociologists to construct grounded typologies of their

subjects based on shared sets of traits, characteristics, and personal histories has a long tradition in the discipline, beginning with the original Chicago school studies and continuing in more recent ethnographic work as well as in quantitatively based cluster analysis. This Chicago school work includes Nels Anderson, *The Hobo: The Sociology of the Homeless Man* (Chicago: University of Chicago Press, 1923); and Frederic M. Thrasher, *The Gang: A Study of 1,313 Gangs in Chicago* (Chicago: University of Chicago Press, 1927). For more recent ethnographic studies, see David A. Snow and Leon Anderson, *Down on Their Luck: A Study of Homeless Street People* (Berkeley: University of California Press, 1993); for examples of quantitative studies that utilize clustering methods, see Andrew Abbott and Alexandra Hrycak, "Measuring Resemblance in Sequence Data: An Optimal Matching Analysis of Musicians' Careers," *American Journal of Sociology* 96 (1990): 144–85; and Mary Blair-Loy, "Career Patterns of Executive Women in Finance: An Optimal Matching Analysis," *American Journal of Sociology* 104 (1999): 1346–97.

5. For example, Daniel was born in Williamsport, Pennsylvania, raised in Greenville, South Carolina, and moved to the city to attend the University of Chicago; Jason, a guitarist, grew up on Long Island in New York and migrated to the Midwest after attending Georgetown University; Greg, a singer and harmonica player, was born in Chicago but was raised in Washington, D.C., and moved back to the city after attending the University of Dayton in Ohio; his band mate Shai hails from Alabama; and so forth.

6. For example, Elliot received an M.A. degree in history from the University of Toronto; Jason graduated from Georgetown; Keith, a bassist, and Dave, a guitarist, both recently graduated from Northwestern University; Daniel attended the University of Chicago.

7. As further symptomatic of their transitional stage in the life course, most of these young musicians are unmarried and live in gentrifying neighborhoods of the city, including Wicker Park and Ukrainian Village. Gentrifying neighborhoods often attract residents whose social characteristics resemble that of the lions of the Chicago blues: unmarried, childless adults with high education levels who value proximity to social, cultural, and entertainment facilities near the city center; see Brian J. L. Berry, "Islands of Renewal in Seas of Decay," in *The New Urban Reality*, ed. Paul Peterson (Washington, D.C.: Brookings Institution, 1985), 83–84. In fact, young cultural producers and other creative workers often seek out affordable housing in gentrifying neighborhoods that offer easy access to central nodes in the artistic labor markets and broader entertainment infrastructure of the city; see Zukin, *Loft Living*, and "Gentrification: Culture and Capital in the Urban Core," *Annual Review of Sociology* 13 (1987): 129–47.

8. Zukin, *Landscapes of Power*, argues that young and educated urban dwellers in pursuance of artistic careers generally maintain low-wage service-oriented jobs within the cultural infrastructure of the city as waiters, bartenders, and the like. However, while some local bluesmen, young and old, do hold jobs in these fields, it is worth noting that younger lions are just as likely to work in higher-income areas of the post-industrial urban labor market, such as in the computer sciences.

9. Examples of the former include Darryl, who attended Columbia University and eventually graduated from the University of Chicago, and Farrell, who graduated with a degree in Latin American studies from Georgetown.

10. In fact, over the course of my fieldwork, Farrell entered the training academy of the Chicago Fire Department, Jack took over the responsibilities of managing and booking acts for B.L.U.E.S. Etcetera, and Darryl continued to pursue a doctorate in philosophy at the University of Illinois at Chicago.

11. In *The Social Order of the Slum*, Suttles describes how neighborhood residents in urban areas organize their daily rounds and social interaction spatially according to distinctions

of race, ethnicity, gender, age, and status. In keeping with this sociological tradition, former students of Suttles have incorporated his theories regarding the ecological manifestations of ordered segmentation into their understandings of local urban hangouts such as bars, liquor stores, cafeterias, and public housing projects; for example, see William Kornblum, *Blue Collar Community* (Chicago: University of Chicago Press, 1974); Anderson, *A Place on the Corner*; Duneier, *Slim's Table*; and Sudhir Alladi Venkatesh, "The Social Organization of Street Gang Activity in an Urban Ghetto," *American Journal of Sociology* 103 (1997): 82–111. Of course, most participants at the club define themselves in terms of a multiplicity of identities, personal characteristics, and dispositions—and therefore spend evenings at the clubs code-switching among several "master statuses." The task of a talented networker (or ethnographer, for that matter) seeking maximum social exposure is to competently negotiate among competing identities throughout the course of an evening.

12. According to Wendy Fonarow, "The Spatial Organization of the Indie Music Gig," in *The Subcultures Reader*, ed. Ken Gelder and Sarah Thornton (London: Routledge, 1997), 367, professionals and other insiders utilize similar tactics of impression management in the back areas of clubs during rock concerts.

13. In contrast, Fonarow, ibid., argues that among insiders in alternative rock subcultures, the ability to appear demonstratively enthusiastic in the spatial zones near the stage areas of music venues does not really exist.

14. Likewise, internal stratification on the basis of local experience, talent, professional success, and social capital exists *within* peer groups as well.

15. Because of this connection, I have named him after the Chicago novelist James T. Farrell, whose *Studs Lonigan: A Trilogy* (Urbana: University of Illinois Press, [1932, 1934, 1935] 1993) has provided fodder for our many barroom conversations about American literature and Chicago history.

16. These cross-generational, interracial relationships recall the pseudo-kinship ties between older and younger men in Chicago's Hyde Park and its surrounding working-class neighborhoods as described in Duneier, *Slim's Table*, in which he offers a short account of the improvised son-father relationship between Slim, a black mechanic, and Bart, a older white gentleman who relied on Slim in times of need.

17. Discussions of the pseudo-familial networks that exist among black adults in the urban milieu appear in Liebow, *Tally's Corner*; Carol Stack, *All Our Kin* (New York: Harper and Row, 1974); and Anderson, *A Place on the Corner*.

18. In Jack's remarks, "Doc" and "Gino" refer to Doc Pellegrino and Gino Battaglia, the owners of Kingston Mines and Blue Chicago, respectively.

19. The boredom and near nausea reported by many blues musicians who play the same set of familiar standards during their performances appears to be a common problem among all different kinds of musicians, including classically trained orchestral players. As one reed instrumentalist complains during an interview in Robert R. Faulkner, *Hollywood Studio Musicians* (Chicago: Aldine Publishing, 1971), 71, "It would be all right if you could play different music all the time in the symphony. But what can a guy think when he's going out to do the Brahms C Minor for the thirty-first time?"

20. On the attitudes of service workers toward their customers, see Hochschild, *The Managed Heart*; Leidner, *Fast Food, Fast Talk*; and Newman, *No Shame in My Game*.

21. Becker, *Outsiders*, 89–90.

22. On the subcultural use of the term *square*, see Becker, *Outsiders*, 85–100; for examples

of its usage, also see Mailer, "The White Negro"; and Ned Polsky, *Hustlers, Beats, and Others* (Garden City, N.Y.: Anchor, 1969).

23. Becker, *Outsiders*, 92.

24. Sonny's repertoire consists mostly of folk-blues songs composed between the two World Wars by artists such as Brownie McGhee, Sonny Terry, Blind Boy Fuller, Elizabeth Cotton, and the Rev. Gary Davis: the audience member in Sonny's story confuses the styles of these traditional blues songs with the folk-rock genre popularized during the 1960s folk music revival by artists like Bob Dylan, Joan Baez, and Simon and Garfunkel, and in the 1970s by post-hippie singer-songwriters like Cat Stevens, James Taylor, and Carole King. On the folk revival and its influence on popular rock music, see Charlie Gillett, *The Sound of the City: The Rise of Rock and Roll* (New York: Outerbridge and Dienstfrey, 1970); Simon Frith, *Sound Effects: Youth, Leisure, and the Politics of Rock 'n' Roll* (New York: Pantheon, 1981); Marcus, *Mystery Train*, and *The Old, Weird America*; Todd Gitlin, *The Sixties: Years of Hope, Days of Rage* (New York: Bantam, 1987); Cantwell, *When We Were Good*; and Geoffrey O'Brien, "Recapturing the American Sound," *New York Review of Books* (April 9, 1998): 45–51.

25. Farrell's remark echoes the optimistic attitude suggested by a jazz musician interviewed by Becker in *Outsiders*, 95.

> I enjoy playing more when there's someone to play for. You kind of feel like there isn't much purpose in playing if there's nobody there to hear you. I mean, after all, that's what music's for—for people to hear and get enjoyment from. That's why I don't mind playing corny too much. If anyone enjoys it, then I kind of get a kick out of it. I guess I'm kind of a ham. But I like to make people happy that way.

26. Peterson, *Creating Country Music*, suggests these contradictory definitions of authenticity—originality and conventionality—in his analysis of the history of country music recording.

27. For example, see Polsky, *Hustlers, Beats and Others*; Hall and Jefferson, *Resistance through Rituals*; and Hebdige, *Subculture*.

28. In *Hell's Angels* (New York: Ballantine, 1965), gonzo journalist Hunter S. Thompson documents the rise of the outlaw motorcycle gang and their particular fashion sense (or lack thereof, as some might suggest).

29. Kembrew McLeod, "Authenticity within Hip-Hop and Other Cultures Threatened with Assimilation," *Journal of Communication* 49 (1999): 134–50, describes how authenticity is conceptualized in the context of hip-hop and rap music.

30. Tiger matches his disdain for club owners with his comparable contempt for local music journalists and critics. Over the past few decades, the local network of professionals engaged in the production of blues music and its affectations have widened to encompass greater numbers of journalists, critics, and other sources of influence. These cultural authorities serve as effective "gatekeepers" capable of suppressing the careers of individual as well as groups of musicians. Consequently, bluesmen find themselves trapped in a wicked paradox: musicians who may potentially retain more subcultural *status* relative to these emergent professionals nevertheless maintain significantly less *power* in the structural hierarchy of the city's blues market. For this reason, musicians understandably perceive themselves as underdogs who must struggle to find gigs, make a living, and somehow succeed unscathed by the barbs of local journalists as well as club owners.

Still, blues musicians tend to dismiss negative reviews as wrongheaded, or at least irrelevant, a strategy not uncommon among other creative workers who often find themselves the target of similarly unwanted publicity, such as actors, artists, and, of course, writers. Tiger revealed his own derision of music critics to me a few days after receiving a negative write-up in an annual Chicago Blues Festival preview in the *Chicago Reader*, a local weekly newspaper. The preview reported the following:

> If Dave "Slim" Douglas represents hope for the future of Chicago blues, Tiger exemplifies what's wrong with the present. Technically he's an admirable player, but he needs to prove it all the time, stoking his over-the-top pyrotechnics with too much wah-wah and then pumping them through an arena-rock set-up. [actual names replaced]

When I ask Tiger for his thoughts on the article a few days after its publication, he shrugs it off: "I pay no attention to that kind of thing . . . I just do my own thing, and if they like it, great, if not, whatever. People are always going to be saying something about you. You just have to ignore it and keep doing what you're doing. Yeah, pay no attention to what that guy said about me."

31. Camille Severino, "Working Women of the Blues," *In the Mix* (June 1998): 26.

32. Valois "See Your Food" Cafeteria provides the setting for Duneier, *Slim's Table*, another Chicago ethnography.

33. On this stylistic shift in the blues, see Keil, *Urban Blues*; and Haralambos, *Right On*.

34. By the same token, it seems reasonable to assume that occupational success and aesthetic taste may be closely related to one another. For example, if survivors like Jack and Darryl define musical merit and value according to a set of criteria that differs from the tastes of mainstream audiences, their musical careers may suffer as an unintended consequence of their persistent search for authenticity. Then again, in a discussion over an early draft of this book, Darryl suggested to me that while it may be the case that his tradition-based brand of authenticity may not be popular among most mainstream audiences, he does not regard this tension as necessarily problematic, as he never desired commercial success in the first place—only the ability to play and enjoy the blues in a manner compatible with his notions of authenticity.

35. Throughout the history of the blues tradition, definitions of authenticity have faced constant revisions as a consequence of mercurial changes in production, marketing, consumption, and the ideological content of appropriate discursive fields. In popular music, dominant notions of authenticity are *always* up for grabs.

36. According to Peterson, *Creating Country Music*, competing sets of definitions structure how art worlds evaluate the authenticity of cultural objects and their creators. On the one hand, authenticity can refer to a strict adherence to an idealized form, whether in elitist notions of culture as a "study of perfection," as articulated by Matthew Arnold, *Culture and Anarchy* (New Haven: Yale University Press, [1865] 1994), or more populist and essentialist notions of "genuine" culture; on the latter, see Edward Sapir, "Culture: Genuine and Spurious," in *Culture, Language, and Personality*, ed. David G. Mandelbaum (Berkeley: University of California Press, 1949). In the arts, traditional and revivalist movements such as the 1930s folk song revival and the rise of neoclassicism in American jazz in the 1980s adhere to this definition of authenticity. In contrast, the term can also refer to the originality, uniqueness, and creativity of a particular object, style, or artist; historically, this definition of the authentic has been hailed by avant-garde movements from bebop jazz to punk rock; for example, on bebop see DeVeaux, *The Birth of Bebop*; and Nisenson, *Blue*; on punk, see Hebdige, *Subculture*; and Greil Marcus, *Lipstick Traces: A Secret History of the Twentieth Century* (Cambridge: Harvard University Press, 1989). Among Chicago blues musicians, survivors generally adhere to the first definition of authenticity, while lions and players tend to follow the second.

37. Even avant-garde artists like Louis ensure that their audiences will approve of their adherence to genre conventions by committing themselves to set lists padded with familiar standards.

38. On genres as socially constructed and highly ambiguous classificatory systems, see Richard A. Peterson, "The Production of Cultural Change: The Case of Contemporary Country Music," *Social Forces* 45 (1978): 292–314; Becker, *Art Worlds*; and Paul DiMaggio, "Classification in Art," *American Sociological Review* 52 (1987): 440–55.

39. The differences in the critical remarks made by Farrell and the more traditionalist orientations of Darryl and Jack provide an example of the internal differentiation that exists *within* subcultural groups. While Farrell's divergence from the ideologies espoused by his fellow survivors cannot be explained by any single variable, his remarks certainly resonate with his contrary and skeptical disposition toward the contemporary affectations of commercialism, including the increased proliferation of local cultural authorities in the city.

40. Certainly, the success of such an ideological move would further delegitimize the attempts of his audiences and students to confuse the songs in his traditional folk-blues repertoire with Top 40 "folk" melodies like "Cat's in the Cradle" and songs by rock artists like Tom Petty.

Chapter 5

1. While hip-hop music originated, like urban blues, in a context of racial segregation and ghetto-poor neighborhood conditions, its incorporation into dominant production, promotional, and distribution channels, as well as its popularity among a diverse and international market of consumers, has made it the music industry's top-selling format; see Rose, *Black Noise*; and McLeod, "Authenticity within Hip-Hop."

2. On the use of black urban styles as a marketing tool in contemporary advertising, see Klein, *No Logo*; on the use of John Lee Hooker and Howlin' Wolf in recent advertising campaigns for Pepsi and the Gap, see James Porter, "Nothin' but the Blues," *New City* (December 2, 1999), 8–9.

3. Rowe, *Chicago Blues*.

4. On the marketplace surrounding the West Side's Maxwell Street area, see Wirth, *The Ghetto*; Ira Berkow, *Maxwell Street: Survival in a Bazaar* (Garden City, N.Y.: Doubleday, 1977); and Irving Cutler, *The Jews of Chicago: From Shetl to Suburb* (Urbana: University of Illinois Press, 1996); on its blues culture, see Paul Oliver, *Conversation with the Blues* (Cambridge: Cambridge University Press, 1965); Rodney Wanker, "Maxwell Street, Sunday Morning," *Chicago Reader* (October 1, 1971), 8; and David Whiteis, "Last Dance at the Carnival of the Soul," *Chicago Reader* (September 2, 1994).

5. Ed Morris, *Old Town Holiday Booklet* (1961); reprinted in "Life and Legend in Old Town," *Old Town/Wells Guide Book* 2, no. 1 (summer 1965).

6. *Old Town Newsletter* 1, no.1 (May 1962).

7. Margaret Stockton Warner, "The Renovation of Lincoln Park: An Ecological Study of Neighborhood Change," Ph.D. diss., University of Chicago (1979).

8. For example, see *Old Town/Wells Guide Book*; "Chicago: City on the Lake," *Plymouth Traveler* 6, no. 1 (1965); Jory Graham, *Chicago: An Extraordinary Guide* (Chicago: Rand McNally, 1967); and *Old Town Guidebook* (1968).

9. *Old Town Guidebook*, 22.

10. On the national scope of the 1960s folk music revival, see Cantwell, *When We Were Good*; and Marcus, *The Old, Weird America*.

11. In bombastic and colorful prose, gonzo journalist Hunter S. Thompson describes the mercurial state of relations between the New Left (and their hippie subcultural factions) and outlaw motorcycle gangs during the 1960s in *Hell's Angels*, 290–301, 312–23; as does Tom Wolfe

in his equally experimental and pseudo-ethnographic *The Electric Kool-Aid Acid Test* (New York: Bantam, 1968), 149–61. For a more sociological account, see Gitlin, *The Sixties*, 210–11.

12. Graham, *Chicago*, 87.

13. Roy Newquist, *Fielding's Guide to Chicago* (New York: Fielding, 1970), 116.

14. Gitlin, *The Sixties*, 393.

15. In this manner, blues music became attractive to mainstream whites in Chicago after Old Town's more intense folk and blues fans popularized and promoted it in accessible North Side bars. In this context, these consumers served as grassroots-level cultural gatekeepers, signaling their preferences for the blues to more general commercial audiences. The rising popularity of other roots-oriented folk music genres followed a similar pathway; see Cantwell, *When We Were Good*. In contrast, Thornton, *Club Cultures*, poses a counterpoint to this type of argument by problematizing the actual distinction between mainstream and subcultural consumers in the context of popular music.

16. Warner, "The Renovation of Lincoln Park," 47–49.

17. According to ibid., 46, land values on Wells Street had more than doubled by 1968.

18. Ibid., 47.

19. Ibid., 59.

20. Ibid., 127.

21. James Steck, "Growing Up with Kingston Mines," *Chicago Reader* (March 12, 1976), 10.

22. Susan Nelson, Jon Anderson, and Abra Anderson, eds., *Serendipity City* (1971), 9.

23. Pete Welding, "Gambler's Blues: Shakey Jake," *Living Blues* 10 (autumn 1972): 13.

24. Warner, "The Renovation of Lincoln Park," 57, 59; Gitlin, *The Sixties*, 323.

25. Sally Banes et al., *Sweet Home Chicago: The Real City Guide* (Chicago: Chicago Review Press, 1974), 71.

26. Steck, "Growing Up with Kingston Mines," 10–11.

27. Harold Hotelling, "Stability in Competition," *Economic Journal* (1929), provides the classic economic model to explain why some kinds of businesses are likely to cluster in space. Social scientists frequently use similar theories of competition to explain how rational decision making on the part of businesses, organizations, and even political parties can engender cultural and ideological isomorphism in those fields as well; see Anthony Downs, *An Economic Theory of Democracy* (New York: Harper and Row, 1957); and Paul DiMaggio and Walter W. Powell, "The Iron Cage Revisited: Institutional Isomorphism and Collective Rationality in Organizational Fields," *American Sociological Review* 52 (1983): 147–60.

28. In contrast to the successes of B.L.U.E.S. during the 1980s, Jack and Hecko both blame the financial troubles of B.L.U.E.S. Etcetera, a blues club located about a mile north of B.L.U.E.S. on a sparse commercial strip of Belmont Avenue in the community area of Lakeview, on a *lack* of spatial clustering in the area. According to Jack:

> Well, between you and me, B.L.U.E.S. Etcetera is closing—we sold it. It hasn't been doing well for a couple of years . . . in fact, our gross has dropped by two-thirds. Part of the problem is a communication breakdown and a lack of agreement among the partners about how to aggressively promote the club to tourists, and so we haven't, and the overhead for such a large space is just too expensive for us to maintain if we can't pack it with tourists consistently. Another problem is that the neighborhood isn't right: there isn't lots of foot traffic on that side of Belmont, and the cabs don't zip down that street as much as they do the busier streets like Halsted Street.

While Jack only partially attributes the club's closing to its relative spatial isolation and lack of surrounding "foot traffic," Hecko blames its troubles solely on the distance between B.L.U.E.S. Etcetera and other North Side attractions closer to the downtown area:

> Even in the ten years that we were involved with B.L.U.E.S. Etcetera, we could never get the conventioneers to go that extra mile, *literally*, to B.L.U.E.S. Etcetera. . . . I mean, we had better acts, better-known acts—but we could not get the conventioneers to come that extra mile. They'd come to Halsted Street . . . but they wouldn't go there. God knows we tried for six, seven, eight years.

29. Steck, "Growing Up with Kingston Mines," 10–11. Note the similarities between Steck's discussion of the "hipeoisie" and David Brooks's recent social commentary on so-called "bourgeoisie bohemians" in *Bobos in Paradise: The New Upper Class and How They Got There* (New York: Simon and Schuster, 2000).

30. Of course, whether these neighborhoods actually *were* such bastions of community solidarity may be subject to debate. On the social construction of idealist and romanticized images of community life, see Gusfield, *Community*; Hummon, *Commonplaces*; and Griswold, "The Writing on the Mud Wall."

31. Nick Gravenites, "Bad Talkin' Bluesman," *Blues Revue* 22 (April/May 1996): 14.

32. Graham, *Chicago*, 85.

33. Jim O'Neal, "Reader's Guide to Blues: The Blues Capital," *Chicago Reader* (September 28, 1973), 29.

34. Jim O'Neal, "Reader's Guide to Blues," *Chicago Reader* (September 26, 1975), 31–33.

35. Herb Nolan, "Arts and Fun," *Chicago Tribune* (November 21, 1976).

36. Jim O'Neal, "Reader's Guide to Blues: Searching for Real Chicago Blues," *Chicago Reader* (September 27, 1974), 16.

37. O'Neal, "Reader's Guide to Blues" (1975), 31–33.

38. George Andrews, ed., *The Grey City Guide* (Chicago: University of Chicago, 1976).

39. Banes et al., *Sweet Home Chicago*, 69.

40. On the rise of middle- and upper-class American tourism in formerly war-torn cities in Southeast Asia, see Pico Iyer, *Video Night in Katmandu and Other Reports from the Not-So-Far East* (New York: Vintage, 1989); and Brooks, *Bobos in Paradise*.

41. For instance, from 1970 to 1990, population levels decreased in Grand Boulevard from 80,150 to 35,897; from 1980 to 1990, unemployment levels increased from 24 percent to 34 percent as the percentage of poor residents grew from 51 percent to 64 percent and average annual incomes decreased from $11,016 (in 1990 US$) to $8,371; see Chicago Fact Book Consortium, *Local Community Fact Book: Chicago Metropolitan Area 1990*. All 1980 dollar amounts related to changes in income and land value have been adjusted using the 1990 Consumer Price Index, Table 764 of the 1990 edition of the *Statistical Abstract of the United States*, in order to reflect real value in 1990 U.S. dollars.

42. For further analyses of the impact of these changes on the fate of black inner-city neighborhoods in Chicago, see William Julius Wilson, *The Truly Disadvantaged* (Chicago: University of Chicago Press, 1987), and *When Work Disappears*; Wacquant and Wilson, "Poverty, Joblessness, and the Social Transformation of the Inner City"; Marta Tienda and Haya Stier, "Joblessness and Shiftlessness: Labor Force Activity in Chicago's Inner City," in *The Urban Underclass*, ed. Christopher Jencks and Paul E. Peterson (Washington, D.C.: Brookings, 1991); Massey and Denton, *American Apartheid*; Jeffrey D. Morenoff and Robert J. Sampson, "Violent Crime and the Spatial Dynamics of Neighborhood Transition: Chicago, 1970–1990," *Social Forces* 76 (1997): 31–64; Pattillo-McCoy, *Black Picket Fences*; and Sampson, Morenoff, and Earls, "Beyond Social Capital."

43. It should also be noted that among black (as well as white) audiences, more contemporary, youth-oriented music genres such as hip-hop are far more popular than the blues, and this shift in leisure tastes may also explain why struggling black neighborhoods in Chicago have such a difficult time maintaining local blues venues; on the popularity of hip-hop among black audiences, see Rose, *Black Noise*; and McLeod, "Authenticity within Hip-Hop."

44. In contrast to their South Side and West Side counterparts, small North Side bars like B.L.U.E.S. pay bands a premium wage ranging from $250 to $400 per weeknight gig, and $600 to $800 for a Friday or Saturday night performance.

45. As quoted in Daniel Brogan, "Gutbucket Blues," *Chicago Tribune* (November 23, 1986). In Brogan's interview with Williams, the bandleader also emphasizes the instability of the West Side neighborhoods as a disincentive for performing there: "Anything, though[,] is better than the West Side's rough and tumble clubs. [According to Williams,] 'I was having fun, but the gigs that we were getting were in real gutter clubs. . . . Real rough places, lots of drunks falling on your instruments.' "

46. I base this assertion on research I conducted in 1996, when I analyzed the content of sixty Chicago guidebooks published between 1945 and 1995. While my sample (consisting of the entire collection of local guidebooks [1945–95] archived at the Chicago Historical Society at that time) was not randomly selected, its size makes me extremely confident in the strength of this assertion; see David Grazian, "Sweet Home Chicago: Constructing a Sociology of Local Urban Cultural Processes," M.A. thesis, Department of Sociology, University of Chicago (1996). Interestingly enough, this shift in publishing content paralleled efforts by intellectuals, publishers, and other cultural authorities to depict Chicago in terms of its historical past rather than its present. In *The Man-Made City* (Chicago: University of Chicago Press, 1990), Gerald D. Suttles argues that the city's romanticization of its urban history drastically increased in the 1970s. Suttles demonstrates this trend through a content analysis of books in print written on the subject of Chicago in which he finds that while the number of contemporary studies of Chicago published prior to 1970 (and still in print) is nearly double that of historical works, this trend completely reverses after 1970, when historical studies outnumber their contemporary counterparts two to one.

47. Weimar Port, *Chicago the Pagan* (Chicago: Judy Publishing, 1953), 112–14, 153; grammatical errors appear in the original.

48. Jack Lait and Lee Mortimer, *Chicago Confidential* (New York: Crown, 1950), 47–48, 52.

49. Jim O'Neal, "The Undisputed Blues Capital," *Chicago Reader* (September 29, 1972).

50. As Logan and Molotch, *Urban Fortunes*, argue, "auxiliary players" such as metropolitan newspapers, publishers, cultural institutions, and professional sports franchises all play a role in enhancing the symbolic landscapes of cities in the interests of increasing circulation rates, ticket sales, and merchandising profits that are generated through local urban growth; also see Suttles, "The Cumulative Texture of Local Urban Culture."

51. Suttles, ibid.; on the "stickiness" of ideas, see Malcolm Gladwell, *The Tipping Point: How Little Things Can Make a Big Difference* (Boston: Little, Brown, 2000).

52. Nolan, "Arts and Fun."

53. Earl Calloway, "Mr. Ricky's Hosts Blues Blowout," *Chicago Defender* (May 14, 1996), 16.

54. Like metropolitan newspapers, the sales potential of city guidebooks rises when local tourism and population growth increases.

55. Bates, *The Best of Chicago.*

56. Amy Teschner, ed., *Sweet Home Chicago: The Real City Guide* (1993).

57. For example, see Anderson, *Imagined Communities*; Hobsbawm and Ranger, *The Invention of Tradition*; Eviatar Zerubavel, "Easter and Passover: On Calendars and Group Identity," *American Sociological Review* 47 (1982): 284–89; and Ozouf, *Festivals and the French Revolution*.

58. Of course, the question of whether at least some of these figures became celebrities as a *result* of their Chicago affiliation remains subject to debate. Recent studies in literary criticism and the sociology of literature emphasize the institutional, organizational, commercial, and ideological factors that explain artistic canon formation; see Gaye Tuchman and Nina E. Fortin, "Fame and Misfortune: Edging Women Out of the Great Literary Tradition," *American Journal of Sociology* 90 (1984): 72–96; Sarah M. Corse, "Nations and Novels," and *Nationalism and Literature: The Politics of Culture in Canada and the United States* (Cambridge: Cambridge University Press, 1997); and Wendy Griswold and Fredrik Engelstad, "Does the Center Imagine the Periphery? State Support and Literary Regionalism in Norway and the United States," *Comparative Social Research* 17 (1998): 129–75.

59. Certainly, as I argue in chapter 2, many of the out-of-towners who attend local blues clubs internalize the assertions made by city boosters and image marketers.

60. See Spear, *Black Chicago*; and Rowe, *Chicago Blues*.

61. Spear, *Black Chicago*, 141.

62. In fact, between 1940 and 1950, Mississippi alone lost one-fourth of its entire black population; see Rowe, *Chicago Blues*, 27. On the postwar migration of southern blacks to Chicago, see Hirsch, *Making the Second Ghetto*; and Massey and Denton, *American Apartheid*.

63. "Gregg Parker to Join Buddy Guy at Blues Fest Opener," *Chicago Defender* (June 4, 1997).

64. Nolan, "Arts and Fun."

65. Similarly, on the sociology of how cultural authorities construct the reputations of historical figures through the careful manipulation of the past, see Gary Alan Fine, "Reputational Entrepreneurs and the Memory of Incompetence: Melting Supporters, Partisan Warriors, and Images of President Harding," *American Journal of Sociology* 101 (1996): 1159–93.

66. For a critique of the vulgar uses of reflection theory, see Wendy Griswold, "American Character and the American Novel: An Expansion of Reflection Theory in the Sociology of Literature," *American Journal of Sociology* 86 (1981): 740–65.

67. Oliver, *Blues Fell This Morning*, 4.

68. Ibid., 10–11.

69. Davis, *The History of the Blues*, 3.

70. Titon, *Early Downhome Blues*, 43.

71. See Palmer, *Deep Blues*; and Davis, *The History of the Blues*.

72. Indeed, blues musicians emerged from the Delta to record in all of these cities as well as Chicago; see Palmer, *Deep Blues*.

73. On the cumulative yet relatively stable quality of the respository of images associated with particular cities, see Suttles, "The Cumulative Texture of Local Urban Culture."

74. Laurence J. Hyman, *Going to Chicago: A Year on the Chicago Blues Scene* (San Francisco: Woodford, 1990), 14.

Chapter 6

1. On the impact of these post-industrial shifts on the cultural landscapes of urban downtown areas, see Sassen, *The Mobility of Labor and Capital*, and *The Global City*; Harvey, *The*

Condition of Postmodernity; Soja, *Postmodern Geographies*; Zukin, *Landscapes of Power*, and *The Cultures of Cities*; Boyer, "Cities for Sale"; and Hannigan, *Fantasy City.*

2. On the marketing of local artistic movements as a strategy of city boosterism in New York City, see Zukin, *Loft Living*, and *The Cultures of Cities.*

3. On the Cultural Chicago program, see Jennifer Dorsey, "Culture Is the Focus of Chicago Promotion," *Travel Weekly* (April 10, 1997): 16.

4. "Birthdays at the Cultural Center," City of Chicago, Department of Cultural Affairs (April 1998).

5. Dorsey, "Culture Is the Focus of Chicago Promotion."

6. "Chicago Neighborhood Tours," Chicago Office of Tourism (1998).

7. In addition, CNT runs special non-neighborhood-specific "heritage" tours that celebrate the artistic, cultural, and historical contributions of local Italian, Puerto Rican, Irish, and Jewish immigrants as well as gays and lesbians.

8. In Chicago a number of private organizations target black tourists by offering custom tours of Bronzeville, including the Black Metropolis Convention and Tourism Council, Black Coutours, and Tour Black Chicago. Likewise, Blues University runs tours of local South Side blues bars: their fifteen-dollar package generally includes shuttle bus transportation and admission to Bronzeville clubs such as the Checkerboard Lounge, 113 Club, and the New Bonanza Lounge (as well as downtown clubs like Blue Chicago and Koko Taylor's Celebrity). In New York Harlem Spirituals, Inc., conducts gospel, jazz, and "soul food" tours of Harlem's historical districts. See Melita Marie Garza, "Tour Buses Veer Off Beaten Path," *Chicago Tribune* (July 7, 1997); Isabel Wilkerson, "A Great Escape, a Dwindling Legacy," *New York Times* (February 15, 1998); and Jeff Johnson, "Blues Legend Master of Solo Act," *Chicago Sun-Times* (February 4, 2000).

9. Not only do the tours tend to attract older passengers among these consumer groups, but among local residents, tour passengers often include former neighborhood residents desiring to visit their old haunts and stomping grounds.

10. While Mandie and Sarah demurred when asked these critical questions about the condition of the city's poor black neighborhoods, my colleague and friend Chad Broughton, who accompanied me on the trip, volunteered a thorough set of sociological and political explanations to the passengers. Apparently, this made Mandie and Sarah very uncomfortable, and perhaps as a result I was refused a follow-up interview with Mandie.

11. The Little Black Pearl Workshop is a nonprofit organization that trains inner-city children and young adults in arts and crafts and sells their finished products to the general public. In addition, the galleries of the workshop showcase traveling exhibits as well as pieces made by local artists.

12. On Willie Dixon's Blues Heaven Foundation, see Flynn McRoberts, "It's the Rebirth of Blues Landmark," *Chicago Tribune* (September 17, 1997), 1.

13. While the CNT program relies on corporate underwriting from Sears, Roebuck and Co., which extended $200,000 over three years to the Office of Tourism, the city provided matching funds. In addition, the project drew on a financial pool of $10 million in Chicago Empowerment Zone resources for cultural facility expansions; see Garza, "Tour Buses Veer Off Beaten Path." In September 1997 *Crain's Chicago Business* reported that each of the six cultural centers with retail sites under construction received $20,000 in goods and services to outfit the space, and another $4,000 was to be extended to buy merchandise. These cultural centers include the West Side's Beth-Anne Cultural and Performing Arts Center and Duncan YMCA Community

Service Center, and Greater Grand Crossing's ETA Creative Arts Foundation; see Anne Moore, "Artisan Belief: Tourists Will Buy Wares," *Crain's Chicago Business* (September 20, 1997).

14. Chicago Department of Cultural Affairs (1998).

15. Moore, "Artisan Belief."

16. Ibid.

17. Of course, insofar as they often provide valuable programs and services to their communities, these cultural centers certainly serve a greater set of local needs than might other tourist attractions.

18. The city promotes this "city of neighborhoods" image through its "Neighborhoods Alive!" program and various streetscape renovation projects. For an example of the latter, see Dirk Johnson, "Chicago Hails District as Symbol of Gay Life," *New York Times* (August 27, 1997).

19. In New York Big Apple Greeters offers a program in which residents from local communities lead tourists on private tours of their neighborhoods, while Harlem Spirituals, Inc., conducts special gospel, jazz, and "soul food" tours of Harlem's historic districts; see Garza, "Tour Buses Veer Off Beaten Path."

20. In *The Man-Made City*, Suttles uses this point to wage a critique against "growth-machine" theories of urban planning and development, such as those put forth in Harvey Molotch, "The City as a Growth Machine," *American Journal of Sociology* 82 (1976): 309–32; and Logan and Molotch, *Urban Fortunes*.

21. See Greg Kot, "Fest Overcomes Poor Start, Cool Weather and Variety of Competition," *Chicago Tribune* (June 8, 1998), sec. 5, pp. 1, 4.

22. On the relationship between private corporate interests and local boosterism, see Logan and Molotch, *Urban Fortunes*.

23. While these squeeze bottles proudly announce "Saluting Chicago's Great Blues Traditions" on their side, accompanying brochures offer a more serious discussion of cetirizine HCl, an allergy medication manufactured and heavily promoted by Zyrtec.

24. At the Billy Goat Tavern and Grill's booth, servers yell, "Cheeseburger!! Cheeseburger!!"—words immortalized by John Belushi in a celebrated *Saturday Night Live* sketch.

25. In addition to the four primary performance stages, the festival hosts a Best Buy stage run by its corporate sponsor and a Route 66 stage, which serves more as a warm-up area than a performing space.

26. Although these seats are free to the public on a first-come, first-served basis, local critics and musicians have suggested that if the festival were willing to charge money for their use, money could be raised to assist the city in hiring more expensive artists. According to local blues journalist Bill Dahl, "1998 Chicago Blues Festival," *Chicago Reader* (May 29, 1998):

> Proven star power was a scarce commodity at last year's Chicago Blues Festival. The shortage was so acute that Buddy Guy—the only household name in the lineup—told the local press he was less impressed with his costars. He even remarked that the annual festival might benefit from charging a small fee for the prime seats at Petrillo Music Shell—a proposition previously championed by more than a few blues insiders, but never by someone wielding Guy's clout.

27. For a discussion on the iconography of cities, see R. Richard Wohl and Anselm L. Strauss, "Symbolic Representation and the Urban Milieu," *American Journal of Sociology* 63 (1958): 523–32; Suttles, "The Cumulative Texture of Local Urban Culture"; Zukin, *Landscapes of Power*; on Chicago's contemporary iconographic landscape, see Charles Osgood, "City Scrap-

book," *Chicago Tribune* (May 7, 1997), 1, 3; and Rick Morrissey, "A Tango between an Icon and a City," *Chicago Tribune* (June 3, 1998), 1.

28. The attribution of fantastic images to the various performance stages of the festival echoes a familiar strategy employed in contemporary theme parks like Disney World; see Zukin, *Landscapes of Power*, 217–50, and *The Cultures of Cities*, 49–77; Michael Sorkin, "See You in Disneyland," in *Variations on a Theme Park: The New American City and the End of Public Space* (New York: Hill and Wang, 1992); and M. Gottdiener, *Postmodern Semiotics: Material Culture and the Forms of Postmodern Life* (Oxford: Blackwell, 1995).

29. *Chicago Blues Festival*, Official Program (1997), 33; (1998), 33.

30. Ibid. (1999), 37.

31. Ibid. (1998), 33.

32. After explaining to Barry that Homesick James did, in fact, perform on Maxwell Street years ago, I offered him a brief history of the oral tradition in folk-blues composition and recording, employing Blind Lemon Jefferson's "Matchbox Blues" and Robert Johnson's "Walking Blues" as examples of how blues composers borrow common musical phrases and lyrics from one another.

33. *Chicago Blues Festival*, Official Program (1997), 33; (1998), 33.

34. Ibid. (1999), 37.

35. On the police harassment of homeless persons and other marginalized citizens in the urban milieu, see Davis, *City of Quartz*; Snow and Anderson, *Down on Their Luck*; Smith, *The New Urban Frontier*; and Duneier, *Sidewalk*.

36. Similarly, in *Sidewalk* Duneier discusses the innovative early-morning strategies employed by street entrepreneurs in their desperate attempts to secure desirable spaces to sell their merchandise.

37. The sad irony of their arrangement is that if Rosa's ever becomes a popular weeknight club, Dustin will have a demonstrably harder time procuring gigs there.

38. George's criticism resonates with the ambivalent review that appeared in the *Chicago Tribune* on that day. In a piece entitled "Blues Tease," Chicago *Tribune* (June 6, 1998), sec. 1, p. 2, music critic Greg Kot reports:

> What a tease. Just as Ray Charles got cooking on the opening night of the 15th annual Chicago Blues Festival at the Petrillo Music Shell, curfew sent everybody home wanting more. Charles played barely 50 minutes Thursday. . . . Charles was in excellent voice, saturating "A Fool for You" with lust, "Hallelujah I Love Her So" with ecstasy and "Drown in My Own Tears" with pathos. The call-and-response with his longtime female backing singers, the Raeletts, gave Charles' secular hymns a sanctified urgency, particularly when Mabel John—a Raelett who went on to score several minor hits on the Memphis' Stax label in the '60s—added her robust voice to the exchanges. But the obligatory finale of "What'd I Say" came all too soon. It made for an abrupt end to what originally had been an intelligently conceived evening of piano-based blues, but which instead turned into somewhat of a rushed hodgepodge.

39. According to local law, Section 4–268-020 of the Municipal Code of the City of Chicago "prohibits all persons from performing in a public area without first obtaining a street performers' permit under Section 4–268-030. Thus, no one, other than performers scheduled to perform on stage as part of the event, may perform within the perimeter of any special event sponsored by the City in Grant Park without such a permit."

40. It should be noted that during the time I spent with Dustin's band, the police never harassed them for any other reason and never approached me in search of a license. In fact, the

officers patrolling the intersection stood behind the crowd during their sets and seemed to enjoy listening to the music, and during one break they approached the band to ask when they would get to hear more music. In contrast, many other street musicians at the festival and in the city at large find themselves the targets of police harassment on a regular basis; see Neal Pollack, "Pushed Off the Platform," *Chicago Reader* (May 14, 1999), sec. 1, p. 1; and Howard Reich, "Vanishing Acts?" *Chicago Tribune* (June 20, 1999), sec. 7, p. 1. For a sociological treatment of the difficulties faced by buskers and other street entrepreneurs, see Whyte, *City*, 25–55; and Duneier, *Sidewalk*.

41. The city designates only six spaces where street musicians may perform, and two of them are located in a remote area away from the pedestrian traffic of the festival.

42. This strategy allows the festival organizers to justify dispersing these performers to remote areas of the park.

Chapter 7

1. See Phil Vettel, "Cool Times in a Hot Town," *Chicago Tribune* (August 10, 1997), sec. 8, p. 1.

2. Rick Bragg, "Driving the Blues Trail, in Search of a Lost Muse," New York *Times* (19 April 2002).

3. Garza, "Tour Buses Veer Off Beaten Path."

4. See Marilyn Wood, *Frommer's Toronto* (New York: Macmillan, 1997).

5. On the festishization of the "new" in contemporary culture, see Michael Lewis, *The New New Thing: A Silicon Valley Story* (New York: W. W. Norton, 2000); and Greg Urban, *Metaculture: How Culture Moves through the World* (Minneapolis: University of Minnesota Press, 2001).

6. Langdon Winner, "Silicon Valley Mystery House," in *Variations on a Theme Park: The New American City and the End of Public Space*, ed. Michael Sorkin (New York: Hill and Wang, 1992); and Amy McConnell, *Fodor's 98: San Francisco* (New York: Fodor's Travel Publications, 1997), 75–77; also see Richard D. Lloyd, "The Digital Bohemia," a paper presented at the ninety-sixth annual meetings of the American Sociological Association, Anaheim, Calif., August 21, 2001.

7. In *No Logo*, 45–46, Klein similarly argues that the Gap commercial featuring the Prima song may have been instrumental in launching the recent swing revival.

8. See Ferguson, "A Cultural Field in the Making."

9. Quoted in Jim Quinn, "The Making of Morimoto," *Philadelphia Magazine* (January 2002): 74.

10. On the consolidation of the music industry, see "The Big Ten," *Nation* 7, no. 14 (January 2002): 27–30.

11. Michael Azerrad, *Our Band Could Be Your Life: Scenes from the American Indie Underground, 1981–1991* (Boston: Little, Brown, 2001), offers a history of this period in rock, devoting particularly close attention to the careers of thirteen bands: Beat Happening, Big Black, Black Flag, Butthole Surfers, Dinosaur Jr, Fugazi, Hüsker Dü, Minor Threat, the Minutemen, Mission of Burma, Mudhoney, the Replacements, and Sonic Youth.

12. Quoted in Thomas Frank, "Alternative to What?" in *Commodify Your Dissent: Salvos from the Baffler*, ed. Frank and Matt Weiland (New York: W. W. Norton, 1997), 148, in which he provides a illuminating and critical discussion of the rise of alternative rock; also see Azerrad, *Our Band Could Be Your Life*. On Minor Threat and the emergence of straightedge hardcore

punk music, see Robert T. Wood, "The Indigenous, Nonracist Origins of the American Skinhead Subculture," *Youth and Society* 31 (1999): 131–51; on the Slits and other proto-riot grrrl bands, see Joanne Gottlieb and Gayle Wald, "Smells Like Teen Spirit: Riot Grrrls, Revolution and Women in Independent Rock," in *Microphone Fiends: Youth Music and Youth Culture*, ed. Andrew Ross and Tricia Rose (New York: Routledge, 1994); and Simon Reynolds and Joy Press, *The Sex Revolts: Gender, Rebellion, and Rock 'n' Roll* (Cambridge: Harvard University Press, 1995).

13. Steve Albini, "The Problem with Music," in *Commodify Your Dissent: Salvos from the Baffler*, ed. Frank and Matt Weiland (New York: W. W. Norton, 1997), 164–65.

14. McLeod, "Authenticity within Hip-Hop"; N. R. Kleinfield, "Guarding the Borders of the Hip-Hop Nation," in *How Race Is Lived in America: Pulling Together, Pulling Apart* (New York: Times Books, 2001).

15. Quoted in McLeod, "Authenticity within Hip-Hop," 140.

16. Quoted in ibid, 143.

17. Quoted in ibid., 145; emphasis in original.

18. On the subcultural world of the rave underground, see Thornton, *Club Cultures*; Collin and Godfrey, *Altered State*; Malbon, *Clubbing*; and Reynolds, *Generation Ecstasy*.

19. This increased news coverage amounted to what British cultural theorists refer to as a "moral panic"; for instance, see Stanley Cohen, *Folk Devils and Moral Panics* (New York: St. Martin's, 1980); and John Springhall, *Youth, Popular Culture and Moral Panics: Penny Gaffs to Gangsta-Rap, 1830–1996* (New York: St. Martin's, 1998). On the emergence of the moral panic surrounding the contemporary rave scene, see Thornton, *Club Cultures*.

20. Thornton, *Club Cultures*, 99.

21. John Leland, "For Rock Bands, Selling Out Isn't What It Used to Be," *New York Times Magazine* (March 11, 2001).

22. Quoted in McLeod, "Authenticity within Hip-Hop," 143.

23. Kleinfield, "Guarding the Borders of the Hip-Hop Nation," 217–18.

24. Quoted in McLeod, "Authenticity within Hip-Hop," 140.

Abbott, Andrew. *Department and Discipline: Chicago Sociology at One Hundred.* Chicago: University of Chicago Press, 1999.

———. "Los Angeles and the Chicago School: A Comment on Michael Dear." *City and Community* 1 (2002): 33–38.

———. *The System of Professions: An Essay on the Division of Expert Labor.* Chicago: University of Chicago Press, 1988.

———. "Of Time and Space: The Contemporary Relevance of the Chicago School." *Social Forces* 75 (1997): 1149–82.

———. "What Do Cases Do?" In *What Is a Case?*, ed. Charles Ragin and Howard Becker. Cambridge: Cambridge University Press, 1992.

Abbott, Andrew, and Alexandra Hrycak. "Measuring Resemblance in Sequence Data: An Optimal Matching Analysis of Musicians' Careers." *American Journal of Sociology* 96 (1990): 144–85.

Adler, Judith. "Travel as Performed Art." *American Journal of Sociology* 94 (1989): 1366–91.

Albini, Steve. "The Problem with Music." In *Commodify Your Dissent: Salvos from the Baffler*, ed. Thomas Frank and Matt Weiland. New York: W. W. Norton, 1997.

Anderson, Benedict. *Imagined Communities: Reflections on the Origin and Spread of Nationalism.* London: Verso, 1991.

Anderson, Elijah. *A Place on the Corner.* Chicago: University of Chicago Press, 1976.

———. *Streetwise: Race, Class, and Change in an Urban Community.* Chicago: University of Chicago Press, 1990.

Anderson, Nels. *The Hobo: The Sociology of the Homeless Man.* Chicago: University of Chicago Press, 1923.

Andrews, George, ed. *The Grey City Guide.* Chicago: University of Chicago, 1976.

Appadurai, Arjun. "Disjuncture and Difference in the Global Cultural Economy." *Public Culture* 2 (1990): 1–24.

Arnold, Matthew. *Culture and Anarchy.* New Haven: Yale University Press, [1865] 1994.

Atkins, E. Taylor. "Can Japanese Sing the Blues?: 'Japanese Jazz' and the Problem of

Authenticity." In *Japan Pop! Inside the World of Japanese Popular Culture*, ed.
Timothy J. Craig. Armonk, N.Y.: M. E. Sharpe, 2000.

Azerrad, Michael. *Our Band Could Be Your Life: Scenes from the American Indie
Underground, 1981–1991*. Boston: Little, Brown, 2001.

Baker, Houston A. *Blues, Ideology and Afro-American Literature: A Vernacular Theory*.
Chicago: University of Chicago Press, 1984.

Bakhtin, Mikhail. *Rabelais and His World*. Trans. Helene Iswolsky. Bloomington: Indiana
University Press, 1984.

Banes, Sally, et al. *Sweet Home Chicago: The Real City Guide*. Chicago: Chicago Review
Press, 1974.

Baraka, Amiri. "The Great Music Robbery." In *The Music: Reflections on Jazz and Blues*.
New York: William and Morrow, 1987.

Baraka, Amiri, as Leroi Jones. *Blues People: Negro Music in White America*. New York:
William and Morrow, 1963.

———. "Jazz and the White Critic." In *Black Music*. New York: Da Capo, 1968.

Barlow, William. *Looking Up at Down: The Emergence of Blues Culture*. Philadelphia:
Temple University Press, 1989.

Bates, Colleen Dunn, ed. *The Best of Chicago*. New York: Prentice Hall, 1989.

Baumann, Shyon. "Intellectualization and Art World Development: Film in the United
States." *American Sociological Review* 66 (2001): 404–26.

Becker, Howard S. *Art Worlds*. Berkeley: University of California Press, 1982.

———. *Outsiders: Studies in the Sociology of Deviance*. Glencoe, Ill.: Free Press, 1963.

Beisel, Nicola. "Class, Culture, and Campaigns against Vice in Three American Cities,
1872–1892." *American Sociological Review* 55 (1990): 44–62.

Berkow, Ira. *Maxwell Street: Survival in a Bazaar*. Garden City, N.Y.: Doubleday, 1977.

Berry, Brian J. L. "Islands of Renewal in Seas of Decay." In *The New Urban Reality*, ed. Paul
Peterson. Washington, D.C.: Brookings Institution, 1985.

"The Big Ten." *Nation* 7, no. 14 (January 2002): 27–30.

Binder, Amy. "Constructing Racial Rhetoric: Media Depictions of Harm in Heavy Metal and
Rap Music." *American Sociological Review* 58 (1993): 753–67.

"Birthdays at the Cultural Center." City of Chicago: Department of Cultural Affairs, April
1998.

Blair-Loy, Mary. "Career Patterns of Executive Women in Finance: An Optimal Matching
Analysis." *American Journal of Sociology* 104 (1999): 1346–97.

Bourdieu, Pierre. *Distinction: A Social Critique of the Judgment of Taste*. Trans. Richard Nice.
Cambridge: Harvard University Press, 1984.

———. *Outline of a Theory of Practice*. Cambridge: Cambridge University Press, 1977.

Bourdieu, Pierre, and Loic J. D. Wacquant. *An Invitation to Reflexive Sociology*. Chicago:
University of Chicago Press, 1992.

Boyer, M. Christine. "Cities for Sale: Merchandising History at South Street Seaport." In
Variations on a Theme Park: The New American City and the End of Public Space, ed.
Michael Sorkin. New York: Hill and Wang, 1992.

Bragg, Rick. "Driving the Blues Trail, in Search of a Lost Muse." *New York Times* (April 19,
2002).

Brogan, Daniel. "Gutbucket Blues." *Chicago Tribune* (November 23, 1986).

Brooks, David. *Bobos in Paradise: The New Upper Class and How They Got There*. New York:
Simon and Schuster, 2000.

Bulmer, Martin. *The Chicago School of Sociology: Institutionalization, Diversity, and the Rise of Sociological Research*. Chicago: University of Chicago Press, 1984.

Butler, Judith. *Gender Trouble: Feminism and the Subversion of Identity*. New York: Routledge, 1990.

Calloway, Earl. "Mr. Ricky's Hosts Blues Blowout." *Chicago Defender* (May 14, 1996), 16.

Cantwell, Robert. *When We Were Good: The Folk Revival*. Cambridge: Harvard University Press, 1996.

Charters, Samuel. *The Roots of the Blues: An African Search*. New York: Da Capo Press, 1981.

Chauncey, George. *Gay New York: Gender, Urban Culture, and the Making of the Gay Male World, 1880–1940*. New York: Basic Books, 1994.

Chicago Blues Festival. Official Program, 1997.

Chicago Blues Festival. Official Program, 1998.

Chicago Blues Festival. Official Program, 1999.

"Chicago: City on the Lake." *Plymouth Traveler* 6, no. 1 (1965).

Chicago Department of Cultural Affairs. "New Chicago Neighborhood Tours Invite Visitors and Chicagoans to Discover Ethnic Chicago." News release (February 19, 1998).

Chicago Fact Book Consortium. *Local Community Fact Book: Chicago Metropolitan Area 1990*. Chicago: Academy Chicago, 1995.

"Chicago Neighborhood Tours." Chicago Office of Tourism, 1998.

Chicago Tourism Fact Book. City of Chicago, 1997.

Christenson, James. "Urbanism and Community Sentiment." *Social Science Quarterly* 60 (1979): 387–400.

Clifford, James. *The Predicament of Culture: Twentieth-Century Ethnography, Literature and Art*. Cambridge: Harvard University Press, 1988.

Cohen, Erik. "Authenticity and Commoditization in Tourism." *Annals of Tourism Research* 15 (1988): 371–86.

Cohen, Stanley. *Folk Devils and Moral Panics*. New York: St. Martin's, 1980.

Coleman, James S. "A Vision for Sociology." *Society* 32 (1994): 29–34.

Collin, Matthew, and John Godfrey. *Altered State: The Story of Ecstasy Culture and Acid House*. London: Serpent's Tail, 1997.

Cooley, Charles Horton. "The Social Self—the Meaning of 'I.' " In *On Self and Social Organization*, ed. Hans-Joachim Schubert. Chicago: University of Chicago Press, [1902] 1998.

Corse, Sarah M. *Nationalism and Literature: The Politics of Culture in Canada and the United States*. Cambridge: Cambridge University Press, 1997.

———. "Nations and Novels: Cultural Politics and Literary Use." *Social Forces* 73, no. 4 (1995): 1279–308.

Crane, Diana. *Fashion and Its Social Agendas: Class, Gender, and Identity in Clothing*. Chicago: University of Chicago Press, 2000.

Cressey, Paul G. *The Taxi-Dance Hall*. Chicago: University of Chicago Press, 1932.

Cruz, Jon. *Culture on the Margins*. Princeton: Princeton University Press, 1999.

Cutler, Irving. *The Jews of Chicago: From Shetl to Suburb*. Urbana: University of Illinois Press, 1996.

Dahl, Bill. "1998 Chicago Blues Festival." *Chicago Reader* (May 29, 1998).

———. "Stale Home Chicago." *Chicago Tribune* (March 15, 1996), sec. 5, p. 1.

Davis, Angela Y. *Blues Legacies and Black Feminism*. New York: Pantheon, 1998.

Davis, Francis. *The History of the Blues*. New York: Hyperion, 1995.

Davis, Fred. *Yearning for Yesterday: A Sociology of Nostalgia*. New York: Free Press, 1979.

Davis, Mike. *City of Quartz: Excavating the Future in Los Angeles*. New York: Vintage, 1992.

Dear, Michael. "Los Angeles and the Chicago School: Invitation to a Debate." *City and Community* 1 (2002): 5–32.

DeVault, Marjorie L. "Novel Readings: The Social Organization of Interpretation." *American Journal of Sociology* 95 (1990): 887–921.

DeVeaux, Scott. *The Birth of Bebop: A Social and Musical History*. Berkeley: University of California Press, 1997.

Diaz, Katharine A. "Chicago: Your Kind of Town." *Corporate and Incentive Travel* (August, 1997): 62–65.

DiMaggio, Paul. "Classification in Art." *American Sociological Review* 52 (1987): 440–55.

———. "Cultural Entrepreneurship in 19th Century Boston." In *Rethinking Popular Culture*, ed. Chandra Mukerji and Michael Schudson. Berkeley: University of California Press, 1991.

DiMaggio, Paul, and Francie Ostrower. "Participation in the Arts by Black and White Americans." *Social Forces* 63 (1990): 753–78.

DiMaggio, Paul, and Walter W. Powell. "The Iron Cage Revisited: Institutional Isomorphism and Collective Rationality in Organizational Fields." *American Sociological Review* 52 (1983): 147–60.

Dorsey, Jennifer. "Culture Is the Focus of Chicago Promotion." *Travel Weekly* (April 10, 1997): 16.

Downs, Anthony. *An Economic Theory of Democracy*. New York: Harper and Row, 1957.

Drake, St. Clair, and Horace R. Cayton. *Black Metropolis: A Study of Negro Life in a Northern City*. New York: Harper and Row, 1945.

Du Bois, W. E. B. *The Philadelphia Negro: A Social Study*. Philadelphia: University of Pennsylvania Press, [1899] 1996.

Duneier, Mitchell. *Sidewalk*. New York: Farrar, Straus and Giroux, 1999.

———. *Slim's Table: Race, Respectability and Masculinity*. Chicago: University of Chicago Press, 1992.

Dyer, Richard. *Heavenly Bodies: Film Stars and Society*. New York: St. Martin's, 1986.

Eco, Umberto. *Travels in Hyperreality*. San Diego: Harcourt Brace Jovanovich, 1986.

Ehrenhalt, Alan. *The Lost City: The Forgotten Virtues of Community in America*. New York: Basic Books, 1995.

Ehrenreich, Barbara. *Nickel and Dimed: On (Not) Getting by in America*. New York: Metropolitan Books, 2001.

Erenberg, Lewis A. *Steppin' Out: New York Nightlife and the Transformation of American Culture, 1890–1930*. Chicago: University of Chicago Press, 1981.

———. *Swingin' the Dream: Big Band Jazz and the Rebirth of American Culture*. Chicago: University of Chicago Press, 1998.

Erickson, Bonnie H. "What Is Good Taste Good for?" *Canadian Review of Sociology and Anthropology* 28 (1991): 255–78.

Evans, David. *Big Road Blues*. New York: Da Capo, 1987.

Fanon, Frantz. *Black Skin, White Masks*. Trans. Charles Lam Markmann. New York: Grove, 1967.

Farrell, James T. *Studs Lonigan: A Trilogy*. Urbana: University of Illinois Press, [1932, 1934, 1935] 1993.

Faulkner, Robert R. *Hollywood Studio Musicians*. Chicago: Aldine Publishing, 1971.

Ferguson, Priscilla Parkhurst. "A Cultural Field in the Making: Gastronomy in 19th-Century France." *American Journal of Sociology* 104 (1998): 597–641.

Fine, Gary Alan. "The Culture of Production: Aesthetic Choices and Constraints in Culinary Work." *American Journal of Sociology* 97 (1992): 1268–94.

———. "Popular Culture and Social Interaction: Production, Consumption and Usage." *Journal of Popular Culture* 11, no 2 (1977): 453–56.

———. "Reputational Entrepreneurs and the Memory of Incompetence: Melting Supporters, Partisan Warriors, and Images of President Harding." *American Journal of Sociology* 101 (1996): 1159–93.

———., ed. *A Second Chicago School? The Development of a Postwar American Sociology.* Chicago: University of Chicago Press, 1995.

Finnegan, Ruth. *Tales of the City: A Study of Narrative and Urban Life.* Cambridge: Cambridge University Press, 1998.

Fischer, Claude. *To Dwell among Friends: Personal Networks in Town and City.* Chicago: University of Chicago Press, 1982.

Fish, Stanley. *Is There a Text in This Class? The Authority of Interpretive Communities.* Cambridge: Harvard University Press, 1980.

Flerlage, Raeburn. *Chicago Blues.* Toronto: ECW Press, 2000.

Fonarow, Wendy. "The Spatial Organization of the Indie Music Gig." In *The Subcultures Reader*, ed. Ken Gelder and Sarah Thornton. London: Routledge, 1997.

Frank, Thomas. "Alternative to What?" In *Commodify Your Dissent: Salvos from the Baffler*, ed. Thomas Frank and Matt Weiland. New York: W. W. Norton, 1997.

Frith, Simon. *Sound Effects: Youth, Leisure, and the Politics of Rock 'n' Roll.* New York: Pantheon, 1981.

Gabler, Neil. *Life the Movie: How Entertainment Conquered Reality.* New York: Vintage, 2000.

Gans, Herbert. *The Urban Villagers: Group and Class in the Life of Italian-Americans.* New York: Free Press, 1962.

Garfinkel, Harold. *Studies in Ethnomethodology.* Cambridge: Polity, 1967.

Garon, Paul. *Blues and the Poetic Spirit.* New York: Da Capo, 1978.

Garza, Melita Marie. "Tour Buses Veer Off Beaten Path." *Chicago Tribune* (July 7, 1997).

Giddens, Anthony. *The Constitution of Society: Outline of the Theory of Structuration.* Cambridge: Polity, 1984.

Giddins, Gary. *Visions of Jazz: The First Century.* New York: Oxford University Press, 1998.

Gillett, Charlie. *The Sound of the City: The Rise of Rock and Roll.* New York: Outerbridge and Dienstfrey, 1970.

Gilroy, Paul. *"There Ain't No Black in the Union Jack": The Cultural Politics of Race and Nation.* Chicago: University of Chicago Press, 1991.

Gitlin, Todd. *The Sixties: Years of Hope, Days of Rage.* New York: Bantam, 1987.

Gladwell, Malcolm. *The Tipping Point: How Little Things Can Make a Big Difference.* Boston: Little, Brown, 2000.

Glaeser, Andreas. *Divided in Unity: Identity, Germany, and the Berlin Police.* Chicago: University of Chicago Press, 2000.

Gleason, Ralph J. "Can the White Man Sing the Blues?" *Jazz and Pop* (1968): 28–29.

Gluckman, Max. *Order and Rebellion in Tribal Africa.* New York: Free Press, 1963.

Goffman, Erving. *Frame Analysis: An Essay on the Organization of Experience.* Boston: Northeastern University Press, 1974.

———. *The Presentation of Self in Everyday Life.* Garden City, N.Y.: Anchor Books, 1959.

———. "Where the Action Is." In *Interaction Ritual: Essays on Face-to-Face Behavior.* New York: Pantheon, 1967.

Gottdiener, M. "Hegemony and Mass Culture: A Semiotic Approach." *American Journal of Sociology* 90 (1985): 979–1001.

———. *Postmodern Semiotics: Material Culture and the Forms of Postmodern Life.* Oxford: Blackwell, 1995.

Gottlieb, Joanne, and Gayle Wald. "Smells Like Teen Spirit: Riot Grrrls, Revolution and Women in Independent Rock." In *Microphone Fiends: Youth Music and Youth Culture*, ed. Andrew Ross and Tricia Rose. New York: Routledge, 1994.

Graham, Jory. *Chicago: An Extraordinary Guide.* Chicago: Rand McNally, 1967.

Gravenites, Nick. "Bad Talkin' Bluesman." *Blues Revue* 22 (April/May 1996): 14.

Grazian, David. "Sweet Home Chicago: Constructing a Sociology of Local Urban Cultural Processes." Master's thesis, Department of Sociology, University of Chicago, 1996.

———. "Uniform of the Party: The Impact of Fashion on Collegiate Subcultural Integration." Henry Rutgers honors thesis, Department of Sociology, Rutgers University, 1994.

"Gregg Parker to Join Buddy Guy at Blues Fest Opener." *Chicago Defender* (June 4, 1997).

Griswold, Wendy. "American Character and the American Novel: An Expansion of Reflection Theory in the Sociology of Literature." *American Journal of Sociology* 86 (1981): 740–65.

———. *Bearing Witness: Readers, Writers, and the Novel in Nigeria.* Princeton: Princeton University Press, 2000.

———. "The Fabrication of Meaning: Literary Interpretation in the United States, Great Britain, and the West Indies." *American Journal of Sociology* 92, no. 5 (March 1987): 1077–117.

———. "The Writing on the Mud Wall: Nigerian Novels and the Imaginary Village." *American Sociological Review* 57 (1992): 709–24.

Griswold, Wendy, and Fredrik Engelstad. "Does the Center Imagine the Periphery? State Support and Literary Regionalism in Norway and the United States." *Comparative Social Research* 17 (1998): 129–75.

Gusfield, Joseph. *Community: A Critical Response.* New York: Harper and Row, 1978.

Haley, Alex. *The Autobiography of Malcolm X.* New York: Ballantine, 1965.

Hall, John. "The Capital(s) of Cultures: A Nonholistic Approach to Status Situations, Class, Gender, and Ethnicity." In *Cultivating Differences: Symbolic Boundaries and the Making of Inequality*, ed. Michele Lamont and Marcel Fournier. Chicago: University of Chicago Press, 1992.

Hall, Stuart, and Tony Jefferson. *Resistance through Rituals: Youth Subcultures in Post-War Britain.* London: Routledge, 1976.

Halle, David. *Inside Culture: Art and Class in the American Home.* Chicago: University of Chicago Press, 1993.

Hamilton, Charles V. *The Black Preacher in America.* New York: William Morrow and Company, 1972.

Hannerz, Ulf. *Exploring the City: Inquiries toward an Urban Anthropology.* New York: Columbia University Press, 1980.

Hannigan, John. *Fantasy City: Pleasure and Profit in the Postmodern Metropolis.* London: Routledge, 1998.

Haralambos, Michael. *Right On: From Blues to Soul in Black America*. New York: Drake, 1975.

Harvey, David. *The Condition of Postmodernity*. Cambridge, Mass.: Blackwell, 1990.

Hasse, John Edward. *Beyond Category: The Life and Genius of Duke Ellington*. New York: Da Capo, 1995.

Hebdige, Dick. *Subculture: The Meaning of Style*. London: Routledge, 1979.

Hemingway, Ernest. *The Sun Also Rises*. New York: Charles Scribner's Sons, 1927.

Herrnstein, Richard J., and Charles Murray. *The Bell Curve: Intelligence and Class in American Life*. New York: Free Press, 1994.

Hirsch, Arnold R. *Making the Second Ghetto: Race and Housing in Chicago, 1940–1960*. Cambridge: Cambridge University Press, 1983.

Hobsbawm, Eric, and Terence Ranger, eds. *The Invention of Tradition*. Cambridge: Cambridge University Press, 1983.

Hochschild, Arlie Russell. *The Managed Heart*. Berkeley: University of California Press, 1983.

hooks, bell. "Eating the Other: Desire and Resistance." In *Black Looks: Race and Representation*. Boston: South End Press, 1992.

————. "Marketing Blackness: Class and Commodification." In *Killing Rage: Ending Racism*. New York: Henry Holt, 1995.

————. "Selling Hot Pussy: Representations of Black Female Sexuality in the Cultural Marketplace." In *Black Looks: Race and Representation*. Boston: South End Press, 1992.

Horowitz, Irving Louis. "Authenticity and Originality in Jazz: Toward a Paradigm in the Sociology of Music." *Journal of Jazz Studies* 1 (1973): 57–63.

Hotelling, Harold. "Stability in Competition." *Economic Journal* (1929).

Hughes, Everett Cherrington. "Dilemmas and Contradictions of Status." *American Journal of Sociology* 50 (1945): 353–59.

Hughes, Langston. "Minstrel Man." In *The New Negro: Voices of the Harlem Renaissance*, ed. Alain Locke. New York: Atheneum, [1925] 1992.

Huizinga, Johan. *Homo Ludens: A Study of the Play-Element in Culture*. Boston: Beacon Press, 1955.

Hummon, David. *Commonplaces: Community Ideology and Identity in American Culture*. Albany: State University of New York Press, 1990.

Hyman, Laurence J. *Going to Chicago: A Year on the Chicago Blues Scene*. San Francisco: Woodford, 1990.

Ignatiev, Noel. *How the Irish Became White*. New York: Routledge, 1995.

Iyer, Pico. *Video Night in Katmandu and Other Reports from the Not-So-Far East*. New York: Vintage, 1989.

Jacobs, Jane. *The Death and Life of Great American Cities*. New York: Vintage, 1961.

Jacobson, Matthew Frye. *Whiteness of a Different Color: European Immigration and the Alchemy of Race*. Cambridge: Harvard University Press, 1998.

Johnson, Dirk. "Chicago Hails District as Symbol of Gay Life." *New York Times* (August 27, 1997).

Johnson, Jeff. "Blues Legend Master of Solo Act." *Chicago Sun-Times* (February 4, 2000).

Kammen, Michael. *American Culture, American Tastes: Social Change and the 20th Century*. New York: Knopf, 1999.

Kasarda, John D., and Morris Janowitz. "Community Attachment in Mass Society." *American Sociological Review* 39 (1974): 328–39.

Katz, Jack. *How Emotions Work*. Chicago: University of Chicago Press, 1999.

Keil, Charles. *Urban Blues*. Chicago: University of Chicago Press, 1966.

Keiser, John A. *The Vice Lords: Warriors of the Street*. New York: Holt, Rinehart and Winston, 1969.

Kennedy, Michael. *The Concise Oxford Dictionary of Music*. London: Oxford University Press, 1980.

Kenney, William Howland. *Chicago Jazz: A Cultural History, 1904–1930*. New York: Oxford University Press, 1993.

Kerouac, Jack. *On the Road*. New York: Viking, 1957.

Klein, Naomi. *No Logo: Taking Aim at the Brand Bullies*. New York: Picador, 1999.

Kleinfield, N. R. "Guarding the Borders of the Hip-Hop Nation." In *How Race Is Lived in America: Pulling Together, Pulling Apart*. New York: Times Books, 2001.

Kornblum, William. *Blue Collar Community*. Chicago: University of Chicago Press, 1974.

Kot, Greg. "Blues Tease." *Chicago Tribune* (June 6, 1998), sec. 1, p. 2.

———. "Fest Overcomes Poor Start, Cool Weather and a Variety of Competition." *Chicago Tribune* (June 8, 1998), sec. 5, pp. 1, 4.

Lait, Jack, and Lee Mortimer. *Chicago Confidential*. New York: Crown, 1950.

Lamont, Michele, and Annette Lareau. "Cultural Capital: Gaps and Glissandos in Recent Theoretical Developments." *Sociological Theory* 6 (1988): 153–68.

Lawrence, A. H. *Duke Ellington and His World: A Biography*. New York: Routledge, 2001.

Lees, Gene. *Cats of Any Color: Jazz, Black and White*. New York: Oxford University Press, 1994.

Leidner, Robin. *Fast Food, Fast Talk: Service Work and the Routinization of Everyday Life*. Berkeley: University of California Press, 1993.

Leland, John. "For Rock Bands, Selling Out Isn't What It Used to Be." *New York Times Magazine* (March 11, 2001).

Levine, Lawrence. *Black Culture and Black Consciousness: Afro-American Thought from Slavery to Freedom*. Oxford: Oxford University Press, 1977.

Lewis, David Levering. *When Harlem Was in Vogue*. New York: Oxford University Press, 1981.

Lewis, Michael. *The New New Thing: A Silicon Valley Story*. New York: W. W. Norton, 2000.

Liebow, Elliot. *Tally's Corner: A Study of Negro Streetcorner Men*. Boston: Little, Brown, 1967.

Lincoln, Bruce. *Discourse and the Construction of Society*. New York: Oxford University Press, 1992.

Lloyd, Richard D. "The Digital Bohemia." Paper presented at the 96th annual meetings of the American Sociological Association, Anaheim, Calif., August 21, 2001.

Logan, John R., and Harvey L. Molotch. *Urban Fortunes: The Political Economy of Place*. Berkeley: University of California Press, 1987.

Loseke, Donileen R., and Spencer E. Cahill. "Actors in Search of a Character: Student Social Workers' Quest for Professional Identity." *Symbolic Interaction* 9, no. 2 (1986): 245–58.

Lott, Eric. *Love and Theft: Blackface Minstrelsy and the American Working Class*. New York: Oxford University Press, 1993.

Lowenthal, David. *The Past Is a Foreign Country*. Cambridge: Cambridge University Press, 1985.

MacCannell, Dean. *The Tourist: A New Theory of the Leisure Class*. New York: Schocken, 1976.

Mailer, Norman. "The White Negro: Superficial Reflections on the Hipster." San Francisco: City Lights, 1957.

Malbon, Ben. *Clubbing: Dancing, Ecstasy and Vitality*. New York: Routledge, 1999.

Malinowski, Bronislaw. *Argonauts of the Western Pacific*. New York: E. P. Dutton, [1922] 1961.

Marcus, Greil. *Lipstick Traces: A Secret History of the Twentieth Century*. Cambridge: Harvard University Press, 1989.

———. *Mystery Train: Images of America in Rock 'n' Roll Music*. New York: Plume, 1975.

———. *The Old, Weird America: The World of Bob Dylan's Basement Tapes*. New York: Henry Holt, 2001.

Massey, Douglas S., and Nancy A. Denton. *American Apartheid: Segregation and the Making of the Underclass*. Cambridge: Harvard University Press, 1993.

Mauss, Marcel. *The Gift: Forms and Functions of Exchange in Archaic Societies*. New York: W. W. Norton, 1967.

May, Reuben A. Buford. *Talking at Trena's: Everyday Conversations at an African American Tavern*. New York: New York University Press, 2001.

McConnell, Amy. *Fodor's 98: San Francisco*. New York: Fodor's Travel Publications, 1997.

McLeod, Kembrew. "Authenticity within Hip-Hop and Other Cultures Threatened with Assimilation." *Journal of Communication* 49 (1999): 134–50.

McRobbie, Angela. *British Fashion Design: Rag Trade or Image Industry?* New York: Routledge, 1998.

McRoberts, Flynn. "It's the Rebirth of Blues Landmark." *Chicago Tribune* (September 17, 1997), 1.

Melbin, Murray. "Night as Frontier." *American Sociological Review* 43 (1978): 3–22.

Melnick, Jeffrey. *A Right to Sing the Blues: African Americans, Jews, and American Popular Song*. Cambridge: Harvard University Press, 1999.

Merrill, Hugh. *The Blues Route*. New York: William Morrow, 1990.

Merton, Robert K. "The Thomas Theorem and the Matthew Effect." *Social Forces* 74 (1995): 379–422.

Mezzrow, Mezz, and Bernard Wolfe. *Really the Blues*. New York: Random House, 1946.

Molotch, Harvey. "The City as a Growth Machine." *American Journal of Sociology* 82 (1976): 309–32.

Molotch, Harvey, William Freudenburg, and Krista E. Paulsen. "History Repeats Itself, but How? City Character, Urban Tradition, and the Accomplishment of Place." *American Sociological Review* 65 (2000): 791–823.

Moore, Anne. "Artisan Belief: Tourists Will Buy Wares." *Crain's Chicago Business* (September 20, 1997).

Morenoff, Jeffrey D., and Robert J. Sampson. "Violent Crime and the Spatial Dynamics of Neighborhood Transition: Chicago, 1970–1990." *Social Forces* 76 (1997): 31–64.

Morris, Ed. *Old Town Holiday Booklet* (1961). Reprinted in "Life and Legend in Old Town." *Old Town/Wells Guide Book*, vol. 2, no. 1 (summer 1965).

Morrissey, Rick. "A Tango between an Icon and a City." *Chicago Tribune* (June 3, 1998), 1.

Mukerji, Chandra. "Artwork: Collection and Contemporary Culture." *American Journal of Sociology* 84 (1978): 348–65.

Nelson, Susan, Jon Anderson, and Abra Anderson, eds. *Serendipity City*, 1971.

Newman, Katherine S. *No Shame in My Game: The Working Poor in the Inner City*. New York: Vintage, 2000.

Newquist, Roy. *Fielding's Guide to Chicago*. New York: Fielding, 1970.

Nisenson, Eric. *Blue: The Murder of Jazz*. New York: Da Capo Press, 2000.

Nolan, Herb. "Arts and Fun." *Chicago Tribune* (November 21, 1976).

Oakley, Giles. *The Devil's Music: A History of the Blues*. London: Da Capo, 1997.

O'Brien, Geoffrey. "Recapturing the American Sound." *New York Review of Books* (April 9, 1998): 45–51.

Old Town Guidebook. 1968.

Old Town Newsletter 1, no.1 (May 1962).

Old Town/Wells Guide Book. 2, no. 1 (summer 1965).

Oldenburg, Ray. *The Great Good Place*. New York: Paragon House, 1989.

Oliver, Paul. *Blues Fell This Morning: Meaning in the Blues*. Cambridge: Cambridge University Press, 1960.

O'Neal, Jim. *Conversation with the Blues*. Cambridge: Cambridge University Press, 1965.

———. "Reader's Guide to Blues." *Chicago Reader* (September 26, 1975), 31, 33.

———. "Reader's Guide to Blues: The Blues Capital." *Chicago Reader* (September 28, 1973), 29.

———. "Reader's Guide to Blues: Searching for Real Chicago Blues." *Chicago Reader* (September 27, 1974), 16, 33.

———. "The Undisputed Blues Capital." *Chicago Reader* (September 29, 1972).

Osgood, Charles. "City Scrapbook," *Chicago Tribune* (May 7, 1997), 1, 3.

Ozouf, Mona. *Festivals and the French Revolution*. Trans. Alan Sheridan. Cambridge: Harvard University Press, 1988.

Palmer, Bryan D. *Cultures of Darkness: Night Travels in the Histories of Transgression*. New York: Monthly Review Press, 2000.

Palmer, Robert. *Deep Blues*. New York: Penguin Books, 1981.

Park, Robert E. "The Natural History of the Newspaper." In *The City*, ed. Robert E. Park, Ernest W. Burgess, and Roderick D. McKenzie. Chicago: University of Chicago Press, 1925.

Pattillo-McCoy, Mary. *Black Picket Fences: Privilege and Peril among the Black Middle Class*. Chicago: University of Chicago Press, 1999.

———. "Church Culture as a Strategy of Action in the Black Community." *American Sociological Review* 63 (1998): 767–84.

Peterson, Richard A. *Creating Country Music: Fabricating Authenticity*. Chicago: University of Chicago Press, 1997.

———. "The Production of Cultural Change: The Case of Contemporary Country Music." *Social Forces* 45 (1978): 292–314.

———. "Understanding Audience Segmentation: From Elite and Mass to Omnivore and Univore." *Poetics* 21 (1992): 243–58.

Peterson, Richard A., and Albert Simkus. "Musical Tastes Mark Occupational Status Groups." In *Cultivating Differences: Symbolic Boundaries and the Making of Inequality*, ed. Michele Lamont and Marcel Fournier. Chicago: University of Chicago Press, 1992.

Pollack, Neal. "Pushed Off the Platform." *Chicago Reader* (May 14, 1999), sec. 1, p. 1.

Polsky, Ned. *Hustlers, Beats, and Others*. Garden City, N.Y.: Anchor, 1969.

Port, Weimar. *Chicago the Pagan.* Chicago: Judy Publishing, 1953.

Porter, James. "Nothin' but the Blues." *New City* (December 2, 1999), 8–9.

Pratt, Ray. *Rhythm and Resistance: Explorations in the Political Uses of Popular Music.* New York: Praeger, 1990.

Putnam, Robert D. *Bowling Alone: The Collapse and Revival of American Community.* New York: Simon and Schuster, 2000.

Quinn, Jim. "The Making of Morimoto." *Philadelphia Magazine* (January 2002): 72.

Radway, Janice. *Reading the Romance: Women, Patriarchy, and Popular Literature.* Chapel Hill: University of North Carolina Press, 1984.

Randel, Don Michael. *Harvard Concise Dictionary of Music.* Cambridge: Belknap, 1978.

Reckless, Walter C. *Vice in Chicago.* Chicago: University of Chicago Press, 1933.

Reich, Howard. "Vanishing Acts?" *Chicago Tribune* (June 20, 1999), sec. 7, p. 1.

Reynolds, Simon. *Generation Ecstasy: Into the World of Techno and Rave Culture.* New York: Routledge, 1999.

Reynolds, Simon, and Joy Press. *The Sex Revolts: Gender, Rebellion, and Rock 'n' Roll.* Cambridge: Harvard University Press, 1995.

Robertson, Pamela. *Guilty Pleasures: Feminist Camp from Mae West to Madonna.* Durham, N.C.: Duke University Press, 1996.

Rogin, Michael. *Blackface, White Noise: Jewish Immigrants in the Hollywood Melting Pot.* Berkeley: University of California Press, 1996.

Rose, Tricia. *Black Noise: Rap Music and Black Culture in Contemporary America.* Hanover, N.H.: Wesleyan University Press, 1994.

Rowe, Mike. *Chicago Blues: The City and the Music.* London: Da Capo, 1975.

Rudinow, Joel. "Race, Ethnicity, Expressive Authenticity: Can White People Sing the Blues?" *Journal of Aesthetics and Art Criticism* 52 (1994): 127–37.

Salzinger, Leslie. "A Maid by Any Other Name: The Transformation of 'Dirty Work' by Central American Immigrants." In *Ethnography Unbound: Power and Resistance in the Modern Metropolis,* ed. Michael Burawoy et al. Berkeley: University of California Press, 1991.

Sampson, Robert J. "Local Friendship Ties and Community Attachment in Mass Society: A Multilevel Systemic Model." *American Sociological Review* 53 (1988): 766–79.

———. "Studying Modern Chicago." *City and Community* 1 (2002): 45–48.

Sampson, Robert J., Jeffrey D. Morenoff, and Felton Earls. "Beyond Social Capital: Spatial Dynamics of Collective Efficacy for Children." *American Sociological Review* 64 (1999): 633–60.

Sampson, Robert J., and Stephen W. Raudenbush. "Systematic Social Observation of Public Spaces: A New Look at Disorder in Urban Neighborhoods." *American Journal of Sociology* 105 (1999): 603–51.

Sandburg, Carl. "Chicago." In *Chicago Poems.* New York: Henry Holt, 1916.

Sapir, Edward. "Culture: Genuine and Spurious." In *Culture, Language, and Personality,* ed. David G. Mandelbaum. Berkeley: University of California Press, 1949.

Sassen, Saskia. *The Global City: New York, London, Tokyo.* Princeton: Princeton University Press, 1991.

———. *The Mobility of Labor and Capital: A Study in International Investment and Labor Flow.* Cambridge: Cambridge University Press, 1988.

Schudson, Michael. "On Tourism and Modern Culture." *American Journal of Sociology* 84 (1979): 1249–58.

Severino, Camille. "Working Women of the Blues." *In the Mix* (June 1998): 24–28.

Sewell, William H., Jr. "A Theory of Structure: Duality, Agency, and Transformation." *American Journal of Sociology* 98 (1992): 1–29.

Shakespeare, William. *As You Like It.* London: Cambridge University Press, 1968.

Shively, Jo Ellen. "Cowboys and Indians: Perceptions of Western Films among American Indians and Anglos." *American Sociological Review* 57 (1992): 725–34.

Smith, Dennis. *The Chicago School: A Liberal Critique of Capitalism.* New York: St. Martin's, 1988.

Smith, Neil. *The New Urban Frontier: Gentrification and the Revanchist City.* London: Routledge, 1996.

Snow, David A., and Leon Anderson. *Down on Their Luck: A Study of Homeless Street People.* Berkeley: University of California Press, 1993.

Soja, Edward W. *Postmodern Geographies: The Reassertion of Space in Critical Social Theory.* London: Verso, 1989.

Sontag, Susan. "Notes on Camp." In *A Susan Sontag Reader.* New York: Farrar, Straus and Giroux, [1964] 1982.

Sorkin, Michael. "See You in Disneyland." In *Variations on a Theme Park: The New American City and the End of Public Space,* ed. Michael Sorkin. New York: Hill and Wang, 1992.

Spear, Allan. *Black Chicago: The Making of a Negro Ghetto, 1890–1920.* Chicago: University of Chicago Press, 1967.

Springhall, John. *Youth, Popular Culture and Moral Panics: Penny Gaffs to Gangsta-Rap, 1830–1996.* New York: St. Martin's, 1998.

Stack, Carol. *All Our Kin.* New York: Harper and Row, 1974.

Steck, James. "Growing Up with Kingston Mines." *Chicago Reader* (March 12, 1976), 10–11.

Steinberg, Stephen. *The Ethnic Myth: Race, Ethnicity, and Class in America.* Boston: Beacon Press, 1989.

Suttles, Gerald D. "The Cumulative Texture of Local Urban Culture." *American Journal of Sociology* 90 (1984): 283–304.

———. *The Man-Made City.* Chicago: University of Chicago Press, 1990.

———. *The Social Construction of Communities.* Chicago: University of Chicago Press, 1972.

———. *The Social Order of the Slum.* Chicago: University of Chicago Press, 1968.

Swidler, Ann. "Culture in Action: Symbols and Strategies." *American Sociological Review* 51 (1986): 273–86.

Teschner, Amy, ed. *Sweet Home Chicago: The Real City Guide,* 1993.

Thomas, W. I., and Dorothy Swaine Thomas. *The Child in America: Behavior Problems and Programs.* New York: Knopf, 1928.

Thompson, Hunter S. *Fear and Loathing in Las Vegas: A Savage Journey to the Heart of the American Dream.* New York: Fawcett, 1971.

———. *Hell's Angels.* New York: Ballantine, 1965.

Thornton, Sarah. *Club Cultures: Music, Media and Subcultural Capital.* Hanover, N.H.: Wesleyan University Press, 1996.

Thrasher, Frederic M. *The Gang: A Study of 1,313 Gangs in Chicago.* Chicago: University of Chicago Press, 1927.

Tienda, Marta, and Haya Stier. "Joblessness and Shiftlessness: Labor Force Activity in

Chicago's Inner City." In *The Urban Underclass*, ed. Christopher Jencks and Paul E. Peterson. Washington, D.C.: Brookings, 1991.

Titon, Jeff Todd. *Early Downhome Blues*. Chapel Hill: University of North Carolina Press, 1977.

Tooze, Sandra B. *Muddy Waters: The Mojo Man*. Toronto: ECW Press, 1997.

Townsend, Audarshia. "Playing Hard to Get." *Chicago Tribune* (December 16, 1999), 1, 10.

Tuchman, Gaye, and Nina E. Fortin. "Fame and Misfortune: Edging Women Out of the Great Literary Tradition." *American Journal of Sociology* 90 (1984): 72–96.

Turner, Victor. *The Ritual Process: Structure and Anti-Structure*. Ithaca: Cornell University Press, 1969.

Ulanov, Barry. *Duke Ellington*. New York: Da Capo, 1975.

———. *A History of Jazz in America*. New York: Viking, 1952.

Urban, Greg. *Metaculture: How Culture Moves through the World*. Minneapolis: University of Minnesota Press, 2001.

Venkatesh, Sudhir Alladi. "The Social Organization of Street Gang Activity in an Urban Ghetto." *American Journal of Sociology* 103 (1997): 82–111.

Vettel, Phil. "Cool Times in a Hot Town." *Chicago Tribune* (August 10, 1997), sec. 8, p. 1.

Wacquant, Loic J. D., and William Julius Wilson. "Poverty, Joblessness, and the Social Transformation of the Inner City." In *Welfare Policy for the 1990s*, ed. Phoebe H. Cottingham and David T. Ellwood. Cambridge: Harvard University Press, 1989.

Wanker, Rodney. "Maxwell Street, Sunday Morning." *Chicago Reader* (October 1, 1971), 8.

Warner, Margaret Stockton. "The Renovation of Lincoln Park: An Ecological Study of Neighborhood Change." Ph.D. diss., University of Chicago, 1979.

Welding, Pete. "Gambler's Blues: Shakey Jake." *Living Blues* 10 (autumn 1972): 13.

Wellman, Barry. "The Community Question: The Intimate Networks of East New Yorkers." *American Journal of Sociology* 84 (1979): 1201–31.

Whiteis, David. "Last Dance at the Carnival of the Soul." *Chicago Reader* (September 2, 1994).

Whyte, William Foote. *Street Corner Society*. Chicago: University of Chicago Press, 1940.

Whyte, William H. *City: Rediscovering the Center*. New York: Doubleday, 1988.

Wilkerson, Isabel. "A Great Escape, a Dwindling Legacy." *New York Times* (February 15, 1998).

Williams, Raymond. *The Country and the City*. London: Chatto and Windus, 1973.

Willis, Paul. *Common Culture*. Boulder, Colo.: Westview, 1990.

———. *Learning to Labor*. New York: Columbia University Press, 1977.

Wilson, William Julius. *The Declining Significance of Race: Blacks and Changing American Institutions*. Chicago: University of Chicago Press, 1978.

———. *The Truly Disadvantaged*. Chicago: University of Chicago Press, 1987.

———. *When Work Disappears. The World of the New Urban Poor*. New York: Vintage, 1996.

Winner, Langdon. "Silicon Valley Mystery House." In *Variations on a Theme Park: The New American City and the End of Public Space*, ed. Michael Sorkin. New York: Hill and Wang, 1992.

Wirth, Louis. *The Ghetto*. Chicago: University of Chicago Press, 1956.

Wohl, R. Richard, and Anselm L. Strauss. "Symbolic Representation and the Urban Milieu." *American Journal of Sociology* 63 (1958): 523–32.

Wolfe, Tom. *The Electric Kool-Aid Acid Test*. New York: Bantam, 1968.

Wood, Marilyn. *Frommer's Toronto*. New York: Macmillan, 1997.

Wood, Michael. "Nostalgia or Never: You Can't Go Home Again." *New Society* 7 (1974): 343–46.

Wood, Robert T. "The Indigenous, Nonracist Origins of the American Skinhead Subculture." *Youth and Society* 31 (1999): 131–51.

Zerubavel, Eviatar. "Easter and Passover: On Calendars and Group Identity." *American Sociological Review* 47 (1982): 284–89.

Zolberg, Vera L. "Barrier or Leveler? The Case of the Art Museum." In *Cultivating Differences: Symbolic Boundaries and the Making of Inequality*, ed. Michele Lamont and Marcel Fournier. Chicago: University of Chicago Press, 1992.

Zorbaugh, Harvey Warren. *The Gold Coast and the Slum*. Chicago: University of Chicago Press, [1929] 1976.

Zuberi, Tukufu. *Thicker than Blood: How Racial Statistics Lie*. Minneapolis: University of Minnesota Press, 2001.

Zukin, Sharon. *The Cultures of Cities*. Cambridge: Blackwell, 1995.

———. "Gentrification: Culture and Capital in the Urban Core." *Annual Review of Sociology* 13 (1987): 129–47.

———. *Landscapes of Power: From Detroit to Disney World*. Berkeley: University of California Press, 1991.

———. *Loft Living: Culture and Capital in Urban Change*. Baltimore: Johns Hopkins University Press, 1982.

Page references in italic refer to photographs.

Black Belt of Chicago. *See* South Side of Chicago; West Side of Chicago

black culture: church culture, 6, 244–45 n. 6; club decor, 43, 82; commodification, 147–53; hip-hop music, 165–66, 236–37, 268 n. 1, 270–71 n. 43

black minstrelsy, 44

blacks: black working-class stereotype, 14; neighborhood blues clubs, 166–67, 178, 182–87; popularity of the blues, 20, 34, 54, 155, 158, 270–71 n. 43. *See also* racial issues

Bland, Bobby "Blue," 16, 152, 155, 158, 216

Blind Lemon Jefferson, 127

Blue Chicago club, 20, 43, 72, 74, *75*, *164*, 252 n. 35

Blue Flame club, 178

blues, 14–16; scale, 106–7, 114–15; style, 34. *See also* musical structure

Blues and the Poetic Spirit (Garon), 39–40

Blues Brothers, 72, 142–43

B.L.U.E.S. club, *xvi*, 1–4, 19, 73–77, *118*, 243 n. 2; American Sociological Association, 241; band wages, 271 n. 44; beginnings, 174–76; musicians, 135–37; perks, 23, 99–100; regulars, 87–124; romance and relationships, 95–98; sanctuary for musicians, 117–20; special events, 92, 122, 136, 263 n. 33

B.L.U.E.S. Etcetera club, 19, 23–24, 73–74, 259 n. 29, 269–70 n. 28; jam sessions, 106–12, 261 n. 20, 262–63 nn. 27–29; musicians, 135

Blues Fell This Morning (Oliver), 39, 194–95

Blues Harbor club, 9

Blues Heaven Foundation, 205

Blues Nazis, 162–63

Blues People (Baraka), 39

The Blues Route (Merrill), 8–9

Boston Blackie, 90

Bourdieu, Pierre, 21

Bragg, Rick, 230

Bronzeville neighborhood, 202–6, 273 n. 8

Broonzy, Big Bill, 129, 131, 162, 191

brotherhood of strangers, 98–100

Broughton, Charles, 273 n. 10

Brown, James, 130, 160, 162

Buddy Guy's Legends club, 3–4, 20, 55, 106, 253 n. 47

Bulls club, 168

Burgess, Ernest, 25

Burns, Jimmy, 121, 132, 136

Calvin (musician), 97–98, 223

Carol's Coming Out Pub, 172

Carter, Clarence, 158

Cayton, Horace, 25

Celebrity club, 3–4

Chad (musician), 83–85, 143–46

Charles, Ray, 159–60, 162–63, 221, 275 n. 38

Checkerboard Lounge, 19, *53*, *185*, 253 nn. 47–49; American Sociological Association visit, 241; cover charge, 57, 254 n. 57; neighborhood, 20, 179, 181, 183–84, 204; tourism, 51–56, 186, 204

Cheers (fictitious Boston pub), 92–93

Chicago, 12–16; blues legacy, 187–96, 272 nn. 59, 65, 72; downtown, 2–3, 51, 55, 73–77, 199–203, 209–10, 253 n. 54; historical development of the blues, 165–92; "Home of the Blues," 255–56 n. 11. *See also* specific neighborhoods

Chicago: An Extraordinary Guide (Graham), 169, 179

Chicago Blues Archive, 26

Chicago Blues Festival, 27–28, 30–31, 208–27, *212*; corporate sponsorships, 209–10, 274 n. 25; Crossroads stage, 211–13; Front Porch stage, 214–16; Juke Joint stage, 213–14, 216; musician, *198*; Petrillo Music Shell, 210–11, *212*, 274 n. 26; Ray Charles performance, 221, 275 n. 38; street musicians, 218–27, *226*, 275 n. 36, 275–76 nn. 39–42

Chicago Bulls, 94, 210–11

Chicago Confidential (Lait and Mortimer), 188

Chicago Cultural Center, 27, 199–200

Chicago Defender, 190–91

Chicago Historical Society, 26

Chicago Magazine, 86

Chicago Neighborhood Tours, 27, 200–8, 273 nn. 7, 9, 13

Chicago Reader, 27, 173–74, 179–80, 189

Chicago school of urban sociology, 25–26, 248 n. 26

menus. *See* food

merchandising of music, 3–4, 7–9, 26, 42–43, 245 n. 10, 251–52 n. 34; anti-commercialism of regulars, 103–4; Chicago Blues Festival, 209–10, 224; corporate sponsorships, 199–200; electronica, 237–38; hip-hop music, 236–37, 239–40; House of Blues club, 72–73; independent (indie) rock, 234–36, 239, 276 n. 11; logos and symbols, 7, 43, 120, 263 n. 32; Lollapalooza tour, 235; MTV, 235; roles of club owners, 139–41, 149–53, 174–76, 266 n. 30; souvenir shops, 43, 205, 252 n. 35, 273 n. 11; Woodstock twenty-fifth anniversary, 235

Merrill, Hugh, 8–9

Method Man (hip-hop artist), 237

methodology, 17–28, 243 n. 1, 245–46 nn. 19–20, 247–48 n. 25, 271 n. 46

Michael (musician), 142–43

Mickey (regular), 100–2, 218

Mike (bouncer), 89

Mississippi Delta blues. *See* Delta blues

Moby (electronica artist), 16, 238

Mojo Kings, 218–19

Montgomery, Little Brother, 191

Moonlight club, 183

moral order of the blues club, 90–94

Morimoto (Iron Chef), 233–34

Morris, Ed, 167

Mortimer, Lee, 188

Morton, Jelly Roll, 204

Mother Blues club, 168–69

Mr. Lee's Chateau, 183

Muddy Waters, 16, 42, 152; creation of urban blues style, 66; early Chicago blues scene, 34–35, 129, 131, 155, 160, 167; growth of Old Town, 169

musical genres, 16, 155, 158–63, 267 n. 37; boogie-woogie piano, 34; Delta blues, 34, 85, 214–16, 259 n. 30; electronica, 237–38; feminist/camp style, 47, 252 n. 44; folk music, 39, 168–69, 171, 266 n. 24, 268 n. 11, 269 n. 15; hip-hop music, 165, 236–37, 239–40, 268 n. 1, 270–71 n. 43; independent (indie) rock, 234–36, 239, 276 n. 11; innovation, 16, 153–63, 267 nn. 34–36, 268 n. 39, 270–71 n. 43; jump blues, 34; popular music, 5, 234–40;

R&B, 254 n. 1; rock, 20, 35, 127–28, 152, 154; soul, 52; swing dance/big band, 232; urban electric blues, 66, 155

musical structure of the blues, 15–16, 34, 106–7, 114–15; instrumentation, *126*, 155; jazz, 161; lyrics, 244 n. 5, 259 n. 30, 275 n. 32. *See also* musical genres

musicians, 23–25, *126*, *148*, 243 n. 1; as audience members, 23, 121–22; celebrities, 3–4, 152, 192, 199–200, 272 n. 58; Chicago Blues Festival, *198*; compensation, 71–72; competition for authenticity, 137–44; creativity, 147–53; criticism of audiences, 139–44, 266 nn. 25, 30; criticism of other musicians, 137–39, 155–58, 263 n. 1; day jobs, 128–29, 132–34, 264 n. 8; financial concerns, 71–72, 110, 136–37, 151–53, 184, 205, 215, 224, 260 n. 5, 262–63 n. 29, 271 nn. 44–45; guest performances, 121–22, 263 n. 35; importance of skill, 25, 33–34, 112, 249 n. 1; jam sessions, 105–12; mentoring, 106–12, 131; musical education, 129–30; need for sanctuary, 117–20, 263 n. 35; nocturnal capital, 83–84; nocturnal self, 108–11; partners and family life, 97–98, 260 nn. 5–6; peer groups, 128–34, 263–64 n. 4, 265 n. 14; preferred places to play, 71–72, 74, 76, 86, 100; professional development, 106–12, 262 n. 25; racial demographics, 14, 20–21, 30, 36–38; racial stereotypes, 29–30, 35, 83–84, 137–46, 149–50, 183–84, 248–49 n. 31; recognition outside of Chicago, 131–32; regulars, *88*; at Smoke Daddy, 83–84; social *vs.* performing roles, 94–98, 134–37, 216, 264–65 nn. 11–12, 265 nn. 16–17; street performing, 218–27, *226*, 275 n. 36, 275–76 nn. 39–42; subcultural cool, 112–16, 262 n. 26; views of authenticity, 125–63. *See also* performance

"Mustang Sally," 140

Myers, Dave, 89, 131–32, 136, 184, 215, 218

Myopic bookstore, 78

Mystery Spot secondhand store, 80

Nashville, 230–31

national culture, 70–71

"Stairway to Heaven," 126–27
Starr, Stephen, 233
Steck, James, 173–74
stereotypes, 11–14, 40–51, 252 nn. 39–40;
    age, 56–57, 254 n. 55; black minstrelsy,
    44; black neighborhoods, 179–82,
    187–88; definitions of blues, 14–16;
    female, 47–50; folklorist/academics, 146;
    male, 44–47; preachers, 144–45, 223;
    racial, 29–30, 36–38, 194–95, 248–49 n.
    31, 251 nn. 26, 28; sexual, 44–51, 57–58,
    144–45, 252 n. 41; stock characters,
    44–51, 144–46, 252 nn. 39–40; tourism,
    245 n. 12; white musicians, 137–46
Steve (bouncer/musician), 95, 136
stock characters. See stereotypes
street performing, 218–27, 226, 275 n. 36,
    275–76 nn. 39–42
subcultural cool, 91, 112–16, 260 n. 2, 262 n.
    26; hip-hop music, 236–37; rave
    underworld, 239
subcultures, 26–28, 244 n. 5, 258–59 n. 28;
    among musicians, 128–34, 263 nn. 1, 3
suburban clubs, 76
Sullivan, Ed, 152
Sunnyland Slim, 2, 111, 176, 191, 262 n. 24
survivors, 133–35, 144–46, 150, 155–57,
    216, 225, 264 n. 9, 264–65 nn. 11–13, 268
    n. 39
Suzanne (waitress), 89–90, 103–5, 261 nn.
    13–14, 16–17
"Sweet Home Chicago" (Robert Johnson),
    4, 6, 8, 12, 31, 48, 140, 149
Sweet Home Chicago guidebook, 172, 182,
    191–92
swing dancing, 232
symbols of authenticity, 13–14, 17, 22–25,
    36–38

Tail Dragger, 51, 89–90, 95, 131–32, 183–84
The Taxi-Dance Hall (Cressey), 26
Taylor, Johnnie, 155, 161
Taylor, Koko, 3–4, 152
Tex (musician), 85
Theresa's Tavern, 178, 181
Thicker than Blood: How Racial Statistics
    Lie (Zuberi), 41
third places, 96–97
Thomas, Dorothy Swaine, 17

Thomas, W. I., 17
Thompson, Hunter S., 240, 268 n. 11
Thornton, Sarah, 238–39
"The Thrill Is Gone" (B.B. King), 140
Thurman, L. C., 57
Tiger (musician), 59; financial aspects of
    blues career, 151; musical education,
    129–30; opinions of the current blues
    scene, 147–49; opinions of the media,
    161–62, 266–67 n. 30; performance style,
    45–46; treatment of musicians, 71–72
tourism, 3, 9, 27–31, 36, 86, 243–44 n. 4, 245
    n. 12, 253 n. 51; anti-tourism, 51–52,
    76–77, 253 n. 50; Chicago Blues Festival,
    208–27; Chicago Neighborhood Tours,
    200–8, 273 nn. 7, 9, 13; commodification
    of the blues, 20–22, 65–72; Cultural
    Chicago program, 197–200; economic
    development, 204–8; entertainment
    infrastructure, 2–3, 8–9, 21, 70, 256 nn.
    15–16; growth of blues as tourist
    industry, 175–96; guidebooks and
    publicity, 187–92, 271 nn. 46, 54;
    nocturnal self, 63–65, 254–55 n. 3;
    promotion, 187–92, 269–70 n. 28, 271
    nn. 46, 50, 272 n. 65; racism, 187–92;
    South Side clubs, 186–87; staged
    authenticity, 12, 245 n. 12; targeting
    blacks, 273 n. 8; urban authenticity,
    229–34. See also commodification of the
    blues in Chicago
The Tourist (MacCannell), 12
Trife (rapper), 239–40
Twilight restaurant, 78

University of Chicago/Department of
    Sociology, 9–10, 25–26, 248 n. 26
urban authenticity, 192–96, 229–34;
    Chicago Neighborhood Tours, 200–8;
    cosmopolitanism, 211, 217; Cultural
    Chicago program, 199–200; danger,
    172–73, 181–82, 187–92, 196; fantasy
    and idealized worlds, 232, 240–42;
    identities of place, 255 n. 8, 255–56 nn.
    11–12; intimacy, 73–77, 98–99; street
    musicians, 219–25; West Town, 83–86.
    See also community
urban bohemians, 77–82
urban electric blues, 66